The American

Slavery, 1760–1865

An Anthology of Sources

The American Debate over Slavery, 1760–1865

An Anthology of Sources

Edited, with an Introduction and Notes, by

Howard L. Lubert, Kevin R. Hardwick,
& Scott J. Hammond

Hackett Publishing Company, Inc.
Indianapolis/Cambridge

19 18 17 16   1 2 3 4 5 6 7

For further information, please address
Hackett Publishing Company, Inc.
P.O. Box 44937
Indianapolis, Indiana 46244-0937

www.hackettpublishing.com

Cover design by Rick Todhunter
Interior design by Elizabeth L. Wilson
Composition by Aptara, Inc.

Library of Congress Cataloging-in-Publication Data
Names: Lubert, Howard L. (Howard Leslie), 1966– editor. | Hardwick, Kevin R.,
    1961– editor. | Hammond, Scott J., editor.
Title: The American debate over slavery, 1760–1865 : an anthology of sources /
    edited, with an introduction and notes, by Howard L. Lubert, Kevin R. Hardwick,
    & Scott J. Hammond.
Description: Indianapolis : Hackett Publishing Company, Inc., 2016. | Includes
    bibliographical references and index.
Identifiers: LCCN 2016030288| ISBN 9781624665356 (pbk.) | ISBN
    9781624665363 (cloth)
Subjects: LCSH: Slavery—United States—History—Sources. | African Americans—
    History—To 1863—Sources.
Classification: LCC E441 .A5769 2016 | DDC 306.3/620973—dc23
LC record available at https://lccn.loc.gov/2016030288

Contents

Chapter Three: 1818–1830

Chapter Four: 1831–1846

Chapter Five: 1847–1853

Chapter Six: 1854–1865

DEDICATION

To the memory of those held in human bondage.

ACKNOWLEDGMENTS

We would like to recognize those family members and colleagues who have helped us from time to time with this project. For helping transcribe portions of the congressional debates over Missouri, we thank Caroline Lubert and Sarah Lubert. We also would like to acknowledge the assistance of our colleagues in the Department of History, especially David Dillard and Andrew Witmer, for their occasional advice about the book. We also extend thanks to the History and Political Science Departments and to the Dean's office in James Madison University's College of Arts and Letters for their financial assistance with this project; to our anonymous reviewers for their helpful comments on the manuscript, to Leslie Connor for copyediting the manuscript and Lauren Hill for proofreading it; and to Rick Todhunter, our editor at Hackett, for his patience and continued encouragement.

Finally, we would like to acknowledge our parents, Marvin and Elaine Lubert, Charlie D. Hardwick and Alison S. Hardwick, and the memory of Neil and Gilberdean Hammond, for all their enduring and unconditional love and support.

NOTE REGARDING TRANSCRIPTIONS

In a small number of instances we have modernized spelling and punctuation in order to make a document easier to read. Where possible, however, we have maintained original spelling, formatting, and punctuation.

General Introduction

When Parliament enacted the Stamp Act in 1765, American colonists were angered and frightened—not by the size of the tax, but because they questioned its legality. To be subject to taxes levied by a legislature to which they sent no representatives, and over which they had no political control, would in effect subject them to absolute power. It would, James Otis famously wrote in 1764, deprive the colonists of their property without their consent, thereby making them "slaves."[1] A few years later, John Dickinson likewise argued that compliance with the Townsend Acts would make the colonists "SLAVES."[2] This anxiety over slavery provoked Samuel Johnson's acerbic question, "How is it that we hear the loudest yelps for liberty among the drivers of negroes?"[3]

The frequency with which the colonists invoked the term "slavery" to describe their own situation may surprise readers today. Chattel slavery was legal—and actual slaves existed—in all thirteen of the American colonies. Didn't the colonists perceive the inconsistency between their pleas and the fact that they held Africans in slavery? The answer is, yes, they did. That recognition was one important consequence of the imperial crisis leading to the American Revolution. The issue of chattel slavery was placed irrevocably on the agenda of the new nation.

Prior to 1765, slavery was not widely debated in the American colonies. A notable exception occurred within the Quaker community, the Society of Friends. Here the efforts of John Woolman and Anthony Benezet were particularly influential. In 1766, following the 1754 publication of his book *Some Considerations on the Keeping of Negroes*, Woolman campaigned throughout Delaware and Maryland's Eastern Shore, bearing testimony against slaveholding and persuading many slave owners, including Quakers, to manumit their slaves. Benezet opened a school for black children in 1770, and in 1775 he formed the first American anti-slavery association, the Society for the Relief of Free Negroes Unlawfully Held in Bondage. As David Brion Davis has observed,

---

1. James Otis, *The RIGHTS of the British Colonies Asserted and proved . . .* (London: J. Almon, 1764), 105.

2. John Dickinson to the *Pennsylvania Chronicle and Universal Advertiser*, Letter VII, January 11, 1768, in *Empire and Nation: Letters from a Farmer in Pennsylvania (John Dickinson). Letters from the Federal Farmer (Richard Henry Lee)*, ed. Forrest McDonald (Indianapolis: Liberty Fund, 1999), 44.

3. Samuel Johnson, *Taxation No Tyranny: An Answer to Resolutions and Address of the American Congress* (London: T. Cadell, 1775), 89.

it is difficult to "exaggerate the central role Quakers played in initiating and sustaining the first antislavery movements."[4]

The Quaker challenge to slavery mostly emerged, along with secular anti-slavery arguments, during the American revolutionary period. As the imperial crisis deepened, the colonists increasingly acknowledged the inconsistency between their appeals to natural rights, liberty, and republican government on the one hand, and chattel slavery on the other. In 1773 George Mason, future drafter of the Virginia Bill of Rights, warned that slavery "is daily contaminating the minds and morals or our people. Every gentleman here is born a petty tyrant. . . . Taught to regard a part of our own species in the most abject and contemptible degree below us, we lose that idea of the dignity of man which the hand of nature has implanted in us."[5] George Washington, the most famous and popular American, declared it to be "among my first wishes to see some plan adopted . . . by which slavery in this country may be abolished by slow, sure, & imperceptible degrees."[6]

Given this, why did slavery continue? First, we must acknowledge that despite increasing criticism of slavery, the prevailing popular sentiment remained ambiguous. While statements decrying the slave trade and the institution of slavery itself multiplied, the defense of slavery also strengthened. For example, a pro-slavery petition written in 1785 by the citizens in Amelia County argued that to abolish slavery in Virginia would be to betray the Revolution. "We risked our Lives and Fortunes, and waded through Seas of Blood," they wrote, "that our Property might be secure."[7]

A second reason the Framers did not abolish slavery was that with three European powers bordering the newly independent states, survival of the continental union was the predominant issue, and survival required a stronger general government. Creating such a government was not possible, however, if it cut too deeply into the interests of any particular state or region. Delegates from the northern states were keen to provide Congress with the authority to place tariffs on imports; delegates from the south—especially South Carolina and Georgia—were intent on protecting the African slave trade. The various interests were reconciled in a bargain, what William Lloyd Garrison would later famously if provocatively refer to as a "covenant with death" and an "agreement with Hell."[8]

---

4. David Brion Davis, *The Problem of Slavery in the Age of Revolution, 1770–1823* (Ithaca, NY: Cornell University Press, 1975), 215.

5. George Mason, "Extracts from the Virginia Charters," in *The Papers of George Mason*, ed. Robert A. Rutland (Chapel Hill: University of North Carolina Press, 1970), 173.

6. George Washington to John Francis Mercer, September 9, 1786, in *The Papers of George Washington*, Confederation Series, vol. 4 (April 2, 1786–January 31, 1787), ed. Theodore Crackel (Charlottesville: University Press of Virginia, 1995), 243.

7. See document 9 in Chapter 1.

8. "Repeal of the Union," *The Liberator* XII, no. 18 (May 6, 1842), 71.

The compromise was subject to interpretation. For many, like General Charles C. Pinckney of South Carolina, the compromise was, in the main, beneficial to slaveholders. While the new Constitution granted power to Congress to ban the importation of slaves from abroad, it could not ban such importations in the original thirteen states until 1808. Moreover, slave owners obtained a new federal guarantee that runaway slaves would be returned to their owners; and Pinckney claimed that because congressional authority was restricted to those powers expressly declared in Article I, Congress was prohibited from emancipating slaves. "In short," he said, "considering all circumstances, we have made the best terms for the security of this species of property it was in our power to make."[9]

James Wilson and others reacted differently. Under the Articles of Confederation, Wilson observed, Congress had no authority to ban the African slave trade. Under the proposed Constitution, it could ban the trade entirely in 1808. "I consider this as laying the foundation for banishing slavery out of the country," he added, "and though the period is more distant than I could wish, yet it will produce the same kind, gradual change, which was pursued in Pennsylvania."[10] William Heath of Massachusetts might not have been quite as sanguine; he remained doubtful that southern states would emancipate their slaves after 1808. But he did observe that under the Constitution Congress could ban the "migration or importation" of slaves into new states, adding that under the Northwest Ordinance Congress had declared that new states "shall be republican, and that there shall be no slavery in them."[11] Heath foresaw a nation in which, over time, slavery would be contained and isolated to the southern states.

The views of Wilson and Heath were widely accepted in the early years of the republic. These men had reason to believe that encouraging signs pointed toward the slow but certain eradication of slavery. The Northwest Ordinance of 1787 banned slavery in the national domain. Most states had already banned the African slave trade. Pennsylvania passed a gradual abolition law in 1780; New Hampshire passed a similar law in 1783, and Connecticut and Rhode Island followed. Virginia passed a manumission law in 1782; and Massachusetts, after the *Quok Walker* ruling, in effect abolished the institution. Events after the Constitution's ratification also seemed to justify optimism. Between 1794 and 1803 Congress passed four separate laws aimed at restricting American involvement in the African slave trade. Then, on January 1, 1808

---

9. See document 3 in Chapter 2.
10. See document 2 in Chapter 2.
11. William Heath, speech before the Massachusetts Ratifying Convention, January 30, 1788, in *The Debates in the Several State Conventions on the Adoption of the Federal Constitution as Recommended by the General Convention at Philadelphia in 1787*, vol. II, 2nd ed., ed. Jonathan Elliot (Washington, D.C., 1836), 115.

(the first day it could legally do so), Congress banned the importation of slaves to the United States. Many people perceived a trend toward total abolition. For many Americans, like Joseph Sidney, there was reason to celebrate. "['T]is not an illusion of fancy, 'tis a truth recorded in the annals," Sidney proclaimed in 1809, "that no African, nor a single individual descended from African ancestors, shall henceforth be imported into this country as a slave. What a stride is this towards the total abolition of slavery in America! what a progress towards the consummation of our fondest hopes!"[12]

But there were ominous signs, too. When in February 1790 the House of Representatives received two petitions against the slave trade, a debate erupted over how they should be received. Josiah Parker of Virginia wanted the House to consider the petitions; indeed, the previous May he had proposed a duty on the importation of slaves, arguing that a tax would help dissuade the practice and wipe "off the stigma under which America labored." Thomas Scott of Pennsylvania agreed, rejecting the claim that "any person can be said to acquire property in another" and promising his support for "every constitutional measure likely to bring about [the] total abolition [of the slave trade]."[13]

Representatives from the Deep South, however, aggressively defended slavery. James Jackson of Georgia, claiming the support of history and Scripture, "supposed the master had a qualified property in his slave." Moreover, slavery was common in Africa; thus, American slavery was "only a change of one slavery for another," with one difference: Africans were better off in America, "where they have a master, bound by the ties of interest and law, to provide for their support and comfort in old age or infirmity." The southern States, he assured his fellow delegates, would "never suffer themselves to be divested of their property without a struggle." Thomas Tudor Tucker of South Carolina was even more direct: should Congress attempt a general emancipation, it "would never be submitted to by the southern States without a civil war."[14]

Anti-slavery petitions kept coming. When Absalom Jones' petition arrived in 1799, beseeching Congress to take action against the kidnapping of free blacks and criticizing the Fugitive Slave Act of 1793, tempers again flared. John Rutledge of South Carolina was particularly incensed. Interpreting the petition as a call for total emancipation, he asked his fellow congressmen, "Would calmness be consistent if entering wedges were prepared to ruin the property of whole estates?" "Yes," he insisted, "we deem this as an entering wedge to an

---

12. John Sidney, "An Oration Commemorative of the Abolition of the Slave Trade in the United States, Delivered before the Wilberforce Philanthropic Association, in the City of New York on the Second of January, 1809" [1–2], Schomburg Center for Research in Black Culture, Manuscripts, Archives and Rare Books Division, New York Public Library Digital Collections, accessed March 10, 2016, http://digitalcollections.nypl.org/items/510d47e3-fd58-a3d9-e040-e00a18064a99.
13. See document 5 in Chapter 2.
14. See document 5 in Chapter 2.

inevitable loss of our property." He then warned that emancipation in America would result in the same death and destruction that followed emancipation in Haiti.[15]

Dire warnings against universal emancipation did not discourage the efforts of many Americans to promote abolition. But as the free black population increased, achieving this goal grew more elusive. Indeed, the number of free blacks in the United States was rapidly increasing. In 1790 an estimated sixty thousand free blacks lived in the United States; by 1830 that number would increase fivefold. Public discussion, and new anxieties, over the status of free blacks increased. Formerly "progressive" states like Pennsylvania considered legislation aimed at regulating this population. In Virginia, John Taylor's influential *Arator* called for the colonization of free blacks, a policy embraced in 1816 by the newly formed American Colonization Society (ACS).

Many white Americans genuinely saw colonization as a step toward total abolition. James Madison hung on to this belief well into the 1830s. Black leaders, however, were skeptical. Richard Allen was convinced that the design concealed behind colonization was to better secure the slave population, and he poignantly affirmed that "this land which we have watered with our tears and blood, is now our mother country and we are well satisfied to stay where wisdom abounds, and the gospel is free."[16] Three years later David Walker would quote Allen, and the words spoken by Henry Clay and John Randolph of Roanoke at the founding meeting of the ACS, in his angry condemnation of American slavery.

Why not simply emancipate slaves without colonization? As members of the Frederick County, Virginia, chapter of the ACS—a chapter sincerely committed to total abolition—explained, "A manumitted slave remains a negro still, and must ever continue in a state of political bondage. . . . Who would submit to a negro president or a negro chief justice?" The result, they argued, would be a disloyal population "prone to . . . rebellion."[17] Similarly, Thomas Dew argued that emancipation without colonization would for freed blacks result in a "life of endless mortification and disappointment." Expecting freedom and equality, emancipated blacks would soon discover that "custom or prejudice . . . would degrade them to the condition of slaves."[18] For many Americans, political power could not be shared among the races, nor were political and social equality obtainable or desirable.

It was their belief in the essential equality of the Negro as much as anything else in their program that made the Garrisonian abolitionists radical. Why

---

15. See document 7 in Chapter 2.
16. See document 13 in Chapter 3.
17. See document 11 in Chapter 3.
18. See document 1 in Chapter 4.

did Northerners insist on attaching emancipation to "expatriation?" Angelina Grimké asked. The "North is most dreadfully afraid of Amalgamation," and fearing "this consequence might flow from emancipation, she is determined to resist all efforts at emancipation without expatriation."[19]

Fierce racial prejudice was prevalent even among people opposed to slavery, and to free blacks, such prejudice was as enchaining as the shackles worn by slaves. "It is true that in . . . this State [New York], there are men, like myself," Theodore Wright proclaimed before an anti-slavery convention in 1836, "who are not subjected to the lash. . . . But sir, still we are slaves . . . we feel the chain galling us. . . ."[20] These deeply rooted prejudices convinced even some African Americans, like Martin Delany, that for free and enslaved blacks expatriation was the only path to true freedom.

Prejudice constrained the policies that even the most sympathetic would propose. John Bingham, future author of the Fourteenth Amendment, objected to Oregon's proposed constitution because it violated the privileges and immunities of U.S. citizens, a class of people that Bingham argued included free blacks. At the same time, he assured Congress that the "natural rights"—those "rights common to all men" which all republican governments uphold—excluded "political rights."[21] Assuring free blacks the right to a jury trial or the benefit of the writ of habeas corpus did not mean they would be permitted to vote. From our perspective Bingham's position suggests prejudice, but to his contemporaries, who were accustomed to denying free blacks every right of citizenship, Bingham's insistence that free blacks were citizens and thus entitled to basic rights seemed radical.

This same perspective should likewise frame how we interpret the words and actions of Abraham Lincoln. It has become popular for interpreters to parse Lincoln's words for evidence of racist sentiments, but when Lincoln reappeared on the political scene in the 1850s, the nation's views on slavery had changed radically since its founding. Lincoln found a Congress, and a nation, embracing legislation predicated on the assumption that slavery was morally permissible, a position he rejected and which he insisted "the fathers of the republic . . . rejected." According to Lincoln, the Framers' intent, reflected in the Constitution, was to ensure the extinction of slavery. Slavery, he claimed, "is hid away, in the constitution, just as an afflicted man hides away a wen or a cancer, which he dares not cut out at once, lest he bleed to death; with the promise, nevertheless, that the cutting may begin at the end of a given time."[22]

---

19. See document 8 in Chapter 4.
20. See document 9 in Chapter 4.
21. See document 7 in Chapter 6.
22. See document 3 in Chapter 6.

In fact, the Constitution's position on slavery was heatedly contested. Recall the earlier tracings of a pro-slavery reading of the Constitution articulated by General Pinckney. At the core of pro-slavery constitutionalism was the claim that "the general government can never emancipate [slaves], for no such authority is granted; and it is admitted, on all hands, that the general government has no powers but what are expressly granted by the Constitution."[23] Such a claim could be, and was, challenged. The Constitution does not limit Congress to powers *expressly* granted. Moreover, constitutional provisions, while falling short of total abolition, could be interpreted as permitting congressional action to contain slavery where it existed. The "migration and importation" clause along with the guarantee that new states form republican governments were interpreted as empowering Congress to ban slavery in new states. This view was strengthened in 1819 when John Jay publicly endorsed it. Others, like Robert Walsh, Jr., added that the commerce clause permitted Congress to suppress "the transportation of slaves, *for sale*, from one state to another, as well as from a state to a territory" and that Congress had the authority "to keep the territories and new states altogether free from the bane of negro slavery."[24]

While Walsh and others, like Representative James Tallmadge from New York, were convinced that Congress could prevent the introduction of slaves into the western territories, others disagreed. James Madison, the foremost authority on the Constitution, disputed this reading of the migration or importation clause, even while he maintained slavery to be an evil for which he sought a political solution. John Scott, representing the territorial government of Missouri, observed that the three-fifths clause was "not restricted to the States" that existed in 1787, noting that Kentucky, Louisiana, and Mississippi had all joined the Union after 1788 as slave states. On what grounds, he asked, could slavery be banned from Missouri? Indeed, as Philip Barbour of Virginia saw it, the privileges and immunities clause guaranteed to citizens in Missouri the "same privileges with a citizen of Virginia [to] hold a slave."[25]

These opposing interpretations would persist until the Civil War. Opponents of slavery pushed an anti-slavery reading. For abolitionists like Theodore Weld, slavery in the nation's capital could (and must) be abolished immediately, for Article I, Section 8 gave Congress authority to "exercise exclusive legislation, in all cases whatsoever" over the nation's capital.[26] Alvan Stewart perceived in the Fifth Amendment the constitutional ground for emancipation.[27] More generally, men like Lysander Spooner and Gerrit

---

23. See document 3 in Chapter 2.
24. See document 5 in Chapter 3.
25. See document 2 in Chapter 3.
26. See document 14 in Chapter 4.
27. See document 13 in Chapter 4.

Smith argued that the Constitution was anti-slavery. At the core of those arguments was a presumption that slavery was antithetical to the natural law in which the Constitution was rooted. Anti-slavery constitutionalists invoked the British ruling in *Stuart v. Somerset* (1772), which had been widely reported in the colonies. These reports were not entirely accurate, but no matter; Lord Mansfield wrote that slavery "*must* take its Rise from *positive* Law; the Origin of it can in no Country or Age, be traced back to any other Source,"[28] and thenceforth the *Somerset* case was offered as proof that slavery was inconsistent with natural law.

The claim that slavery was incompatible with natural law, however, did not refute the claim that the Constitution, as positive law, recognized the institution of slavery. Disputes over how to "read" the Constitution—as pro- or anti-slavery—opened a rift in the abolitionist movement. For Garrisonian abolitionists, the Constitution was a "sordid, trucking, cowardly" compromise that granted legal status to slavery.[29] Even if the language of the Constitution was not explicit, decades of legal rulings and legislation proved the Constitution to permit slavery. The moral imperative for Garrisonians was clear: if the Constitution supported slavery, then one must forswear behavior that would legitimize it. No abolitionist, Wendell Phillips explained, could "consistently take office under it, or swear to support it."[30] By the 1830s, other abolitionists argued that emancipation required more than moral suasion; direct political action was necessary. Establishing the Liberty Party in late 1839, James Birney and others called on abolitionists to commit their votes to the cause.

Slavery's apologists agreed with Garrison that the Constitution protected slavery. This claim was sanctioned by the U.S. Supreme Court in *Dred Scott v. Sandford*. Writing for the Court, Chief Justice Roger B. Taney argued that slaves were a form of property. Since property was guaranteed in the Fifth Amendment, he concluded that the "right of property in a slave is distinctly and expressly affirmed in the Constitution."[31] Lincoln would take great exception with that claim: "I believe that the right of property in a slave *is not* distinctly and expressly affirmed in the Constitution," he argued during his famous debates with Stephen Douglas. Equally troubling for Lincoln was the fact that Taney's ruling, and Douglas' insistence that he "don't care whether slavery is voted up or down," seemed predicated on the assumption that there was nothing inherently wrong with slavery.[32] Thomas Cobb made this assumption explicit the following year, when, contravening the claim in *Somerset*, he held

---

28. As reported in the *Virginia Gazette*, ed. Alexander Purdie and John Dixon (August 27, 1772), 3.
29. See document 1 in Chapter 6.
30. See document 21 in Chapter 4.
31. See document 4 in Chapter 6.
32. See document 6 in Chapter 6.

that Negro slavery was consistent with natural law and, therefore, that Negro slavery was presumed legal in a country until and unless that nation explicitly prohibited it.[33]

Cobb's claim was hardly new. Apologists for slavery had been anticipating his argument for decades. For example, as South Carolina governor George McDuffie explained, "servitude, in some form, is one of the essential . . . elements of which all political communities are composed."[34] James Henry Hammond echoed this sentiment. "In all social systems there must be a class to do the menial duties, to perform the drudgery of life," what Hammond called the "mud-sill" of society.[35] For McDuffie, Hammond, Dew, George Fitzhugh, John Calhoun, and many other opinion leaders in the South, the existence of an enslaved class in an otherwise free society was as natural as summer rain in Charleston. The North had its slaves, too, they argued, but rather than relying on Negro chattel slaves, the North enslaved free whites through the system of wages. Wage slavery, they claimed, was far worse than chattel slavery, for it enslaved men not suitable for slavery. Moreover, these white "slaves" possessed political power, and were they to use that power effectively, they could overturn the social and political order.

Happily for all, slavery's proponents argued, the South had discovered a docile race, one able to withstand the climate, to labor when commanded, and whose happiness depended on submission. African Negroes, McDuffie pronounced, "have all the qualities that fit them for slaves, and not one of those that would fit them to be freemen." To liberate them would be futile. "The capacity to enjoy freedom is an attribute not to be communicated by human power," he asserted. "It is an endowment of God," one "conferred . . . only upon those who are qualified to enjoy it." Until the "Ethiopian can change his skin," emancipation would be harmful to slave and master alike.[36]

In short, to men like James Henry Hammond, slavery had become "the greatest of all the great blessings which a kind Providence has bestowed upon our glorious region."[37] It was essential to the Negro's happiness, and it eliminated the class envy that existed between rich and poor whites in free-market societies. As Thomas Dew explained, "Color alone is here the badge of distinction, the true mark of aristocracy, and all who are white are equal in spite of the variety of occupation."[38] Accordingly, McDuffie declared "domestic slavery [to be] the cornerstone of our republican edifice." "No patriot," he added,

---

33. Thomas R. R. Cobb, *An Inquiry into the Law of Negro Slavery in the United States of America* (Savannah, 1858).

34. See document 7 in Chapter 4.

35. See document 5 in Chapter 6.

36. See document 7 in Chapter 4.

37. See document 10 in Chapter 4.

38. See document 1 in Chapter 4.

"who justly estimates our privileges will tolerate the idea of emancipation, at any period, however remote." Slavery had become essential to the preservation of white liberty.[39]

This was the environment Lincoln and Bingham faced in the 1850s. Slavery's advocates advanced constitutional arguments in its defense and proclaimed it essential to democracy. Race prejudice was deeply and widely engrained in the culture. Even Henry Clay, a man whom Lincoln admired and who claimed to be "no friend of slavery," rejected any plan that would promote the "equal social condition" of both black and white.[40] It's not surprising, then, that Stephen Douglas repeatedly accused Lincoln of promoting racial equality. Politically, Lincoln could not ignore such race-baiting, and as Lucas Morel notes, at times what Lincoln says regarding the rights of blacks "sounds poorly to modern ears." But as Morel astutely points out, "in all of Lincoln's writings, including the [1858 Lincoln-Douglas] debates, he never says blacks are *naturally* inferior to whites."[41] Before Lincoln could ask whites to accept civil and political rights for blacks, he first had to persuade them that blacks had natural rights. Lincoln understood that to end slavery, he had to save the Union; and that to save the Union, he had to put slavery on a path to extinction. Achieving both goals meant getting white Americans to start adjusting their attitudes toward blacks. Frederick Douglass perceived the delicate balance Lincoln had to maintain, and the ease with which his actions and words might be misconstrued as anti-black. Speaking at the unveiling of the Freedmen's Monument in Washington, D.C., Douglass observed that "viewed from the genuine abolition ground, Mr. Lincoln seemed tardy, cold, dull, and indifferent; but measuring him by the sentiment of his country, a sentiment he was bound as a statesman to consult, he was swift, zealous, radical, and determined."[42] In his rejection of the "mud-sill" theory, and in his majestic words at Gettysburg, Lincoln sought to remind Americans that the nation was founded on the principles of freedom and dignity for all.

---

39. See document 7 in Chapter 4.
40. See document 15 in Chapter 4.
41. Lucas E. Morel, "Lincoln, Race, and the Spirit of '76," *Perspectives on Political Science* 39 (January–March 2010): 6–7.
42. Frederick Douglass, "Oration in Memory of Abraham Lincoln," in *Frederick Douglass: Selected Speeches and Writings*, ed. Philip S. Foner (Chicago: Chicago Review Press, 2000), 221.

Chapter One: 1760–1786

Introduction

On August 24, 1774, one month after Parliament enacted the last of the Coercive Acts and just two weeks prior to the meeting of the First Continental Congress in Philadelphia, George Washington wrote a letter to his friend Bryan Fairfax concerning the ongoing crisis with Britain. For Washington, as for most colonists, the central dispute with Britain remained unchanged: namely, locating the line distinguishing parliamentary authority from the authority of the colonial governments. Washington would "not undertake to say where the Line between Great Britain and the Colonies should be drawn," but he added that he was "clearly of [the] opinion that one ought to be drawn; & our Rights clearly ascertaind." He then offered the following observation: "I could wish . . . that the dispute had been left to Posterity to determine, but the Crisis is arrivd when we must assert our Rights, or Submit to every Imposition that can be heap'd upon us; till custom and use, will make us as tame, & abject Slaves, as the Blacks we Rule over with such arbitrary Sway."[1]

It was not unusual for the American colonists to invoke the rhetoric of slavery when condemning parliamentary measures. Beginning with passage of the Stamp Act in 1765, many colonists perceived a parliamentary plot to enslave them. At first, the colonists objected to parliamentary taxation. They argued that to be taxed by a legislature in which they were not represented would render their property and rights insecure. By 1774, the argument had widened: the colonists could only be bound by laws to which they had consented. Because they were not represented in Parliament (and thus did not consent to parliamentary measures), Parliament could claim no legal authority whatsoever over them. To be governed by an unelected Parliament was to be subject to an uncontrollable, unaccountable, and therefore arbitrary power. Arbitrary power was rightly deemed incompatible with liberty, and Washington (and others) recognized in chattel slavery the same deprivation of liberty that they feared would be the consequence of Parliament's actions in the colonies.

Washington's reference to a "Line" further reminds us that the colonists were acutely sensitive to local rule. Parliament's actions in 1774, particularly

---

1. George Washington to Bryan Fairfax, August 24, 1774, in *The Papers of George Washington*, Colonial Series, vol. 10 (March 21, 1774–June 15, 1775), ed. W. W. Abbot and Dorothy Twohig (Charlottesville: University Press of Virginia, 1995), 155.

the Quebec Act, threatened to strip authority from the popularly elected colonial assemblies. In that sense, recent parliamentary measures were incompatible with the rights of the colonies as corporate bodies (what later would be called "states' rights"). The heightened sensitivity to the rights of the colonies as independent political societies is a leading principle in the Declaration of Independence, one that indelibly shaped the Articles of Confederation. When Washington and others spoke in this period of legislative action to abolish slavery, they referred to state—not national—authority.

Washington and others of like mind had reason to trust that the states would undertake meaningful action to end slavery. By 1776, colonists up and down the Atlantic seaboard were accustomed to living with slavery. One consequence of the American Revolution was that it forced colonists to confront the contradiction between their own emerging political identity and the institution of slavery. Colonial disquiet with slavery was reinforced by an emerging evangelical critique of the institution. Quakers, among others, on both sides of the Atlantic began to organize in opposition to slavery and in particular against the slave trade. In 1787 British Quakers (along with Anglicans Thomas Clarkson and Granville Sharp) established an organization dedicated to eradicating the infernal trade. In the colonies, Quakers like Jonathan Woolman and Anthony Benezet were among the earliest and most effective voices against slavery.

In general, the revolutionary era was marked by growing moral and political objections to the African slave trade. By the mid-1780s, a number of states had liberalized their manumission laws, passed gradual abolition laws, or banned slavery outright. Political leaders warned of the incompatibility of chattel slavery with republican institutions. In 1773 George Mason described slavery as a "slow Poison, which is daily contaminating the Minds & Morals of our People." Every slaveholder "is born a petty Tyrant," he argued. According to Mason, the slave owner, "practiced in Acts of Despotism & Cruelty," will grow "callous to the Dictates of Humanity." The danger was clear. "Habituated from our Infancy to trample upon the Rights of Human Nature," he warned, "every generous, every liberal Sentiment, if not extinguished, is enfeebled in our Minds. And in such an infernal School are to be educated our future Legislators & Rulers."[2] How could a free republic be maintained when its leaders and its citizens were daily trained in the practice of arbitrary power? Thomas Jefferson would famously echo these concerns a few years later, in his *Notes on the State of Virginia*.

Yet, Mason owned slaves, as did Jefferson, Patrick Henry, and other revolutionaries. "Would any one believe that I am Master of Slaves of my own

---

2. George Mason, "Extracts from the Virginia Charters," in *The Papers of George Mason*, ed. Robert A. Rutland (Chapel Hill: University of North Carolina Press, 1970), 173.

purchase!" Patrick Henry exclaimed in 1773, articulating an uneasiness with slavery increasingly felt in the American colonies. "I am drawn along by [the] general inconvenience of living without them, I will not, I cannot justify it."[3] Henry Laurens expressed similar discomfort. Writing to his son John, he noted that he "was born in a country where slavery had been established by British kings and parliaments," and that he had "found the Christian religion and slavery growing under the same authority and cultivation." Nevertheless, he abhorred slavery. He continued:

> The day I hope is approaching when, from principles of gratitude as well as justice, every man will strive to be foremost in showing his readiness to comply with the Golden Rule. Not less than twenty thousand pounds sterling would all my Negroes produce if sold at public auction tomorrow. I am not the man who enslaved them; they are indebted to Englishmen for that favour; nevertheless I am devising means for manumitting many of them, and for cutting off the entail of slavery. Great powers oppose me—the laws and customs of my country, my own and the avarice of my countrymen. What will my children say if I deprive them of so much estate? These are difficulties, but not insuperable. I will do as much as I can in my time, and leave the rest to a better hand.[4]

For many Americans, slavery was a way of life and an important source of wealth. The fact that slaves were viewed as property, and that the protection of property rights was a leading cause of the Revolution, prompted resistance to state efforts to liberalize manumission laws or abolish the institution outright. The 1785 petition by the Free Inhabitants of Amelia County (Virginia) is a good case in point. In sum, the American Revolution had sparked criticisms of slavery to the point that supporters of slavery felt compelled more actively to defend the institution—something that had been rare in earlier decades. While most of the white inhabitants of North America remained deeply racist, anti-slavery sentiments and early anti-slavery organizations began to emerge, prefiguring the arguments and efforts of future foes of slavery.

---

3. Patrick Henry to Robert Pleasants, January 18, 1773. See document 2 in this chapter.
4. John Laurens to Henry Laurens, August 14, 1776, in *A South Carolina Protest against Slavery: Being a Letter from Henry Laurens . . . to His Son . . .* (New York: G. P. Putnam, 1861), 20–21.

DOCUMENTS

1. Anthony Benezet, *A Short Account of That Part of Africa Inhabited by the Negroes* (1762)

Anthony Benezet (1713–1784) of Pennsylvania was instrumental in spearheading Quaker opposition to slavery. Here Benezet rejected the claim that enslaved blacks would have met the same fate in Africa, described the Middle Passage, and argued that the slave trade will stifle Christianity in Africa. The book consists of a lengthy essay on the slave trade, in which Benezet quoted extensively from earlier writings, after which he appended excerpts from a 1760 pamphlet. We include portions of both, below.

A SHORT ACCOUNT OF THE Slave-trade, &c.

. . . A lamentable and shocking Instance of the Influence which the Love of Gain has upon the Minds of those who yield to its Allurements, even when contrary to the Dictates of Reason, and the common Feelings of Humanity, appears in the Prosecution of the *Negro Trade*. . . . An Evil of so deep a Dye, and attended with such dreadful Consequences, that no well-disposed Person . . . who knows the Tyranny, Oppression and Cruelty with which this iniquitous Trade is carried on, can be a silent and innocent Spectator. How many Thousands of our harmless Fellow Creatures have, for a long Course of Years, fallen a Sacrifice to that selfish Avarice, which gives Life to this compli-cated Wickedness. The Iniquity of being engaged in a Trade, by which so great a Number of innocent People are yearly destroyed, in an untimely and miser-able Manner, is greatly aggravated from the Consideration that we, as a People, have been peculiarly favored with the Light of the Gospel; that Revelation of Divine Love, which the Angels introduced to the World, by a Declaration of *Peace on Earth, and Good Will to Men—of every Nation, Kindred, Tongue and People*. . . .

It is frequently alledged, in excuse for this Trade, that the Negroes Sold in our Plantations, are mostly Persons who have been taken Prisoners in those Wars which arise amongst themselves, from their mutual Animosities; and that these Prisoners would be sacrificed to the Resentment of those who have taken them Captive, if they were not purchased and brought away by the Europeans. It is also represented, that the Negroes are generally a stupid, savage People, whose Situation in their own Country is necessitous and unhappy, which has induced many to believe, that the bringing them from their Native Land is rather a Kindness than an Injury. . . .

[T]he *Negroes* are generally a sensible humane and sociable People, and that their Capacity is as good, and as capable of Improvement as that of the WHITES. . . .

And as to the common Arguments alleged in Defense of the Trade, *viz.*, That the *Slaves* sold to the *Europeans* are Captives taken in War, who would be destroyed by their Conquerors if not thus purchased; it is without Foundation: For although there were doubtless Wars amongst the *Negroes* before the *Europeans* began to trade with them, yet certain it is, that since that Time, those Calamities have prodigiously increased, which is principally owing to the Solicitations of white People, who have instigated the poor *Africans* by every Method, even the most iniquitous and cruel, to procure Slaves to load their Vessels, which they freely and gladly purchase without any Regard to the Precepts of the Gospel, the Feelings of Humanity, or the common Dictates of Reason and Equity. . . .

From what has been said, it may be concluded that the *Negroes* might have been happy, if the *Europeans* had not bore the Name only, but had, indeed, acted the Part of Christians, in using their Endeavours, by Example as well as Precept, to make them acquainted with the glad Tidings of the Gospel, and with that change of Heart, and Redemption from Sin, which Christianity proposes; this, if attended to, would have necessarily been productive of the peaceable Fruits of Righteousness; Innocence and Love, would have reigned in the Room of Animosities and Bloodshed . . . ; thus the Christians instead of provoking the Vengeance of a Jealous GOD, would have been the happy Instruments of compleating these poor *Africans* Happiness. But the Reverse has happened; the Europeans, forgetful of their Profession and Duty, as Men and Christians, have conducted in such a Manner, as must necessarily raise in the Minds of the Thoughtful and well-disposed *Negroes*, the utmost Scorn and Detestation of the Christian Name. They have made all other Considerations give way to an insatiable Desire of Gain, and are become the principal and moving Cause of the most abominable and dreadful Scene, that was, perhaps, ever acted upon this Globe. . . .

EXTRACTS *from* a Pamphlet, *intituled*, Two Dialogues on the Man-Trade, *Printed in* London, *in the Year* 1760 [included in Benezet's *Short Account of That Part of Africa* . . .]

. . . Man-stealers were, by the Law of *Moses*, punished with Death. *He that stealeth a Man, or if he be found in his Hand, he shall surely be put to Death,*

Exod. xxi. 16. And in the New Testament, 1 Tim. 10. Man-stealers are reck-
oned amongst the very worst of Men. Can any Thing be more cruel and barbarous, than to seize upon human Creatures, and take them away by Force
from their native Country, from their Friends and Relations, for ever . . . and
drive them, like Hogs, to Market, there to be sold for Slaves for Life? . . . What
Monsters in Nature then, destitute of all Humanity and Compassion, must
they be, who are guilty of it. The black Men have the same natural Affection
for their Kindred, and as strong, as we have. To sell and buy human Creatures . . . , to trade in Men, as you would in brute Creatures, or any other
Commodities, is really impious as well as cruel. Man is a noble Creature, made
but a little lower than the Angels, and crowned with Glory and Honour. He is
the Offspring of GOD; therefore, thus to debase him, and to bring him down
upon a Level with the Brutes, yea with Things inanimate, is great Impiety, it is
an high Affront offered to him, who is the kind and merciful Father of us all,
who hath made of one Blood all Nations of Men to dwell on the Face of the
Earth, and hath united them all in one Body by the Ties of Nature. . . .

The Captain of the *Guiney* Ship, when he has finished his Marketing, when
he has bought as many reasonable Creatures as he wants, and is full freighted,
having on board (we will say) Two Hundred of them, coupled in Irons, and
closely crammed up in a Ship of about One Hundred Tons Burthen, he sets
out for one of our Plantations, and may be two or three Months on the Voyage;
during which Time, from the Filth and Stench that must be among them,
occasioned by their being put down under Deck, and penn'd together in so
little Room, Distempers break out among them, and carry off a great many, a
Fifth, or Fourth, yea, sometimes a third Part of them. . . . I remember I read
an Account in one of the News-Papers last Year; a Ship, belonging to *Liverpool,*
that had a Hundred and Ninety Slaves on board, Eighty of whom died on
the Voyage. . . . Taking all the Slaves together, that are brought on board our
Ships yearly, from the Coast of *Africa*, where they are bought by our *Guiney*
Merchants, I think one may venture to affirm, that, at least, a Tenth Part of
them die on the Voyage. . . .

What a sad dreadful Affair then is this Man-Trade, whereby so many Thousands of our Fellow rational Creatures lose their Lives, are, truly and properly
speaking, murdered every Year; I do not think there is an Instance of so great
Barbarity and Cruelty carried on in any Part of the World, as is this, Year after
Year. It is enough to make one tremble, to think what a Load of Guilt lies
upon this Nation, on this Account, and that the Blood of Thousands of poor
innocent Creatures, murdered every Year, in carrying on this cursed Trade, cry
aloud to Heaven for Vengeance.

2. Patrick Henry, Letter to Robert Pleasants (January 18, 1773)

In this letter, eventually published in the nineteenth century, Patrick Henry (1736–1799) asserted that slavery conflicts with Scripture and natural justice. This letter would later be cited as evidence that the American Founders desired to see slavery abolished.

I take this oppo[rtunity] to acknowledge the receipt of A[nthony] Benezets Book against the Slave Trade. I thank you for it. It is not a little surprising that Christianity, whose chief excellence consists in softening the human heart, in cherishing & improving its finer Feelings, should encourage a Practice so totally repugnant to the first Impression of right & wrong. What adds to the wonder is that this Abominable Practice has been introduced in ye. most enlightened Ages. Times that seem to have pretentions to boast of high Improvements in the Arts, Sciences, & refined Morality, h[ave] brought into general use, & guarded by many Laws, a Species of Violence & Tyranny, which our more rude & barbarous, but more honest Ancestors detested. Is it not amazing, that at a time, when ye. Rights of Humanity are defined & understood with precision, in a Country above all others fond of Liberty, that in such an Age, & such a Country we find Men, professing a Religion ye. most humane, mild, meek, gentle & generous; adopting a Principle as repugnant to humanity as it is inconsistant with the Bible and destructive to Liberty.

Every thinking honest Man rejects it in Speculation, how few in Practice from conscienscious Motives? The World in general has denied [the] People a share of its honours, but the Wise will ascribe to [you] a just Tribute of virtuous Praise, for [the] Practice of a train of Virtues among which y[ou]r disagreement to Slavery will be principally ranked.—I cannot but wish well to a people whose System imitates ye. Example of him whose Life was perfect.—And believe m[e], I shall honour the Quakers for their noble Effort to abolish Slavery. It is equally calculated to promote moral & political Good.

Would any one believe that I am Master of Slaves of my own purchase! I am drawn along by [the] general inconvenience of living without them, I will not, I cannot justify it. However culpable my Conduct, I will so far pay my devoir to Virtue, as to own the excellence & rectitude of her Precepts, & to lament my want of conforming to them.—

I believe a time will come when an oppo[rtunity] will be offered to abolish this lamentable Evil.—Every thing we can do is to improve it, if it happens in our day, if not, let us transmit to our descendants together with our Slaves, a pity for their unhappy Lot, & an abhorrence for Slavery. If we cannot reduce this wished for Reformation to practice, let us treat the unhappy victims with lenity, it is [the] furthest advance we can make toward Justice. [We owe to the] purity of our Religion to shew that it is at variance with that Law which warrants Slavery.—

3. Benjamin Rush, *An Address to the Inhabitants of the British Settlements in America on the Slavery of the Negroes in America* (1773)

In this pamphlet Dr. Benjamin Rush (1746–1813) refuted claims that Scripture defends slavery or that slavery serves as a means to spread the Gospel. Rush suggested that slavery is a "national crime," which, if not confronted, will elicit divine "national punishments," a warning common among abolitionists and famously repeated in Abraham Lincoln's Second Inaugural Address. The footnotes below are original to Rush.

. . . Without entering into the History of the facts which relate to the Slave Trade, I shall proceed to combat the principal arguments which are used to support it.

I need hardly to say anything in favour of the Intellects of the Negroes, or of their capacities for virtue and happiness, although these have been supposed, by some, to be inferior to those of the inhabitants of Europe. The accounts which travelers give us of their ingenuity, humanity, and strong attachment to their parents, relations, friends and country, show us that they are equal to the Europeans, when we allow for the diversity of temper and genius which is occasioned by climate. We have many well-attested anecdotes of as sublime and disinterested virtue among them as ever adorned a Roman or a Christian character. Slavery is so foreign to the human mind, that the moral faculties, as well as those of the understanding are debased, and rendered torpid by it. All the vices which are charged upon the Negroes in the southern colonies and the West-Indies, such as Idleness, Treachery, Theft, and the like, are the genuine offspring of slavery. . . .

Nor let it be said, in the present Age, that their black color (as it is commonly called) either subjects them to, or qualifies them for slavery. The vulgar notion of their being descended from Cain, who was supposed to have been marked with this color, is too absurd to need refutation. . . .

. . . [T]here are some who have gone so far as to say that Slavery is not repugnant to the Genius of Christianity, and that it is not forbidden in any part of the Scripture. . . . [W]e are told the Jews kept the Heathens in perpetual bondage.[5] The design of providence in permitting this evil, was probably to prevent the Jews from marrying amongst strangers, to which their intercourse with them upon any other footing than that of slaves, would naturally have inclined them.[6] Had this taken place . . . the intention of Providence in keeping them a distant people, in order to accomplish the promise made to Abraham, that "in his seed all the nations of the earth should be blessed," would have been defeated. . . . But with regard to their own countrymen, it is plain, perpetual slavery was not tolerated. Hence, at the end of seven years or in the year of the jubilee, all the Hebrew slaves were set at liberty.[7] . . . But if, in the partial Revelation which God made, of his will to the Jews, we find such testimonies against slavery, what may we not expect from the Gospel, the Design of which was to abolish all distinctions of name and country? While the Jews thought they complied with the precepts of the law, in confining the love of their neighbor "to the children of their own people," Christ commands us to look upon all mankind even our Enemies[8] as our neighbors and brethren, and "in all things, to do unto them whatever we would wish they should do unto us." He tells us further that his "Kingdom is not of this World," and therefore constantly avoids saying any thing that might interfere directly with the Roman or Jewish Governments: and although he does not call upon masters to emancipate their slaves, or slaves to assert that Liberty wherewith God and Nature had made them free, yet there is scarcely a parable or a sermon in the whole history of his life, but what contains the strongest arguments against Slavery. Every prohibition of Covetousness, Intemperance, Pride, Uncleanness, Theft, and Murder, which he delivered, every lesson of meekness, humility, forbearance, Charity, Self-denial, and brotherly-love, which he taught, are leveled against this evil. . . .

There are some amongst us who cannot help allowing the force of our last argument, but plead as a motive for importing and keeping slaves, that they become acquainted with the principles of the religion of our country. This is like justifying highway robbery because part of the money acquired in this manner was appropriated to some religious use. Christianity will never be propagated by any other methods than those employed by Christ and His

---

5. Levit. xxv. 44, 45, 46.

6. That marriage with strangers was looked upon as a crime among the Jews, we learn from Ezra ix. 1 to 6, also from the whole of chapter x.

7. Deuteronomy xxiv. 7.

8. This is strongly inculcated in the story of the good Samaritan, Luke X.

Apostles. Slavery is an engine as little fitted to that purpose as Fire or the Sword. A Christian Slave is a contradiction in terms. . . .

But it will be asked, What steps shall we take to remedy this Evil, and what shall we do with those Slaves we have already in this Country?

The first thing I would recommend to put a stop to slavery in this country, is to leave off importing slaves. For this purpose let our assemblies unite in petitioning the king and parliament to dissolve the African committee of merchants: It is by them that the trade is chiefly carried on to America. We have the more reason to expect relief from an application at this juncture, as by a late decision in favor of a Virginia slave in Westminster-Hall, the Clamors of the whole nation are raised against them. Let such of our countrymen as engage in the slave trade, be shunned as the greatest enemies to our country, and let the vessels which bring the slaves to us, be avoided as if they bore in them the Seeds of that forbidden fruit, whose baneful taste destroyed both the natural and the moral world. As for the Negroes amongst us, who, from having acquired all the low vices of slavery, or who from age or infirmities are unfit to be set at liberty, I would propose, for the good of society, that they should continue the property of those with whom they grow old, or from whom they contracted those vices and infirmities. But let the young Negroes be educated in the principles of virtue and religion—let them be made to limit the time of their servitude, and to entitle them to all the privileges of free-born British subjects. . . .

And now my countrymen, What shall I add more to rouse up your Indignation against Slave-keeping. . . . Think of the bloody Wars which are fomented by it among the African nations, or if these are too common to affect you, think of the pangs which attend the dissolution of the ties of nature in those who are stolen from their relations. Think of the many thousands who perish by sickness, melancholy, and suicide, in their voyages to America. Pursue the poor devoted victims to one of the West India islands, and see them exposed there to public sale. Hear the cries, and see their looks of tenderness at each other, upon being separated. Mothers are torn from their Daughters, and Brothers from Brothers, without the liberty of a parting embrace. Their master's name is now marked upon their breasts with a red hot iron. But let us pursue them into Sugar Field: and behold a scene still more affecting than this—See! . . . [S]ome of them, overcome with heat and sickness, seek to refresh themselves by a little rest. But, behold an Overseer approaches them. In vain they sue for pity. He lifts up his Whip, while streams of Blood follow every stroke. . . . Behold, one covered with stripes, into which melted wax is poured—another tied down to a block or a stake—a third suspended in the air by his thumbs—a fourth—I cannot relate it. Where now is Law or Justice? Let us fly to them to step in for their relief. . . . See here one without a limb, whose only crime was an attempt to regain his Liberty, another led to a Gallows for stealing a morsel of Bread, to which his labor gave him a better title than his master—a third famishing on a gibbet—a fourth, in a flame of Fire! His shrieks pierce the heavens. O God! Where is thy Vengeance! O Humanity, Justice, Liberty, Religion—where have ye fled? . . .

Ye men of Sense and Virtue—Ye advocates for American Liberty, rouse up and espouse the cause of Humanity and general Liberty. Bear a testimony against a vice which degrades human nature, and dissolves that universal tie of benevolence which should connect all the children of men together in one great Family. The plant of liberty is of so tender a Nature, that it cannot thrive long in the neighborhood of slavery. Remember the eyes of all Europe are fixed upon you, to preserve an asylum for freedom in this country, after the last pillars of it are fallen in every other quarter of the Globe.

But chiefly—ye Ministers of the Gospel . . . let your zeal keep pace with your opportunities to put a stop to slavery. While you enforce the duties of "tithe and cumin," neglect not the weightier laws of justice and humanity. Slavery is an Hydra of sin, and includes in it every violation of the precepts of the Law and the Gospel. In vain will you command your flocks to offer up the incence of Faith and Charity, while they continue to mingle the Sweat and blood of Negro slaves with their sacrifices. . . . Remember that national crimes require national punishments, and without declaring what punishment awaits this evil, you may venture to assure them, that it cannot pass with impunity, unless God shall cease to be just and merciful.

4. Richard Nisbet, *Slavery Not Forbidden by Scripture, Or a Defense of the West Indian Planter* (1773)

Responding to Benjamin Rush, Richard Nisbet (n.d.), who came to Philadelphia in the 1770s from the West Indies, where he had owned slaves, defended slavery through scriptural interpretation. Denying that slaves were brutalized, he argued that slavery served to improve their condition.

. . . SLAVERY, like all other human institutions, may be attended with its particular abuses, but that is not sufficient totally to condemn it, and to reckon every one unworthy the society of men who owns a negro.

If precedent constitutes law, surely it can be defended, for it has existed in all ages. The Scriptures, instead of forbidding it, declare it lawful. The divine legislator, Moses, says—"Both thy bond-men and thy bond-maids, which thou shalt have, shall be of the heathen that are round about you: of them shall ye buy, and of their families that are with you, which they beget in your land: and they shall be your possession. And ye shall take them for a possession, they shall be your bond-men forever" [*Leviticus* xxv. 44, 45, 46]. . . .

In another place, giving laws concerning servants, he says—"And if a man smite his servant or his maid, with a rod, and he die under his hand, he shall be surely punished; notwithstanding, if he continue a day or two, he shall not be punished: for he is his money" [*Exodus* xxi. 20].

Killing a servant on the spot it seems was punished, though not capitally: for in the same chapter, he mentions six capital crimes, and always expresses in the most direct terms that the delinquent shall suffer death. We cannot easily infer the same meaning from the word *punished*. He probably meant a pecuniary fine. . . . The words *his money*, plainly convey the idea of property, as if he were talking of an ox or an ass.

It must be observed, that these laws, which are so much in favour of the master, seem to have been applicable only to Hebrew servants. . . . [S]laves for life . . . lay under still greater disadvantages. The heathens and strangers appear to have been held in so small estimation, by Moses and the Jews, that it is likely that he did not think it worth while to give any laws concerning them, and left it in the will of the master, to treat them as he thought proper. . . .

Our Saviour's general maxims of charity and benevolence, cannot be mentioned as proofs against slavery. If the custom had been held in abhorrence by Christ and his disciples, they would, no doubt, have preached against it in direct terms. . . .

If this writer [Benjamin Rush] had confined himself to the impropriety of slavery in this, and some of the other colonies, and treated the subject in an unprejudiced manner, his labours might have been useful. . . . But his proposal of settling the West-Indies entirely with whites, and giving the Negroes their liberty, could never come from a man of common sense. The Author of the *Address* has, certainly, never been in the sugar islands, and consequently, whatever he mentions, concerning them, must be from a confused hear-say, not from experience.

I IMAGINE there are above four-hundred thousand Negroes in the British Islands: Can he point out a plan to procure the same number of whites in their stead? Or, if they could be got, would not there be a necessity for vast reinforcements, to supply the place of those cut off by disease? Where is the money to be raised to make satisfaction to the Planters for the loss of their property? . . .

It is now time to indulge, for a moment, the commercial supposition, that government were . . . by act of parliament, [to] declare all the negroes free; many of the richest British subjects must immediately become beggars, and the sugar colonies (not to mention those that produce rice and indigo) will be deserted. The nation must consequently pay above four millions a year, to foreigners, for that commodity, the revenue will be reduced more than another million, and the surest vent for our manufactures would be lost. By such terrible drains, Britain would be rendered quite defenceless, and she must soon fall as easy prey to France, or some of her other powerful neighbours; and thus, by freeing the Africans, Britons, themselves, must become abject slaves to despotick power. . . .

. . . He has represented the West-India planters as a set of hardened monsters, who, whip their slaves without any cause—ravish their women—torment both sexes with melted wax and fire—suspend them in the air by the thumbs, and wantonly indulge themselves in every species of cruelty. He says these pictures are taken from real life. I should be glad to know his authority.

. . . For my part, I never knew a single instance of such shocking barbarities, and every West-Indian with whom I have conversed on the subject, has made the same declaration. . . .

I have no intentions to insinuate, that the planters do not bestow proper correction when it is necessary. If they were totally neglectful in this particular, they would neither be lovers of justice, nor consult the happiness of their slaves. . . . The negroes of a very indulgent, easy master, for the most part, become compleat villains. They not only injure their master's property, but likewise are a nuisance to the neighbourhood, and for their flagrant crimes are often punished by the laws; which might have been prevented if they had been checked in proper time. You have no chance to acquire the esteem of negroes by never correcting them for a fault; they are sure to laugh at your folly. It is a universal remark, that almost every insurrection in the West-Indies, has been hatched on the estates of over-indulgent masters, and ten to one, his favorite servants are the ringleaders, and strike the first blow. . . .

[Benjamin Rush] would make us believe, that negroes are often put to death, by the laws, for such a trifling transgression as stealing a bit of bread. . . . They are never capitally punished, except for the most flagrant crimes—none condemned without the clearest proofs—notorious acts of theft, which in England would bring any person to the gallows, are only punished with a few stripes. . . . Once in a dozen years, perhaps, a Negro has been *burnt* or *gibbeted* for an atrocious murder: But have there not been instances of people suffering the former punishment in England; and much severer tortures than either, are common among the most civilized nations in Europe. The accusation of their being *starved*, is equally groundless. A planter will deny himself the common necessaries of life, rather than let his negroes want, for he cannot expect them to work, unless they are properly fed. . . .

. . . Though one cannot talk with any degree of certainty, with regard to the situation of the Africans, in their own country, yet . . . on the whole, it seems probable, that they are a much inferior race of men to the whites in every respect. . . . They are, in their own country, said to be utterly unacquainted with arts, letters, manufactures, and everything which constitutes civilized life. I never could observe the Africans have the most distant idea of a Supreme Being, or that they paid him the smallest worship. . . . They seem to be utterly unacquainted with friendship, gratitude, and every tie of the same kind. Great pains are taken to give a high coloring to the affecting scenes between relations when parted at a sale; but I appeal to everyone who has ever been present, at the disposal of a cargo, if he has not seen these creatures, separated from their nearest relations without looking after them, or wishing them farewell. . . .

A Negro may be said to have few cares, and less reason to be anxious about to-morrow, than any other individual of our species. . . . The Negro, it is true, cannot easily change his master, but to make amends for this inconvenience, he enjoys the singular advantage, over his brother in freedom, of being attended with care during sickness, and of having the same provision in old age, as in the days of his youth. [T]he more children he has, the richer he becomes; for the moment a child is born, the parents receive the same quantity of food for its support . . . and in case of their own death, if they have any reflection, they will quit the world with the certainty, of their children being brought up with the same care they formerly experienced themselves.

5. Thomas Jefferson, Notes from a Meeting of the Committee of the Continental Congress on the Articles of Confederation (July 12, 1776)

Under the Articles of Confederation, the continental government raised revenue through quotas levied on the states in proportion to their wealth. How properly to measure state wealth provoked debate. Slaveholding interests were loath to count slaves for this purpose, but others disagreed, and Congress ultimately based taxes on land values. In 1783, when Congress once more considered using population to calculate taxes, the debate over counting slaves again erupted, introducing the three-fifths compromise later adopted by the Framers of the U.S. Constitution.

On Friday July 12. The Committee appointed to draw the Articles of Confederation reported them, and . . . those articles were debated which determined the proportion or quota of money which each state should furnish to the common treasury. . . . The first of these articles were expressed in the original draught in these words. "Art. XI. All charges of war & all other expenses that shall be incurred for the common defense, or general welfare, and allowed by the United States assembled, shall be defrayed out of a common treasury, which shall be supplied by the several colonies in proportion to the number of inhabitants of every age, sex & quality, except Indians not paying taxes, in each colony. . . ."

Mr. [Samuel] Chase [of Maryland] moved that the quotas should be fixed, not by the number of inhabitants of every condition, but by that of the "white inhabitants." . . . He considered the number of inhabitants as a tolerably good criterion of property, and that this might always be obtained. He therefore thought it the best mode which we could adopt, with one exception only. He observed that Negroes are property, and as such cannot be distinguished from the lands or personalities held in those States where there are few slaves, that the surplus of profit which a Northern farmer is able to lay by, he invests in cattle, horses, &c. whereas a Southern farmer lays out that same surplus in slaves. There is no more reason therefore for taxing the Southern states on the farmer's head, & on his slave's head, than the Northern ones on their farmer's heads & the heads of their cattle, that the method proposed would therefore tax the Southern states according to their numbers & their wealth conjunctly, while the Northern would be taxed on numbers only: that Negroes in fact should not be considered as members of the state more than cattle & that they have no more interest in it.

Mr. John Adams [of Massachusetts] observed that the numbers of people were taken by this article as an index of the wealth of the state, & not as subjects of taxation, that as to this matter it was of no consequence by what name you called your people, whether by that of freemen or of slaves. That in some countries the laboring poor were called freemen, in others they were called slaves; but that the difference as to the state was imaginary only. . . . Certainly 500 freemen produce no more profits, no greater surplus for the payment of taxes than 500 slaves. Therefore the state in which are the laborers called freemen should be taxed no more than that in which are those called slaves. Suppose by any extraordinary operation of nature or of law one half the laborers of a state could in the course of one night be transformed into slaves: would the state be made the poorer or the less able to pay taxes? . . . It is the number of laborers which produce the surplus for taxation, and numbers therefore indiscriminately, are the fair index of wealth. That it is the use of the word "property" here, & its application to some of the people of the state, which produces the fallacy. How does the Southern farmer procure slaves? Either by importation or by purchase from his neighbor. If he imports a slave, he adds one to the number of laborers in his country, and proportionably to its profits & abilities to pay taxes. If he buys from his neighbor it is only a transfer of a laborer from one farm to another, which does not change the annual produce of the state, & therefore should not change its tax. That if a Northern farmer works ten laborers on his farm, he can, it is true, invest the surplus of ten men's labor in cattle: but so may the Southern farmer working ten slaves. That a state of one hundred thousand freemen can maintain no more cattle than one of one hundred thousand slaves. Therefore they have no more of that kind of property. That a slave may indeed from the custom of speech be more properly called the wealth of his master, than the free laborer might be called the wealth of his employer: but as to the state, both were equally its wealth, and should therefore equally add to the quota of its tax.

Mr. [Benjamin] Harrison [of Virginia] proposed as a compromise, that two slaves should be counted as one freeman. He affirmed that slaves did not do so much work as freemen; and doubted if two effected more than one. . . .

Mr. [James] Wilson [of Pennsylvania] said that if this amendment should take place the Southern colonies would have all the benefit of slaves, whilst the Northern ones would bear the burden. That slaves increase the profits of a state, which the Southern states mean to take to themselves; that they also increase the burthen of defense, which would of course fall so much the heavier on the Northern. That slaves occupy the places of freemen and eat their food. Dismiss your slaves & freemen will take their places. It is our duty to lay every discouragement on the importation of slaves. . . . That other kinds of property were pretty equally distributed through all the colonies: there were as many cattle, horses, & sheep, in the North as the South, & South as the North; but not so as to slaves. That experience has shown that those colonies have been always able to pay most which have the most inhabitants, whether they be black or white, and the practice of the Southern colonies has always been to make every farmer pay poll taxes upon all his laborers whether they be black or white. He acknowledges indeed that freemen work the most; but they consume the most also. They do not produce a greater surplus for taxation. The slave is neither fed nor clothed so expensively as a freeman. Again white women are exempted from labor generally, but Negro women are not. In this then the Southern states have an advantage as the article now stands. It has sometimes been said that slavery is necessary because the commodities they raise would be too dear for market if cultivated by freemen; but now it is said that the labor of the slave is the dearest. . . .

Dr. [John] Witherspoon [of New Jersey] was of opinion that the value of lands & houses was the best estimate of the wealth of a nation, and that it was practicable to obtain such a valuation. This is the true barometer of wealth. The one now proposed is imperfect in itself, and unequal between the States. . . .

6. Alexander Hamilton, Letter to John Jay (March 14, 1779)

Here Alexander Hamilton (1755–1804) endorsed a proposal advanced by Colonel John Laurens that sought to address the shortage of soldiers in the South by raising a regiment of black troops in exchange for their freedom. The South Carolina Assembly ultimately rejected this scheme. Hamilton's letter expresses sympathy toward slaves and suggests that blacks were not inferior.

Dear Sir,

Col. Laurens, who will have the honor of delivering you this letter, is on his way to South Carolina, on a project, which I think, in the present situation of affairs there, is a very good one and deserves every kind of support and encouragement. This is to raise two three or four battalions of Negroes; with the assistance of the government of that state, by contributions from the owners in proportion to the number they possess. . . .

It appears to me, that an expedient of this kind, in the present state of Southern affairs, is the most rational, that can be adopted, and promises very important advantages. Indeed, I hardly see how a sufficient force can be collected in that quarter without it; and the enemy's operations there are growing infinitely serious and formidable. I have not the least doubt, that the Negroes will make very excellent soldiers, with proper management; and I will venture to pronounce, that they cannot be put in better hands than those of Mr. Laurens. . . . It is a maxim with some great military judges, that with sensible officers soldiers can hardly be too stupid. . . . I mention this, because I frequently hear it objected to the scheme of embodying Negroes that they are too stupid to make soldiers. This is so far from appearing to me a valid objection that I think their want of cultivation (for their natural faculties are probably as good as ours) joined to that habit of subordination which they acquire from a life of servitude, will make them sooner become soldiers than our White inhabitants. Let officers be men of sense and sentiment, and the nearer the soldiers approach to machines perhaps the better.

I foresee that this project will have to combat much opposition from prejudice and self-interest. The contempt we have been taught to entertain for the blacks, makes us fancy many things that are founded neither in reason nor experience; and an unwillingness to part with property of so valuable a kind will furnish a thousand arguments to show the impracticability or pernicious tendency of a scheme which requires such a sacrifice. But it should be considered, that if we do not make use of them in this way, the enemy probably will; and that the best way to counteract the temptations they will hold out will be to offer them ourselves. An essential part of the plan is to give them their freedom with their muskets. This will secure their fidelity, animate their courage, and I believe will have a good influence upon those who remain, by opening a door to their emancipation. This circumstance, I confess, has no small weight in inducing me to wish the success of the project; for the dictates of humanity and true policy equally interest me in favor of this unfortunate class of men. . . .

7. Chief Justice William Cushing, Notes on *Quok Walker v. Nathaniel Jennison* (1783)

In this trial, the Massachusetts Supreme Court ruled that slavery was incompatible with the state's constitution. While the court's ruling was not written down, Cushing's instructions to the jury survive. The state constitution did not expressly prohibit slavery, but without legal support the institution could not survive. By 1790, slavery had disappeared from Massachusetts.

. . . As to the doctrine of slavery and the right of Christians to hold Africans in perpetual servitude, and sell and treat them as we do our horses and cattle, that (it is true) has been heretofore countenanced by the Province Laws formerly, but nowhere is it expressly enacted or established. It has been a usage—a usage which took its origin from the practice of some of the English nations, and the regulations of British government respecting the then Colonies, for the benefit of trade and wealth. But whatever sentiments have formerly prevailed in this particular or slid upon us by the example of others, a different idea has taken place with the people of America, more favorable to the natural rights of mankind, and to that natural, innate desire of Liberty, with which Heaven (without regard to color, complexion, or shape of noses-features) has inspired all the human race. And upon this ground our Constitution of Government, by which the people of this Commonwealth have solemnly bound themselves, sets out with declaring that all men are born free and equal—and that every subject is entitled to liberty, and to have it guarded by the laws, as well as life and property—and in short is totally repugnant to the idea of being born slaves. This being the case, I think the idea of slavery is inconsistent with our own conduct and Constitution; and there can be no such thing as perpetual servitude of a rational creature, unless his liberty is forfeited by some criminal conduct or given up by personal consent or contract. . . .

8. Methodist Petition to Abolish Slavery in Virginia (November 1785)

In the 1780s, Methodists throughout the states condemned slavery, advocating emancipation and instructing abolition among their communicants. Inspired by the Gospel, Methodists petitioned for abolition in the Virginia state legislature that convened in 1785.

To the Honorable Gentlemen of the State of Virginia; The Petition of the underwritten Electors of the said State.

Humbly Sheweth: That your Petitioners are clearly and fully persuaded that Liberty is the Birthright of Mankind, the right of every rational Creature without exception, who has not forfeited that right to the laws of his Country: That the Body of Negroes in this State have been robbed of that right without any such Forfeiture, and therefore ought in Justice to have their right restored: That the Glorious and ever Memorable Revolution can be Justified on no other principles, but what do plead with greater force for the Emancipation of our Slaves; in proportion as the Oppression exercised over them exceeds the Oppression formerly exercised by Great Britain over these States. That the Argument, "They were Prisoners of War, when they were Originally purchased," is utterly invalid, for no right of Conquest can Justly subject any Man to perpetual Slavery, much less his posterity: That the Riches & Strength of every Country consists in the number of its Inhabitants who are Interested in the support of its Government; and therefore to bind the Vast Body of Negroes to the State by the powerful ties of Interest will be the highest Policy. That the Argument drawn from the difference of Hair, Features, and Color, are so beneath the Man of Sense, much more the Christian, that we would insult the Honorable Assembly by enlarging upon them. That the fear of the Enormities which the Negroes may commit, will be groundless, at least if the Emancipation be gradual, as the Activity of the Magistrates and the provision of Houses of Correction where Occasion may require, will easily Suppress the gross, flagrant, Idleness either of Whites or Blacks. But above all, that deep Debasement of Spirit, which is the necessary Consequence of Slavery, incapacitates the human Mind (except in a few instances) for the Reception of the Noble and enlarged principles of the Gospel. . . . That of Consequence, Justice, mercy and Truth, every Virtue that can Adorn the Man or the Christian, the Interest of Religion, the honor & real Interest of the State, and the Welfare of Mankind do unanswerably, uncontrollably plead for the Removal of this grand Abomination; And therefore that we humbly entreat the Honorable the Assembly, as their Superior Wisdom may dictated to them, to pursue the most Prudential, but effectual Method for the immediate or Gradual Extirpation of Slavery. . . .

9. Amelia County Pro-Slavery Petition (November 10, 1785)

Responding to the Methodist initiative, slavery apologists in the Virginia Southside and Piedmont submitted numerous counter-petitions. The Amelia County petition, excerpted here, uses Scripture to defend slavery, expressing fears about the consequences of emancipation, and demands that the legislature repeal the recently enacted manumission law.

The Remonstrance and Petition of the Free Inhabitants of Amelia County [Virginia]

Gentlemen,

When the British Parliament usurped a Right to dispose of our Property without our Consent, we dissolved the Union with our Parent Country, and established a Constitution and Form of Government of our own, that our Property might be secure, in Future. In Order to effect this we risked our Lives and Fortunes, and waded through Seas of Blood. By the favorable Interposition of Providence our Attempt was crowned with Success. We were put in the Possession of our Rights of Liberty and Property: And these Rights [are] as well secured, as they can be by any human Constitution or Form of Government. But notwithstanding this, we understand a very subtle and daring Attempt is made to dispossess us of a very important Part of our Property. An Attempt set on Foot, we are informed, by the Enemies of our Country, Tools of the British Administration, and supported by certain Men among us of considerable Weight, To WREST FROM US OUR SLAVES, by an Act of the Legislature for a general Emancipation of them. An attempt unsupported by Scripture or sound Policy.

It is unsupported by Scripture. For we find that under the Old Testament Dispensation, Slavery was permitted by the Deity himself. Thus, Leviticus Ch. 25. Ver. 44, 45, 46. "Both thy Bond Men and Bond Maids, which thou shalt have, shall be of the Heathen that are round about you; of them shall ye buy Bond Men and Bond Maids. Moreover, of the Children of the Strangers that do sojourn among you, of them shall ye buy, and of their Families that are with you, which they beget in your Land, and they shall be your Possession, and ye shall take them as an Inheritance, for your Children after you, to inherit them for a Possession; they shall be your Bond-men forever." This Permission to buy and inherit Bond-men and Bond-maids, we have Reason to conclude, continued through all the Revolutions of the Jewish Government, down to the Advent of our Lord. And we do not find, that either he or his Apostles abridged it. The Freedom promised to his Followers, is a Freedom from the Bondage of Sin and Satan, and from the Dominion of Mens' Lusts and Passions; but as to their Outward Condition, whatever that was before they embraced the Religion of Jesus, whether Bond or Free, it remained the same afterwards. This St. Paul expressly asserts I Cor. Chap. 7. Ver. 20. where he is speaking directly to this very Point, "Let every Man abide in the same Calling, wherein he is called"; and Ver. 24. "Let every Man wherein he is called, therein abide with God." Thus it is evident the said Attempt is unsupported by Scripture.

It is also exceedingly impolitic. For it involves in it, and is productive of Want, Poverty, Distress, and Ruin to the Free Citizen; Neglect, Famine and Death to the black Infant and superannuated Parent; The Horrors of all the Rapes, Murders, and Outrages, which a vast Multitude of unprincipled, unpropertied, revengeful, and remorseless Banditti are capable of perpetrating; inevitable Bankruptcy to the Revenue, and consequently Breach of public Faith, and Loss of Credit with foreign Nations; and, lastly, sure and final Ruin to this now flourishing free and happy Country.

We therefore, your Petitioners and Remonstrants, do solemnly adjure and humbly pray you that you will discountenance and utterly reject every Motion and Proposal for emancipating our Slaves; that as the Act lately made, empowering the Owners of Slaves to liberate them, hath produced, and is still productive of, very bad Effects, you will immediately and totally repeal it; and that as many of the Slaves, liberated by that Act, have been guilty of Thefts and Outrages, Insolences and Violences, destructive to the Peace, Safety, and Happiness of Society, you will make effectual Provision for the due Government of them.

10. Thomas Jefferson, *Notes on the State of Virginia* (completed by 1785; final and revised publication in 1787)

In his influential book Notes on the State of Virginia, *Thomas Jefferson (1743–1826) presented an early example of "scientific" racism, expressing a number of the prejudices that many Americans have long ascribed to African Americans. Jefferson sought to explain why emancipation without colonization is not a viable option. He claimed that biologically determined racial differences disqualify some races from the practice of self-government, a claim that he later qualified. However, he argued that slavery violates natural law, issuing a warning about its moral and political effects on the health of American democracy. He maintained that race prejudice "is still a powerful obstacle" to emancipation, and for the remainder of his life advocated emancipation with colonization.*

Query XIV

. . . It will probably be asked, Why not retain and incorporate the blacks into the state, and thus save the expense of supplying, by importation of white settlers, the vacancies they will leave? Deep rooted prejudices entertained by the whites; ten thousand recollections, by the blacks, of the injuries they have sustained; new provocations; the real distinctions which nature has made; and many other circumstances, will divide us into parties, and produce convulsions which will probably never end but in the extermination of the one or the other race. To these objections, which are political, may be added others, which are physical and moral. The first difference which strikes us is that of color. Whether the black of the negro resides in the reticular membrane between the skin and scarf-skin, or in the scarf-skin itself; whether it proceeds from the color of the blood, the color of the bile, or from that of some other secretion, the difference is fixed in nature, and is as real as if its seat and cause were better known to us. And is this difference of no importance? Is it not the foundation of a greater or less share of beauty in the two races? Are not the fine mixtures of red and white, the expressions of every passion by greater or less suffusions of color in the one, preferable to that eternal monotony, which reigns in the countenances, that immoveable veil of black which covers all the emotions of the other race? Add to these, flowing hair, a more elegant symmetry of form, their own judgment in favor of the whites, declared by their preference of them, as uniformly as is the preference of the Oranootan for the black women over those of his own species. The circumstance of superior beauty, is thought worthy attention in the propagation of our horses, dogs, and other domestic animals; why not in that of man? Besides those of color, figure, and hair, there are other physical distinctions proving a difference of race. They have less hair on the face and body. They secrete less by the kidneys, and more by the glands of the skin, which gives them a very strong and disagreeable odor. This greater degree of transpiration renders them more tolerant of heat, and less so of cold, than the whites. Perhaps too a difference of structure in the pulmonary apparatus, which a late ingenious experimentalist has discovered to be the principal regulator of animal heat, may have disabled them from extricating, in the act of inspiration, so much of that fluid from the outer air, or obliged them in expiration, to part with more of it. They seem to require less sleep. A black, after hard labor through the day, will be induced by the slightest amusements to sit up till midnight, or later, though knowing he must be out with the first dawn of the morning. They are at least as brave, and more adventuresome. But this may perhaps proceed from a want of forethought, which prevents their seeing a danger till it be present. When present, they do not go through it with more coolness or steadiness than the whites. They are more ardent after their female: but love seems with them to be more an eager desire, than a tender delicate mixture of sentiment and sensation. Their griefs are transient. Those numberless afflictions, which render it doubtful whether heaven has given life to us in mercy or in wrath, are less felt, and sooner forgotten with them. In general, their existence appears to participate more of sensation than reflection. To this must be ascribed their disposition to sleep when abstracted from their diversions, and unemployed in labor. An animal whose body is at rest, and who does not reflect, must be disposed to sleep of course. Comparing them by their faculties of memory, reason, and imagination, it appears to me, that in memory they are equal to the whites; in reason much inferior, as I think one could scarcely be found capable of tracing and comprehending the investigations of Euclid; and that in imagination they are dull, tasteless, and anomalous. It would be unfair to follow them to Africa for this investigation. We will consider them here, on the same stage with the whites. . . . Most of them indeed have been confined to tillage . . . yet many have been so situated, that they might have availed themselves of the conversation of their masters; many have been brought up to the handicraft arts, and from that circumstance have always been associated with the whites. Some have been liberally educated. . . . The Indians, with no advantages of this kind, will often carve figures on their pipes not destitute of design and merit. . . . They astonish you with strokes of the most sublime oratory; such as prove their reason and sentiment strong, their imagination glowing and elevated. But never yet could I find that a black had uttered a thought above the level of plain narration; never see even an elementary trait of painting or sculpture. In music they are more generally gifted than the whites with accurate ears for tune and time. . . . Whether they will be equal to the composition of a more extensive run of melody, or of complicated harmony, is yet to be proved. Misery is often the parent of the most affecting touches in poetry. Among the blacks is misery enough, God knows, but no poetry. Love is the peculiar oestrum of the poet. Their love is ardent, but it kindles the senses only, not the imagination. Religion indeed has produced a Phyllis Whately [Wheatley]; but it could not produce a poet. The compositions published under her name are below the dignity of criticism. . . .

The improvement of the blacks in body and mind, in the first instance of their mixture with the whites, has been observed by every one, and proves that their inferiority is not the effect merely of their condition of life. We know that among the Romans, about the Augustan age especially, the condition of their slaves was much more deplorable than that of the blacks on the continent of America. . . . Yet notwithstanding these and other discouraging circumstances among the Romans, their slaves were often their rarest artists. They excelled too in science, insomuch as to be usually employed as tutors to their master's children. Epictetus, Terence, and Phaedrus, were slaves. But they were of the race of whites. It is not their condition then, but nature, which has produced the distinction. Whether further observation will or will not verify the conjecture, that nature has been less bountiful to them in the endowments of the head, I believe that in those of the heart she will be found to have done them justice. That disposition to theft with which they have been branded, must be ascribed to their situation, and not to any depravity of the moral sense. . . .

Notwithstanding these considerations which must weaken their respect for the laws of property, we find among them numerous instances of the most rigid integrity, and as many as among their better instructed masters, of benevolence, gratitude, and unshaken fidelity. The opinion, that they are inferior in the faculties of reason and imagination, must be hazarded with great diffidence. . . . Advance it therefore as a suspicion only, that the blacks, whether originally a distinct race, or made distinct by time and circumstances, are inferior to the whites in the endowments both of body and mind. It is not against experience to suppose, that different species of the same genus, or varieties of the same species, may possess different qualifications. Will not a lover of natural history then, one who views the gradations in all the races of animals with the eye of philosophy, excuse an effort to keep those in the department of man as distinct as nature has formed them? This unfortunate difference of color, and perhaps of faculty, is a powerful obstacle to the emancipation of these people. Many of their advocates, while they wish to vindicate the liberty of human nature, are anxious also to preserve its dignity and beauty. Some of these, embarrassed by the question "What further is to be done with them?" join themselves in opposition with those who are actuated by sordid avarice only. Among the Romans emancipation required but one effort. The slave, when made free, might mix with, without staining the blood of his master. But with us a second is necessary, unknown to history. When freed, he is to be removed beyond the reach of mixture. . . .

Query XVIII

. . . There must doubtless be an unhappy influence on the manners of our people produced by the existence of slavery among us. The whole commerce between master and slave is a perpetual exercise of the most boisterous passions, the most unremitting despotism on the one part, and degrading submissions on the other. Our children see this, and learn to imitate it; for man is an imitative animal. This quality is the germ of all education in him. From his cradle to his grave he is learning to do what he sees others do. If a parent could find no motive either in his philanthropy or his self-love, for restraining the intemperance of passion towards his slave, it should always be a sufficient one that his child is present. But generally it is not sufficient. The parent storms, the child looks on, catches the lineaments of wrath, puts on the same airs in the circle of smaller slaves, gives a loose to his worst of passions, and thus nursed, educated, and daily exercised in tyranny, cannot but be stamped by it with odious peculiarities. The man must be a prodigy who can retain his manners and morals undepraved by such circumstances. And with what execrations should the statesman be loaded, who permitting one half the citizens thus to trample on the rights of the other, transforms those into despots, and these into enemies, destroys the morals of the one part, and the *amor patriae* of the other. For if a slave can have a country in this world, it must be any other in preference to that in which he is born to live and labor for another: in which he must lock up the faculties of his nature, contribute as far as depends on his individual endeavors to the evanishment of the human race, or entail his own miserable condition on the endless generations proceeding from him. With the morals of the people, their industry also is destroyed. For in a warm climate, no man will labor for himself who can make another labor for him. This is so true, that of the proprietors of slaves a very small proportion indeed are ever seen to labor. And can the liberties of a nation be thought secure when we have removed their only firm basis, a conviction in the minds of the people that these liberties are of the gift of God? That they are not to be violated but with his wrath? Indeed I tremble for my country when I reflect that God is just: that his justice cannot sleep for ever: that considering numbers, nature and natural means only, a revolution of the wheel of fortune, an exchange of situation, is among possible events: that it may become probable by supernatural interference! The Almighty has no attribute which can take side with us in such a contest.—But it is impossible to be temperate and to pursue this subject through the various considerations of policy, of morals, of history natural and civil. We must be contented to hope they will force their way into everyone's mind. I think a change already perceptible, since the origin of the present revolution. The spirit of the master is abating, that of the slave rising from the dust, his condition mollifying, the way I hope preparing, under the auspices of heaven, for a total emancipation, and that this is disposed, in the order of events, to be with the consent of the masters, rather than by their extirpation.

11. George Washington, Letter to Robert Morris (April 12, 1786)

In this letter, George Washington (1732–1799) addressed efforts by Quakers to emancipate slaves, particularly the slaves of slave owners visiting Pennsylvania. Pennsylvania had enacted a gradual abolition law in 1780, rendering aid to runaway slaves illegal. While the law did not apply to "domestic slaves attending upon delegates in congress from the other American states" or to persons "passing through or sojourning in this state," this letter reveals ongoing efforts by Quakers to secure emancipation. Southerners increasingly complained about Northern interference in reclaiming fugitive slaves.

Dear Sir:

I give you the trouble of this letter at the instance of Mr. Dalby of Alexandria; who is called to Philadelphia to attend what he conceives to be a vexatious lawsuit respecting a slave of his, whom a Society of Quakers in the city (formed for such purposes) have attempted to liberate. . . . And if the practice of this Society of which Mr. Dalby speaks, is not discountenanced, none of those whose misfortune it is to have slaves as attendants, will visit the City if they can possibly avoid it; because by so doing they hazard their property; or they must be at the expense (and this will not always succeed) of providing servants of another description for the trip.

I hope it will not be conceived from these observations, that it is my wish to hold the unhappy people, who are the subject of this letter, in slavery. I can only say that there is not a man living who wishes more sincerely than I do, to see a plan adopted for the abolition of it; but there is only one proper and effectual mode by which it can be accomplished and that is by Legislative authority; and this, as far as my suffrage will go, shall never be wanting. But when slaves who are happy and contented with their present masters, are tampered with and seduced to leave; when a conduct of this sort begets discontent on one side and resentment on the other, and when it happens to fall on a man, whose purse will not measure with that of the Society, he looses [*sic*] his property for want of means to defend it; it is oppression in the latter case, and not humanity in any, because it introduces more evils than it can cure.

Chapter Two: 1787–1817

Introduction

When South Carolina revised its state constitution in 1790, it retained its existing fifty-acre requirement for voting; it also added a new requirement that members of the state's House of Representatives own "a settled freehold estate of five hundred acres of land and ten negroes, or . . . real estate of the value of one hundred and fifty pounds sterling, clear of debt."[1] The state's constitutional linkage of slaveholding to office holding, reflecting the interests of the state's plantation owners, would not end until 1865. One might contend that such institutionalization of the slave interest was not unprecedented. After all, Article I, Section 2 of the U.S. Constitution apportioned seats in the U.S. House of Representatives "by adding to the whole Number of free Persons" three-fifths "of all other persons," namely, slaves.[2] Eventually, religious leaders like Theodore Parker and political leaders like Salmon P. Chase would decry the "slave power," which they linked in part to that provision.

The existence of a stronger national government after 1788 redirected the debate over slavery. From this point forward arguments about slavery, and the national government's authority over and obligations toward it, would take place in Congress as well as in the state legislatures. At the same time, what the Constitution wrought with respect to slavery would remain a hotly contested issue. The drafting and text of the Constitution are more complicated than cries of "slave power" suggest. Consider Madison's "Virginia Plan." This initial blueprint for a new constitution proposed to apportion seats in Congress according to the number of free inhabitants. When dispute over apportionment erupted between small and large states, it was James Wilson—a Pennsylvanian who personally objected to slavery—who initially suggested adoption of the three-fifths clause.[3]

Despite any personal misgivings, Wilson observed that reasonable objections to the provision "must be overruled by the necessity of compromise." This observation was confirmed the next day, when William Davie of North Carolina

---

1. If the officeholder was not a resident in his election district, he was required to possess a "settled freehold estate therein of the value of five hundred pounds sterling, clear of debt."
2. This provision was altered by Section 2 of the Fourteenth Amendment.
3. This provision had first been proposed in 1783 by the Confederation Congress in its effort to amend the rule for apportioning quotas of revenue. Wilson offered the proposal on July 11, 1787.

insisted that his state "would never confederate on any terms that did not rate [slaves] at least as 3/5."[4] The issue was complicated by the fact that the apportionment rule was intended to address two issues: taxation and representation. Compromise was necessary to reach agreement on a new constitution and thereby achieve the delegates' paramount goal: sustaining the Union. If the Union were to break apart, the states would fall prey to European powers, or tensions already brewing between the states would flare into real conflict. A more powerful national government was needed to address both dangers.

Meanwhile, legal developments in numerous states seemed to signal a slow but steady shift in public attitudes against slavery. Action at the state level was particularly noteworthy, for it was assumed that laws regarding slavery and manumission, like other laws dealing with the health, safety, and welfare of people, were the purview of the state governments. Accordingly, the debates over slavery at the Constitutional Convention, and in the various state ratifying conventions, were in fact less predominant than documents in this chapter might suggest. Yes, slavery was debated—at times, passionately. Overall, however, the problem of slavery was not a leading *national* concern in the drafting and ratifying conventions.

If that's the case, why include excerpts from the conventions? Because unlike the Articles of Confederation, which delegated no authority whatsoever to the general government on the subject of slavery, the new Constitution did delegate some (albeit limited) authority. Even before the Constitution was ratified, disagreement arose over the extent and nature of that power. James Wilson regretted that greater restrictions were not placed on the slave trade, "but so far as it operates," he stated, "it presents us with the pleasing prospect that the rights of mankind will be acknowledged and established throughout the Union. [T]he lapse of a few years, and Congress will have power to exterminate slavery from within our borders."[5] At the same time, leaders in South Carolina were satisfied that they had "obtained a representation" for their "property," and that slave owners had "obtained a right to recover our slaves in whatever part of America they may take refuge, which is a right we had not before."[6] In short, whereas previously the issue of slavery (at the national level) had been

---

4. Wilson made his remark on July 11; Davie made his on July 12. See Max Farrand, ed., *The Records of the Federal Convention of 1787*, rev. ed., vol. 1 (New Haven, CT: Yale University Press, 1966), 587 and 593, respectively.

5. James Wilson, speech to the Pennsylvania Ratifying Convention, December 4, 1787, in *The Debates in the Several State Conventions on the Adoption of the Federal Constitution as Recommended by the General Convention at Philadelphia in 1787*, vol. II, 2nd ed., ed. Jonathan Elliot (Washington, D.C., 1836), 484.

6. Charles Cotesworth Pinckney, Speech to the South Carolina House of Representatives, January 17, 1788. See document 3 in this chapter.

primarily a moral and religious one, the new Constitution now made it political and legal as well.

Critics of the slave trade wasted no time petitioning Congress. Petitions from Quakers, abolitionist societies, and African American leaders pressed Congress, urging it to "step to the very verge of the power vested in you for discouraging every species of traffic in the persons of our fellow-men" and suggesting that congressional action might lead to a general emancipation.[7] Some members of Congress supported these petitions. "I look upon the slave trade to be one of the most abominable things on earth," Pennsylvania congressman Thomas Scott declared in 1790. "If there was neither God nor devil," he continued, "I should oppose it upon the principles of humanity, and the law of nature."[8]

Such claims provoked various responses. Some representatives, particularly from the Deep South, defended the slave trade and the institution of slavery generally. If one is "guided by that evidence upon which the Christian system is founded," Georgia congressman James Jackson asserted, one "will find that religion is not against it."[9] Others, like Michael Stone of Maryland, worried "that if Congress took any measures indicative of an intention to interfere with the kind of property alluded to, it would sink it in value very considerably, and might be injurious to a great number of the citizens, particularly in Southern States. . . ."[10] The southern states "would never have entered into the Confederation," William Smith of South Carolina added, "unless their property had been guaranteed to them, for such is the state of agriculture in that country, that without slaves it must be abandoned. Why will these people, then, make use of arguments to induce the slave to turn his hand against his master?"[11]

Many others stopped short of defending the institution, offering an apology of sorts for it by denying responsibility for its introduction into the colonies. By this account, slavery was an inherited evil—something thrust upon the colonists by the British government, but for which they were not morally culpable. Jefferson included such a charge in his draft of the Declaration—it was removed from the final published version—and it continued to find expression. "It was the British Government that transmitted them down to us when

---

7. Petition from the Pennsylvania Society for the Abolition of Slavery, February 3, 1790. See document 5 in this chapter.

8. Thomas Scott, speech to the U.S. House of Representatives, February 12, 1790. See document 5 in this chapter.

9. James Jackson, speech to the U.S. House of Representatives, February 12, 1790. See document 5 in this chapter.

10. Michael Stone, speech to the U.S. House of Representatives, February 11, 1790. See document 5 in this chapter.

11. William Smith, speech to the U.S. House of Representatives, February 12, 1790. See document 5 in this chapter.

in a colonized state," James Jones of Georgia asserted in a debate over a petition from Absalom Jones and others. Of course, the suggestion that the British foisted slavery on unwilling colonists did not mean that the Americans, now free from British control, should keep slaves. "But being here," Jones added, "and being the property of individuals after obtaining our common liberty and forming our Federal compact, property and safety were guaranteed to every individual and State in the Confederation. How can this House meddle with that part of our property? The General Government has no power over it."[12]

The obstacles to emancipation were not merely pecuniary. Deep-rooted racism also infected the discussion of slavery and emancipation. In some cases, racism buttressed arguments for slavery. For defenders of slavery like James Jackson, emancipation would actually harm the slaves. "It was the fashion of the day to favor the liberty of slaves," he stated. "He would not go into a discussion of the subject; but he believed it was capable of demonstration that they were better off in their present situation than they would be if they were manumitted. What are they to do if they are discharged? Work for a living? Experience has shown us they will not."[13]

Slavery's opponents exhibited similar racist attitudes. Racism made it difficult to perceive a viable plan for abolishing slavery. In his *Notes on the State of Virginia*, Jefferson famously argued that free blacks and whites could not live together peaceably. Years later, South Carolina congressman William Smith would quote from Jefferson's *Notes* to show "that Negroes were by nature an inferior race of beings" and that "emancipation would be attended with one or other of these consequences; either that a mixture of the races would denigrate the whites, without improving the blacks, or that it would create two separate classes of people in the community involved in inveterate hostility, which would terminate in the massacre and extirpation of one or the other."[14] Smith himself did not oppose slavery—in fact, he associated it with the commercial health of the Union—but many, like Jefferson, objected to slavery while harboring profound racial prejudice.

If as Jefferson and others suggested emancipation might lead to a race war, there were only two options: keep Negroes in chains, or make their emancipation contingent on removing them from the country. Jefferson had advocated emancipation with colonization in his *Notes*, and the idea of combining emancipation with colonization continued to gain adherents. That colonization schemes proliferated in the early decades of the nineteenth century is not

12. James Jones, speech to the U.S. House of Representatives, January 2, 1800. See document 7 in this chapter.
13. James Jackson, speech to the U.S. House of Representatives, May 13, 1789. See document 4 in this chapter.
14. William Smith, speech to the House of Representatives, March 17, 1790. See document 5 in this chapter.

surprising, for the population of free blacks was growing rapidly. Between 1790 and 1800 it nearly doubled; it nearly doubled again by 1810, to almost 190,000.

People supported colonization for different reasons. Some, like John Randolph and John Taylor, argued that colonizing free blacks would actually help "secure the property of every master." Speaking before the American Colonization Society in 1816, Randolph observed that the

> population of free negroes was viewed by every slave holder as one of the greatest sources of the insecurity, and also unprofitableness, of slave property; that they serve to excite in their fellow beings a feeling of discontent, of repining at their situation, and that they act as channels of communication not only between different slaves, but between the slaves of different districts; that they are the depositories of stolen goods, and the promoters of mischief. In a worldly sense of view, then, without entering into the general question, apart from those higher and nobler motives which had been well presented to the meeting, the owners of slaves were interested in throwing this population out of the bosom of the people.[15]

Others were in fact guided by those "higher and nobler motives." Many advocates for colonization understood slavery to be both a political and moral evil. At the same time, many of them harbored racial prejudice. Henry Clay spoke for many when he noted that the "unconquerable prejudices resulting from their color" meant that blacks could "never . . . amalgamate with the free whites of this country."[16] If true, this presented a serious problem. For could it be supposed, John Taylor asked, "that the Negroes could be made free, and yet kept from property and equal civil rights. . . ?" Either blacks would have to be granted equal rights—an unfathomable idea even for most men of noble ideals—or their efforts to achieve equality would result in "catastrophe."[17] From this perspective, colonization was a moderate solution to the problem of slavery, for it would bring about abolition gradually while permanently removing blacks from America—thereby ensuring political, economic, and social stability. Colonization had some advocates in the black community, too. Paul Cuffee, for example, was an early proponent. Confident that free blacks would never be accepted in America, he undertook to bring them to Sierra Leone.

---

15. "The Meeting on the Colonization of Free Blacks," *Daily National Intelligencer* (Washington, D.C.), December 24, 1816, 2.

16. Ibid. Clay's remarks are also quoted by David Walker in his *Appeal* (see document 15 in Chapter 3).

17. See document 10 in this chapter.

Most African American leaders, however, offered a scathing indictment of colonization as well as of slavery and racial prejudice. "No people in the world make louder pretensions to 'liberty, equality, and the rights of man,' than the people of the South," remarked Joseph Sidney, speaking at an event held at Liberty Hall in Philadelphia in 1809. "And yet, strange as it may appear, there is no spot in the United States, where oppression reigns with such unlimited sway."[18] Colonization was no answer, for according to James Forten and other leaders in the African American community, colonization would once again tear black families apart; it would be detrimental to blacks who were colonized; and it would strengthen and thus perpetuate the institution of slavery. Instead, Sidney, Forten, and other black leaders demanded that the principles of the Declaration be honored. "Are we not to be considered as men," Forten movingly asked? "Has the God who made the white man and the black, left any record declaring us a different species[?] Are we not sustained by the same power, supported by the same food, hurt by the same wounds, pleased with the same delights, and propagated by the same means[?] And should we not then enjoy the same liberty, and be protected by the same laws[?]"[19]

DOCUMENTS

1. Philadelphia Constitutional Convention Debates, as recorded by James Madison (1787)

Not a predominant issue at the Constitutional Convention, slavery nonetheless arose amid discussions over representation and taxation. Various delegates spoke out against the slave trade, and a few expressed moral outrage toward the institution of slavery. But other delegates made it clear that a constitutional agreement was predicated on protecting the institution. The overriding urgency of Union, combined with political interests and the belief

---

18. Joseph Sidney, "An Oration Commemorative of the Abolition of the Slave Trade in the United States, Delivered before the Wilberforce Philanthropic Association, in the City of New-York, on the Second of January, 1809," [5], Schomburg Center for Research in Black Culture, Manuscripts, Archives and Rare Books Division, New York Public Library Digital Collections, accessed March 10, 2016, http://digitalcollections.nypl.org/items/510d47e3-fd58-a3d9-e040-e00a18064a99.

19. See document 9 (Letter II) in this chapter.

*that slavery was already disappearing, led the delegates to consider slavery
"in a political light only."*

WEDNESDAY, JULY 11, 1787

Mr. RANDOLPH's motion requiring the Legislature to take a periodical census for the purpose of redressing inequalities in the Representation, was resumed. . . .

Mr. WILLIAMSON . . . moved that Mr. Randolph's proposition be postpond. in order to consider the following "that in order to ascertain the alterations that may happen in the population & wealth of the several States, a census shall be taken of the free white inhabitants and 3/5 ths. of those of other descriptions on the 1st. year after this Government shall have been adopted and every year thereafter; and that the Representation be regulated accordingly."

Mr. BUTLER & Genl. PINKNEY insisted that blacks be included in the rule of Representation, equally with the Whites: and for that purpose moved that the words "three fifths" be struck out. . . .

Mr. GHORUM. This ratio was fixed by Congs. as a rule of taxation. Then it was urged by the Delegates representing the States having slaves that the blacks were still more inferior to freemen. At present when the ratio of representation is to be established, we are assured that they are equal to freemen. The arguments on ye. former occasion had convinced him that 3/5 was pretty near the just proportion and he should vote according to the same opinion now.

Mr. BUTLER insisted that the labour of a slave in S. Carola. was as productive & valuable as that of a freeman in Massts., that as wealth was the great means of defence and utility to the Nation they were equally valuable to it with freemen; and that consequently an equal representation ought to be allowed for them in a Government which was instituted principally for the protection of property, and was itself to be supported by property.

Mr. MASON, could not agree to the motion, notwithstanding it was favorable to Virga. because he thought it unjust. It was certain that the slaves were valuable, as they raised the value of land, increased the exports & imports, and of course the revenue, would supply the means of feeding & supporting an army, and might in cases of emergency become themselves soldiers. As in these important respects they were useful to the community at large, they ought not to be excluded from the estimate of Representation. He could not however regard them as equal to freemen and could not vote for them as such. . . .

The next clause as to 3/5 of the negroes considered. . . .

Mr. WILSON did not well see on what principle the admission of blacks in the proportion of three fifths could be explained. Are they admitted as Citizens? then why are they not admitted on an equality with White Citizens? are they admitted as property? then why is not other property admitted into the computation? These were difficulties however which he thought must be overruled by the necessity of compromise. . . .

WEDNESDAY, AUGUST 22, 1787

. . . Mr. SHERMAN was for leaving the clause as it stands. He disapproved of the slave trade; yet as the States were now possessed of the right to import slaves, as the public good did not require it to be taken from them, & as it was expedient to have as few objections as possible to the proposed scheme of Government, he thought it best to leave the matter as we find it. He observed that the abolition of Slavery seemed to be going on in the U. S. & that the good sense of the several States would probably by degrees compleat it. . . .

Col. MASON. This infernal trafic originated in the avarice of British Merchants. The British Govt. constantly checked the attempts of Virginia to put a stop to it. The present question concerns not the importing States alone but the whole Union. The evil of having slaves was experienced during the late war. Had slaves been treated as they might have been by the Enemy, they would have proved dangerous instruments in their hands. . . . He mentioned the dangerous insurrections of the slaves in Greece and Sicily. . . . Maryland & Virginia he said had already prohibited the importation of slaves expressly. N. Carolina had done the same in substance. All this would be in vain if S. Carolina & Georgia be at liberty to import. The Western people are already calling out for slaves for their new lands, and will fill that Country with slaves if they can be got thro' S. Carolina & Georgia. Slavery discourages arts & manufactures. The poor despise labor when performed by slaves. They prevent the immigration of Whites, who really enrich & strengthen a Country. They produce the most pernicious effect on manners. Every master of slaves is born a petty tyrant. They bring the judgment of heaven on a Country. As nations can not be rewarded or punished in the next world they must be in this. By an inevitable chain of causes & effects providence punishes national sins, by national calamities. He lamented that some of our Eastern brethren had from a lust of gain embarked in this nefarious traffic. . . . He held it essential in every point of view that the Genl. Govt. should have power to prevent the increase of slavery.

Mr. ELSWORTH. As he had never owned a slave could not judge of the effects of slavery on character: He said however that if it was to be considered in a moral light we ought to go farther and free those already in the Country.— As slaves also multiply so fast in Virginia & Maryland that it is cheaper to raise than import them, whilst in the sickly rice swamps foreign supplies are necessary, if we go no farther than is urged, we shall be unjust towards S. Carolina & Georgia. Let us not intermeddle. As population increases poor laborers will be so plenty as to render slaves useless. Slavery in time will not be a speck in our Country. Provision is already made in Connecticut for abolishing it. And the abolition has already taken place in Massachusetts. As to the danger of insurrections from foreign influence, that will become a motive to kind treatment of the slaves.

Mr. PINKNEY. If slavery be wrong, it is justified by the example of all the world. He cited the case of Greece, Rome & other antient States; the sanction given by France, England, Holland & other modern States. In all ages one half of mankind have been slaves. If the Southern States were let alone they will probably of themselves stop importations. He wd. himself as a Citizen of S. Carolina vote for it. An attempt to take away the right as proposed will produce serious objections to the Constitution which he wished to see adopted.

General PINKNEY declared it to be his firm opinion that if himself & all his colleagues were to sign the Constitution & use their personal influence, it would be of no avail towards obtaining the assent of their Constituents. S. Carolina & Georgia cannot do without slaves. As to Virginia she will gain by stopping the importations. Her slaves will rise in value, & she has more than she wants. It would be unequal to require S. C. & Georgia to confederate on such unequal terms. . . . He contended that the importation of slaves would be for the interest of the whole Union. The more slaves, the more produce to employ the carrying trade; the more consumption also, and the more of this, the more of revenue for the common treasury. He admitted it to be reasonable that slaves should be dutied like other imports, but should consider a rejection of the clause as an exclusion of S. Carola. from the Union. . . .

Mr. GERRY thought we had nothing to do with the conduct of the States as to Slaves, but ought to be careful not to give any sanction to it.

Mr. DICKENSON considered it as inadmissible on every principle of honor & safety that the importation of slaves should be authorised to the States by the Constitution. The true question was whether the national happiness would be promoted or impeded by the importation, and this question ought to be left to the National Govt. not to the States particularly interested. . . . Greece and Rome were made unhappy by their slaves. He could not believe that the Southn. States would refuse to confederate on the account apprehended; especially as the power was not likely to be immediately exercised by the Genl. Government. . . .

Mr. KING thought the subject should be considered in a political light only. If two States will not agree to the Constitution as stated on one side, he could affirm with equal belief on the other, that great & equal opposition would be experienced from the other States. He remarked on the exemption of slaves from duty whilst every other import was subjected to it, as an inequality that could not fail to strike the commercial sagacity of the Northn. & middle States. . . .

Genl. PINKNEY . . . moved to commit the clause that slaves might be made liable to an equal tax with other imports which he thought right & which would remove one difficulty that had been started.

Mr. RUTLEDGE. If the Convention thinks that N. C. S. C. & Georgia will ever agree to the plan, unless their right to import slaves be untouched, the expectation is vain. The people of those States will never be such fools as to give up so important an interest. . . .

Mr. GOVr. MORRIS wished the whole subject to be committed including the clauses relating to taxes on exports & to a navigation act. These things may form a bargain among the Northern & Southern States. . . .

2. James Wilson, Speech in the Pennsylvania Ratifying Convention (December 3, 1787)

While slavery was a more peripheral issue in the state ratification conventions, delegates nevertheless addressed it. This document and the next represent the variety within this debate. In Pennsylvania, James Wilson (1742–1798) applauded the Constitution as a step toward abolition. In South Carolina, General Charles Cotesworth Pinckney (1746–1825) embraced it as a guarantee of slavery's perpetuation.

. . . With respect to the clause restricting Congress from prohibiting the *migration or importation of such persons* as any of the states now existing shall think proper to admit, prior to the year 1808, the honorable gentleman says that this clause is not only dark, but intended to grant to Congress, for that time, the power to admit the importation of *slaves*. No such thing was intended. But I will tell you what was done, and it gives me high pleasure that so much was done. Under the present Confederation, the states may admit the importation of slaves as long as they please; but by this article, after the year 1808, the Congress will have power to prohibit such importation, notwithstanding the disposition of any state to the contrary. I consider this as laying the foundation for banishing slavery out of this country; and though the period is more distant than I could wish, yet it will produce the same kind, gradual change, which was pursued in Pennsylvania. It is with much satisfaction I view this power in the general government, whereby they may lay an interdiction on this reproachful trade: but an immediate advantage is also obtained; for a tax or duty may be imposed on such importation, not exceeding ten dollars for each person; and this, sir, operates as a partial prohibition; it was all that could be obtained. I am sorry it was no more; but from this I think there is reason to hope, that yet a few years, and it will be prohibited altogether; and in the mean time, the *new* states which are to be formed will be under *the control* of Congress in this particular, and slaves will never be introduced amongst them. The gentleman says that it is unfortunate in another point of view: it means to prohibit the introduction of white people from Europe, as this tax may deter them from coming amongst us. A little impartiality and attention will discover the care that the Convention took in selecting their language. The words are, "the migration or importation of such persons, &c., shall not be prohibited by Congress prior to the year 1808, but a tax or duty may be imposed on such importation." It is observable here that the term *migration* is dropped, when a tax or duty is mentioned, so that Congress have power to impose the tax only on those imported.

3. Charles Cotesworth Pinckney, Speech in the South Carolina House of Representatives over the Calling of a State Ratifying Convention (January 17, 1788)

. . . General Pinckney . . . As we have found it necessary to give very extensive powers to the federal government both over the persons and estates of the citizens, we thought it right to draw one branch of the legislature immediately from the people, and that both wealth and numbers should be considered in the representation. We were at a loss, for some time, for a rule to ascertain the proportionate wealth of the states. At last we thought that the productive labor of the inhabitants was the best rule for ascertaining their wealth. In conformity to this rule, joined to a spirit of concession, we determined that representatives should be apportioned among the several states, by adding to the whole number of free persons three fifths of the slaves. We thus obtained a representation for our property. . . .

The general then said he would make a few observations on the objections which the gentleman had thrown out on the restrictions that might be laid on the African trade after the year 1808. On this point your delegates had to contend with the religious and political prejudices of the Eastern and Middle States, and with the interested and inconsistent opinion of Virginia, who was warmly opposed to our importing more slaves. I am of the same opinion now as I was two years ago . . . that, while there remained one acre of swamp-land uncleared of South Carolina, I would raise my voice against restricting the importation of negroes. I am as thoroughly convinced as that gentleman is, that the nature of our climate, and the flat, swampy situation of our country, obliges us to cultivate our lands with negroes, and that without them South Carolina would soon be a desert waste. . . .

By this settlement we have secured an unlimited importation of negroes for twenty years. Nor is it declared that the importation shall be then stopped; it may be continued. We have a security that the general government can never emancipate them, for no such authority is granted; and it is admitted, on all hands, that the general government has no powers but what are expressly granted by the Constitution, and that all rights not expressed were reserved by the several states. We have obtained a right to recover our slaves in whatever part of America they may take refuge, which is a right we had not before. In short, considering all circumstances, we have made the best terms for the security of this species of property it was in our power to make. We would have made better if we could; but, on the whole, I do not think them bad. . . .

4. Debates in the U.S. Congress: House of Representatives (May 13, 1789)

No sooner had the first Congress convened than Virginia congressman Josiah Parker introduced a proposal to tax imported slaves. The following year, Congress was petitioned to exercise its limited powers over the slave trade. The following documents exemplify the debate between delegates from the upper and lower South. On behalf of the lower South, Georgia congressman James Jackson accused states like Virginia of seeking to restrain the trade from self-interest. Parker expressed a genuine objection both to the trade and to slavery itself, invoking the Declaration of Independence and claiming that the practice violated "Revolution principles." When petitions were read into the record, delegates—especially from the lower South—reacted angrily, claiming that the petitions demanded "total emancipation," a belief that led Thomas Tudor Tucker to warn that emancipation by congressional statute would precipitate civil war.

The House again resolved itself into a Committee of the whole on the Impost Bill, Mr. Page in the Chair.

Mr. [Fisher] Ames [of Massachusetts] moved to insert china, crockery-ware, and gunpowder; he thought them articles of luxury. . . .

Mr. [Josiah] Parker [of Virginia] moved to insert a clause in the bill, imposing a duty on the importation of slaves, of ten dollars each person. He was sorry that the constitution prevented Congress from prohibiting the importation altogether; he thought it a defect in that instrument that it allowed of such a practice; it was contrary to the Revolution principles, and ought not to be permitted; but as he could not do all the good he desired, he was willing to do what lay in his power. . . .

Mr. [Roger] Sherman [of Connecticut] approved of the object of the motion, but he did not think this bill was proper to embrace the subject. He could not reconcile himself to the insertion of human beings as an article of duty, among goods, wares, and merchandise. He hoped it would be withdrawn for the present, and taken up hereafter as an independent subject.

Mr. [James] Jackson [of Georgia], observing the quarter from which this motion came, said it did not surprise him. . . . He recollected that Virginia was an old settled State, and had her complement of slaves; so she was careless of recruiting her numbers by this means; the natural increase of her imported blacks was sufficient for their purpose; but he thought gentlemen ought to let their neighbors get supplied, before they imposed such a burthen upon the importation. . . . He knew this business was viewed in an odious light to the eastward, because the people were capable of doing their own work, and had no occasion for slaves; but gentlemen will have some feeling for others; they will not try to throw all the weight upon those who have assisted in lightening their burthens; they do not wish to charge us for every comfort and enjoyment of life, and at the same time take away the means of procuring them. . . .

Mr. Parker [of Virginia] . . . Although the gentleman from Connecticut [Mr. Sherman] had said, that they ought not to be enumerated with goods, wares, and merchandise, he believed they were looked upon by the African traders in this light. He knew it was degrading the human species to annex that character to them; but he would rather do this than continue the actual evil of importing slaves a moment longer. He hoped Congress would do all that lay in their power to restore to human nature its inherent privileges, and, if possible, wipe off the stigma under which America labored. The inconsistency in our principles, with which we are justly charged, should be done away, that we may show, by our actions, the pure beneficence of the doctrine we hold out to the world in our Declaration of Independence. . . .

Mr. Jackson [of Georgia] said, it was the fashion of the day to favor the liberty of slaves. He would not go into a discussion of the subject; but he believed it was capable of demonstration that they were better off in their present situation than they would be if they were manumitted. What are they to do if they are discharged? Work for a living? Experience has shown us they will not. Examine what has become of those in Maryland; many of them have been set free in that State. Did they turn themselves to industry and useful pursuits? No, they turn out common pickpockets, petty larceny villains. And is this mercy, forsooth, to turn them into a way in which they must lose their lives; for when they are thrown upon the world, void of property and connexions, they cannot get their living but by pilfering. What is to be done for compensation? Will Virginia set all her negroes free? Will they give up the money they cost them, and to whom? When this practice comes to be tried there, the sound of liberty will lose those charms which make it grateful to the ravished ear. But our slaves are not in a worse situation than they were on the coast of Africa. It is not uncommon there for the parents to sell their children in peace; and in war, the whole are taken and made slaves together. In these cases, it is only a change of one slavery for another; and are they not better here, where they have a master, bound by the ties of interest and law, to provide for their support and comfort in old age or infirmity, in which, if they were free, they would sink under the pressure of woe for want of assistance? . . .

Mr. [James] Madison [of Virginia]. I cannot concur with gentlemen who think the present an improper time or place to enter into a discussion of the proposed motion. . . . There may be some inconsistency in combining the ideas which gentlemen have expressed, that is, considering the human race as a species of property; but the evil does not arise from adopting the clause now proposed; it is from the importation to which it relates. Our object in enumerating persons on paper with merchandise, is to prevent the practice of actually treating them as such, by having them in future forming part of the cargoes of goods, wares, and merchandise to be imported into the United States. The motion is calculated to avoid the very evil intimated by the gentleman. . . .

I conceive the constitution, in this particular, was formed in order that the Government, whilst it was restrained from laying a total prohibition, might be able to give some testimony of the sense of America with respect to the African trade. . . . It is to be hoped, that by expressing a national disapprobation of this trade, we may destroy it, and save ourselves from reproaches, and our posterity the imbecility ever attendant on a country filled with slaves. . . .

5. Debates in the U.S. Congress: House of Representatives (February 11–March 17, 1790)

Thursday, February 11: Mr. Fitzsimons [of Pennsylvania] presented the following Address to the Senate and House of Representatives of the United States.

To the Senate and the House of Representatives of the United States

The Address of the people called Quakers in their annual assembly convened.

[A]s professors of faith in that ever blessed all-perfect Lawgiver, whose injunctions remain of undiminished obligation on all who profess to believe in him, "whatsoever ye would that men should do unto you, do you even so unto them;" we apprehend ourselves religiously bound to request your serious Christian attention, to the deeply interesting subject whereon our religious society, in their annual assembly, on the tenth month, 1783, addressed the then Congress, who, though the Christian rectitude of the concern was by the Delegates generally acknowledged, yet not being vested with the powers of Legislation, they declined promoting any public remedy against the gross national iniquity of trafficking in the persons of fellow-men; but divers of the Legislative bodies of the different States, on this Continent, have since manifested their sense of the public detestation due to the licentious wickedness of the African trade for slaves, and the inhuman tyranny and blood guiltiness inseparable from it: the debasing influence whereof most certainly tends to lay waste the virtue, and of course, the happiness of the people.

[W]e find it indispensably incumbent on us, as a religious body, assuredly believing that both the true temporal interest of nations and eternal well-being of individuals, depend on doing justly, loving mercy, and walking humbly before God . . . to attempt to excite your attention to the affecting subject . . . whether it be not an essential part of the duty of your exalted station, to exert upright endeavors to the full extent of your powers, to remove every obstruction to public righteousness, which the influence of artifice of particular persons, governed by the narrow mistaken views of self-interest, has occasioned, and whether, notwithstanding such seeming impediments, it be not in reality within your power to exercise justice and mercy, which, if adhered to, we cannot doubt, must produce the abolition of the slave trade. . . .

Mr. [Josiah] Parker [of Virginia] . . . I hope, Mr. Speaker, the petition of these respectable people will be attended to with all the readiness the importance of its object demands. . . .

Mr. Michael J. Stone [of Maryland] feared that if Congress took any measures indicative of an intention to interfere with the kind of property alluded to, it would sink it in value very considerably, and might be injurious to a great number of the citizens, particularly in Southern States. . . .

Mr. James Jackson [of Georgia] . . . I apprehend, if through the interference of the General Government the slave trade was abolished, it would evince to the people a disposition towards a total emancipation, and they would hold their property in jeopardy. Any extraordinary attention of Congress to this petition may have, in some degree, a similar effect. I would beg to ask those, then, who are desirous of freeing the Negroes, if they have funds sufficient to pay for them? If they have, they may come forward on that business with some propriety; but, if they have not, they should keep themselves quiet, and not interfere with a business in which they are not interested. [Is] the whole morality of the United States confined to the Quakers? Are they the only people whose feelings are to be consulted on this occasion? Is it to them we owe our present happiness? Was it they who formed the Constitution? Did they, by their arms or contributions, establish our independence? I believe they were generally opposed to that measure: why, then, on their application should we injure men who, at the risk of their lives and fortunes, secured to the community their liberty and property? If Congress pay any uncommon degree of attention to their petition, it will furnish just ground of alarm to the Southern States. But why do these men set themselves up in such a particular manner against slavery? Do they understand the rights of mankind, and the disposition of Providence, better than others? If they were to consult that book, which claims our regard, they will find that slavery is not only allowed but commended. Their Savior, who possessed more benevolence and commiseration than they pretend to, has allowed of it: and if they fully examine the subject, they will find that slavery has been no novel doctrine since the days of Cain; but be these things as they may, I hope the House will order the petition to lie on the table, in order to prevent an alarm to our Southern brethren. . . .

Friday, February 12: The following memorial of the Pennsylvania Society for promoting the Abolition of Slavery, the relief of free Negroes unlawfully held in bondage, and the improvement of the condition of the African race, was presented and read.

The Memorial Respectfully Showeth, . . .

. . . That mankind are all formed by the same Almighty Being, alike objects of his care, and equally designed for the enjoyment of happiness, the Christian religion teaches us to believe, and the political creed of America fully coincides with the position. Your memorialists, particularly engaged in attending to the distresses arising from slavery, believe it their indispensable duty to present this subject to your notice. They have observed, with real satisfaction, that many important and salutary powers are vested in you for "promoting the welfare and securing the blessings of liberty to the people of the United States;" and as they conceive, that these blessings ought rightfully to be administered, without distinction of color, to all descriptions of people, so they indulge themselves in the pleasing expectation, that nothing which can be done for the relief of the unhappy objects of their care will be either omitted or delayed.

From a persuasion that equal liberty was originally the portion, and is still the birth-right of all men; and influenced by the strong ties of humanity, and the principles of their institution, your memorialists conceive themselves bound to use all justifiable endeavors to loosen the bounds of slavery, and promote a general enjoyment of the blessings of freedom. Under these impressions, they earnestly entreat your serious attention to the subject of slavery; that you will be pleased to countenance the restoration of liberty to those unhappy men, who alone, in this land of freedom are degraded into perpetual bondage, and who, amidst the general joy of surrounding freemen, are groaning in servile subjection; that you will devise means for removing this inconsistency from the character of the

American people; that you will promote mercy and justice towards this distressed race, and that you will step to the very verge of the power vested in you for discouraging every species of traffic in the persons of our fellow-men.

Benjamin Franklin, *President*
Philadelphia February 3, 1790

Mr. Thomas Tudor Tucker [of South Carolina] was sorry the petition had a second reading, as he conceived it contained an unconstitutional request, and from that consideration he wished it thrown aside. He feared the commitment of it would be a very alarming circumstance to the Southern States; for if the object was to engage Congress in an unconstitutional measure, it would be considered as an interference with their rights, the people would become very uneasy under the Government, and lament that they ever put additional powers into their hands. He was surprised to see another memorial on the same subject; and that signed by a man who ought to have known the Constitution better. He thought it a mischievous attempt, as it respected the persons in whose favor it was intended. It would buoy them up with hopes, without a foundation, and as they could not reason on the subject, as more enlightened men would, they might be led to do what they would be punished for, and the owners of them, in their own defense, would be compelled to exercise over them a severity they were not accustomed to. Do these men expect a general emancipation of slaves by law? This would never be submitted to by the southern States without a civil war. . . .

Mr. Thomas Scott [of Pennsylvania]—I cannot entertain a doubt that the memorial is strictly agreeable to the Constitution. . . . We can, at present, lay our hands upon a small duty of ten dollars; I would take this, and if it is all that we can do, we must be content: but I am sorry that the framers of the Constitution did not go further, and enable us to interdict the traffic entirely; for I look upon the slave trade to be one of the most abominable things on earth; and if there was neither God nor devil, I should oppose it upon the principles of humanity, and the law of nature. I cannot, for my part, conceive how any person can be said to acquire a property in another; is it by virtue of conquest? Some have dared to advance this monstrous principle, that the conqueror is absolute master of his conquest; that he may dispose of it as his property, and treat it as he pleases; but, enough of those who reduce men to the state of transferable goods, or use them like beasts of burden, who deliver them up as property or patrimony to others. Let us argue on the principles countenanced by reason and becoming humanity; the petitioners view the subject in a religious light, but I do not stand in need of religious motives to induce me to reprobate the traffic in human flesh . . . and to support every constitutional measure likely to bring about its total abolition.

Mr. James Jackson [of Georgia] differed with the gentleman last up, and supposed the master had a qualified property in his slave. He said the contrary doctrine would go to the destruction of every species of personal service. The gentleman said, he did not stand in need of religion to induce him to reprobate slavery, but if he is guided by that evidence upon which the Christian system is founded, he will find that religion is not against it. He will see from Genesis to Revelations, the current setting strong that way. There never was a government on the face of the Earth, but what permitted slavery. The purest sons of freedom in the Grecian Republics, the citizens of Athens and Lacedaemon, all had slaves. On this principle, the nations of Europe are associated; it is the basis of the feudal system. But suppose all this to have been wrong, let me ask the gentleman if it is good policy to bring forward a business at this moment, likely to light up the flame of civil discord; for the people of the Southern States will resist one tyranny as soon as another? The other parts of the Continent may bear them down by force of arms, but they will never suffer themselves to be divested of their property without a struggle. . . .

Mr. William L. Smith of South Carolina . . . When we entered into this confederacy, we did it from political, not from moral motives, and I do not think my constituents want to learn morals from the petitioners; I do not believe they want improvement in their moral systems; if they do, they can get it at home. . . .

I said the States would never have entered into the Confederation, unless their property had been guaranteed to them, for such is the state of agriculture in that country, that without slaves it must be abandoned. Why will these people, then, make use of arguments to induce the slave to turn his hand against his master? We labor under difficulties enough from the ravages of the late war. A gentleman can hardly come from that country with a servant or two, either to this place or Philadelphia, but there are persons trying to seduce his servants to leave him: and, when they have done this, the poor wretches are obliged to rob their master, in order to obtain a subsistence; all those, therefore, who are concerned in this seduction, are accessories to robbery. . . .

Mr. Elbridge Gerry [of Massachusetts] thought the interference of Congress fully compatible with the Constitution, and could not help lamenting the miseries to which the natives of Africa were exposed by this inhuman commerce. He never contemplated the subject without reflecting what his own feelings would be, in case himself, his children, or friends were placed in the same deplorable circumstances. He then adverted to the flagrant acts of cruelty which are committed in carrying on that traffic; and asked, whether it can be supposed that Congress has no power to prevent such abuses? He then referred to the Constitution, and pointed out the restrictions laid on the General Government respecting the importation of slaves. It was not, he presumed, in the contemplation of any gentleman in this House to violate that part of the

Constitution; but that we have a right to regulate this business, is as clear as that we have any rights whatever. . . .

Tuesday, March 17: . . .

Mr. William L. Smith (of South Carolina) said he lamented that this subject had been brought before the House . . . because he foresaw . . . that it was a subject of a nature to excite the alarms of the Southern members, who would not view, without anxiety, any interference in it on the part of Congress. . . .

The memorials from the Quakers contained, in his opinion, a very indecent attack on the character of those States which [possess] slaves. . . . He could not but consider it as calculated to fix a stigma of the blackest nature on the State he had the honor to represent, and to hold its citizens up to public view as men divested of every principle of honor and humanity. Considering it in that light, he felt it incumbent on him not only to refute those atrocious calumnies, but to resent the improper language made use of by the memorialists. . . .

The memorial from the Pennsylvania Society applied, in express terms, for an emancipation of slaves, and the report of the committee appeared to hold out the idea that Congress might exercise the power of emancipating after the year 1808; for it said that Congress could not emancipate slaves prior to that period. He remarked, that either the power of manumission still remained with the several States, or it was exclusively vested in Congress; for no one would contend that such a power would be concurrent in the several States and the United States. . . .

He applied these principles to the case in question; and asked, whether the Constitution had, in express terms, vested the Congress with the power of manumission? Or whether it restrained the States from exercising that power? . . . But admitting that Congress had the authority to manumit slaves in America, and were disposed to exercise it, would the Southern States acquiesce in such a measure without a struggle? Would the citizens of that country tamely suffer their property to be torn from them? Would even the citizens of the other States, which did not possess this property, desire to have all the slaves let loose upon them? Would not such a step be injurious even to the slaves themselves? It was well known that they were an indolent people, improvident, averse to labor: when emancipated, they would either starve or plunder. Nothing was a stronger proof of the absurdity of emancipation than the fanciful schemes which the friends to the measure had suggested, one was to ship them out of the country, and colonize them in some foreign region. This plan admitted that it would be dangerous to retain them within the United States after they were manumitted: but surely it would be inconsistent with humanity to banish these people to a remote country, and to expel them from their native soil, and from places to which they had a local attachment. It would be no less repugnant to the principles of freedom, not to allow them to remain here, if they desired it. How could they be called freemen, if they were against their consent, to be expelled [from] the country? Thus did the advocates for emancipation acknowledge that the blacks, when liberated, ought not to remain here to stain the blood of the whites by a mixture of the races.

. . . But allowing that a practicable scheme of general emancipation could be devised, there can be no doubt that the two races would remain distinct. It is known, from experience, that the whites had such an idea of their superiority over the blacks, that they never even associated with them; even the warmest friends to the blacks kept them at a distance, and rejected all intercourse with them. Could any instance be quoted of their intermarrying; the Quakers asserted that nature had made all men equal, and that the difference of color should not place Negroes on a worse footing in society than the whites; but had any of them ever married a Negro, or would any of them suffer their children to mix their blood with that of a black? They would view with abhorrence such an alliance.

Mr. Smith then read some extracts from Mr. Jefferson's *Notes on Virginia*, proving that Negroes were by nature an inferior race of beings; and that whites would always feel a repugnance at mixing their blood with blacks. Thus, he proceeded, that respectable author, who was desirous of countenancing emancipation, was, on a consideration of the subject, induced candidly to avow that the difficulties appeared insurmountable. The friends to manumission had said, that by prohibiting the further importation of slaves, and by liberating those born after a certain period, a gradual emancipation might take place, and that in process of time the very color would be extinct, and there would be none but whites. He was at a loss to learn how that consequence would result. If the blacks did not intermarry with the whites, they would remain black to the end of time; for it was not contended that liberating them would whitewash them; if they would intermarry with the whites, then the white race would be extinct, and the American people would be all of the mulatto breed. In whatever light, therefore, the subject was viewed, the folly of emancipation was manifest. . . .

A proper consideration of this business must convince every candid mind, that emancipation would be attended with one or other of these consequences; either that a mixture of the races would denigrate the whites, without improving the blacks, or that it would create two separate classes of people in the community involved in inveterate hostility, which would terminate in the massacre and extirpation of one or the other. . . . The negroes would not be benefitted by it; free negroes never improve in talents, never grow rich, and continue to associate with the people of their own color. This is owing either to the natural aversion the whites entertain towards them, and an opinion of the superiority of their race, or to the natural attachment the blacks have to those of their own color; in either case, it proves that they will, after manumission, continue a distinct people, and have separate interests. . . .

This is not an object of general concern, for I have already proved that it does not weaken the Union; but admit that it did, will the abolition of slavery strengthen South Carolina? It can only be cultivated by slaves; the climate, the nature of the soil, ancient habits, forbid the whites from performing the labor. Experience convinces us of the truth of this. . . . If the slaves are emancipated, they will not remain in that country—remove the cultivators of the soil, and the whole of the low country, all the fertile rice and indigo swamps will be deserted, and become a wilderness. . . . If the low country is deserted, where will be the commerce, the valuable exports of that country, the large revenue raised from its imports and from the consumption of the rich planters? In a short time, the Northern and Eastern States will supply us with their manufactures; if you depopulate the rich low country of South Carolina and Georgia, you will give us a blow which will immediately recoil on yourselves. [T]he States are links of one chain: if we break one, the whole must fall to pieces. . . .

6. Absalom Jones, Petition to the U.S. Congress (1799)

In 1799 Congress received a petition seeking relief for free blacks who were abducted and sold into slavery. Led by Absalom Jones (1746–1818), the petitioners reproved the federal Fugitive Slave Act for encouraging the enslavement of free blacks. Some congressional delegates argued that Congress must receive such petitions and that slavery was akin to a destructive "cancer." Others, arguing against receiving such petitions, denied that the authors enjoyed the right to petition Congress as the petitioners were not included among "we, the people."

To the President, Senate, and House of Representatives of the United States.

The petition of the People of Colour, Freemen, within the City and Suburbs of Philadelphia:

Humbly sheweth That thankful to God our Creator and to the Government under which we live, for the blessing and benefit extended to us in the enjoyment of our natural right to Liberty, and the protection of our Persons and property from the oppression and violence, to which so great a number of like colour and National Descent are subjected; We feel ourselves bound from a sense of these blessings to continue in our respective allotments, and to lead honest and peaceable lives, rendering due submission to the Laws, and exciting and encouraging each other thereto, agreeable to the uniform advice of our real friends of every denomination. Yet, while we feel impress'd with grateful sensations for the Providential favours we ourselves enjoy, We cannot be insensible of the condition of our afflicted Brethren, suffering under various circumstances in different parts of these States; but deeply sympathizing with them, We are incited by a sense of Social duty and humbly conceive ourselves authorized to address and petition you in their behalf, believing them to be objects of representation in your public Councils, in common with ourselves and every other class of Citizens within the Jurisdiction of the United States, according to the declared design of the present Constitution . . . as set forth in the preamble thereto in the following words viz. "We the People of the United States in order to form a more perfect union, establish Justice, insure domestick tranquility, provide for the Common Defence, and to secure the blessings of Liberty to ourselves and posterity, do ordain." We apprehend this solemn Compact is violated by a trade carried on in a clandestine manner to the Coast of Guinea, and another equally wicked practiced openly by Citizens of some of the Southern States upon the waters of Maryland and Delaware: Men sufficiently callous as to qualify for the brutal purpose, are employed in kidnapping those of our Brethren that are free, and purchasing others of such as claim a property in them; thus these poor helpless victims like droves of Cattle are seized, fettered, and hurried into places provided for this most horrid traffic, such as dark cellars and garrets. . . . After a sufficient number is obtained, they are forced on board vessels, crouded under hatches, and without the least commiseration, left to deplore the sad separation of the dearest ties in nature, husband from wife and Parents from children; thus pack'd together they are transported to Georgia and other places, and there inhumanly exposed to sale: Can any Commerce, trade, or transaction, so detestably shock the feelings of Man, or degrade the dignity of his nature equal to this, and how increasingly is the evil aggravated when practiced in a Land, high in profession of the benign doctrines of our blessed Lord, who taught his followers to do unto others as they would they should do unto them! . . . We do not ask for the immediate emancipation of all, knowing that the degraded State of many and their want of education, would greatly disqualify for such a change; yet humbly desire you may exert every means in your power to undo the heavy burdens, and prepare the way for the oppressed to go free, that every yoke may be broken.

The Law not long since enacted by Congress called the Fugitive Bill, is, in its execution found to be attended with circumstances peculiarly hard and distressing, for many of our afflicted Brethren in order to avoid the barbarities wantonly exercised upon them, or thro fear of being carried off by those

Men-stealers, have been forced to seek refuge by flight; they are then hunted by armed Men, and under colour of this law, cruelly treated, shot, or brought back in chains to those who have no just claim upon them.

In the Constitution, and the Fugitive bill, no mention is made of Black people or Slaves; therefore if the Bill of Rights, or the declaration of Congress are of any validity, we beseech that as we are men we may be admitted to partake of the Liberties and unalienable Rights therein held forth; firmly believing that the extending of Justice and equity to all Classes would be a means of drawing down the blessings of Heaven upon this Land, for the Peace and Prosperity of which, and the real happiness of every member of the Community, we fervently pray.

Philadelphia, 30th of December, 1799.

Absalom Jones and others, 73 subscribers.

7. Debates in the U.S. Congress: House of Representatives, in Response to a Petition from Absalom Jones, et al. (January 2–3, 1800)

Thursday, January 2: Mr. Robert Waln [of Pennsylvania] presented a petition of Absalom Jones and others, free men of color, of the city and county of Philadelphia . . . which he moved to have referred to the committee appointed to inquire whether any and what alterations ought to be made in the existing law prohibiting the slave trade from the United States to any foreign place or country. . . .

Mr. John Rutledge Jr. [of South Carolina] thought any reference at all very improper; he hoped it would be laid on the table, and with a view never to be called up hereafter. Petitions of this sort had repeatedly come before the House, only with the difference of transfer of hands. . . . Those gentlemen who used to come forward, to be sure, had not avowedly come forward again, but had now put it into the hands of the black *gentlemen.* They now tell the House these people are in slavery—I thank God they are! If they were not, dreadful would be the consequences. They say they are not represented. To be sure a great number of them are not. Farther, they say they are sent to the Southern States. Who can prevent that? Persons possessing slaves have a right to send them there if they choose. They tell you that they are brought from Africa. This matter is in a train to be prevented, the subject being now in the hands of a committee. Already has too much of this new-fangled French philosophy of liberty and equality found its way and was too apparent among these *gentlemen* in the Southern States, by which nothing would do but their liberty. . . .

Mr. George Thatcher [of Massachusetts] . . . If Congress had not power to legislate on the African trade, then why did they say it was with a committee? . . . Would any gentleman say that it was policy not to legislate about 700,000 enemies, in the very body of the United States? While they were slaves they were enemies. He declared a greater evil than the very principle could not exist; it was a cancer of immense magnitude, that would some time destroy the body politic, except a proper legislation should prevent the evil. . . .

Mr. John Brown [of Rhode Island] said he was in hopes that every member belonging to the Northern States would have seen by this time the impropriety of encouraging slaves to come from the Southern States to reside as vagabonds and thieves among them, and have been tired of the bad policy. No subject surely was so likely to cause a division of the States as that respecting slaves. He did not hold a slave in the world, he said, but he was as much for supporting the rights and property of those who did, as though he was a slave owner. He considered this as much personal property as a farm or a ship, which was incontestably so. . . .

We want money, said Mr. Brown, we want a navy; we ought therefore to use the means to obtain it. We ought to go farther than has yet been proposed, and repeal the bills in question altogether, for why should we see Great Britain getting all the slave trade to themselves; why may not our country be enriched by that lucrative traffic? . . .

Mr. [Samuel] Dana [of Connecticut] said if the petition before the House contained nothing but a farrago of the French metaphysics of liberty and equality, he should think that it was likely to produce some of the dreadful scenes of St. Domingo. Or if he believed it was only the effects of a religious fanaticism in a set of men who thought they were doing their duty, though he thought the subject quite out of the power of Congress, he might be disposed to think it quite wrong. But when he perceived a petition, addressed in language which was very decent, and which expressly declared that the petitioners did not wish the House to do what was inconsistent with the Constitution, but only asked an amelioration of the severities under which people of their color labored, he thought it ought to be received and committed. . . .

Mr. James Jones [of Georgia] . . . First, the petitioners contemplated that those people (the slaves) ought to be represented, "with *us* and the rest of the citizens of the United States." Then they speak of the Federal compact, in which they consider those people as interested in common with others, under these words: "we, the people of the United States of America," &c. I would ask gentlemen whether, with all their philanthropy, they would wish to see those people sitting by their sides deliberating in the councils of the nation? He presumed not. They go on farther and say, "We do not ask for the immediate emancipation of all, but we ask you to prepare the way for the oppressed to go free, that every yoke might be broken, thus keeping up the principle to do unto others as you would they should do unto you." The words need only be read to convince every man what is the tendency of their request. The gentleman farther says, that 700,000 men are in bondage. I ask him how he would remedy this evil as he calls it? But I do not think it is any evil; would he have these people turned out in the United States to ravage, murder, and commit every species of crime? I believe it might have been happy for the United States if these people had never been introduced amongst us, but I do believe that they have been immensely benefited by coming amongst us. It was the British Government that transmitted them down to us when in a colonized state, but being here, and being the property of individuals after obtaining our common liberty and forming our Federal compact, property and safety were guaranteed to every individual and State in the Confederation. How can this House meddle with that part of our property? The General Government has no power over it. . . .

Mr. Jonas Platt [of New York] . . . Although, agreeably to the Constitution, Congress could not make any laws to prevent the emigration or importation of any persons whom the several States should, at the adoption thereof, think proper to admit, yet Congress could, and had made laws relative to fugitives from justice and previous to the year 1800. It was this law they prayed the amelioration of, and that the power of persons over their slaves might be limited, and that the law might be so amended as to prevent its violation. It was for that, and not for the general abolition of slavery they prayed, and surely they ought to be heard; their prayer ought to be committed for that purpose.

He disclaimed the least desire, but an abhorrence, of any principle that would rob persons of their property, but at the same time he was not such a dupe to *words* as to be of the opinion held up by a gentleman that because the French had used the words "reason" and "philosophy" he should discard them, and with them humanity! . . .

Friday, January 3: . . . The House resumed unfinished business of yesterday, on the resolution for referring certain parts of the petition of Absalom Jones and others. . . .

Mr. [John] Rutledge [Jr., of South Carolina] thought it a little extraordinary that when gentlemen from some parts of the Union were positively assured that very serious, nay, dreadful effects, must be the inevitable consequence of their discussions on this subject, they still would persist. He used strong words, he said, because no others would be appropriate. Gentlemen recommended the subject to be calmly argued. Would gentlemen feel calm if measures were taken to destroy most of their property? Would calmness be consistent if entering wedges were prepared to ruin the property of whole estates? If ever it was justi-fiable to be warm on any subject in the House, it surely was on an occasion like the present, when imminent danger is in view. Yes we deem this as an entering wedge to an inevitable loss of our property, if persisted in. It appeared by the gentlemen's arguments that he had just been reading the philosopher Brissot.

Three emissaries from St. Domingo appeared in the hall of the [National] Convention, demanding the emancipation of their species from slavery. The Convention were told it would operate as an entering wedge that would go to the destruction of property, and the loss of one of the finest islands in the world; that it would be murderous in the extreme; that it would open scenes which had never been practiced since the destruction of Carthage; that a whole rich country would be buried in blood; that thousands would instantly be reduced to abject penury; that the first towns in that fine island would be reduced to a heap of ashes. But those gentlemen said no it cannot be, all our desires originate in philanthropy—we wish to do good! But sir, we have lived to see these dreadful scenes. . . . Most important consequences may be the result. . . . [W]e know the situation of things there, although they do not, and not knowing we deprecate it. There have been emissaries amongst us in the Southern States; they have begun their war upon us; and actual organization has commenced; we have had them meeting in their club room, and debating on that subject, and determinations have been made. . . .

I recollect that gentlemen in France used arguments like the gentleman from Massachusetts: "We can indemnify these proprietors." But how did they do it, or how can it be done?—Not at all. Farther, we are told these things would take place, we need not be alarmed; it was inevitable; that it was rea-sonable and unavoidable. Sir, it never will take place. There is one alternative which will save us from it, but that alternative I deprecate very much; that is, that we are able to take care of ourselves, and if driven to it, we will take care of ourselves. . . .

8. Thomas Jefferson, Letter to Rufus King, U.S. Minister to Great Britain (July 13, 1802)

Here Jefferson expressed a growing fear of slave insurrections stirred by Gabriel's Rebellion, which resulted in the execution of twenty-six black men alleged to have been ringleaders. Jefferson questioned the criminality of the participants, and sensed interest among some political leaders in finding milder punishments in response to future insurrections.

Dear Sir—The course of things in the neighbouring islands of the West Indies appears to have given a considerable impulse to the minds of the slaves in different parts of the U.S. A great disposition to insurgency has manifested itself among them, which, in one instance, in the state of Virginia, broke out into actual insurrection. This was easily suppressed: but many of those concerned, (between 20 and 30, I believe) fell victims to the law. So extensive an execution could not but excite sensibility in the public mind, and beget a regret that the laws had not provided, for such cases, some alternative, combining more mildness with equal efficacy. The legislature of the state, at a subsequent meeting, took the subject into consideration, and have communicated to me through the governor of the state, their wish that some place could be provided, out of the limits of the U.S. to which slaves guilty of insurgency might be transported; and they have particularly looked to Africa as offering the most desirable receptacle. We might for this purpose, enter into negociations with the natives, on some part of the coast, to obtain a settlement. . . . But there being already such an establishment on that coast by the English Sierre Leone Company, made for the express purpose of colonizing civilized blacks to that country, it would seem better, by incorporating our emigrants with theirs, to make one strong rather than two weak colonies. This would be the more desirable because the blacks settled at Sierre Leone, having chiefly gone from these states would often receive among those we should send, their acquaintances and relations. The object of this letter, therefore, is to ask the favor of you to enter into conference with such persons private and public as would be necessary to give us permission to send thither the persons under contemplation. It is material to observe that they are not felons, or common malefactors, but persons guilty of what the safety of society, under actual circumstances, obliges us to treat as a crime, but which their feelings may represent in a far different shape. They are such as will be a valuable acquisition to the settlement already existing there, and well calculated to cooperate in the plan of civilization. . . .

9. James Forten, *Letters from a Man of Colour, on a Late Bill before the Senate of Pennsylvania* (1813)

Responding to a proposed Pennsylvania law designed to ban further immigration of free blacks, James Forten (1766–1842) asserted that the state constitution is color-blind. Forten exposed the prejudice and abuse faced daily by African Americans throughout Pennsylvania, and he suggested that while public opinion shapes the law, the law, in turn, equally shapes public attitudes and behavior.

LETTER I.

. . . We hold this truth to be self-evident, that GOD created all men equal, and is one of the most prominent features in the Declaration of Independence, and in that glorious fabric of collected wisdom, our noble Constitution. This idea embraces the Indian and the European, the Savage and the Saint, the Peruvian and the Laplander, the white Man and the African, and whatever measures are adopted subversive of this inestimable privilege, are in direct violation of the letter and the spirit of our Constitution. . . .

These thoughts were suggested by the promulgation of a late bill, before the Senate of Pennsylvania, to prevent the emigration of people of color into this state. It was not passed into a law at this session and must in consequence lay over until the next, before when we sincerely hope, the white men, whom we should look upon as our protectors, will have become convinced of the inhumanity and impolicy of such a measure, and forbear to deprive us of those inestimable treasures, Liberty and Independence. This is almost the only state in the Union wherein the African have justly boasted of rational liberty and the protection of the laws, and shall it now be said they have been deprived of that liberty, and publicly exposed for sale to the highest bidder? Shall colonial inhumanity that has marked many of us with shameful stripes, become the practice of the people of Pennsylvania, while Mercy stands weeping at the miserable spectacle? People of Pennsylvania, descendants of the immortal Penn, doom us not to the unhappy fate of thousands of our countrymen in the Southern States and the West Indies; despise the traffic in blood, and the blessing of the African will forever be around you. Many of us are men of property, for the security of which, we have hitherto looked to the laws of our blessed state, but should this become a law, our property is jeopardized, since the same power which can expose to sale an unfortunate fellow creature, can wrest from him those estates which years of honest industry have accumulated. Where shall the poor African look for protection, should the people of Pennsylvania consent to oppress him? We grant there are a number of worthless men belonging to our color, but there are laws of sufficient rigor for their punishment, if properly and duly enforced. . . . If there are worthless men, there are also men of merit among the African race, who are useful members of Society. The truth of this let their benevolent institutions and the numbers clothed and fed by them witness. Punish the guilty man of color to the utmost limit of the laws, but sell him not [to] slavery! If he is in danger of becoming a public charge prevent him! If he is too indolent to labor for his own subsistence, compel him to do so; but sell him not to slavery. By selling him you do not make him better, but commit a wrong, without benefiting the object of it or society at large.

Many of our ancestors were brought here more than one hundred years ago; many of our fathers, many of ourselves, have fought and bled for the independence of our country. Do not then expose us to sale. Let not the spirit of the father behold the son robbed of that liberty which he died to establish, but let the motto of our legislators, be—"The Law knows no distinction." . . .

LETTER II.

Those patriotic citizens, who, after resting from the toils of an arduous war, which achieved our independence and laid the foundation of the only reasonable Republic upon earth, associated together, and for the protection of those inestimable rights for the establishment of which they had exhausted their blood and treasure, framed the Constitution of Pennsylvania, have by the ninth article declared, "that all men are born equally free and independent, and have certain inherent and indefeasible rights, among which are those of enjoying life and liberty." Under the restraint of wise and well administered laws, we cordially unite in the above glorious sentiment, but by the bill upon which we have been remarking, it appears as if the committee who drew it up mistook the sentiment expressed in this article, and do not consider us as men, or that those enlightened statesmen who formed the constitution upon the basis of experience intended to exclude us from its blessings and protection. If the former, why are we not to be considered as men[?] Has the God who made the white man and the black, left any record declaring us a different species[?] Are we not sustained by the same power, supported by the same food, hurt by the same wounds, pleased with the same delights, and propagated by the same means[?] And should we not then enjoy the same liberty, and be protected by the same laws[?]—We would wish not to legislate, for our means of information and the acquisition of knowledge are, in the nature of things, so circumscribed, that we must consider ourselves incompetent to the task: but let us, in legislation be considered men. It cannot be that the authors of our Constitution intended to exclude us from its benefits, for just emerging from unjust and cruel emancipation, their souls were too much affected with their own deprivations to commence the reign of terror over others. They knew we were deeper skinned than they were, but they acknowledged us as men, and found that many an honest heart beat beneath a dusky bosom. They felt that they had no more authority to enslave us, than England had to tyrannize over them. They were convinced that if amenable to the same laws in our actions, we should be protected by the same laws in our rights and privileges. Actuated by these sentiments they adopted the glorious fabric of our liberties, and declaring "all men" free, they did not particularize white and black, because they never supposed it would be made a question whether we were men or not. Sacred be the ashes, and deathless be the memory of those heroes who are dead;

and revered be the persons and the characters of those who still exist and lift the thunders of admonition against the traffic in blood. . . .

LETTER IV.

I proceed again to the consideration of the bill of unalienable rights belonging to black men. . . . And let me here remark, that this unfortunate race of humanity, although protected by our laws, are already subject to the fury and caprice of a certain set of men, who regard neither humanity, law nor privilege. They are already considered as a different species, and little above the brute creation. They are thought to be objects fit for nothing else than lordly men to vent the effervescence of their spleen upon, and to tyrannize over, like the bearded Musselman over his horde of slaves. Nay, the Musselman, thinks more of his horse, than the generality of people do of the despised black!—Are not men of color sufficiently degraded? Why then increase their degradation. It is a well known fact, that black people, upon certain days of public jubilee, dare not to be seen after twelve o'clock in the day, upon the field to enjoy the times; for no sooner do the fumes of that potent devil, Liquor, mount into the brain, than the poor black is assailed like the destroying Hyena or the avaricious Wolf! I allude particularly to the Fourth of July—Is it not wonderful, that the day set apart for the festival of Liberty, should be bused [abused] by the advocates of Freedom, in endeavouring to sully what they profess to adore. If men, though they know that the law protects all, will dare, in defiance of law, to execute their hatred upon the defenseless black, will they not by the passage of this bill, believe him still more a mark for their venom and spleen—Will they not believe him completely deserted by authority, and subject to every outrage brutality can inflict—too surely they will, and the poor wretch will turn his eyes around to look in vain for protection. Pause, ye rulers of a free people, before you give us over to despair and violation—we implore you, for the sake of humanity, to snatch us from the pinnacle of ruin, from that gulf, which will swallow our rights, as fellow creatures; our privileges, as citizens; and our liberties, as men! . . .

LETTER V.

. . . By the third section of this bill, which is its peculiar hardship, the police officers are authorized to apprehend any black, whether a vagrant or a man of reputable character, who cannot produce a Certificate that he has been registered. He is to be arrayed before a justice, who thereupon is to commit him to prison! The jailor is to advertise a Freeman, and at expiration of six months, if no owner appears for this degraded black, he is to be exposed to sale, and if not sold to be confined at hard labour for seven years!—Man of feeling, read this!—No matter who, no matter where. The Constable, whose antipathy generally against the black is very great, will take every opportunity of hurting his feelings! Perhaps, he sees him at a distance and having a mind to raise the boys in hue and cry against him, exclaims, "Halloa! Stop the Negro?"—The boys, delighting in the sport immediately begin to hunt him, and immediately from a hundred tongues, is heard the cry—"Hoa, Negro, where is your Certificate!"—Can any thing be conceived more degrading to humanity! Can any thing be done more shocking to the principal of Civil Liberty!—A person arriving from another state, ignorant of the existence of such a law, may fall a victim to its cruel oppression. But he is to be advertised, and if no owner appears—How can an owner appear for a man who is free and belongs to no one!—If no owner appears, he is exposed for sale!—Oh, inhuman spectacle: found in no unjust act convicted of no crime, he is barbarously sold like the produce of the soil, to the highest bidder, or what is still worse, for no crimes, without the inestimable privilege of a trial by his peers, doomed to the dreary walls of a prison for the term of seven tedious years! . . .

. . . Pennsylvania has always been a refuge from slavery, and to this state the Southern black, when freed, has flown for safety. . . . When masters in many of the Southern states, which they frequently do, free a particular black, unless that black leaves the state in so many hours any person resident of the said state, can have him arrested and again sold to Slavery. . . . I have known persons of this description sold three times after being first emancipated. Where shall he go? Shut every state against him, and, like Pharoah's kine, drive him into the sea.—Is there no spot on earth that will protect him! Against their inclination, his ancestors were forced from their homes by trades in human flesh, and even under such circumstances, the wretched offspring are denied the protection you afforded to brutes. . . .

10. John Taylor, *Arator* (1814)

John Taylor of Caroline (1753–1824) viewed the population of free blacks living in the slaveholding states anxiously. Assuming a link between free blacks and insurrection, he also claimed that free blacks (whom he characterizes as a separate "race or nation") are detrimental to agriculture, a grave concern as Southern agriculture "entirely depends on slaves." Responding to Jefferson, Taylor argued that slavery cultivates virtue among blacks, and an appreciation of equality and liberty among whites.

Number 13

Slavery

. . . I allude to the policy of introducing by law into society, a race, or nation of people between the masters and slaves, having rights extremely different from either, called free Negroes and Mulattoes. It is not my intention to consider the peril to which this policy exposes the safety of the country, by the excitement of insurrection, with which it perpetually goads the slaves, the channels for communication it affords, and the reservoir for recruits it provides. I shall only observe, that it was this very policy, which first doomed the whites, and then the mulattoes themselves, to the fate suffered by both in St. Domingo. . . . Being defined by experience in that country, and by expectation in this, it is unnecessary for me to consider the political consequences of this policy.

My present object is to notice its influence on agriculture. This so entirely depends on slaves in a great proportion of the union, that it must be deeply affected by whatever shall indispose them to labor, render them intractable, or entice them into a multitude of crimes and irregularities. A free Negro and Mulatto class is exactly calculated to effect all these ends. They live upon agriculture as agents or brokers for disposing stolen products. . . .

They wound agriculture in the two modes of being an unproductive class living upon it, like a stock-jobber or capitalist class, and of diminishing the utility of the slaves. This latter mode might be extended to a multitude of particulars, among which rendering the slaves less happy, compelling masters to use more strictness, disgusting them with agriculture itself, and greatly diminishing their ability to increase the comforts, and of course the utility of slaves, would be items deeply trenching upon its prosperity. It is however unnecessary to prove what every agriculturalist in the slave states experimentally knows, namely, that his operations are greatly embarrassed, and his efforts retarded, by circumstances having the class of free Negroes for their cause.

The only remedy is to get rid of it. . . . The situation of the free Negro class is exactly calculated to force it into every species of vice. Cut off from most of the rights of citizens, and from all the allowances of slaves, it is driven into every species of crime for subsistence; and destined to a life of idleness, anxiety and guilt. The slaves more widely share in its guilt, than in its fraudulent acquisitions. They owe to it the perpetual pain of repining at their own condition by having an object of comparison before their own eyes, magnified by its idleness and thefts with impunity, into a temptation the most alluring to slaves; and will eventually owe to it the consequences of their insurrection. . . .

It may be easily effected by purchasing of Congress lands sufficient for their subsistence in states where slavery is not allowed, and giving them the option of removing to those lands, or emigrating wherever they please. . . .

Number 14

Slavery, continued.

Societies are instituted to control and diminish the imperfections of human nature, because without them it generates ignorance, savageness and depravity of manners. Those best constituted, cannot however cure it of a disposition to command, and to live by the labor of others; it is eternally forming sub-societies for acquiring power and wealth, and to these perfidious, ambitious, avaricious or unconstitutional sub-societies, the liberty and property of the rest of the body politic has universally fallen prey. [H]itherto the most perfect society for the public good, has never been able to defend itself against sub-societies in some for advancing the wealth or power of a faction or a particular interest. . . .

The attempt will undoubtedly terminate according to the nature of man, as it has once already terminated; but its catastrophe ought rather to be courted than avoided if the author of the notes on Virginia [Th. Jefferson] is right in the following quotations. "The whole commerce between master and slave," he says, "is a perpetual exercise of the most boisterous passions, the most unremitting despotism on one part, and degrading submissions on the other. . . . The man must be a prodigy who can retain his manners and morals undepraved by such circumstances. The Almighty has no attribute which can take side with us in such a contest.". . .

If Mr. Jefferson's assertions are correct, it is better to run the risk of national extinction, by liberating and fighting the blacks, than to live abhorred by God, and consequently hated of man. If they are erroneous, they ought not to be admitted as arguments for the emancipating policy. . . .

. . . To me it seems, that slaves are too far below, and too much in the power of the master, to inspire furious passions; that such are nearly as rare and disgraceful towards slaves as towards horses; that slaves are more frequently the objects of benevolence than of rage; and hardly ever suffered to tyrannize over them; that they open instead of shut the sluices of benevolence in tender minds; and that fewer good public or private characters have been raised in countries enslaved by some faction of particular interest, than in those where personal slavery existed.

I conjecture the cause of this to be, that vicious and mean qualities become despicable in the eyes of freemen from their association with the character of slaves. Character, like condition is contrasted, and as one contrast causes us to love liberty better, so the other causes us to love virtue better. Qualities odious in themselves, become more contemptible, when united with the most degraded class of men, than when seen in our equals; and pride steps in to aid the struggles of virtue. Instead of fearing that children imbibe the qualities of slaves, it is probable, that the circumstance of seeing bad qualities in slaves will contribute to their virtue.

For the same reason the submission and flattery of slaves will be despised, and cause us rather to hate servility than to imbibe a dictatorial arrogance. . . . It is the submission and flattery of equals, which fills men with the impudent and wicked wish to dictate, and an impatience of free opinion and fair discussion. . . .

Virtue and vice are naturally unavoidably coexistent in the moral world, as beauty and deformity are in the animal; and one is the only mirror in which the other can be seen, and therefore, in the present state of man, one cannot be destroyed without the other. It may be thus that personal slavery has constantly reflected the strongest rays of civil liberty and patriotism. . . . Perhaps the sight of slavery and its vices may inspire the mind with an affection for liberty and virtue. . . .

Let it not be supposed that I approve of slavery because I do not aggravate its evils, or prefer a policy which must terminate in a war of extermination. The chapter on the manners of slave-holders before quoted, concludes with an intimation, that the consent of the masters to a general emancipation, or their own extirpation, were the alternatives between which they had to choose. Such a hint from a profound mind is awful. It admits an ability in the blacks, though shackled by slavery, to extirpate the whites, and proposes to increase this ability by knocking off their shackles. Such a hint adds force to the recommendation in the previous essay for separating the enslaved and free blacks, as some security against the prognosticated extirpation. . . .

Number 28

Labor

. . . The history of parties in its utmost malignity is but a feint mirror for reflecting the consequences of a white and a black party. If badges and names have been able to madden men in all ages, up to robbery and murder in their most atrocious forms, no doubt can exist of the consequences of placing two nations of distinct colors and features on the same theater, to contend, not about sounds and signs, but for wealth and power.

And yet an amiable and peaceful religious sect, have been long laboring with some success, to plunge three fourths of the union, into a civil war of a complexion so inveterate, as to admit of no issue, but the extermination of one entire party. . . . The French revolution, bottomed upon as correct abstract principles and sounder practical hopes, turned out to be a foolish and mischievous speculation; what then can be expected from making republicans of negro slaves, and conquerors of ignorant infuriated barbarians? . . .

But what will not enthusiasm attempt? It attempted to make freemen of the people of France; the experiment pronounced that they were incapable of liberty. It attempted to compound a free nation of black and white people in St. Domingo. The experiment pronounced that one color must perish. And now rendered blinder by experience, it proposes to renew the last experiment, though it impressed truth by sanctions of inconceivable horror; and again to create a body politic, as monstrous and unnatural as a mongrel half white man and half Negro.

Do these hasty, or in the language of exact truth, fanatic philosophers, patriots or Christians, suppose that the Negroes could be made free, and yet kept from property and equal civil rights . . . ? As rivals for rule with whites, the collision would be immediate, and the catastrophe speedy. Divested of equal civil rights and wealth to prevent this rivalship, but endowed with personal liberty, they would constitute the most complete instrument for invasion or ambition, hitherto forged throughout the entire circle of human folly. . . .

11. James Forten and Russell Perrott, An Address to the Humane and Benevolent Inhabitants of the City and County of Philadelphia (1817)

Gathering in Philadelphia in August 1817, an assembly representing free blacks and led by James Forten and Russell Perrott (ca. 1791–1824) protested the colonization plans previously proposed by the American Colonization Society. Forten and Perrott, who believed progress toward abolition was under way, criticized the ACS, fearing ulterior motives to use colonization as a means to perpetuate slavery.

The free people of colour, assembled together, under circumstances of deep interest to their happiness and welfare, humbly and respectfully lay before you this expression of their feelings and apprehensions.

Relieved from the miseries of slavery, many of us by your aid, possessing the benefits which industry and integrity in this prosperous country assure to all its inhabitants, enjoying the rich blessings of religion, by opportunities of worshiping the only true God, under the light of Christianity, each of us according to his understanding; and having afforded to us and to our children the means of education and improvement; we have no wish to separate from our present homes, for any purpose whatever. Contented with our present situation and condition we are not desirous of increasing their prosperity, but by honest efforts and by the use of those opportunities for their improvement, which the constitution and laws allow to all. It is therefore with painful solicitude, and sorrowing regret, we have seen a plan for colonizing the free people of colour of the United States on the coast of Africa, brought forward under the auspices and sanction of gentlemen whose names give value to all they recommend, and who certainly are among the wisest, the best, and the most benevolent of men, in this great nation.

If the plan of colonizing is intended for our benefit and those who now promote it will never seek our injury, we humbly and respectfully urge that it is not asked for by us; nor will it be required by any circumstances, in our present or future condition, as long as we shall be permitted to share the protection of the excellent laws, and just government which we now enjoy, in common with every individual of the community.

We therefore . . . with humble and grateful acknowledgments to those who have devised it, renounce, and disclaim every connection with it, and respectfully but firmly declare our determination not to participate in any part of it.

If this plan of colonization now proposed is intended to provide a refuge and a dwelling for a portion of our brethren, who are now held in slavery in the South, we have other and stronger objections to it, and we entreat your consideration of them.

The ultimate and final abolition of slavery in the United States is, under the guidance and protection of a just God, progressing. Every year witnesses the release of numbers of the victims of oppression, and affords new and safe assurances that the freedom of all will in the end be accomplished. As they are thus by degrees relieved from bondage, our brethren have opportunities for instruction and improvement; and thus they become in some measure fitted for their liberty.—Every year, many of us have restored to us by the gradual, but certain march of the cause of abolition—parents, from whom we have been long separated—wives and children, whom we had left in servitude—and brothers, in blood as well as in early sufferings, from whom we had been long parted.

But if the emancipation of our kindred shall, when the plan of colonization shall go into effect, be attended with transportation to a distant land, and shall be granted on no other condition, the consolation for our past sufferings and of those of our colour, who are in slavery, which have hitherto been, and under the present situation of things, would continue to be afforded to us and to them, will cease for ever. The cords, which now connect them with us will be stretched by the distance to which their ends will be carried until they break; and all the sources of happiness, which affection and connection, and blood bestow, will be ours or theirs no more.

Nor do we view the colonization of those who may become emancipated by its operation among our southern brethren, as capable of producing their happiness. Unprepared by education, and a knowledge of the truths of our blessed religion, for their new situation, those who will thus become colonists will themselves be surrounded by every suffering which can afflict the members of the human family.

Without arts, without habits of industry, and unaccustomed to provide by their own exertions and foresight for their wants, the colony will soon become the abode of every vice and the home of every misery. Soon will the light of Christianity, which now dawns among that section of our species, be shut out by the clouds of ignorance, and their day of life be closed, without the illuminations of the Gospel.

To those of our brethren who shall be left behind, there will be assured perpetual slavery and augmented sufferings.—Diminished in numbers the slave population of the southern states, which by its magnitude alarms its proprietors, will be easily secured. Those among their bondmen, who feel that they should be free, by rights which all mankind have from God and from nature, and who thus may become dangerous to the quiet of their masters, will be sent to the colony; and the tame and submissive will be retained, and subjected to increased rigor. Year after year will witness these means to assure safety and submission among their slaves; and the southern masters will colonize only those whom it may be dangerous to keep among them. The bondage of a large portion of our brethren will thus be rendered perpetual.

Should the anticipations of misery and want among the colonists, which with great deference we have submitted to your better judgment, be realized; to emancipate and transport to the colony, will be held forth by slave-holders as the worst and heaviest of punishments, and they will be threatened and successfully used to enforce increased submission to their wishes and subjection to their commands.

Nor ought the sufferings and sorrows, which must be produced by an exercise of the right to transport and colonize such only of their slaves as may be selected by the slave-holders escape the attention and consideration of those whom with all humility we now address. Parents will be torn from their children—husbands from their wives—brothers from brothers—and all the heart-rending agonies which were endured by our forefathers when they were dragged into bondage from Africa will be again renewed, and with increased anguish. The shores of America will like the sands of Africa be watered by the tears of those who will be left behind. Those who shall be carried away will roam childless, widowed, and alone, over the burning plains of Guinea.

. . . We humbly, respectfully, and fervently entreat and beseech your disapprobation of the plan of colonization now offered by "the American society for colonizing the free people of color in the United States."—Here, in the city of Philadelphia, where the voice of the suffering sons of Africa was first heard; where was first commenced the work of abolition, on which Heaven hath smiled, for it could have had success only from the Great Maker; let not a purpose be assisted which will stay the cause of the entire abolition of slavery in the United States, and which may defeat it altogether; which proffers to those who do not ask for them what it calls benefits, but which they consider injuries; and which must insure to the multitudes whose prayers can only reach you through us, misery, and sufferings, and perpetual slavery.

Chapter Three: 1818–1830

Introduction

Looking backward from 1818, when Missouri applied for statehood, one could have perceived the containment of slavery and anticipated the slow but inexorable extinction of the institution. While only three states had legally abolished slavery by the time the Constitution was adopted in 1788, numerous other states would subsequently enact gradual abolition laws. A national colonization society (the American Colonization Society, or ACS) had been created, advocating the relocation of freed slaves to western Africa, which for some members was a necessary means toward abolition. Moreover, in 1787, while the Constitution was being drafted, the Confederation Congress banned slavery in the Northwest Territory. The Constitution, by permitting a complete ban on the slave trade as early as 1808, seemed to anticipate slavery's obsolescence. Many Americans perceived the slave trade to be a moral anathema and deemed ending it instrumental to the eventual abolition of slavery itself. When Russell Perrott stated that the "abolition of the slave trade should be hailed by every lover of genuine liberty as the commencement of that happy era, in which Freedom shall reign to the 'furthest verge of the green earth,'" he was articulating a common sentiment.[1]

Of course, a different view of affairs in 1818 was possible. Many supporters of the ACS actually endorsed colonization for the sake of perpetuating slavery. Thousands of blacks were still held in bondage in New York, New Jersey, and even in Pennsylvania. Slaves were actually owned in Illinois and Indiana, in spite of the Northwest Ordinance, a fact that has prompted some scholars to reassess the Founders' commitment to ending slavery. Economic motivations were also important. If in the 1780s slavery had been viewed as economically less efficient than free labor, the invention of the cotton gin, the settlement of the cotton delta in Mississippi and Alabama, and the growing importance of slavery to economic growth in the British West Indies, Brazil, and elsewhere demonstrated that chattel slavery was now more than economically viable—it was lucrative.[2]

---

1. Russell Perrott, *An Oration on the Abolition of the Slave Trade, Delivered on the First of January, 1812, at the African Church of St. Thomas* (Philadelphia: James Maxwell, 1812).
2. On this point, see David Brion Davis, "The Significance of Excluding Slavery from the Old Northwest in 1787," *Indiana Magazine of History* 84 (March 1988): 78–80.

Still, even though slavery lingered in most northern states in a comparatively limited way, by 1820 slavery in America had taken on a decidedly regional hue. Moreover, the gradualist approach to abolition in the North should not be mistaken for uncertainty about the morality of slavery. As historian David Brion Davis notes, by the 1780s anti-slavery principles had become a viable element in American (and British) moral and political discourse. Increasingly Americans who thought about the problem of slavery determined that a gradualist approach, including a focus on banning the slave trade, was the responsible and most effective means to achieving the goal of complete abolition. That helps explain the symbolic importance of the Ordinance of 1787. When Congress considered extending the 1787 ban to the Mississippi Territory in 1798 and the newly purchased Louisiana Territory in 1804, it demurred, acknowledging the large number of slaves who had previously been brought there under English, Spanish, and French laws. But in 1787 the number of slaves living in the region covered by the Northwest Ordinance was small; the institution had not yet taken hold. And while the law was ambiguous about the status of slaves living in the territories prior to passage of the ordinance, its ban on slavery was politically important. As Davis suggests, its very ambiguity deterred settlers from bringing slaves to the territory. As a result, federal law had effectively prevented slavery from taking root in the Northwest Territory.[3]

That helps explain why Missouri's application for statehood ignited a major national crisis over slavery. Permitting slavery in Missouri appeared to presage the spread of slavery throughout the vast Louisiana Territory. To men like James Tallmadge, prohibiting slavery in Missouri (and by extension, the rest of the Louisiana Territory) was necessary to promote the principles embodied in the Declaration of Independence, for maintaining the Union, and for the eventual abolition of slavery nationwide. "Extend your view across the Mississippi," Tallmadge implored, "look down the long vista of futurity" and one can see an American empire "inhabited by the hardy sons of American freemen . . . owners of the soil on which they live, and interested in the institutions which they labor to defend. . . . But, sir, . . . extend slavery—this bane of man, this abomination of heaven—over your extended empire, and you prepare its dissolution."[4] Missouri statehood held considerable symbolic significance as well as real political and economic consequences. Accordingly, debate over the conditions for Missouri statehood provoked unprecedented, exhaustive, and heated arguments about slavery in America from moral, religious, political, economic, and constitutional perspectives.

The controversy over Missouri statehood was resolved through compromise. Congress permitted Missouri to enter the Union as a slave state; Maine entered

---

3. Ibid., 82–84.
4. See document 3 in this chapter.

as a free state; and slavery was "forever prohibited" in territory obtained from France and which lay north of the 36°30' line, which was Missouri's southern border. Some leaders applauded the legislation, believing that the divisive issue of slavery had been permanently removed from American politics. Other leaders, however, were not so sanguine. Jefferson agreed that the issue was "hushed . . . for the moment. But this is a reprieve only," he added, "not a final sentence. A geographical line, coinciding with a marked principle, moral and political, once conceived and held up to the angry passions of men, will never be obliterated; and every new irritation will mark it deeper and deeper."[5] Rufus King agreed, writing that "the Missouri question . . . is given out to be settled, but nothing is less true. Its influence will increase, its magnitude also."[6] And future president Andrew Jackson, warning that the Missouri question would be the "entering wedge to separate the union," and echoing Southern opinion, questioned the motives of Tallmadge and others. "It is a question of political asscendency, and power," he wrote, "and the Eastern interest are determined to succeed regardless of the consequences. . . . I hope I may not live to see the evils that must grow out of this wicked design of Demagogues, who talk about humanity, but whose sole object is self agrandisement regardless of the happiness of the nation."[7] Those warnings were almost realized the following year, when debate in Congress nearly erupted over a provision of the Missouri constitution that barred free blacks from entering the state. Henry Clay helped avoid another fight by persuading Congress to agree that the provision would "never be construed to authorize the passage of any law . . . by which any citizen, of either of the states in this Union, shall be excluded from the enjoyment of any of the privileges and immunities to which such citizen is entitled under the constitution of the United States."[8]

Of course, whether free blacks were citizens was itself still an open question, and thus Clay's provision, while successful in getting the Missouri constitution approved, didn't resolve the underlying issues. More generally, we should not equate the banning of slavery from a state or territory with a commitment to social and political equality. Keeping a territory free of slaves was also often a way to keep it free of blacks. Keeping the soil "free" typically meant keeping it free for whites. In fact, despite Clay's provision, laws severely regulating or prohibiting the migration of free blacks into states and territories, along with laws disenfranchising and marginalizing

---

5. See document 10 in this chapter.

6. Rufus King to J. A. King, March 18, 1820, in *The Life and Correspondence of Rufus King*, vol. 6 (1816–1827), ed. Charles R. King (New York: G. P. Putnam's Sons, 1900), 303.

7. Andrew Jackson to A. J. Donelson, April 16, 1820, in *The Papers of Andrew Jackson*, vol. 4, *1816–1820* (Knoxville: University of Tennessee, 1994), 367.

8. Resolution Providing for the Admission of the State of Missouri into the Union, *United States Statutes at Large*, 16th Cong., 2d Sess., 3:645 (1821).

free blacks, would be enacted in Ohio, Illinois, Indiana, and elsewhere. It was in part a draconian Ohio law that led David Walker in 1830 to publish his fiery *Appeal to the Coloured Citizens of the World*. The impassioned tone of that work would be a harbinger of the emotional intensity that would characterize abolitionism in the decade to come.

DOCUMENTS

1. Rufus King, Two Speeches on the Missouri Bill, Delivered before the U.S. Senate (1819)

Here Rufus King (1755–1827) defended an amendment, introduced by New York representative James Tallmadge, requiring Missouri to enter the Union as a free state. In the following three documents, which include excerpts from the extended congressional debates over this amendment, King and others debate slavery as a constitutional issue and question its political ramifications. Would allowing slavery in the West promote or inhibit abolition? Is free or slave labor more productive? Does the Constitution's guarantee of republican government empower Congress to ban slavery in new states? Does the "territories clause" grant Congress such power? Would the privileges and immunities clause be violated by such a ban? Some feared that banning slavery would inflame sectional tensions. Others insisted that slavery was never recognized by the Constitution and that its spread would besmirch the national character. Perhaps most compelling is the full-throated commitment expressed by several delegates to sacrificing life for country in the event of civil war.

February 11th and 14th, 1819

. . . The question respecting slavery in the old thirteen States had been decided and settled before the adoption of the Constitution, which grants no power to Congress to interfere with, or to change what had been so previously settled. The slave States, therefore, are free to continue or to abolish slavery. Since the year 1808 Congress have possessed power to prohibit and have prohibited the further migration or importation of slaves into any of the old thirteen States, and at all times, under the Constitution, have had power to prohibit such migration or importation into any of the new States or territories of the United States. The Constitution contains no express provision respecting slavery in a new State that may be admitted into the Union. . . . Congress may, therefore, make it a condition of the admission of a new State, that slavery shall be forever prohibited within the same. . . .

The United States . . . [became] proprietors of the extensive territory northwest of the river Ohio, [and] although the confederation contained no express provision upon the subject, Congress . . . assumed as incident to their office, the power to dispose of this territory; and for this purpose, to divide the same into distinct States, to provide for the temporary government of the inhabitants thereof, and for their ultimate admission as new States into the Federal Union. The ordinance for those purposes, which was passed by Congress in 1787 . . . provides, "that there shall be neither slavery nor involuntary servitude in the said territory." . . .

The State of Virginia, which ceded to the United States her claims to this territory, consented by her delegates in the old Congress to this ordinance— not only Virginia, but North Carolina, South Carolina, and Georgia, by the unanimous votes of their delegates in the old Congress, approved of the ordinance of 1787, by which slavery is forever abolished in the territory northwest of the river Ohio. . . .

Without the votes of these States, the ordinance could not have passed. . . . Slavery had long been established in these States—the evil was felt in their institutions, laws, and habits, and could not easily or at once be abolished. But these votes so honorable to these States, satisfactorily demonstrate their unwillingness to permit the extension of slavery into the new States which might be admitted by Congress into the Union. The States of Ohio, Indiana, and Illinois . . . have been admitted by Congress into the Union, on the condition and conformably to the article of compact, contained in the ordinance of 1787, and by which it is declared that there shall be neither slavery nor involuntary servitude in any of the said States.

Although congress possess the power of making the exclusion of slavery a part or condition of the act admitting a new state into the union, they may in special cases, and for sufficient reasons, forbear to exercise this power. Thus Kentucky and Vermont were admitted as new states into the union, without making the abolition of slavery the condition of their admission. . . .

Admitting this construction of the constitution, it is alleged that the power by which congress excluded slavery from the states northwest of the river Ohio, is suspended in respect to the states that may be formed in the province of Louisiana. The article of the treaty referred to declares, "That the inhabitants of the territory shall be incorporated in the union of the United States, and admitted as soon as possible, according to the principles of the federal constitution, to the enjoyment of all rights, advantages and immunities of citizens of the United States. . . ."

. . . The first clause of this stipulation will be executed by the admission of Missouri as a new state into the union; . . . such admission will impart to the inhabitants of Missouri, "all the rights, advantages, and immunities" which citizens of the United States derive from the constitution thereof;—these rights may be denominated federal rights, are uniform throughout the union, and are common to all its citizens. But the rights derived from the constitution and laws of the states, which may be denominated state rights, in many particulars differ from each other. Thus, while the federal rights of the citizens of Massachusetts and Virginia are the same, their state rights are however dissimilar,—slavery being forbidden in one, and permitted in the other state. This difference arises out of the constitutions and laws of the two states, in the same manner as the difference in the rights of the citizens of these states to vote for representatives in congress arises out of the state laws and constitution: in Massachusetts, every person of lawful age and possessing property of any sort, of the value of two hundred dollars, may vote for representatives to congress;—in Virginia, no person can vote for representatives to congress unless he be a freeholder. As the admission of a new state into the union confers upon its citizens only the rights denominated federal, and as these are common to the citizens of all the states . . . it follows that the prohibition of slavery in Missouri will not impair the federal rights of its citizens; and that such prohibition is not restrained by the clause of the treaty which has been cited. . . .

If Congress possess the power to exclude slavery from Missouri, it still remains to be shown that they ought to do so. . . .

The rule for apportionment of taxes [see Article I, Section 2] is not necessarily the most equitable rule for the apportionment of representatives among the States; property must not be disregarded in the composition of the first rule, but frequently is overlooked in the establishment of the second. A rule which might be approved in respect to taxes, would be disapproved in respect to representatives; one individual possessing twice as much property as another, might be required to pay double the taxes of such other; but no man has two votes to another's one; rich or poor, each has but a single vote in the choice of representatives. In the dispute between England and the colonies, the latter denied the right of the former to tax them, because they were not represented in the English Parliament. [T]he true meaning . . . of this principle of the English constitution is, that a colony or district is not to be taxed which is not represented; not that its number of representatives shall be ascertained by its quota of taxes. If three-fifths of the slaves are virtually represented, or their owners obtain a disproportionate power in legislation, and in the appointment of the President of the United States, why should not other property be virtually represented, and its owners obtain a like power in legislation, and in the choice of the President? . . . To secure to the owners of property in slaves greater political power than is allowed to the owners of other and equivalent property, seems to be contrary to our theory of the equality of personal rights, inasmuch as the citizens of some States thereby become entitled to other and greater political power than the citizens of other States. . . . According to the last census, the whole number of slaves within the United was 1,191,364, which entitles the States possessing the same to twenty representatives, and twenty presidential electors more than they would be entitled to, were the slaves excluded. By the last census, Virginia contained 582,104 free persons, and 392,518 slaves. In any of the States where slavery is excluded, 582,104 free persons would be entitled to elect only sixteen representatives, while in Virginia, 582,104 free persons, by the addition of three-fifths of her slaves, become entitled to elect, and do in fact elect, twenty-three representatives, being seven additional ones on account of her slaves. . . .

The equality of rights, which includes an equality of burdens, is a vital principle in our theory of government, and its jealous preservation is the best security of public and individual freedom; the departure from this principle in the disproportionate power and influence, allowed to the slaveholding States, was a necessary sacrifice to the establishment of the Constitution. The effect of this concession has been obvious in the preponderance which it has given to the slaveholding States over the other States. Nevertheless, it is an ancient settlement, and faith and honor stand pledged not to disturb it. But the extension of this disproportionate power to the new States would be unjust and odious. . . .

2. Debates in the U.S. Congress: House of Representatives (February 15, 1819)

Mr. John W. Taylor of New York spoke. . . . Our votes this day will determine whether the high destinies of this region, and of these generations, shall be fulfilled, or whether we shall defeat them by permitting slavery, with all its baleful consequences, to inherit the land. . . .

I [remind] my opponents of their own declarations on the subject of slavery. How often, and how eloquently, have they deplored its existence among them? What willingness, nay, what solicitude have they not manifested to be relieved from this burden? How have they wept over the unfortunate policy that first introduced slaves into this country! How have they disclaimed the guilt and shame of that original sin, and thrown it back upon their ancestors. . . . Gentlemen have now an opportunity of putting their principles into practice; if they have tried slavery and found it a curse; if they desire to dissipate the gloom with which it covers their land; I call upon them to exclude it from the Territory in question; plant not the seeds in this uncorrupt soil; let not our children, looking back to the proceedings of this day, say of them, as they have been constrained to speak of their fathers, "we wish their decision had been different; we regret the existence of this unfortunate population among us; but we found them here: we know not what to do with them; it is our misfortune, we must bear it with patience." . . .

Mr. Chairman, one of the gentlemen from Kentucky (Mr. Clay) has pressed into his service the cause of humanity. He has pathetically urged us to withdraw our amendment and suffer this unfortunate population to be dispersed over the country. He says they will be better fed, clothed and sheltered, and their whole condition will be greatly improved. Sir, true humanity disowns his invocation. The humanity to which he appeals is base coin; it is counterfeit, it is that humanity which seeks to palliate disease by the application of nostrums, which scatter its seeds through the whole system—which saves a finger to-day, but amputates the arm to-morrow. Sir, my heart responds to the call of humanity; I will zealously unite in any practicable means of bettering the condition of this oppressed people. I am ready to appropriate a territory to their use, and to aid them in settling it—but I am not willing, I never will consent to declare the whole country west of the Mississippi a market overt for human flesh. In vain will you enact severe laws against the importation of slaves, if you create for them an additional demand, by opening the western world to their employment. . . .

. . . If slavery shall be tolerated, the country will be settled by rich planters, with their slaves; if it shall be rejected, the emigrants will chiefly consist of the poorer and more laborious classes of society. . . . If the rejection of slavery will tend to discourage emigration from the South, will not its admission have the same effect in relation to the North and East? Whence came the people who, with a rapidity never before witnessed have changed the wilderness between the Ohio and Mississippi into fruitful fields; who have erected there, in a period almost too short for the credibility of future ages, three of the freest and most flourishing States in our Union? They came from the eastern hive. . . . Do you believe that these people will settle in a country where they must take rank with Negro slaves? Having neither the ability nor will to hold slaves themselves, they labor cheerfully while labor is honorable; make it disgraceful, they will despise it. . . .

An argument has been urged by a gentleman from Virginia (Mr. Barbour) against the proposed amendment, connected with our revenues. He said, that by prohibiting the further introduction of slaves into the proposed State, we should reduce the price and diminish the sales of our public lands. In my opinion, the effect would be precisely the reverse. . . . But, should the fact be otherwise, I entreat gentlemen to consider whether it become the high character of an American Congress to barter the present happiness and future safety of unborn millions for a few pieces of pelf, for a few cents on an acre of land. For myself, I would no sooner contaminate the national Treasury with such ill-gotten gold, than I would tarnish the fame of our national ships by directing their employment in the African slave trade. But, whatever may be the influence of the subject in controversy upon the original price of land, it must be evident to all men of observation that its ultimate and permanent effects are very prejudicial to agricultural improvement. . . . Had not slavery been introduced into Maryland, her numerous and extensive old fields, which now appear to be worse than useless, would long since have supported a dense population of industrious freemen, and contributed largely to the strength and resources of the State. Who has travelled along the line which divides that State from Pennsylvania, and has not observed that no monuments are necessary to mark the boundary; that it is easily traced by following the dividing lines between farms highly cultivated and plantations laying open to the common and overrun with weeds; between stone barns and stone bridges on one side, and stack cribs and no bridges on the other; between a neat, blooming, animated, rosy-cheeked peasantry on the one side, and a squalid, slow-motioned, black population on the other? . . .

Mr. Timothy Fuller [of Massachusetts] said, that . . . above all, the Constitution expressly makes a republican form of government in the several States a fundamental principle. . . . It clearly, therefore, is the duty of Congress, before admitting a new sister into the Union, to ascertain that her constitution or form of government is republican. Now, sir, the amendment proposed by the gentleman from New York, Mr. Tallmadge, merely requires that slavery shall be prohibited in Missouri. Does this imply anything more than that its constitution shall be republican? The existence of slavery in any State is so far a departure from republican principles. The Declaration of Independence . . . defines the principle on which our National and state Constitutions are all professedly founded. The second paragraph of that instrument begins thus: "We hold these truths to be self-evident—that all men are created equal—that they are endowed by their Creator with certain inalienable rights—that among these are life, liberty, and the pursuit of happiness." Since, then, it cannot be denied that slaves are men, it follows that they are in a purely republican government born free, and are entitled to liberty and the pursuit of happiness. [Mr. Fuller was here interrupted by several gentlemen, who thought it improper to question in debate the republican character of the slaveholding States, which had also a tendency, as one gentlemen (Mr. Edward Colston, of Virginia), said to deprive those States of the right to hold slaves as property, and he adverted to the probability that there might be slaves in the gallery listening to the debate.] Mr. Fuller assured the gentlemen that nothing was further from his thoughts than to question on that floor the right of Virginia and other states, which held slaves when the Constitution was established, to continue to hold them. . . .

My reason, Mr. Chairman, for recurring to the Declaration of our Independence, was to draw from an authority admitted in all parts of the Union a definition of the basis of republican government. If, then, all men have equal rights, it can no more comport with the principles of a free Government to exclude men of a certain color from the enjoyment of "liberty and the pursuit of happiness," than to exclude those who have not attained a certain portion of wealth, or a certain stature of body; or to found the exclusion on any other capricious or accidental circumstance. Suppose Missouri, before her admission as a State were to submit to us her constitution, by which no person could elect, or be elected to any office, unless he possessed a clear annual income of twenty thousand dollars; and suppose we had ascertained that only . . . a very small number of persons had such an estate; would this be anything more or less than a real aristocracy, under a form nominally republican? [S]ir, it is demonstrable that the exclusion of the black population from all political freedom, and making them the property of the whites, is an equally palpable invasion of right and abandonment of principle. If we do this in the admission of new States, we violate the Constitution, and we have not now the excuse which existed when our National Constitution was established. Then, to effect a concert of interests, it was proper to make concessions. The States where slavery existed not only claimed the right to continue it, but it was manifest that a general emancipation of slaves could not be asked of them. Their political existence would have been in jeopardy; both masters and slaves must have been involved in the most fatal consequences.

. . . The States then holding slaves are permitted, from the necessity of the case, and for the sake of union, to exclude the republican principle so far, and only so far, as to retain their slaves in servitude, and also their progeny, as had been the usage, until they should think it proper or safe to conform to the pure principle by abolishing slavery. . . .

Mr. Philip P. Barbour of Virginia, said that . . . he was decidedly opposed to the amendment. . . . Our power, in relation to this subject, is derived from [Article IV, Section 3, clause 1], which is in these words; "New States may be admitted, by the Congress, into this Union." Now, sir, although, by the next succeeding clause of the same section, "Congress has the power to make all needful rules and regulations, respecting the territory of the United States;" and although, therefore, whilst the proposed State continued a part of our territory . . . it would have been competent for us . . . to make needful rules and regulations—to have established the principle now proposed; yet, the question assumes a totally different aspect when that principle is intended to apply to a State. This term State has a fixed and determinate meaning; in itself, it imports the existence of a political community, free and independent, and entitled to . . . enjoy all those rights of sovereignty which belong to the original states which composed the Federal family, and into an union with which it is to be admitted. Now, sir, although the original States are shorn of many of their beams of sovereignty—such, for example, as that of declaring war, of regulating commerce, &c.; yet we know that, even by an express amendment to the Constitution, all powers not expressly delegated are reserved to the States respectively; and of course the power in question, of deciding whether slavery shall or shall not exist. Gentlemen had said that slavery was prohibited in many of the original States. Does not the House, said Mr. B., at the first glance, perceive the answer to this remark? It is an argument from fact to principle, and in this its utter fallacy consists. It is true that slavery does not exist in many of the original States; but why does it not? Because they themselves, in the exercise of their legislative power, have willed that it shall be so. But, though it does not now exist, it is competent for them, by a law of their own enactment, to authorize it—to call it into existence whenever they shall think fit. Sir, how different would be the situation of Missouri, if the proposed amendment be adopted. . . .

But, sir, this provision would be in violation of another principle of the Constitution, to be found in [Article IV, Section 2, clause 1]; by which it is declared that "the citizens of each State shall be entitled to all privileges and immunities of citizens in the several States." Now, he would ask, whether a citizen of the State of Missouri, who (if this amendment prevail) cannot hold a slave, could . . . be said to enjoy the same privileges with a citizen of Virginia who now may hold a slave, or even with a citizen of Pennsylvania, who, though he cannot now hold one, yet may be permitted by the Legislature of his own State? . . . This part of the Constitution, then also forbids the adoption of the amendment under discussion. . . .

. . . It is said that the like prohibition has been enacted as it respects Ohio and the other States northwest of the river Ohio. [H]e did not hesitate to express it as his desired opinion, that the ordinance which he had just mentioned was utterly void, and, consequently, that those States might introduce slavery amongst them, if they so willed, because . . . [the] prohibition of slavery . . . would unquestionably render those States less sovereign than the original States of the Federal Union. . . .

. . . Throughout all the Southern States, it was well known a very large portion of the population consisted of slaves, who, at the same time, stood towards the white population of the same States in relation of property; although they were considered and treated as the most valuable, as the most favored property; their masters remembered that they were men, and although certainly degraded in the scale of society, by reason of their servitude, we felt for them those sympathies which bind one man to another, though that other may be our inferior. We were attached to them, too, by our prejudices, by our education and habits; in short, such were the feelings of the Southern people towards their slaves, that nothing scarcely but the necessity of the master, or the crime of the slave, would induce him to sell his slave. If the master emigrate, he would carry his slaves with him, not only for the various reasons which he had already stated, but because, going into a wilderness, where much labor was necessary to clear the country, they were, on that account, peculiarly necessary. Under these circumstances, a prohibition of the importation of slaves would in almost every instance, be tantamount to a prohibition of the emigration of the Southern people to the State of Missouri. He asked whether it could be just to adopt such a regulation as would open an illimitable tract of the most fertile land to the Northern party of the United States, and, in effect, entirely shut out the whole Southern people? . . . He hoped, from this view of the subject, the House would be struck with its monstrous injustice.

Let it be remembered that we are not now called upon to decide, whether slavery shall be introduced into this country. [T]he real question is, what disposition shall we make of those slaves who are already in the country? Shall they be perpetually confined on this side of the Mississippi, or shall we spread them over a much larger surface by permitting them to be carried beyond that river? The consequences which would flow from the different systems would furnish a satisfactory answer to these inquiries. The slaves, in the Southern States, bear a very considerable proportion to the whole population. [I]f ever the time shall come when we shall be engaged in war, and they should be excited to insurrection, it is obvious that there must be an immense subduction from the efficiency of the slaveholding section of our country; its actual efficiency would consist only, or nearly so, in the excess of the white beyond the black population; by spreading them over a more extended surface, you secure these advantages; first, by diminishing the proportion which the slaves bear in point of numbers to the whites, you diminish their motives to insurrection. Secondly, that if that even ever should occur, it would obviously be much more easily and certainly suppressed. . . . He thanked God, he felt no alarm upon that subject at present; and that he slept quietly in his bed, notwithstanding the apprehension which some gentlemen seemed to entertain. But, in making the remarks which he did, he looked along the line of time, and wished that our measures should be adapted to the future circumstances of our country. Again, he would ask if it can be good policy to perpetuate fixed boundaries, either natural or artificial, between the slaveholding and non-slaveholding States? He had thought that the great object of our Federal compact was union. The surest possible mode of securing our political union, next to promoting the common defence and general welfare, is to give, as far as possible, every facility to the intercourse between the different sections of this extensive Republic; that, by the attrition which will be the result of that intercourse, the asperities of our mutual prejudices and jealousies may be rubbed off; that the face of our society may present the smooth surface of harmony and good will; and, in short, that we may be knit together by a sympathy of feelings, by a community of habits and manners which ought to bind us together as brothers of the same great political family. Already is the northern part of our country, together with that northwest of the river Ohio, divided from us by those distinguishing names of slaveholding and non-slaveholding. Let us not make the Mississippi another great natural boundary, for the purpose of perpetuating the same distinctions, and dividing our country into castes. . . .

Mr. Arthur Livermore [of New Hampshire] spoke as follows: Mr. Chairman . . . I propose to show what slavery is, and to mention a few of the many evils which follow in its train; and I hope to evince that we are not bound to tolerate the existence of so disgraceful a state of things beyond its present extent, and that it would be impolitic, and very unjust, to let it spread over the whole face of our Western territory. Slavery in the United States is the condition of man subjected to the will of a master, who can make any disposition of him short of taking away his life. In those States where it is tolerated, laws are enacted, making it penal to instruct slaves in the art of reading, and they are not permitted to attend public worship, or to hear the Gospel preached. Thus the light of science and of religion is utterly excluded from the mind, that the body may be more easily bowed down in servitude. The bodies of slaves may, with impunity, be prostituted to any purpose, and deformed in any manner by their owners. The sympathies of nature in slaves are disregarded; mothers and children are sold and separated; the children wring their little hands and expire in agonies of grief, while the bereft mothers commit suicide in despair. How long will the desire of wealth render us blind to the sin of holding both the bodies and souls of our fellow men in chains! But, sir, I am admonished of the Constitution, and told that we cannot emancipate slaves. I know we may not infringe that instrument, and therefore do not propose to emancipate slaves. The proposition before us goes only to prevent our citizens from making slaves of such as have a right to freedom. In the present slaveholding States let slavery continue, for our boasted Constitution connives at it; but do not, for the sake of cotton and tobacco, let it be told to future ages that, while pretending to love liberty, we have purchased an extensive country to disgrace it with the foulest reproach of nations. Our Constitution requires no such thing of us. The ends for which that supreme law was made are succinctly stated in its preface. They are, first, to form a more perfect union, and insure domestic tranquility. Will slavery effect this? Can we, sir, by mingling bond with free, black spirits with white, like Shakespeare's witches in Macbeth, form a more perfect union, and insure domestic tranquility? Secondly, to establish justice. Is justice to be established by subjecting half mankind to the will of the other half? Justice, sir, is blind to colors, and weighs in equal scales the rights of all men, whether white or black. Thirdly, to provide for the common defense, and secure the blessings of liberty. Does slavery add anything to the common defense? Sir, the strength of a Republic is in the arm of freedom. But, above all things, do the blessings of liberty consist in slavery? If there is any sincerity in our profession, that slavery is an ill, tolerated only from necessity, let us not, while we feel that ill, shun the cure which consists only in an honest avowal that liberty and equal rights are the end and aim of all our institutions, and that to tolerate slavery beyond the narrowest limits prescribed for it by the Constitution, is a perversion of them all. . . .

An opportunity is now presented, if not to diminish, at least to prevent, the growth of a sin which sits heavy on the soul of every one of us. By embracing this opportunity, we may retrieve the national character, and in some degree, our own. But if we suffer it to pass unimproved, let us at least be consistent, and declare that our Constitution was made to impose slavery, and not to establish liberty. Let us no longer tell idle tales about the gradual abolition of slavery; away with colonization societies, if their design is only to rid us of free blacks and turbulent slaves; have done also with Bible societies, whose views are extended to Africa and the East Indies, while they overlook the deplorable condition of their sable brethren within our own borders; make no more laws to prohibit the importation of slaves, for the world must see that the object of such laws is alone to prevent the glutting of a prodigious market for the flesh and blood of man, which we are about to establish in the West, and to enhance the price of sturdy wretches, reared like black cattle and horses for sale on our own plantations.

3. Debates in the U.S. Congress: House of Representatives (February 16, 1819)

Mr. [John] Scott, of [the] Missouri [Territory] . . . entertained the opinion that, under the Constitution, Congress had not the power to impose this or any other restriction, or to require of the people of Missouri their assent to this condition, as a prerequisite to their admission into the Union. He contended this from the language of the Constitution itself. . . .

[I]n the second section of that instrument it was provided that "representatives and direct taxes shall be apportioned among the several States which may be included within this Union, according to their respective numbers, which shall be determined by adding to the whole number of free persons, including those bound to service for a term of years, and excluding Indians not taxed, three-fifths of all other persons." This provision was not restricted to the States then formed, and about to adopt the Constitution, but to all those States which might be included within this Union, clearly contemplating the admission of new States thereafter, and providing that to them also should this principle of representation and taxation equally apply. [A] practical exposition had been made by Congress of this part of the Constitution, in the admission of Kentucky, Louisiana, and Mississippi, as States, all of whom were slaveholding States, and to each of them this principle had been extended.

Mr. S. said he considered the contemplated conditions and restrictions, contained in the proposed amendments, to be unconstitutional and unwarrantable, from the provisions of the treaty of cession, by the third article of which it was stipulated, that "the inhabitants of the ceded territory shall be incorporated in the union of the United States, and admitted, as soon as possible, according to the principles of the Federal Constitution, to the enjoyment of all the rights, advantages, and immunities, of citizens of the United States." . . .

Mr. S. would infer from this expression, that it was the understanding of the parties, that so soon as any portion of the territory, of sufficient extent to form a State, should contain the number of inhabitants required by law to entitle them to a Representative on the floor of this House, that they then had the right to make the call for admission, and this admission, when made, was to be, not on conditions that gentlemen might deem expedient, . . . "but according to the principles of the Federal Constitution," and none other. The people of Missouri were, by solemn treaty stipulation, when admitted, to enjoy all the rights, advantages, and immunities of citizens of the United States. Can any gentlemen contend, that, laboring under the proposed restriction, the citizens of Missouri would have all the rights, advantages, and immunities of other citizens of the Union?

Mr. S. thought that if this provision was proper, or within the powers of Congress, they also had the correlative right to say, that the people of Missouri should not be admitted as a State, unless they provided, in the formation of their State constitution, that slavery should be tolerated. Would not those conscientious gentlemen startle at this, and exclaim, *What*, impose on those people slaves, when they do not want them! This would be said to be a direct attack on the State independence. Was it in the power of Congress to annex the present condition, Mr. S. deemed it equally within the scope of their authority to say, what color the inhabitants of the proposed State should be, what description of property, other than slaves, those people should or should not possess, and the quantity of property each man should retain, going upon the Agrarian principle. He would even go further, and say, that Congress had an equal power to enact to what religion the people should subscribe; that none other should be professed, and to provide for the excommunication of all those who did not submit. . . .

Mr. S. said, he would trouble the House no longer; he thanked them for the attention and indulgence already bestowed; but he desired to apprize gentlemen, before he sat down, that they were sowing the seeds of discord in this Union, by attempting to admit States with unequal privileges and unequal rights; that they were signing, sealing, and delivering their own death warrants; that the weapon they were so unjustly wielding against the people of Missouri, was a two-edged sword. From the cumulative nature of power, the day might come when the General Government might, in turn, undertake to dictate to them on questions of internal policy. . . . And, whatever might be the ultimate determination of the House, Mr. S. considered this question big with the fate of Caesar and of Rome. . . .

Mr. [James] Tallmadge, of New York, rose.— . . . When I had the honor to submit to this House the amendment now under consideration, I accompanied it with a declaration, that it was intended to confine its operation to the newly acquired territory across the Mississippi; and I then expressly declared that I would in no manner intermeddle with the slaveholding States, nor attempt manumission in any one of the original States in the Union. Sir, I even went further, and stated that I was aware of the delicacy of the subject, and that I had learned from Southern gentlemen the difficulties and the dangers of having free blacks intermingling with slaves; and, on that account, and with a view to the safety of the white population of the adjoining States, I would not even advocate the prohibition of slavery in the Alabama Territory; because, surrounded as it was by slave-holding States, and with only imaginary lines of division, the intercourse between slaves and free blacks could not be prevented, and a *servile* war might be the result. . . . But, sir, all these reasons cease when we cross the banks of the Mississippi, a newly acquired territory, never contemplated in the formation of our Government, not included within the compromise of mutual pledge in the adoption of our Constitution. . . .

Sir, the honorable gentleman from Missouri, (Mr. Scott) who has just resumed his seat, has told us of the *ides of March*, and has cautioned us to "*beware of the fate of Caesar and of Rome.*" Another gentleman, (Mr. Cobb) from Georgia, in addition to other expressions of great warmth, has said, "that, if we persist, the Union will be dissolved;" and, with a look fixed on me, has told us, "we have kindled a fire which all the waters of the ocean cannot put out, which seas of blood can only extinguish." . . .

Sir, if a dissolution of the Union must take place, let it be so! If civil war, which gentlemen so much threaten, must come, I can only say, let it come! My hold on life is probably as frail as that of any man who now hears me; but, while that hold lasts, it shall be devoted to the service of my country—to the freedom of man. If blood is necessary to extinguish any fire which I have assisted to kindle, I can assure gentlemen, while I regret the necessity, I shall not forbear to contribute my mite. Sir, the violence to which gentlemen have resorted on this subject will not move my purpose, nor drive me from my place. I have the fortune and honor to stand here as the representative of freemen, who possess intelligence to know their rights, who have the spirit to maintain them. . . . I know the will of my constituents, and, regardless of consequences, I will avow it; as their representative, I will proclaim their hatred to slavery in every shape; as their representative, here will I hold my stand, until this floor, with the Constitution of my country which supports it, shall sink beneath me. If I am doomed to fall, I shall at least have the painful consolation to believe that I fall, as a fragment, in the ruins of my country.

Sir, the gentleman from Virginia (Mr. Colston) has accused my honorable friend, from New Hampshire (Mr. Livermore) of "speaking to the galleries," and, by his language, endeavoring to excite a servile war. . . .

Sir, has it already come to this; that in the Congress of the United States— that, in the legislative councils of republican America, the subject of slavery has become a subject of so much feeling—of such delicacy—of such danger, that it cannot safely be discussed? Are members who venture to express their sentiments on this subject to be accused of talking to the galleries, with intent to excite a servile war . . . ? Are we to be told of the dissolution of the Union; of civil war, and of seas of blood? And yet, with such awful threatenings before us, do gentlemen, in the same breath, insist upon the encouragement of this evil; upon the extension of this monstrous scourge of the human race? . . . If its power, its influence, and its impending dangers have already arrived at such a point that it is not safe to discuss it on this floor, and it cannot now pass under consideration as a proper subject for general legislation, what will be the result when it is spread through your widely extended domain? . . . Now is the time. It must now be met, and the extension of the evil must now be prevented, or the occasion is irrevocably lost, and the evil can never be contracted.

Sir, extend your view across the Mississippi, over our newly acquired territory. . . . Look down the long vista of futurity. . . . Behold this extended empire, inhabited by the hardy sons of American freemen . . . owners of the soil on which they live, and interested in the institutions which they labor to defend. . . . But, sir, . . . extend slavery—this bane of man, this abomination of heaven—over your extended empire, and you prepare its dissolution; you turn its accumulated strength into positive weakness; you cherish a canker in your breast; you put poison in your bosom; you place a vulture on your heart—nay, you whet the dagger and place it in the hands of a portion of your population, stimulated to use it, by every tie, human and divine. The envious contrast between your happiness and their misery, between your liberty and their slavery, must constantly prompt them to accomplish your destruction. Your enemies will learn the source and the cause of your weakness. As often as internal dangers shall threaten, or internal commotions await you, you will then realize, that, by your own procurement, you have placed amidst your families, and in the bosom of your country, a population producing at once the greatest cause of individual danger and of national weakness. With this defect, your Government must crumble to pieces, and your people become the scoff of the world. . . .

4. James Madison, Letter to Robert J. Evans (June 15, 1819)

In this letter James Madison (1751–1836) endorsed colonizing African Americans, free and slave, on the condition of restitution for slaveholders. For Madison, slavery was an "evil," but it was "deep rooted and wide-spread." He concluded that any solution must account for the "existing & durable prejudices of the nation." Madison thus suggested that colonization must coincide with emancipation, because prejudice will always guarantee the unjust treatment of blacks.

. . . A general emancipation of slaves ought to be 1. gradual. 2. equitable & satisfactory to the individuals immediately concerned. 3. consistent with the existing & durable prejudices of the nation.

That it ought, like remedies for other deep rooted and wide-spread evils, to be gradual, is so obvious that there seems to be no difference of opinion on that point.

To be equitable & satisfactory, the consent of both the Master & the slave should be obtained. That of the Master will require a provision in the plan for compensating a loss of what he held as property guaranteed by the laws, and recognized by the Constitution. That of the slave, requires that his condition in a state of freedom, be preferable in his own estimation, to his actual one in a state of bondage.

To be consistent with existing and probably unalterable prejudices in the U. S. the freed blacks ought to be permanently removed beyond the region occupied by or allotted to a White population. The objections to a thorough incorporation of the two people are, with most of the Whites insuperable; and are admitted by all of them to be very powerful. If the blacks, strongly marked as they are by Physical & lasting peculiarities, be retained amid the Whites, under the degrading privation of equal rights political or social, they must be always dissatisfied with their condition as a change only from one to another species of oppression; always secretly confederated agst. the ruling & privileged class; and always uncontroulled by some of the most cogent motives to moral and respectable conduct. The character of the freed blacks, even where their legal condition is least affected by their colour, seems to put these truths beyond question. It is material also that the removal of the blacks be to a distance precluding the jealousies & hostilities to be apprehended from a neighboring people stimulated by the contempt known to be entertained for their peculiar features; to say nothing of their vindictive recollections, or the predatory propensities which their State of Society might foster. Nor is it fair, in estimating the danger of Collisions with the Whites, to charge it wholly on the side of the Blacks. There would be reciprocal antipathies doubling the danger.

The colonizing plan on foot, has as far as it extends, a due regard to these requisites; with the additional object of bestowing new blessings civil & religious on the quarter of the Globe most in need of them. The Society proposes to transport to the African Coast, all free & freed blacks who may be willing to remove thither; to provide by fair means, &, it is understood with a prospect of success, a suitable territory for their reception; and to initiate them into such an establishment as may gradually, and indefinitely expand itself. . . .

But the views of the Society are limited to the case of blacks already free, or who may be *gratuitously* emancipated. To provide a commensurate remedy for the evil, the plan must be extended to the great Mass of blacks, and must embrace a fund sufficient to induce the Master as well as the slave to concur in it. Without the concurrence of the Master, the benefit will be very limited as it relates to the Negroes; and essentially defective, as it relates to the U. States; and the concurrence of Masters, must, for the most part, be obtained by purchase. . . .

The object to be obtained, as an object of humanity, appeals alike to all; as a National object, it claims the interposition of the nation. It is the nation which is to reap the benefit. The nation therefore ought to bear the burden.

Happily it . . . is the peculiar fortune, or, rather a providential blessing of the U. S. to possess a resource commensurate to this great object, without taxes on the people, or even an increase of the public debt.

I allude to the vacant territory the extent of which is so vast, and the vendible value of which is so well ascertained. . . .

5. Robert Walsh, Jr., *Free Remarks on the Spirit of the Federal Constitution* (1819)

In the following exchange, Robert Walsh, Jr., (1784–1859) and James Madison debated the meaning of the migration or importation clause of Article I, Section 10. Walsh's arguments that Congress could prohibit both the introduction of slavery in new states and the transportation of slaves between states after 1808 were not novel. In 1787 James Wilson and William Heath made similar arguments during the Pennsylvania ratification debates. The same claim had already emerged in congressional debates over Missouri statehood, with John Jay defending it in a published 1819 letter to Elias Boudinot. Madison rejected this reading, suggesting that congressional efforts to prohibit slavery in new states conflict with other constitutional provisions while raising doubts about the political expediency of such efforts.

. . . The various motives which led to the formal recognition of a power in the federal government to prohibit the importation of slaves, are plainly distinguishable. The traffic was acknowledged to be in itself heinous and disgraceful; the subsequent bondage cruel, unjust, dangerous. A moral and enlightened people, jealous of principle and character, as well as watchful of the general peace and safety, would do nothing not exacted by a supreme necessity, that might enlarge the crying evil and sin; would do all that was practicable to prevent its extension; all that might, without injury or strife, conduce to its extinction. . . .

By the clauses above quoted, the federal government is recognized to have the power of prohibiting at once and for ever, not only the *importation* of slaves from abroad, into the territories and new states, but their *migration*, or removal from the old states into the new or into the territories. The conjecture has been indulged that the Convention employed the words *migration* and *importation* as synonimous. But these words had never been so received either among the proper authorities in language, or in common parlance; neither custom nor etymology would warrant such a use of them. We are not entitled to imagine, that the lettered men and distinguished writers who framed the constitution would, where precision was so important, have confounded terms correctly and commonly understood to be of distinct import; or, in the hypothesis that this was not notoriously the case, have fallen into sheer tautology. If they had intended to vest in Congress no other or further power than that of prohibiting *importation*, they could not have conveyed their meaning more clearly or fully, than by the word *importation* alone. . . .

After what has been said we can hardly doubt, that this general intention was to keep the territories and new states altogether free from the bane of negro slavery. . . . To compass this end, it was indispensible that the federal government should be invested with the power to control the *internal transportation* of slaves—to hinder the introduction of them into the new states from the old. As it cannot be conceived why the faculty should have been reserved to Congress, of prohibiting *at once* the importation or migration of slaves into the territories and new states, unless it were with a view to shut out slavery from them altogether, or prevent its increase,—so it cannot be conceived that, for this purpose, it could have been deemed sufficient, merely to guard against the importation of slaves into them *from abroad.* . . .

All must admit that the federal government possesses the power of suppressing the transportation of slaves, *for sale,* from one state to another, as well as from a state to a territory. The turn of the clause of the Constitution respecting the prohibiting of importation, implies the admission of a previous general power in the federal government to that effect. But this general power was understood to arise out of the other expressly given, of regulating commerce with foreign nations. . . . As the power of regulating commerce "between the several states," is also expressly given, it included in the same manner, that of prohibiting the *commerce* in slaves between those states.

Other reasons besides that of securing the new states and territories from one of the worst of ills, may be suggested for the grant to Congress, of the power of suppressing the internal transportation of slaves for whatever general purpose. The Convention can be supposed to have felt a wish to prevent any occasion being given, for the greater activity of that *internal trading* in human flesh, *the negro-driving,* which is among the most odious and disgraceful incidents of the institution of slavery. They could perceive that, if the removal of slaves to the new states, were not liable to entire suppression, these would form additional lucrative marts serving to incite the traffic just mentioned, and its twin practice—kidnapping. They could not fail, moreover, to be sensible how much the opening and continuance of such vents would, by holding out temptations to cupidity, obstruct that which must have been dear to their hearts—emancipation of individuals in the old states. . . .

6. James Madison, Letter to Robert Walsh, Jr. (November 27, 1819)

. . . As to the intention of the framers of the Constitution in the clause relating to "the migration and importation of persons, &c" the best key may perhaps be found in the case which produced it. The African trade in slaves had long been odious to most of the States, and the importation of slaves into them had been prohibited. Particular States however continued the importation, and were extremely averse to any restriction on their power to do so. In the convention the former States were anxious, in framing a new constitution, to insert a provision for an immediate and absolute stop to the trade. The latter were not only averse to any interference on the subject; but solemnly declared that their constituents would never accede to a Constitution containing such an article. Out of this conflict grew the middle measure providing that Congress should not interfere until the year 1808; with an implication, that after that date, they might prohibit the importation of slaves into the States then existing, & previous thereto, into the States not then existing. . . . The earnestness of S. Carolina & Georgia was further manifested by their insisting on the security in the V article, against any amendment to the Constitution affecting the right reserved to them, & their uniting with the small states, who insisted on a like security for their equality in the Senate. . . .

But some of the States were not only anxious for a Constitutional provision against the introduction of slaves. They had scruples against admitting the term "slaves" into the Instrument. Hence the descriptive phrase, "migration or importation of persons;" the term "migration" allowing those who were scrupulous of acknowledging expressly a property in human beings, to view *imported* persons as a species of emigrants, while others might apply the term to foreign malefactors sent or coming into the country. . . .

But whatever may have been intended by the term "migration" or the term "persons," it is most certain, that they referred exclusively to a migration or importation from other countries into the U. States; and not to a removal, voluntary or involuntary, of slaves or freemen, from one to another part of the U. States. Nothing appears or is recollected that warrants this latter intention. Nothing in the proceedings of the State conventions indicates such a construction there. Had such been the construction it is easy to imagine the figure it would have made in many of the states, among the objections to the constitution, and among the numerous amendments to it proposed by the State conventions, not one of which amendments refers to the clause in question. Neither is there any indication that Congress have heretofore considered themselves as deriving from this Clause a power over the migration of removal of individuals, whether freemen or slaves, from one State to another, whether new or old. . . . Every indication is against such a construction by Congress of their constitutional powers. Their alacrity in exercising their powers relating to slaves is a proof that they did not claim what they did not exercise. They punctually and unanimously put in force the power accruing in 1808 against the further importation of slaves from abroad. They had previously directed their power over American vessels on the high seas, against the African trade. They lost no time in applying the prohibitory power to Louisiana, which having maritime ports, might be an inlet for slaves from abroad. But they forbore to extend the prohibition to the introduction of slaves from other parts of the Union. They had even prohibited the importation of slaves into the Mississippi Territory from *without the limits of the U. S.* in the year 1798, without extending the prohibition to the introduction of slaves from *within those limits*; altho' at the time the ports of Georgia and S. Carolina were open for the importation of slaves from abroad, and increasing the mass of slavery within the U. States. . . .

If these views of the subject be just, a power in Congress to controul the interior migration or removals of persons, must be derived from some other source than Sect. 9, Art. 1; either from the clause giving power "to make all needful rules and regulations respecting the Territory or other property belonging to the U. S. or from that providing for the admission of New States into the Union."

The terms in which the 1st. of these powers is expressed, tho' of a ductile character, cannot well be extended beyond a power over the Territory as property, & a power to make the provisions really needful or necessary for the Govt. of settlers until ripe for admission as States into the Union. It may be inferred that Congress did not regard the interdict of slavery among the needful regulations contemplated by the constitution; since in none of the Territorial Governments created by them, is such an interdict found. The power, however be its import what it may, is obviously limited to a Territory whilst remaining in that character as distinct from that of a State.

As to the power of admitting new States into the federal compact, the questions offering themselves are; whether congress can attach conditions, or the new States concur in conditions, which after admission, would abridge or *enlarge* the constitutional rights of legislation common to the other States; whether Congress can by a compact with a new member take power either to or from itself, or place the new member above or below the equal rank & rights possessed by the others; whether all such stipulations, expressed or implied would not be nullities, and so pronounced when brought to a practical test. It falls within the Scope of your enquiry, to state the fact, that there was a proposition in the convention to discriminate between the old and new States, by an Article in the Constitution declaring that the aggregate number of representatives from the States thereafter to be admitted should never exceed * that of the States originally adopting the Constitution. The proposition happily was rejected. The effect of such a discrimination is sufficiently evident. . . .

For the grounds on which 3/5 of the slaves were admitted into the ratio of representation, I will with your permission, save trouble by referring to No. 54 of the Federalist. In addition, it may be stated that this feature in the Constitution was combined with that relating to the power over Commerce & navigation. In truth these two powers, with those relating to the importation of slaves, & the Articles establishing the equality of representation in the Senate & the rule of taxation, had a complicated influence on each other which alone would have justified the remark, that the Constitution was "the result of mutual deference & Concession." . . .

The *expediency* of exercising a supposed power in Congress, to prevent a diffusion of the slaves actually in the Country, as far as the local authorities may admit them, resolves itself into the probable effects of such a diffusion on the interests of the slaves and of the Nation.

Will it or will it not better the condition of the slaves, by lessening the number belonging to individual masters, and intermixing both with greater masses of free people? Will partial manumissions be more or less likely to take place, and a general emancipation be accelerated or retarded? Will the moral & physical condition of slaves, in the mean time, be improved or deteriorated? . . .

Will the aggregate strength, security, tranquility and harmony of the whole nation be advanced or impaired by lessening the proportion of slaves to the free people in particular sections of it? . . .

On the whole, the Missouri question, as a constitutional one, amounts to the question whether the condition proposed to be annexed to the admission of Missouri would or would not be void in itself, or become void the moment the territory should enter as a State within the pale of the Constitution. And as a question of expediency & humanity, it depends essentially on the probable influence of such restrictions on the quantity & duration of slavery, and on the general condition of slaves in the U. S. . . .

Under one aspect of the general subject, I cannot avoid saying, that . . . the tendency of what has passed and is passing, fills me with no slight anxiety. Parties under some denominations or other must always be expected in a Govt. as free as ours. When the individuals belonging to them are intermingled in every part of the whole Country, they strengthen the Union of the Whole, while they divide every part. Should a State of parties arise, founded on geographical boundaries and other Physical & permanent distinctions which happen to coincide with them, what is to control those great repulsive Masses from awful shocks against each other? . . .

7. Debates in the U.S. Congress: Senate (January 20–February 1, 1820)

As the congressional debate over Missouri statehood proceeded, several members of Congress expressed competing interpretations of the relationship between the Declaration of Independence and the Constitution. If the Declaration's principles did govern the Constitution, as Nathaniel Macon warned, either a war of extermination would follow, or blacks would demand political equality, compelling whites to abandon their "land and houses." The Declaration's principles, Philip Barbour added, were never intended to apply to blacks. Barbour expressed a predominant Southern argument against purportedly innovative efforts to connect the Declaration and the Constitution. Others, like Jonathan Roberts of Pennsylvania, argued that the Declaration's principles directly governed the Constitution, and thus the Constitution afforded no authority to enslave anyone. Using language that would later resonate with Lincoln, he argued that the Constitution was "a righteous consummation of the promises of the Revolution." Also invoking the Declaration, Joshua Cushman held slavery to be a creature of human law, not natural law, thereby subject to regulation or prohibition. Finally, Charles Pinckney offered his view of the history of American slavery since the Revolution and its effect on relations among the states. He blamed the North, envious of the wealth enjoyed in the South as a result of slavery, for unjustly seeking dominance in Congress. Moreover, he claimed, slaves are well-nourished, happy, and carefree, but free blacks are disproportionately numbered among the criminal class. To ban slavery in Missouri, he concluded, would alarm the South, exacerbate current divisions, and precipitate civil war.

Thursday, January 20:

Mr. [Nathaniel] Macon [of North Carolina] . . . [W]hy depart from the good old way, which has kept us in quiet, peace, and harmony—everyone living under his own vine and fig tree, and none to make him afraid? Why leave the road of experience, which has satisfied all, and made all happy, to take this new way, of which we have no experience? The way leads to universal emancipation, of which we have no experience. The Eastern and Middle States furnish none. For years before they emancipated they had but few, and of these a part were sold to the South, before they emancipated. We have not more experience or book learning on this subject than the French Convention had which turned the slaves of St. Domino loose. Nor can we foresee the consequences which may result from this motion, more than the convention did in their decree. A clause in the Declaration of Independence has been read, declaring "that all men are created equal;" follow that sentiment, and does it not lead to universal emancipation? If it will justify putting an end to slavery in Missouri, will it not justify it in the old States? . . .

Massachusetts, Pennsylvania and Virginia, have been often mentioned in the debate; and it has frequently been said, that the two first had emancipated their slaves; from which an inference seemed to be drawn that the other might have done so; emancipation, to these gentlemen, seems to be quite an easy task. It is so where there are but very few; and would be more easy if color did not everywhere place the blacks in a degraded state. Where they enjoy the most freedom, they are there degraded. The respectable whites do not permit them to associate with them, or to be of their company when they have parties. But if it be so easy a task, how happens it that Virginia, which before the Revolution endeavored to put an end to the African slave trade, has not attempted to emancipate? It will not be pretended that the great men of other States were superior, or greater lovers of liberty, than her Randolph, . . . her Washington, her Henry, her Jefferson, her Nelson. None of these ever made the attempt—and their names ought to convince everyone that it is not an easy task in that State. . . . If the words of the Declaration of Independence be taken as part of the Constitution . . . what will be the condition of the Southern country when this shall be carried into execution? Take the most favorable which can be supposed, that no convulsion ensue—that nothing like a massacre or war of extermination takes place, as in St. Domingo: but that the whites and blacks do not marry and produce mulatto States—will not the whites be compelled to move and leave their land and houses and leave the country to the blacks? And are you willing to have black members of Congress? But if the scenes of St. Domingo should be [re-]enacted, would not the tomahawk and scalping knife be mercy?

Friday, January 28:

Mr. [Nicholas] Van Dyke, of Delaware, rose and addressed the Senate as follows: . . . It was . . . not anticipated that the Declaration of Independence would be resorted to, as furnishing a key to the construction of the Constitution of 1787, or that arguments would be drawn from that source to give color to a claim of power under the latter instrument. Much less was it expected that the recital of abstract theoretical principles, in a national manifesto in 1776, would be gravely urged at this day, to prove that involuntary servitude does not lawfully exist within the United States. [T]he distinguished statesmen who pledged to each other, "their lives, their fortunes, and their sacred honor," in support of that declaration, were not visionary theorists; they were men of sound, practical, common sense, and, from the premises assumed, arrived at sound practical conclusions. When we call to mind the state of this young country at that awful moment, struggling for the right of self-government, engaged in war with the most powerful nation of Europe, pressed on all sides with accumulating difficulties and dangers, can it be credited that the Declaration of Independence was designed to dissolve the bonds of social order throughout the States—to reduce all men to a state of nature, and to set at large a host of slaves, the readiest instruments to be employed by the enemy in the work of destruction, in the very bosom of the nation? Think you, sir, that it was meant to invoke the genius of universal emancipation, and to proclaim liberty and equality to every human being who breathed the air, and trod the soil, of this new Republic? The faith of that man who can believe this, is much stronger than mine. No, sir, that manifesto was not intended—was not understood—to abolish or to alter any law then existing in any State for the security of property, or for the regulation of their internal concerns. Self-preservation—a regard for their own personal safety, and that of their families, and a regard for the best interests of the nation—forbade those sages to do such an act. . . .

Tuesday, February 1:

Mr. James Barbour [of Virginia] . . . [B]oth the gentleman from Pennsylvania and New Hampshire have called to their aid the Declaration of Independence, and the sacred principles it consecrates. What has that to do with this question? Who were the parties—the slaves? No. Did slavery not exist in every State of the Union at the moment of its promulgation? Did it enter into any human mind that it had the least reference to this species of population? Is there not at the present moment slaves in the very States from which we hear these novel doctrines?

How has it happened that these doctrines have slept till this moment? Where were they at the adoption of the Constitution, in which slavery is recognized, and the property guaranteed by an express clause? And shall we, the mere creatures of that instrument, presume to question its authority? To every other sanction imposed by our situation, is the solemn oath that we will support it. Where are the consciences of gentlemen who hold this language? But they assure us that they do not mean to touch this property in the old States. What, this eternal, and, as they say, immutable principle, consecrated by this famous instrument, and in support of which we have appealed to God, is to have no obligatory force on the very parties who made it, but attaches instantly cross the Mississippi! What kind of ethics is this that is bounded by latitude and longitude, which is inoperative on the left, but is omnipotent on the right bank of the river? . . .

Mr. [Jonathan] Roberts [of Pennsylvania responded] . . . Without reserve, I deny that there is any power in a State to make slaves, or to introduce slavery where it has been abolished, or where it never existed, or even to permit its existence only as an evil admitting of no immediate remedy. . . . The Constitution provides that new States may be admitted into this Union, and that the United States shall guaranty to every State in this Union a republican form of government. [I]t was declared, on the part of these States, that all men are created equal; that they are endowed by their Creator with certain inalienable rights, among which are life, liberty and the pursuit of happiness; that to secure these rights governments are instituted among men, deriving their just powers from the consent of the governed. Two conclusions most clearly result from these premises; that a government founded on these principles can neither make slaves nor kings. . . .

. . . A new state admitted into the Union . . . must be a State with a Republican government. Though gentlemen have looked abroad to define this phrase, to get at a conveniently enlarged definition, it follows, most clearly, that it stands in the Constitution an insuperable interdict to slave making. . . .

The recognition of slavery in the Constitution will not go far to justify the right to establish it. Why is a circumlocution of words used in that instrument, to designate such persons, instead of one so appropriate as that of slaves? Either because it was considered as a painful word, or, for the better reason, that it was hoped that the Constitution would survive a state of things where the word could be applicable. In either case emancipation must have been looked to as a desirable event, and a righteous consummation of the promises of the Revolution. . . .

Slaves, says the gentlemen from South Carolina (Mr. Smith), are the happiest poor people in the world. . . . I have had occasions to listen before now to comparisons drawn by Southern gentlemen between the laborer of the North and the Southern slave. In ordinary cases such a parallel could hardly justify a reply. The white laborer is always a free man, generally an honest man; often an intelligent and informed man. He knows his rights, and understands his duties. Free laborers, who are housekeepers, are seldom without their newspapers and means of information. These channels of intelligence are everywhere established with us. . . . The relation between laborer and employer, where the latter is a freeman, is that of equals. Each looks to the other for the fulfillment of the covenant between them. . . . Under any aspect, however, there can be no just resemblance, nor any comparison of advantages, common to the freeman and slave. . . .

When gentlemen claim for Missouri this boon of slavery, as it has been called, and paint its advantages, and plead for its legality, let them look at its origin. Whence have they derived their claims as owners and masters? From the violence of savage warfare; from the frauds and crimes of the man-stealer. Here is the foundation of your pretensions. What was originally wrong can never become right, while there is a living subject to suffer. While I most readily admit, a sudden and general emancipation in a large portion of this Union would be the frenzy of madness, I hold it the incumbent duty of all to believe it desirable, and to look and hope for its consummation in the fullness of God's providence. . . .

8. Joshua Cushman, Address before the U.S. House of Representatives (February 14, 1820)

Mr. Cushman [of Massachusetts] addressed the Chair as follows: . . . Happily, the restriction contended for . . . provides . . . that a human being, whatever be his complexion, in the Territory or State of Missouri, shall feel the force of these self-evident truths—*that God created all mankind equal and endowed them with certain inalienable rights*—amongst which are "life, *liberty*, and the pursuit of happiness." Can ingenuity, aided by elocution, fix a stigma on such a just and wise and liberal policy in the opinion of the enlightened world? It is somewhat singular that the gentlemen who are so fastidiously delicate respecting the powers of Congress, should habitually usurp an unwarrantable power over a large portion of their fellow-men. What is your right to make an African your property, but the right of the strongest? . . .

Property itself, sir, if not a creature of the law, by law is modified, restrained, or regulated in its use. In a state of society, respecting many kinds of property, no man has a right to do what he will with his own. It cannot be used by him to the destruction of others. No man is permitted, by law, to set fire to his own house in the midst of a city, however convenient it might be to him to have it consumed. In a number of instances the laws interpose and regulate the property which men have in animals, or restrain or limit their use. If any species of them were becoming noxious to any section of country, or if multiplying them should become hurtful and injurious to the community, laws might be enacted to prevent the mischievous effects.

This reasoning is applicable to every species of property, of every complexion, whether blue, or yellow, or black. If, therefore, you consider your slaves property—and if spreading this species of property over the Missouri would be injurious to the best interest of the nation, as nothing has been stipulated to the contrary, on the principles that regulate other kinds of property, Congress may regulate or prohibit to you the use of this. . . .

To the evils of slavery, where slavery exists by compact, there is, perhaps, no adequate remedy. But not to prevent, where there is a power of prevention, is a strange repugnance of practice to theory. And to diminish the whole quantity of an evil by making it more extensive, by increasing it in a tenfold ratio, appears to me worse than that quackery in the boasted art of healing, which, instead of extracting, should scatter the morbid matter of the diseased part throughout the whole frame, till all that was sound should become infected. . . .

Where there is a demand for any commodity, there the market will be supplied. Open a profitable sale for slaves in the Missouri, and Africans will be brought there to market by all means, and from all quarters. The shortsighted avarice of individuals will elude all your laws, the activity of your peace officers, the vigilance of your fleets or armies. In opposition to all that can be done, there will be fresh importations, and undersellers in the market, which will defeat the hopes which you indulge of gain. There is no way so effectual to prevent this human traffic . . . as to remove all temptation, to render the trade as unprofitable as it is odious. This will be laying the axe at the root of the tree, and giving it a fatal stroke by which it will wither, droop, and die. . . .

9. Charles Pinckney, Address before the U.S. House of Representatives (February 14, 1820)

Mr. PINCKNEY, of South Carolina, addressed the Chair as follows:

[T]he true motive for all this dreadful clamor throughout the Union, this serious and eventful attack on our most sacred and valuable rights and properties, is [for the non-slaveholding states] to gain a fixed ascendency in the representation of Congress. . . .

[L]et us now see who supports this Government; who raises your armies, equips your navies, pays your public debt, enables you to erect forts, arsenals, and dock yards. . . . Who are your real sinews in war, and the best—I had almost said nearly the only—sinews and sources of your commerce in peace? . . .

. . . I ask you who pays the expense, and who, in fact, enables you to go on with your Government at all, and prevents its wheels from stopping? I will show you by the papers which I hold in my hand. This, sir, is your Secretary of the Treasury's report, made a few weeks ago, by which it appears that all the exports of native products, from Maine to Pennsylvania, inclusive, for the last year, amounted to only about eighteen millions of dollars; while those among the slaveholding States, to the southward of Pennsylvania, amounted to thirty-two millions or thereabouts, thereby enabling themselves, or acquiring the right, to import double as much as the others, and furnishing the Treasury with double the amount the Northern and Eastern States do. And here, let me ask, from whence do these exports arise? By whose hands are they made? I answer, entirely by the slaves; and yet these valuable inhabitants, without whom your very Government could not go on, and the labor of two or three of whom in the Southern States is now more valuable to it than the labor of five inhabitants in the Eastern States, the States owning them are denied a representation but for three-fifths on this floor, while the whole of the comparatively unproductive inhabitants of the Northern and Eastern States are fully represented here. Is it just—is this equal? . . .

A great deal has been said on the subject of slavery—that it is an infamous stain and blot on the States that hold them; not only degrading the slave, but the master, and making him unfit for republican government; that it is contrary to religion and the law of God; and that Congress ought to do everything in their power to prevent its extension among the new States.

Now, sir, I should be glad to know how any man is acquainted with what is the will or the law of God on this subject. Has it ever been imparted either to the old or the new world? Is there a single line in the Old or the New Testament, either censuring or forbidding it? I answer without hesitation, no. . . .

Let those acquainted with the situation of the people of Asia and Africa, where not one man in ten can be called a freeman, or whose situation can be compared with the comforts of our slaves, throw their eyes over them, and carry them to Russia, and from the North to the South of Europe, where, except Great Britain, nothing like liberty exists. . . . [T]hen let him come nearer home, and examine into the situation of the free negroes now resident in New York and Philadelphia, and compare them with the situation of our slaves, and he will tell you that, perhaps, the most miserable and degraded state of human nature is to be found among the free negroes of New York and Philadelphia, most of whom are fugitives from the Southern States, received and sheltered in those States. I did not go to New York, but I did to Philadelphia, and particularly examined this subject while there. I saw their streets crowded with idle, drunken negroes, at every corner; and, on visiting their penitentiary, found, to my astonishment, that, out of five hundred convicts there confined, more than one-half were blacks; and, as all the convicts throughout that State are sent to that penitentiary, and, if Pennsylvania contains eight hundred thousand white inhabitants, and only twenty-six thousand blacks, of course the crimes and vices of the blacks in those States are, comparatively, twenty times greater than those of the whites in the same States, and clearly proves that a state of freedom is one of the greatest curses you can inflict on them.

From the opinions expressed respecting the Southern States and the slaves there, it appears to me most clear that the members on the opposite side know nothing of the Southern States, their lands, products or slaves. . . . Sir, when we recollect that our former parent State was the original cause of introducing slavery into America, and that neither ourselves or ancestors are chargeable with it; that it cannot be got rid of without ruining the country, certainly the present mild treatment of our slaves is most honorable to that part of the country where slavery exists. Every slave has a comfortable house, is well fed, clothed, and taken care of; he has his family about him, and in sickness has the same medical aid as his master, and has a sure and comfortable retreat in his old age, to protect him against its infirmities and weakness. During the whole of his life he is free from care, that canker of the human heart, which destroys at least one half of the thinking part of mankind, and from which a favored few, very few, if indeed any, can be said to be free. Being without education, and born to obey, to persons of that description moderate labor and discipline are essential. The discipline ought to be mild, but still, while slavery is to exist, there must be discipline. In this state they are happier than they can possibly be if free. A free black can only be happy where he has some share of education and has been bred to a trade or some kind of business. The great body of slaves are happier in their present situation than they could be in any other, and the man or men who would attempt to give them freedom, would be their greatest enemies. . . .

It will not be a matter of surprise to any one, that so much anxiety should be shown by the slaveholding States, when it is known that the alarm, given by this attempt to legislate on slavery, has led to the opinion, that the very foundations of that kind of property are shaken; that the establishment of the precedent is a measure of the most alarming nature; for, should succeeding Congresses continue to push it, there is no knowing to what length it may be carried.

Have the Northern States any idea of the value of our slaves? At least, sir, six hundred millions of dollars. If we lose them, the value of the lands they cultivate will be diminished in all cases one half, and in many, they will become wholly useless, and an annual income of at least forty millions of dollars will be lost to your citizens; the loss of which will not alone be felt by the non-slave-holding States, but by the whole Union; for, to whom, at present, do the Eastern States, most particularly, and the Eastern and Northern, generally, look for the employment of their shipping, in transporting our bulky and valuable products, and bringing us the manufactures and merchandises of Europe? . . . But, sir, there is an infinitely greater call upon them, and this is the call of justice, of affection and humanity. Reposing at a great distance, in safety, in the full enjoyment of all their Federal and State rights, unattacked in either, or in their individual rights, can they, with indifference, or ought they to risk, in the remotest degree, the consequences which this measure may produce. These may be the division of this Union and a civil war. . . .

10. Thomas Jefferson, Letter to John Holmes (April 22, 1820)

In this famous letter, Jefferson warned that while compromise had momentarily alleviated the heated debate over slavery, the debate over Missouri bode ill for the Union. Note that for Jefferson, emancipation was still a goal—one demanded by justice—but also one more likely to be secured through union rather than disunion.

I thank you, Dear Sir, for the copy you have been so kind as to send me of the letter to your constituents on the Missouri question. It is a perfect justification to them. I had for a long time ceased to read the newspapers or pay any attention to public affairs, confident they were in good hands, and content to be a passenger in our bark to the shore from which I am not distant. But this momentous question, like a fire bell in the night, awakened and filled me with terror. I considered it at once as the knell of the Union. It is hushed indeed for the moment. But this is a reprieve only, not a final sentence. A geographical line, coinciding with a marked principle, moral and political, once conceived and held up to the angry passions of men, will never be obliterated; and every new irritation will mark it deeper and deeper. I can say with conscious truth that there is not a man on earth who would sacrifice more than I would, to relieve us from this heavy reproach, in any *practicable* way. The cession of that kind of property, for so it is misnamed, is a bagatelle which would not cost me in a second thought, if, in that way, a general emancipation and *expatriation* could be effected: and, gradually, and with due sacrifices, I think it might be. But as it is, we have the wolf by the ears, and we can neither hold him, nor safely let him go. Justice is in one scale, and self-preservation in the other. Of one thing I am certain, that as the passage of slaves from one state to another would not make a slave of a single human being who would not be so without it, so their diffusion over a greater surface would make them individually happier and proportionally facilitate the accomplishment of their emancipation, by dividing the burthen on a greater number of coadjutors. An abstinence, too, from this act of power, would remove the jealousy excited by the undertaking of Congress to regulate the condition of the different descriptions of men composing a State. This certainly is the exclusive right of every State, which nothing in the constitution has taken from them and given to the general government. Could Congress, for example, say that the non-freemen of Connecticut shall be freemen, or that they shall not emigrate into any other State?

I regret that I am now to die in the belief that the useless sacrifice of themselves, by the generation of 1776, to acquire self-government and happiness to their country, is to be thrown away by the unwise and unworthy passions of their sons, and that my only consolation is to be, that I live not to weep over it. If they would but dispassionately weigh the blessings they will throw away, against an abstract principle more likely to be effected by union than by scission, they would pause before they would perpetrate this act of suicide on themselves and of treason against the hopes of the world. . . .

11. *The Annual Report of the Auxiliary Society of Frederick County, Virginia, for Colonizing the Free People of Color in the United States* (November 4, 1820)

This annual report of a local chapter of the American Colonization Society reflects the consensus of many Upper South planters in places like Virginia or Maryland. To these planters, slavery was an unmitigated evil; persons of African descent were capable of civilization and suffered real oppression in the United States. Regardless of these assertions, the report concludes that white citizens of the United States were culturally unprepared to accept blacks as equal citizens. Moreover, free black persons represented dangerous examples, because they encouraged insurrection. To many such planters, then, colonization represented a viable and ethically sound solution to the problem of slavery.

Africa, the pride of antiquity, and the original seat of the arts and sciences, has for three hundred years been visited with every act of oppression which could be devised by the tyranny or injustice of mankind. After improving the condition of the ancient nations of Europe and Asia, by instructing them in the principles of civil government and the maxims of philosophy, she has, in modern ages, been rewarded for her services by a system of cruel, inhuman persecution, unparalleled in the annals of the world. By means of the slave trade, that scourge of Africa, the countries bordering on her sea coast have been desolated, her virtues blasted, her peace destroyed, her civilization retarded or converted to barbarism, and her intercourse with foreign nations annihilated, except in the diabolical traffic of human flesh! Our own country is blackened with the victims of slavery, already amounting to nearly two millions of souls; and to contemplate their increase through the vista of futurity is alarming to the patriot and the philanthropist.

While we deprecate the horrors of slavery, it is consoling to reflect that our country, is originally guiltless of the crime, which was legalized by G. Britain under our colonial government, and consummated by commercial avarice, at a time when our powerless legislatures vainly implored the mother country to abolish a trade so impious in its character and dreadful in its consequences. In the year 1772, Virginia discourages the importation of slaves by the imposition of duties, and supplicated the throne to remove the evil; and in 1778, having broken the fetters of British tyranny, she passed a law prohibiting further importation of slaves. The attention of the continental Congress was called to this interesting subject as early as the year 1774, and the opposition then expressed to the slave trade was afterwards effectuated by a law enacted by the constitutional Congress as soon as its delegated powers would permit. . . .

The bare mention of the high objects of our pursuit, ought to convince every reflecting mind of their expediency. What are those objects?

1st. To colonize the free people of color of the United States.

2d. To prepare the way for the gradual emancipation and colonization of our slaves.

3d. To contribute to the abolition of the slave trade.

4th. To perform an act of justice to Africa and her descendants, by restoring her unfortunate children, and by disseminating through that continent the principles of Christianity and civilization.

5th. As a consequence of the preceding propositions, to promote the prosperity of our country and save it from impending ruin.

It was necessary to avow our real objects, since some have falsely charged us with wishing to rivet more strongly the fetters of slavery by removing the free persons of color; whilst others, with no less absurdity, have accused us of an intention to emancipate all the slaves by a compulsory process equally repugnant to our wishes and transcending our authority.

. . . We say it is expedient to colonize the free people of color. In Greece and Rome, emancipated slaves became useful citizens, because nature had branded them with no characteristic difference of complexion. But "can the Ethiopian change his skin?" A manumitted slave remains a negro still, and must ever continue in a state of political bondage; and it is obvious that he who is deprived of the inherent rights of a citizen can never become a loyal subject. Who would submit to a negro president or a negro chief justice? The very idea inspires indignation and contempt. Thus degraded in the scale of existence, the emancipated negro must be habitually prone to infancy and rebellion.

. . . The free negroes corrupt our slaves by urging them to plunder the community and affording a receptacle to the fruits of their depredations; by also inculcating ideas of freedom and independence, which must terminate in insurrection. Some individuals of this class, we readily admit, by their honesty and industry have surrounded themselves with many of the comforts of life; but unfortunately, their example is not less dangerous than that of an emancipated vagabond. By witnessing the situation of his affluent brother, the slave contrasts it with his own, pants for his liberty, becomes discontented and disobedient, and in order to move in the same sphere with the fraternity of freed-men, at the expense of his integrity mimics the dress and manners of fashionable life. From what has been urged, the expediency of removing this nuisance from the community is clearly inferable, both in relation to their interest and ours; and this end can only be attained by means of the colonizing Society.

. . . That slavery is an evil no one can deny. All must desire to cure the disease or mitigate its ravages. If the evil be of fearful magnitude now, what will it be *fifty years hence?* . . .

By thus gradually removing this class of our population, we should not only be liberated from the apprehension of a servile war, at which humanity shudders, but would moreover greatly improve the moral worth of the community. . . .

. . . [I]t is impiously maintained by some, that the poor, unfortunate negroes, are lower than ourselves in the scale of being, and nearly allied to the apes and monkeys! Jacob Oson, a negro of New York, in defending his countrymen from this charge of inferiority, sagaciously remarks: "It is no place to judge of the strength or agility of the tiger in his cage. Furthermore, the majestic state of the lion may be debased by bondage. Let his majesty the lion be unbound, and he will resume his former prerogative. So let us be emancipated from our encumbrances, and then, where ignorance and darkness reign, religion and true science would abound. As a garden uncultivated soon grows to weeds, so is the state of our nation, being enslaved in America for about three hundred years, trodden under foot, and considered as the offscouring of the earth." These are the words of a *negro*, and they have been cited to prove that negroes can feel and think like human beings, though deprived of the power of action. . . .

. . . Rely upon it, the Africans are not brutes, and therefore will return with joy to the land of their ancestors. . . .

12. Rev. Dr. Richard Furman, Exposition of *the Views of the Baptists*, Relative to the *Coloured Population* in the United States (December 24, 1822)

Here Richard Furman (1755–1825) used Scripture and the law of nations to defend the right to hold slaves. Even if the slave trade is deplorable, he argues, it was originally motivated by piety, and blacks have benefited from the institution. Masters bear great responsibilities toward their slaves, including the duty of bringing them the Gospel. Furman warns that efforts to prove that Scripture is incompatible with slavery threaten the peace, and, moreover, provoke masters to deny their slaves religious instruction and thus eternal salvation.

. . . On the lawfulness of holding slaves, considering it in a moral and religious view, the Convention think it their duty to exhibit their sentiments . . . because they consider their duty to God, the peace of the State, the satisfaction of scrupulous consciences, and the welfare of the slaves themselves, as intimately connected with a right view of the subject. They rather, because certain writers on politics, morals and religion, and some of them highly respectable, have advanced positions, and inculcated sentiments, very unfriendly to the principle and practice of holding slaves; and by some these sentiments have been advanced among us, tending in their nature, *directly* to disturb the domestic peace of the State, to produce insubordination and rebellion among the slaves, and to infringe the rights of our citizens; and *indirectly*, to deprive the slaves of religious privileges, by awakening in the minds of their masters a fear, that acquaintance with the Scriptures, and the enjoyment of these privileges would naturally produce the aforementioned effects; because the sentiments in opposition to the holding of slaves have been attributed, by their advocates, to the Holy Scriptures, and to the genius of Christianity. These sentiments, the Convention, on whose behalf I address your Excellency, cannot think just, or well-founded: for the right of holding slaves is clearly established by the Holy Scriptures, both by precept and example. . . .

. . . If the holding of slaves is lawful, or according to the Scriptures; then this Scriptural rule can be considered as requiring no more of the master, in respect of justice . . . than what he, if a slave, could consistently, wish to be done to himself, while the relationship between master and servant should still be continued.

In this argument, the advocates for emancipation blend the ideas of injustice and cruelty with those, which respect the existence of slavery, and consider them as inseparable. But, surely, they may be separated. A bond-servant may be treated with justice and humanity as a servant; and a master may, in an important sense, be the guardian and even father of his slaves.

They become a part of his family, (the whole, forming under him a little community) and the care of ordering it and providing for its welfare, devolves on him. The children, the aged, the sick, the disabled, and the unruly, as well as those, who are capable of service and orderly, are the objects of his care: The labour of these, is applied to the benefit of those, and to their own support, as well as that of the master. Thus, what is effected, and often at a great public expense, in a free community, by taxes, benevolent institutions, bettering houses, and penitentiaries, lies here on the master, to be performed by him, whatever contingencies may happen; and often occasions much expense, care and trouble, from which the servants are free. Cruelty, is, certainly, inadmissible; but servitude may be consistent with such degrees of happiness as men usually attain in this imperfect state of things. . . .

Some difficulties arise with respect to bringing a man, or class of men, into a state of bondage. For crime, it is generally agreed, a man may be deprived of his liberty. But, may he not be divested of it by his own consent, directly, or indirectly given . . . ? [T]he Africans brought to America were, slaves, by their own consent, before they came from their own country, or fell into the hands of white men.

Their law of nations, or general usage, having, by common consent the force of law, justified them, while carrying on their petty wars, in killing their prisoners or reducing them to slavery; consequently, in selling them, and these ends they appear to have proposed to themselves; the nation, therefore, or individual, which was overcome, reduced to slavery, and sold would have done the same by the enemy, had victory declared on their, or his side. Consequently, the man made slave in this manner, might be said to be made so by his own consent, and by the indulgence of barbarous principles. . . .

If the above representation of the Scriptural doctrine, and the manner of obtaining slaves from Africa is just; and if also purchasing them has been the means of saving human life, which there is great reason to believe it has; then, however the slave trade, in present circumstances, is justly censurable, yet might motives of humanity and even piety have been originally brought into operation in the purchase of slaves, when sold in the circumstances we have described. If, also, by their own confession, which has been made in manifold instances, their condition, when they have come into the hands of humane masters here, has been greatly bettered by the change; if it is, ordinarily, really better, as many assert, than that of thousands of the poorer classes in countries reputed civilized and free; and, if, in addition to all other considerations, the translation from their native country to this has been the means of their mental and religious improvement, and so of obtaining salvation, as many of themselves have joyfully and thankfully confessed—then may the just and humane master, who rules his slaves and provides for them, according to Christian principles, rest satisfied, that he is not, in holding them, chargeable with moral evil, nor with acting, in this respect, contrary to the genius of Christianity.

It appears to be equally clear, that those, who by reasoning on abstract principles, are induced to favour the scheme of general emancipation, and who ascribe their sentiments to Christianity, should be particularly careful, however benevolent their intentions may be, that they do not by a perversion of the Scriptural doctrine, through their wrong views of it, not only invade the domestic and religious peace and rights of our Citizens, on this subject; but, also by an intemperate zeal, prevent indirectly, the religious improvement of the people they design, professedly, to benefit; and, perhaps, become, evidently, the means of producing in our country, scenes of anarchy and blood; and all this in a vain attempt to bring about a state of things, which, if arrived at, would not probably better the state of that people; which is thought, by men of observation, to be generally true of the Negroes in the Northern states, who have been liberated. . . .

13. Bishop Richard Allen, Letter to the Editor of the "Freedom's Journal" (November 2, 1827)

In this editorial, Richard Allen (1760–1831) rejected colonization, suggesting that the policy seeks to further subjugate the slaves. Allen observed that America is home for African Americans, and he decried the injustice of enslaving Africans to till the soil for others while denying them access to the bounty they've cultivated. Allen endorsed James Forten's pronouncements that African Americans were "entitled to participate in the blessings of [America's] luxuriant soil" and that "we will never separate ourselves voluntarily from the slave population in this country. . . ." Allen's letter was quoted in full in David Walker's Appeal. Here, we have followed the formatting and punctuation as it appears in the third edition of Walker's appeal, published in 1830.[9]

DEAR SIR: I have for several years been striving to reconcile my mind, to the colonization of Africa in Liberia, but there have always been, and there still remain great and insurmountable objections against the scheme. We are an unlettered people, brought up in ignorance; not one in a hundred can read

---

9. See document 15 in this chapter.

or write; not one in a thousand has a liberal education. Is there any fitness for such to be sent into a far country, among Heathens, to convert or civilize them; when they themselves are neither civilized nor Christianized? . . . Is there any fitness for such people to be colonized in a far country, to be their own rulers? Can we not discern the project of sending the free people of colour away from this country? Is it not for the interest of the slave holder, to select, the free people of colour out of the different states, and send them to Liberia? Will it not make their slaves uneasy to see free men of colour enjoying liberty? It is against the law in some of the southern states, that a person of colour should receive an education under a severe penalty. Colonizationists speak of America being first colonized, but is there any comparison between the two? America was colonized by as wise, judicious, and educated men as the world afforded. William Penn did not want for learning, wisdom, or intelligence. If all the people in Europe and America were as ignorant, and in the same situation as our brethren, what would become of the world; where would be the principle or piety that would govern the people? We were stolen from our mother country and brought here. We have tilled the ground and made fortunes for thousands, and still they are not weary of our services. But they who stay to till the ground must be slaves. Is there no land enough in America, or "corn enough in Egypt?" Why would they send us into a far country to die? See the thousands of foreigners emigrating to America every year; and if there be ground sufficient for them to cultivate, and bread for them to eat; why would they wish to send the first tillers of the land away? Africans have made fortunes for thousands, who are yet unwilling to part with their services; but the free must be sent away, and those who remain must be slaves? I have no doubt that there are many good men who do not see as I do; and who are for sending us to Liberia, but they have not duly considered the subject—they are not men of colour. This land which we have watered with our tears and our blood, is now our mother country and we are well satisfied to stay where wisdom abounds, and the gospel is free.

14. *The State [of North Carolina] v. John Mann* (1829)

John Mann was indicted for the battery and shooting of Lydia, a slave whom he had "rented," an incident provoked by a small infraction on Lydia's part. At trial Mann was convicted, but the state's supreme court overturned the conviction. The opinion, written by Thomas Ruffin (1787–1870), a slave

owner, legally established the relationship between master and slave. Ruffin
grounds his ruling in the "established habits" of the whites and the need for
the complete dominion of the master. Harriet Beecher Stowe would cite this
case as one of the sources for her novel Dred.

RUFFIN, Judge.— . . . The indictment charges a battery on *Lydia*, a slave of
Elizabeth Jones. . . . Here the slave had been *hired* by the Defendant, and was in
his possession; and the battery was committed during the period of hiring. . . .
The enquiry here is, whether a cruel and unreasonable battery on a slave, by
the hirer, is indictable. . . . Our laws uniformly treat the master or other person
having the possession and command of the slave, as entitled to the same extent
of authority. The object is the same—the services of the slave; and the same
powers must be confided. In a criminal proceeding, and indeed in reference
to all other persons but the general owner, the hirer and possessor of a slave,
in relation to both rights and duties, is, for the time being, the owner. . . .
[U]pon the general question, whether the owner is answerable *criminaliter*, for
a battery upon his own slave, or other exercise of authority or force, not forbidden by statute, the Court entertains but little doubt.—That he is so liable,
has never yet been decided; nor, as far as is known, been hitherto contended.
There have been no prosecutions of the sort. The established habits and uniform practice of the country in this respect, is the best evidence of the portion
of power, deemed by the whole community, requisite to the preservation of
the master's dominion. . . . [A]rguments drawn from the well established principles, which confer and restrain the authority of the parent over the child, the
tutor over the pupil, the master over the apprentice, have been pressed on us.
The Court does not recognize their application. There is no likeness between
the cases. They are in opposition to each other, and there is an impassable
gulf between them.—The difference is that which exists between freedom and
slavery—and a greater cannot be imagined. In the one, the end in view is the
happiness of the youth, born to equal rights with that governor, on whom
the duty devolves of training the young to usefulness, in a station which he is
afterwards to assume among freemen. To such an end, and with such a subject,
moral and intellectual instruction seem the natural means; and for the most
part, they are found to suffice. Moderate force is superadded, only to make the
others effectual. If that fail, it is better to leave the party to his own headstrong
passions, and the ultimate correction of the law, than to allow it to be immod-
erately inflicted by a private person. With slavery it is far otherwise. The end
is the profit of the master, his security and the public safety; the subject, one
doomed in his own person, and his posterity, to live without knowledge, and
without the capacity to make any thing his own, and to toil that another may
reap the fruits. [S]uch services can only be expected from one who has no will
of his own; who surrenders his will in implicit obedience to that of another.

Such obedience is the consequence only of uncontrolled authority over the body. There is nothing else which can operate to produce the effect. The power of the master must be absolute, to render the submission of the slave perfect. I most freely confess my sense of the harshness of this proposition, I feel it as deeply as any man can. And as a principle of moral right, every person in his retirement must repudiate it. But in the actual condition of things, it must be so. There is no remedy. This discipline belongs to the state of slavery. They cannot be disunited, without abrogating at once the rights of the master, and absolving the slave from his subjection. It constitutes the curse of slavery to both the bond and free portions of our population. But it is inherent in the relation of master and slave. . . .

We are happy to see, that there is daily less and less occasion for the interposition of the Courts. The protection already afforded by several statutes, that all-powerful motive, the private interest of the owner, the benevolences towards each other, seated in the hearts of those who have been born and bred together, the frowns and deep execrations of the community upon the barbarian, who is guilty of excessive and brutal cruelty to his unprotected slave, all combined, have produced a mildness of treatment, and attention to the comforts of the unfortunate class of slaves, greatly mitigating the rigors of servitude, and ameliorating the condition of the slaves. The same causes are operating, and will continue to operate with increased action, until the disparity in numbers between the whites and blacks, shall have rendered the latter in no degree dangerous to the former, when the police now existing may be further relaxed. . . .

I repeat, that I would gladly have avoided this ungrateful question. But being brought to it, the Court is compelled to declare, that while slavery exists amongst us in its present state, or until it shall seem fit to the Legislature to interpose express enactments to the contrary, it will be the imperative duty of the Judges to recognize the full dominion of the owner over the slave. . . . And this we do upon the ground, that this dominion is essential to the value of slaves as property, to the security of the master, and the public tranquillity, greatly dependent upon their subordination; and in fine, as most effectually securing the general protection and comfort of the slaves themselves.

15. David Walker, *Appeal to the Coloured Citizens of the World* (1830)

Vehemently renouncing colonization, abolitionist David Walker (1785–1830) directly questions the motives of the American Colonial Society. Rejecting claims that Americans were blameless in the introduction of slavery, and ridiculing the pious protestations of Henry Clay and others, Walker condemns their blatant corruption of the Gospel. Were Scripture to justify slavery, then whites, not blacks, should be enslaved, for they emulate Cain. Most important, however, is Walker's defiant argument for resistance and his indignation at the violence suffered by Cincinnati's blacks in 1829, victims of white enforcement of Ohio's Black Code. The brackets in the version we republish below are original to this document.

Article IV:
OUR WRETCHEDNESS IN CONSEQUENCE
OF THE COLONIZING PLAN.

. . . At a meeting which was convened in the District of Columbia, for the express purpose of agitating the subject of colonizing us in some part of the world, Mr. Clay was called to the chair, and having been seated a little while, he rose and spake, in substance, as follows: says he—"That class of the mixt population of our country [coloured people] was peculiarly situated; they neither enjoyed the immunities of freemen, nor were they subjected to the incapacities of slaves, but partook, in some degree, of the qualities of both. From their condition, and the unconquerable prejudices resulting from their colour, they never could amalgamate with the free whites of this country. It was desirable, therefore, as it respected them, and the residue of the population of the country, to drain them off. Various schemes of colonization had been thought of, and a part of our continent, it was supposed by some, might furnish a suitable establishment for them. But, for his part, Mr. C. said, he had a decided preference for some part of the Coast of Africa. There ample provision might be made for the colony itself, and it might be rendered instrumental to the introduction into that extensive quarter of the globe, of the arts, civilization, and Christianity." [Here I ask Mr. Clay, what kind of Christianity? Did he mean such as they have among the Americans—distinction, whip, blood and oppression? I pray the Lord Jesus Christ to forbid it.] "There," said he, "was a peculiar, moral fitness, in restoring them to the land of their fathers, and if instead of the evils and sufferings which we had been the innocent cause of inflicting upon the inhabitants of Africa, we can transmit to her the blessings of our arts, our civilization, and our religion. May we not hope that America will extinguish a great portion of that moral debt which she has contracted to that unfortunate continent?" . . .

Before I proceed any further, I solicit your notice, brethren, to the foregoing part of Mr. Clay's speech, in which he says, (look above) "and if, instead of the evils and sufferings which we had been the innocent cause of inflicting," &c.—What this very learned statesman could have been thinking about, when he said in his speech, "we had been the innocent cause of inflicting," &c., I have never been able to conceive. Are Mr. Clay and the rest of the Americans, innocent of the blood and groans of our fathers and us, their children?—Every individual may plead innocence, if he pleases, but God will, before long, separate the innocent from the guilty, unless something is speedily done—which I suppose will hardly be, so that their destruction may be sure. Oh Americans! let me tell you, in the name of the Lord, it will be good for you, if you listen to the voice of the Holy Ghost, but if you do not, you are ruined!!! . . .

But to return to Mr. Clay, whence I digressed. He says, "it was proper and necessary distinctly to state, that he understood it constituted no part of the object of this meeting, to touch or agitate in the slightest degree, a delicate question, connected with another portion of the coloured population of our country. It was not proposed to deliberate upon or consider at all, any question of emancipation, or that which was connected with the abolition of slavery. It was upon that condition alone, he was sure, that many gentlemen from the South and the West, whom he saw present, had attended, or could be expected to co-operate. It was upon that condition only, that he himself had attended."

That is to say, to fix a plan to get those of the coloured people, who are said to be free, away from among those of our brethren whom they unjustly hold in bondage, so that they may be enabled to keep them the more secure in ignorance and wretchedness, to support them and their children, and consequently they would have the more obedient slaves. For if the free are allowed to stay among the slaves, they will have intercourse together, and, of course, the free will learn the slaves *bad habits*, by teaching them that they are MEN, as well as other people, and certainly *ought* and *must* be FREE.

. . . Now I appeal and ask every citizen of these United States . . . Do you believe that Mr. Henry Clay, late Secretary of State, and now in Kentucky, is a friend to the blacks, further, than his personal interest extends? Is it not his greatest object and glory upon earth, to sink us into miseries and wretchedness by making slaves of us, to work his plantation to enrich him and his family? Does he care a pinch of snuff about Africa—whether it remains a land of Pagans and of blood, or of Christians, so long as he gets enough of her sons and daughters to dig up gold and silver for him? . . . Would he work in the hot sun to earn his bread, if he could make an African work for nothing, particularly, if he could keep him in ignorance and make him believe that God made him for nothing else but to work for him? Is not Mr. Clay a white man, and too delicate to work in the hot sun!! Was he not made by his Creator to sit in the shade, and make the blacks work without remuneration for their services, to support him and his family!!! I have been for some time taking notice of this man's speeches and public writings, but never to my knowledge have I seen any thing in his writings, which insisted on the emancipation of slavery, which has almost ruined his country. Thus we see the depravity of men's hearts, when in pursuit only of gain—particularly when they oppress their fellow creatures to obtain that gain. . . .

Extract from the Speech of Mr. John Randolph, of Roanoke. . . .

. . . "There was a popular work on agriculture, by John Taylor of Carolina [Caroline], which was widely circulated, and much confided in, in Virginia. In that book, much read because coming from a practical man, this description of people, [referring to us half free ones] were pointed out as a great evil. They had indeed been held up as the greater bug-bear to every man who feels an inclination to emancipate his slaves, not to create in the bosom of his country so great a nuisance. If a place could be provided for their reception, and a mode of sending them hence, there were hundreds, nay thousands of citizens who would, by manumitting their slaves, relieve themselves from the cares attendant on their possession. The great slaveholder," Mr. R. said, "was frequently a mere sentry at his own door—bound to stay on his plantation to see that his slaves were properly treated, &c." Mr. R[andolph] concluded by saying, that he had thought it necessary to make these remarks being a slave-holder himself, to shew that, "so far from being connected with abolition of slavery, the measure proposed would prove one of the greatest securities to enable the master to keep in possession his own property."

Here is a demonstrative proof, of a plan got up, by a gang of slave-holders to select the free people of colour from among the slaves, that our more miserable brethren may be the better secured in ignorance and wretchedness, to work their farms and dig their mines, and thus go on enriching the Christians with their blood and groans. What our brethren could have been thinking about, who have left their native land and home and gone away to Africa, I am unable to say. This country is as much ours as it is the whites, whether they will admit it now or not, they will see and believe it by and by. . . .

[Here Walker quotes Bishop Allen's 1827 letter in full. See document 13 in this chapter.—eds.]

. . . I have several times called the white Americans our *natural enemies*—I shall here define my meaning of the phrase. Shem, Ham and Japheth, together with their father Noah and wives, I believe were not natural enemies to each other. When the ark rested after the flood upon Mount Arrarat, in Asia, they (eight) were all the people which could be found alive in all the earth—In fact if Scriptures be true, (which I believe are) there were no other living men in all the earth, notwithstanding some ignorant creatures hesitate not to tell us that we, (the blacks) are the seed of Cain the murderer of his brother Abel. But where or of whom those ignorant and avaricious wretches could have got their information, I am unable to declare. Did they receive it from the Bible? I have searched the Bible as well as they . . . and have never seen a verse which testifies whether we are the seed of Cain or of Abel. Yet those men tell us that we are the seed of Cain, and that God put a dark stain upon us, that we might be known as their slaves!!! Now, I ask those avaricious and ignorant wretches, who act more like the seed of Cain, by murdering—the whites or the blacks? How many vessel loads of human beings, have the blacks thrown into the seas? How many thousand souls have the blacks murdered in cold blood, to make them work in wretchedness and ignorance, to support them and their families?—However, let us be the seed of *Cain, Harry, Dick, or Tom!!!* God will show the whites what we are, yet. I say, from the beginning, I do not think that we were natural enemies to each other. But the whites having made us so wretched, by subjecting us to slavery, and having murdered so many millions of us, in order to make us work for them, and out of devilishness—and they taking our wives, whom we love as we do ourselves—our mothers, who bore the pains of death to give us birth—our fathers and dear little children, and ourselves, and strip and beat us one before the other—chain, hand-cuff, and drag us about like rattlesnakes—shoot us down like wild bears, before each other's faces, to make us submissive to, and work to support them and their families. They (the whites) know well, if we are *men*—and there is a secret monitor in their hearts which tells them we are—they know, I say, if we *are* men, and see them treating us in the manner they do, that there can be nothing in our hearts but death alone, for them, notwithstanding we may appear cheerful, when we see them murdering our dear mothers and wives, because we cannot help ourselves. Man, in all ages and all nations of the earth, is the same. . . .

The whites knowing this, they do not know what to do; they know that they have done us so much injury, they are afraid that we, being men, and not brutes, will retaliate, and woe will be to them; therefore, that dreadful fear, together with an avaricious spirit, and the natural love in them, to be called masters, (which term will yet honour them with to their sorrow) bring them to the resolve that they will keep us in ignorance and wretchedness, as long as they possibly can, and make the best of their time, while it lasts.

Consequently they, themselves, (and not us) render themselves our natural enemies, by treating us so cruel. They keep us miserable now, and call us their property, but some of them will have enough of us by and by—their stomachs shall run over with us; they want us for their slaves, and shall have us to their fill. We are all in the world together!!—I said above, because we cannot help ourselves, (viz. we cannot help the whites murdering our mothers and our wives) but this statement is incorrect—for we can help ourselves; for, if we lay aside abject servility, and be determined to act like men, and not brutes—the murderers among the whites would be afraid to show their cruel heads. . . . Oh! my coloured brethren, all over the world, when shall we arise from this death-like apathy?—And be men! . . .

Thus, we see, my brethren, the two very opposite positions of those great men, who have written respecting this "Colonizing Plan." (Mr. Clay and his slave-holding party,) men who are resolved to keep us in eternal wretchedness, are also bent upon sending us to Liberia. While the Reverend Bishop Allen, and his party, men who have the fear of God, and the welfare of their brethren at heart. The Bishop, in particular, whose labours for the salvation of his brethren, are well known to a large part of those who dwell in the United States, are completely opposed to the plan—and advise us to stay where we are. Now we have to determine whose advice we will take respecting this all important matter, whether we will adhere to Mr. Clay and his slave holding party, who have always been our oppressors and murderers, and who are for colonizing us, more through apprehension than humanity, or to this godly man who has done so much for our benefit, together with the advice of all the good and wise among us and the whites. Will any of us leave our homes and go to Africa? I hope not.

Let them commence their attack upon us as they did on our brethren in Ohio, driving and beating us from our country, and my soul for theirs, they will have enough of it. Let no man of us budge one step, and let slave-holders come to beat us from our country. America is more our country, than it is the whites—we have enriched it with our *blood and tears*. The greatest riches in all America have arisen from our blood and tears:—and will they drive us from our property and homes, which we have earned with our *blood*? They must look sharp or this very thing will bring swift destruction upon them. . . .

. . . Now let us reason—I mean you of the United States, whom I believe God designs to save from destruction, if you will hear. . . . I say, let us reason; had you not better take our body, while you have it in your power, and while we are yet ignorant and wretched, not knowing but a little, give us education, and teach us the pure religion of our Lord and Master, which is calculated to make the lion lay down in peace with the lamb, and which millions of you have beaten us nearly to death for trying to obtain since we have been among you, and thus at once, gain our affection while we are ignorant? Remember Americans, that we must and shall be free and enlightened as you are, will you wait until we shall, under God, obtain our liberty by the crushing arm of power? Will it not be dreadful for you? I speak Americans for your good. We must and shall be free I say, in spite of you. You may do your best to keep us in wretchedness and misery, to enrich you and your children; but God will deliver us from under you. And wo, wo, will be to you if we have to obtain our freedom by fighting. Throw away your fears and prejudices then, and enlighten us and treat us like men, and we will like you more than we do now hate you, and tell us now no more about colonization, for America is as much our country, as it is yours.—Treat us like men, and there is no danger but we will all live in peace and happiness together.

Chapter Four: 1831–1846

Introduction

As the decade of the 1820s came to a close, there were two million slaves in the United States and nearly three hundred thousand free blacks. Those numbers had increased threefold and fivefold, respectively, since 1790, and along with their dramatic increase came a profound change in the national debate over slavery. The rise in the free black population reflected the workings of gradual emancipation laws and the influence of Revolution principles. The growing importance of slave labor in the nineteenth century, however, greatly reduced the number of personal manumissions.

Southerners increasingly viewed free blacks as a threat to political, social, and economic stability. Fear that free blacks would foment insurrection, stoked by actual rebellions in Haiti and Virginia, led legislatures to enact restrictive manumission laws. For example, some states required legislative approval of all manumissions. Others required the master to guarantee that the freed slave would not rely on the public for support. By the mid-1830s, seven states, along with the Florida Territory, had passed laws requiring manumitted slaves to leave the state. Such statutes, the diminishing number of personal manumissions, and the relatively low number of free blacks actually colonized abroad by the American Colonization Society (ACS) severely tested the presumption that gradual manumissions combined with colonization would successfully end slavery in America.

Free blacks were also unwelcome in the free states. Ohio, Illinois, and Indiana banned immigration of free blacks; other states regulated their movements. State laws failed to protect blacks from racially motivated violence; indeed, as James Forten's *Letters from a Man of Colour* (see document 9 in Chapter 2) suggest, state laws often encouraged violence against African Americans. Between 1829 and 1845, blacks were targeted in race riots in Cincinnati, Philadelphia, New York City, and elsewhere.

As the population of free blacks in the North grew, they were increasingly the focus of discriminatory legislation. State laws restricted the types of trades blacks could enter. In 1833 Connecticut passed legislation to prevent Prudence Crandall from educating African American women. New states like Ohio denied blacks the right to vote, while existing states revised their codes to severely limit or rescind entirely the right of blacks to vote. When the Pennsylvania constitutional convention considered similar electoral reform in 1837, Robert Purvis published his *Appeal of Forty Thousand Citizens, Threatened with Disfranchisement.* "Why should tax-paying colored men, any more than other tax-payers, be deprived of the right of voting for their representatives?" he asked. "It was said in the Convention, that this government belongs to the *Whites.*" Purvis rejected this claim. "We lay hold of the principles which Pennsylvania asserted in the hour which tried men's souls— which BENJAMIN FRANKLIN and his eight colleagues, in name of the commonwealth, pledged their lives, their fortunes, and their sacred honor to sustain." Moreover, stripped of the franchise, free blacks would be even more vulnerable to kidnapping by Southern slave catchers. The proposed change, he concluded, marked "the first step towards re-imposing the chains which have now rusted for more than fifty years."[1]

Purvis' comment is revealing. It suggests that for many people committed to ending slavery, the promise of the Missouri Compromise was in jeopardy. No one would be more struck by this loss of faith, or by the belief that a gradual approach to emancipation was morally indefensible, than William Lloyd Garrison. Initially, Garrison supported the ACS and gradual emancipation. By 1829, however, when he partnered with Benjamin Lundy in publishing the abolitionist newspaper, the *Genius of Universal Emancipation,* Garrison was poised to renounce colonization entirely. In a September 2, 1829, editorial, Garrison declared that time had proven colonization was not itself a remedy for slavery. In fact, he warned that reliance on colonization to end slavery would perpetuate the institution. "Crafty advocates of slavery," he wrote, "rejoice at [the popular] delusion" that the ACS was capable of ending slavery.[2]

By 1829, Garrison was voicing most of the positions that as founder, editor, and publisher of *The Liberator* he would advocate forcefully for the next thirty-five years. In a Fourth of July address he delivered earlier that year at Boston's Park Street Church, Garrison called slavery "a gangrene preying upon our vitals—an earthquake rumbling under our feet—a mine accumulating materials for a national catastrophe." He reminded the audience that "all men are born equal." "I am sick of our unmeaning declamation in praise of liberty and equality," he added, and "of our hypocritical cant about the unalienable rights of man." He observed that racial prejudice in the North was stronger than in the South: "Conquer [that Northern prejudice], and the victory [over slavery] is won." Moreover, he asserted that the free states "are constitutionally involved in the guilt of slavery, by adhering to a national compact that

---

1. Robert Purvis, *Appeal of Forty Thousand Citizens, Threatened with Disfranchisement to the People of Pennsylvania* (Philadelphia: Merrihew & Gunn, 1838), 9, 17–18.
2. William Lloyd Garrison, "To the Public," *Genius of Universal Emancipation* (September 2, 1829), in *William Lloyd Garrison, 1805–1879: The Story of His Life as Told by His Children*, vol. 1, *1805–1835*, ed. Wendell Phillips Garrison (Houghton, Mifflin and Company, 1889), 142–44; the quote is located on 143.

sanctions it," and "that they have the right to remonstrate against its continuance, and it is their duty to assist in its overthrow." He concluded that "this monstrous inequality should no longer be tolerated"; that it must be "speedily put down—not by force, but by fair persuasion"; and that "if we must share in the guilt and danger of destroying the bodies and souls of men, *as the price of our Union,* if the slave States will haughtily spurn our assistance, and refuse to consult the general welfare, then the fault is not ours if a separation eventually take place."[3]

On January 1, 1831, in the first issue of *The Liberator,* Garrison announced a significant change in his thoughts on slavery: he now and forever renounced the doctrine of gradual abolition. As he noted in his opening remarks "To the Public," he asked "pardon of my God, of my country, and of my brethren the poor slaves," for having earlier supported colonization, a doctrine he condemned as "full of timidity, injustice and absurdity." He then added some of the most frequently reprinted words in American history:

> I am aware, that many object to the severity of my language; but is there not cause for severity? I *will* be as harsh as truth, and as uncompromising as justice. On this subject, I do not wish to think, or speak, or write, with moderation. No! no! Tell a man whose house is on fire, to give a moderate alarm; tell him to moderately rescue his wife from the hands of the ravisher; tell the mother to gradually extricate her babe from the fire into which it has fallen;— but urge me not to use moderation in a cause like the present. I am in earnest—I will not equivocate—I will not excuse—I will not retreat a single inch—AND I WILL BE HEARD.[4]

In this and subsequent issues, Garrison would proclaim in full-throated voice the major positions he would maintain until slavery was abolished: the reliance on moral persuasion as the means to ending slavery; the rejection of coercion as a legitimate means to combating slavery—even by slaves in response to their condition; the denunciation of the Constitution as a pro-slavery document; the rejection of political activities such as voting and holding office, since such activities required compromise on the question of slavery while lending legitimacy to the Constitution; a call for greater rights for women as well as blacks, and for women to play a more public role as advocates for those causes; and the insistence that the moral purity of the individual (and of the free states) takes precedence over the continued existence of the Union.

---

3. William Lloyd Garrison, "Address at Park Street Church" (July 4, 1829), ibid., 128–30, 132–33, 136.
4. William Lloyd Garrison, "To the Public," *The Liberator* I, no. 1 (January 1, 1831), 1.

Garrisonian abolitionists committed to "immediate abolition," a term that caused confusion and consternation. The ambiguity of the term, and the Garrisonian tendency to publicly harangue and rebuke, led people to misconstrue what immediate abolition stood for. The Garrisonians were often accused of fomenting slave rebellion and for supporting the use of extra-constitutional means to achieve their goal, a claim they vehemently denied. As John Greenleaf Whittier explained, Garrisonian abolitionists rejected "talk of *gradual* abolition, because, as Christians, we find no authority for advocating a *gradual relinquishment of sin*. We say to slaveholders—'Repent NOW—*today*—IMMEDIATELY;'—just as we say to the intemperate—'Break off from vice *at once*.'" Garrisonians opposed "any *political interposition* of the Government, in regard to slavery as it exists in the *States*," he explained, because they considered "any such interference . . . unlawful and unconstitutional." Instead, they aimed "to overthrow slavery by the moral influence of an enlightened public sentiment," which they would accomplish through relentless appeals from the pulpit and the press, appeals that would persistently and insistently invoke the "commands of God," and fearlessly expose "the GUILT of holding *property in man*."[5] This evangelical zeal, this unwavering faith in the effectiveness of moral appeals, gave the Garrisonians a profound sense of purpose.

That zeal, the rapid growth in their numbers, their commitment to immediate abolition, to ending race prejudice, and to political and civil equality provoked intense and hostile response. In many cases, the response came at the hands of racist and pro-slavery mobs. Abolitionist editors like James Birney had their presses destroyed by raging anti-abolitionist mobs; others, like Elijah Lovejoy, lost their lives along with their presses. Routinely called fanatics by their detractors, abolitionist meetings were attacked by mobs; their speakers were assaulted (Garrison himself was dragged through the streets of Boston and nearly lynched by a mob); bounties were placed on their heads; and their publications were seized by mobs and then suppressed by the U.S. Post Office. Even moderate anti-slavery advocates, like Leonard Bacon and Catharine Beecher, rebuked the Garrisonians for both the substance and tone of their arguments.

The Garrisonians eventually encountered their own internal divisions. Some members, including Arthur Tappan and Theodore S. Wright, broke with Garrison over his position on the role of women in public affairs and his criticism of American religious institutions over the slavery question. Other members, including Birney and Whittier, eventually concluded that political action in addition to moral appeals was essential to ending slavery, and in 1839 they formed the Liberty Party (Birney was its first presidential nominee). A rift also opened over constitutional interpretation, with some abolitionists, like

---

5. John Greenleaf Whittier, "Whittier's Reply," *The Liberator* III, no. 33 (August 17, 1833), 1.

Lysander Spooner and Alvan Stewart, contending that the Constitution was an anti-slavery document.[6] That claim contributed to renewed controversy in Congress regarding the national government's authority over slavery, particularly in the nation's capital.

The various attacks on slavery elicited an equally vigorous defense of slavery. Particularly noteworthy was the claim made by Thomas Dew and others that slavery was consistent with republican government. Indeed, in the South there was a "perfect spirit of equality" precisely because the "menial and low offices" were performed by blacks. "Color alone is here the badge of distinction," Dew explained, "and all who are white are equal in spite of the variety of occupation."[7] Moreover, this democracy for whites, based on the forced labor of blacks, was beneficial to the slaves as well. Southerners like Dew depicted free blacks as lazy and unproductive. Lacking direction and initiative, they would become a burden and a danger to the public. They were described as naturally inferior to and incapable of competing economically with whites. Politically and morally they were unsuited to the responsibilities of self-government. However, as slaves they were—it was argued—nourished and well kept; their labors were not hard and they were happy, even carefree. "In a word," South Carolina governor George McDuffie declared, "our slaves are cheerful, contented, and happy, much beyond the general condition of the human race except where those foreign intruders and fatal ministers of mischief, the emancipationists, have tempted them to aspire above the condition to which they have been assigned in the order of providence."[8]

Fantastic as these claims were, they were not unprecedented. But now they grew commonplace among slavery's apologists, and the frequency and insistence with which they were asserted were indeed new. The defense of slavery was no longer excusatory; it had transformed into advocacy of an institution more to be unabashedly promoted than reluctantly defended, a social good to be embraced rather than a necessary evil and unfortunate inheritance to be managed. Now, as John Calhoun famously announced in Congress, slavery "was a good—a great good."[9] Accordingly, for the first time, slavery's advocates, like Governor McDuffie, voiced the intent to maintain slavery in perpetuity. "No patriot who justly estimates our privileges will tolerate the idea of emancipation, at any period, however remote, or on any conditions of pecuniary advantage, however favorable," McDuffie announced.[10] For as James Henry Hammond explained, "Slavery can never be abolished. The doom of Ham has

---

6. See document 13 in this chapter.
7. See document 1 in this chapter.
8. See document 7 in this chapter.
9. See document 11 in this chapter.
10. See document 7 in this chapter.

been branded on the form and features of his African descendants. The hand of fate has united his color and his destiny."[11]

DOCUMENTS

1. Thomas R. Dew, *A Review of the Debate in the Virginia Legislature of 1831 and 1832* (1832)

In reaction to the Nat Turner Rebellion, the Virginia legislature opened discussions on the question of emancipation. In response, Thomas Dew argued that colonization was impractical and, therefore, that slavery must be perpetuated. He depicts free blacks as inherently lazy, preferring a brutish life to the industry of "civilized" man. Dew further claims that emancipation would not bring legal or social equality. Long-engrained habits and prejudices would determine social and political arrangements; free blacks would consequently lead disappointing lives and foment insurrections. Finally, Dew rejects Jefferson's claim that slavery is inimical to republican government.

. . . It is well known, that during the last summer, in the county of Southampton in Virginia, a few slaves, led on by Nat Turner, rose in the night, and murdered in the most inhuman and shocking manner, between sixty and seventy of the unsuspecting whites of that county. The news, of course, was rapidly diffused, and with it consternation and dismay were spread throughout the State, destroying for a time all feeling of security and confidence; and even when subsequent development had proved, that the conspiracy had been originated by a fanatical negro preacher, (whose confessions prove beyond a doubt mental aberration,) and that this conspiracy embraced but few slaves, all of whom had paid the penalty of their crimes, still the excitement remained. . . . In this state of excitement and unallayed apprehension, the Legislature met, and plans for abolition were proposed and earnestly advocated in debate. . . .

1st. Emancipation without Deportation.

. . . As we believe the scheme of deportation utterly impracticable, we have come to the conclusion that in the present great question, the real and decisive

---

11. See document 10 in this chapter.

line of conduct is either abolition [of slavery] without removal, or a steady perseverance in the system now established. . . .

. . . Much was said in the legislature of Virginia about superiority of free labor over slave, and perhaps under certain circumstances this might be true; but in the present instance, the question is between *the relative amounts of labor which may be obtained from slaves before and after their emancipation.* Let us then first commence with our country, where it is well known to everybody, that slave labor is vastly more efficient and productive, than the labor of free blacks.

Taken as a whole class, the latter must be considered the most worthless and indolent of the citizens of the United States. It is well known that throughout the whole extent of our Union, they are looked upon as the very *drones* and *pests* of society. Nor does this character arise from the disabilities and disfranchisement by which the law attempts to guard against them. In the non-slave-holding states, where they have been more elevated by law, this kind of population is in a worse condition and much more troublesome to society, than in the slave holding, and especially in the planting states. Look through all the Northern States, and mark the class upon whom the eye of the police is most steadily and constantly kept—see with what vigilance and care they are hunted down from place to place—and you cannot fail to see, that idleness and improvidence are at the root of all their misfortunes. . . .

. . . Why . . . are our colored free men so generally indolent and worthless among the industrious and enterprising citizens of even our northern and New-England states? . . . It is because there is an inherent and intrinsic cause at work, which will produce its effect under all circumstances. In the free black, the principle of idleness and dissipation triumphs over that of accumulation and the desire to better our condition; the animal part of the man gains the victory over the moral; and he consequently prefers sinking down into the listless inglorious repose of the brute creation, to rising to that energetic activity which can only be generated amid the multiplied, refined and artificial wants of civilized society. The very conception which nine slaves in ten have of liberty, is that of idleness and sloth with the enjoyment of plenty; and we are not to wonder that they should hasten to practice upon their theory so soon as liberated. . . .

[T]here are other circumstances which must not be omitted in an enumeration of the obstacles to emancipation. The blacks have now all the habits and feelings of slaves, the whites have those of masters; the prejudices are formed, and mere legislation cannot remove them. . . . Declare the negroes of the South free to-morrow, and vain will be your decree until you have prepared them for it; you depress, instead of elevating. The law would, in every point of view, be one of the most cruel and inhumane which could possibly be passed. The law would make them freemen, and custom or prejudice . . . would degrade them to the condition of slaves. . . . [I]n the southern states the condition of the free blacks is better than in the northern; in the latter he is told that he is a freeman and entirely equal to the white, and prejudice assigns to him a degraded station. . . . He consequently leads a life of endless mortification and disappointment. . . . In the southern states, law and custom more generally coincide; the former makes no profession which the latter does not sanction, and consequently the free black has nothing to grieve and disappoint him.

[I]f we were to liberate the slaves, we could not, in fact, alter their condition—they would still be virtually slaves; talent, habit, and wealth, would make the white the master still, and the emancipation would only have the tendency to deprive him of those sympathies and kind feelings for the black which now characterize him. . . .

The great evil, however, of these schemes of emancipation, remains yet to be told. They are admirably calculated to excite plots, murders, and insurrections. . . . In the . . . case [of gradual emancipation], you disturb the quiet and contentment of the slave who is left unemancipated; and he becomes the midnight murderer to gain that fatal freedom whose blessings he does not comprehend. In the . . . case [of rapid emancipation], want and invidious distinction will prompt to revenge. [H]is idleness will produce want and worthlessness, and his very worthlessness and degradation will stimulate him to deeds of rapine and vengeance; he will oftener engage in plots and massacres, and thereby draw down on his devoted head the vengeance of the provoked whites. . . .

III. Injustice and Evils of Slavery.

. . .

2dly. [I]t is further said that the moral effects of slavery are of the most deleterious and hurtful kind. . . .

Let us now look a moment to the slave, and contemplate his position. Mr. Jefferson has described him as hating, rather than loving his master, and as losing, too, all that amor patria which characterizes the true patriot. . . . We assert . . . that Mr. Jefferson is not borne out by the fact. We are well convinced that there is nothing but the mere relations of husband and wife, parent and child, brother and sister, which produce a closer tie, than the relation of master and servant. We have no hesitation in affirming, that throughout the whole slave holding country, the slaves of a good master, are his warmest, most constant, and most devoted friends; they have been accustomed to look up to him as their supporter, director and defender. Every one acquainted with southern slaves, knows that the slave rejoices in the elevation and prosperity of his master; and the heart of no one is more gladdened at the successful debut of young master or miss on the great theatre of the world, than that of either the young slave who has grown up with them, and shared in all their sports, and even partaken of all their delicacies—or the aged one who has looked on and watched them from birth to manhood, with the kindest and most affectionate solicitude, and has ever met from them, all the kind treatment and generous sympathies of feeling tender hearts. We have often heard slaveholders affirm, that they would sooner rely upon their slaves for fidelity and attachment in the hour of danger and severe trial, than on any other equal number of individuals; and we all know, that the son or daughter, who has been long absent from the paternal roof, on returning to the scenes of infancy, never fails to be greeted with the kindest welcome and the most sincere and heartfelt congratulations from those slaves among whom he has been reared to manhood. . . .

3dly. . . . It has been contended that slavery is unfavorable to a republican spirit: but the whole history of the world proves that this is far from being the case. . . . Another, and perhaps more efficient cause of this, is the perfect spirit of equality so prevalent among the whites of all the slave holding states. . . . The menial and low offices being all performed by the blacks, there is at once taken away the greatest cause of distinction and separation of the ranks of society. The man to the north will not shake hands familiarly with his servant, and converse, and laugh, and dine with him, no matter how honest and respectable he may be. But go to the south, and you will find that no white man feels such inferiority of rank as to be unworthy of association with those around him. Color alone is here the badge of distinction, the true mark of aristocracy, and all who are white are equal in spite of the variety of occupation. . . .

2. Elizur Wright, Jr., *The Sin of Slavery and Its Remedy* (1833)

Following Garrison's lead, Elizur Wright, Jr. (1804–1885) argued for racial equality, an end to race prejudice, and immediate abolition, using moral appeals to persuade slave owners to acknowledge their sin of slaveholding and to accept their duty to secure justice for their victims. Wright argues that immediate abolition is safe: free blacks would be industrious, and they would not seek vengeance against their former masters. By the late 1830s, Wright joined those who argued for political action beyond Garrison's "moral suasion" in behalf of the abolitionist cause.

. . . UNDER THE GOVERNMENT of God, as exhibited in this world, there is but one remedy for sin, and that is available only by a *repentance*, evidenced by reformation. There is no such thing as holding on to sin with safety. It is not only to be renounced, but the very occasions of it are to be avoided at whatever sacrifice. If thy right hand cause thee to offend, cut it off—if thy right eye, pluck it out. . . . The doctrine of immediate abolition of slavery asks no better authority than is offered by scripture. It is in perfect harmony with the letter and spirit of God's word.

The doctrine may be thus briefly stated. It is the duty of the holders of slaves immediately to restore to them their liberty. . . . It is their duty equitably to restore to them those profits of their labor, which have been wickedly wrested away, especially by giving them that moral and mental instruction—that education, which alone can render any considerable accumulation of property a blessing. It is their duty to employ them as voluntary laborers, on equitable wages. Also, it is the duty of all men to proclaim this doctrine—to urge upon slave-holders *immediate emancipation*, so long as there is a slave—to agitate the consciences of tyrants, so long as there is a tyrant on the globe.

Though this doctrine does not depend, in regard to the slave-holder, upon the safety of immediate emancipation, nor, in regard to the non-slave-holder, on the prospect of accomplishing any abolition at all, but upon the commands of God, yet . . . I am willing to rest the cause on the truth of the following propositions. . . .

1. Immediate abolition is safe.

. . . The immediate abolition of slavery is safe, because, without giving to the slaves any motives to injure their masters, it would take away from them the very strong ones which they now have. Why does the white mother quake at the rustling of a leaf? Why, but that she is conscious that there are those around her, who have been deeply enough provoked to imbrue their hands in her blood, and in that of the tender infant at her breast. And this, while all is cringing servility around her—while every want is anticipated, and the most menial services are performed with apparent delight. But well she knows that it is a counterfeit delight. Well enough she knows, that were *she* subjected to the same degradation to which she subjects others, vengeance would fire her heart, and seek the first occasion to do its fellest deed. . . .

. . . Immediate emancipation would reverse the picture. It would place a motive to love you in the room of every one which now urges the slaves to hate you. . . . Your fields which now lie sterile, or produce but half the crop, because the whip of the driver, although it may secure its motion, cannot give force to the Negro's hoe, would then smile beneath the plough of the freeman—the genial influence of just and equitable wages. . . . Your own estates would be worth double the cash. . . .

Holders of stolen men! Do you still point us to the degraded free blacks of the South, and say they are more miserable than the slaves? We deny the assertion. We appeal to yourselves whether there be any suffering even unto death which you would not endure rather than be slaves—rather than be fed and fattened slaves—rather than to wear a single link of a slave's chain—rather than to submit to slavery even in the abstract principle, apart from all matters of reality. . . .

But what if it were true, that the free black at the South is more miserable than the slave? It would be no argument against that sort of emancipation for which we plead. We plead for no *turning loose, no exile, no kicking out of house and home, but for complete and hearty* JUSTICE. Justice requires that the masters . . . should follow up their acts of emancipation by giving *employment* and affording the means of *education*. . . . We hold the masters bound, individually and in the aggregate, first to LIBERATE and then to ENLIGHTEN the IMMORTAL MINDS that have been abused and debased by their avarice and lust! . . .

2. The firm expression of an enlightened public opinion on the part of non-slave-holders, in favor of instant abolition, is an effectual, and the only effectual, means of securing abolition in any time whatsoever.

Others exclaim, "But how can your scheme of *immediate, instant abolition* be practicable? Can a handful of northern men, or even the combined North, expect to overturn southern society from its foundation in a *moment?*— in the *twinkling of an eye?* What fools! Forsooth you will do nothing against slavery, unless you can do everything, all at once! Heaven deliver *us* from such Quixotism! We are for the gradual abolition, for not attempting more than we can effect." . . .

Now if I may be allowed to make a distinction too elementary to be overlooked by an infant, a doctrine is one thing, and a plan is another. When we say that slave-holders ought all to emancipate their slaves *immediately*, we state a *doctrine* which is *true*. We do not propose a *plan*. Our *plan* . . . is simply this: To promulgate the true *doctrine* of human rights in high places and low places, and all places where there are human beings. . . . Let those who contemn this plan, renounce, if they have not done it already, the Gospel plan for converting the world. . . .

By prosecuting the plan described, we *expect* to see the benevolent, one by one at first, and afterwards in dense masses, awaking, gathering up their armor and rushing to the standard with the resolution to make up for lost time; we expect to see, at length, the full tide of public sympathy setting in favor of the slave. We expect to see him, when escaped from his cruel servitude, greeted by the friends of liberty, at the North. . . . We expect to see the free colored American so educated and elevated in our own land, that it shall be notorious that the slave is BROTHER TO A MAN! In the meantime, we expect to see the great body of slave-holders exasperated, foaming with rage and gnashing their teeth, threatening loudly to secede from the Union! Madly prating about the invasion of sacred rights, the disturbance of their domestic quiet, and the violation of solemn compacts; and with blind infatuation, riveting tighter the fetters of their helpless victims. Nevertheless, we expect to *see* some tyrants, conscience-stricken, loosen their grasp; we expect, with God's good help, to hear the trumpet of the world's jubilee announcing that the *last fetter* has been knocked off from the heel of the *last slave*. . . .

3. Leonard Bacon, "The Abolition of Slavery," in *Slavery Discussed in Occasional Essays, from 1833 to 1846* (first published in the *Quarterly Christian Spectator*, 1833)

In this review of a series of lectures by the abolitionist Amos A. Phelps, Congregational theologian and writer Leonard Bacon (1802–1881) presents a moderate voice on the issue of slaveholding. Like other moderates, Bacon did not necessarily view slaveholding as sinful; he did, however, look forward to the eventual end of the institution, linking the duties of masters to that end, while charging abolitionists like Phelps with recklessly undermining that goal.

It cannot be doubted, that much of the dispute which exists at the present time among those who are seeking the extinction of slavery, is to be ascribed to some mutual misunderstanding in regard to the import of terms. One class of philanthropists . . . insist on what they call the immediate, unqualified, complete abolition of slavery. Another class, whose philanthropy is equally unquestionable, think that though the immediate and universal emancipation of two millions of slaves may be better than the perpetuity of slavery, a progressive and gradual subversion of the fabric of society now existing in the southern States would be much more desirable, as respects the well-being of both the slaves and their masters, and as respects all those great interests of the human race, which are confessedly involved in the result. . . .

The first thing necessary to the adjustment of the controversy, between the two parties of those who cherish a common enmity against slavery, is, that we have a distinct and right understanding of the terms "abolition" and "emancipation," as they are used in this controversy. . . .

We have before us, in the "Preamble and Constitution of the Anti-Slavery Society of Lane Seminary," the following "exposition of immediate emancipation. . . ."

> "By immediate emancipation, we do not mean that the slaves shall be turned loose upon the nation, to roam as vagabonds and aliens—nor
>
> That they shall be instantly invested with all political rights and privileges—nor
>
> That they shall be expelled from their native land to a foreign clime, as the price and condition of their freedom.
>
> But we *do* mean—that instead of being under the unlimited control of a few irresponsible masters, they shall really receive the protection of law;
>
> That the power which is invested in every slaveholder, to rob them of their just dues, to drive them into the field like beasts, to lacerate their bodies, to sell the husband from his wife, the wife from her husband, and children from their parents, shall instantly cease;
>
> That the slaves shall be employed as free laborers, fairly compensated and protected in their earnings;
>
> That they shall be placed under a benevolent or disinterested supervision, which shall secure to them the right to obtain secular and religious knowledge, to worship God according to the dictates of their consciences, and to seek an intellectual and moral equality with the whites."

In this definition . . . the only particular which implies emancipation at all, in the sense of investing the slaves with freedom, is the demand, "that the slaves shall be employed as free laborers." That expression, taken by itself, might be understood to mean, that they are to be immediately free to labor or not to labor at their pleasure, free to find employment for themselves according to their liking, and free to dispose of their earnings according to their own discretion. But against such a construction, the writers seem to have guarded at the outset, by saying, "We do not mean, that the slaves shall be turned loose upon the nation, to roam as vagabonds and aliens." In other words, they do not mean, that the slaves are to be immediately invested with self-control.

This, if we understand the meaning of words, is not immediate emancipation. The slave . . . is not emancipated, till he becomes a free man. You may make the master responsible, and limit his power. You may take the slave out of the power of his master entirely, and put him under an overseer appointed by the public. You may do for his physical comfort, for his protection, for his instruction, whatever seems needful. But he is not emancipated, till he goes forth, like the freed apprentice at the expiration of his indentures, his own master, "loose to roam" whithersoever he pleases. . . .

. . . "Slavery," [Mr. Phelps] tells us . . . means simply, "holding man as property"—simply holding and treating a rational and accountable creature of God, a brother of the human family, as a thing without rights, a mere article of merchandise. The thing, then, which is to be immediately abolished, and the extinction of which is all that is necessarily meant by immediate abolition, if Mr. Phelps' definition of slavery is a true one, is nothing else than the practice of owning men, or rather of assuming and claiming to own them, as chattels. . . .

. . . Our notion of the abolition of slavery, is the ENTIRE DESTRUCTION of that artificial constitution of society, which takes away from one man the power of self-control, and puts him under the protection and control of another. The immediate emancipation of a slave by his master, is the instantaneous dissolution of the relation in that individual instance. The immediate abolition of slavery, in a state or country, is the instantaneous dissolution of that relation between all the masters and all the slaves, by some sudden violence, or by some act of legislation. While the slave is passing through a period of pupilage, controlled by the discretion of another, his emancipation may be in progress, but it is not complete. While the slaves of a country are considered by the law as not yet fully competent to the responsibility of directing their own movements and employments, so long—though the process of abolition may be going forward with great rapidity, and though the result may be as sure as the progress of time, and though the statute-book may have fixed the date at which the slaves shall be left to their own discretion—slavery is not completely abolished.

In taking our stand, then, against immediate emancipation . . . we do not oppose what Mr. Phelps, and men like him, of logical and calculating minds, argue for, under those names. As for the thing which alone they profess to recognize as slavery, we hold it to be invariably sinful. As for the thing, which, when they attempt to speak accurately, they call emancipation, we hold it to be the plainest and first duty of every master. As for the thing, which they describe as the meaning of immediate abolition, we hold it to be, not only practicable and safe, but the very first thing to be done for the safety of a slave-holding country. The immediate abolition against which we protest, as perilous to the Commonwealth and unjust to the slaves, is a different thing from that which the immediate abolitionists think they are urging on the country.

Why, then, dispute about words . . . ? We answer, because words in such a case are not mere breath, but things, and things of great importance in their effect on the public mind, and in their effect on those who use them. . . . [T]here is, in their use of terms, a certain logical sleight-of-hand, which perplexes, irritates and inflames the public, and . . . [which] tends to embitter their philanthropy, and to turn their sense of right into something too much like rancor.

The sophism by which they unwittingly impose on their own minds, and inflame the minds of others, is this: the terms "slavery," "slaveholding," "immediate emancipation," &c., [have] one meaning in their definitions, and . . . another meaning in their denunciations and popular harangues. Thus they define a slaveholder to be one who claims and treats his fellow-men as property—as things—as destitute of all personal rights; one, in a word, whose criminality is self-evident. But the moment they begin to speak of slave-holders in the way of declamation, the word . . . denotes any man who stands in the relation of overseer and governor to those whom the law has constituted slaves; and consequently every man who, in the meaning of the laws, or in the mean-ing of common parlance, is a slave-holder, is denounced, with unmeasured expressions of abhorrence and hate, as an enemy of the species. What is the effect of this on their own minds? What—on the minds of those who happen, from one cause or another, to be ripe for factious and fanatical excitement against the south? What—on the minds of those who, without unraveling the sophistry of the case, know that many a slaveholder is conscientious, and does regard his slaves as brethren? What—on the minds of those slaveholders them-selves, who are conscious of no such criminality? So of immediate emancipa-tion. They define that to be an immediate cessation from the sin of claiming and treating men as chattels; but when they begin to urge this duty, in appeals to popular feeling, the phrase "immediate emancipation," cannot be hindered from meaning an immediate discharge of the slave from all special guardian-ship and government, and his immediate investiture with the power of self-control. This, they are understood to mean by the great mass of those who hear them, and this they do actually imply in many of their appeals. . . .

. . . And what is the effect? The public understands them as demanding immediate and complete emancipation, in the obvious meaning of the terms; and the public at large, north and south, east and west, denounces them as visionary and reckless agitators. Hence it is, that even in those States where the hatred of slavery is most pervading and most intense, the call for an immediate abolition meeting, is so often the signal for some demonstration of popular indignation. . . .

We know it is often said, that any doctrine short of immediate emancipation, puts the conscience of the slaveholder asleep, and justifies him in transmitting slavery unmitigated to another generation. But nothing can be more unwar-ranted than such an assertion. The duty of *immediate emancipation* is one thing. The *immediate duty* of emancipation is another thing. That duty, the present duty of beginning the emancipation of his slaves . . . which shall infallibly result in their complete liberation, at the earliest date consistent with their well-being, may be urged at once on every slaveholder as a direct and indisputable corollary from the great law of love. Such a process, under whatever form it may be commenced, must imply at the outset, that, in the estimation of the master at least, the slave is no longer a chattel, but a person; no longer a thing, but a man, invested with the majesty of God's image, and endowed with the rights that belong to God's intelligent and accountable creature.

Here, then, let the public sentiment of the country speak out for the emancipation of slaves, and for the abolition of slavery. This is the gradual abolition which we stand ready always to advocate. . . . Let it be everywhere insisted on, as the first point to be carried, that to hold men as property, to claim them, and use them, and dispose of them, as things without personality, and without rights, is a sin, with which neither humanity nor religion can have any compromise. . . . On this point, the feeling in the free states is unanimous, and has been for these forty years. . . .

Nor will it be found impracticable to discuss this point at the south, or to convince even slaveholders of the wrong of claiming their slaves as "property, in the same sense with their brood mares. . . ." It is not impracticable; for there are hundreds of masters there, who are convinced already, and who act on the conviction, that they stand to their slaves, not in the relation of ownership over property, but in the relation of guardianship and government over men, intelligent, and invested by the God of nature with the rights of humanity, yet ignorant, dependent, and, but for the master, defenceless. By the power, not indeed of heat, and smoke, and fury, but of light and love, that conviction may be made to spread, till, having first pervaded the churches there of every denomination, it shall become the strong conviction of the popular mind. . . . Then will the keystone of the mighty fabric of oppression have been taken away; and legislation will have begun, effectually, the abolition of slavery. . . .

4. Richard H. Colfax, *Evidence against the Views of the Abolitionists, Consisting of Physical and Moral Proofs, of the Natural Inferiority of the Negroes* (1833)

Richard Colfax, adopting a prime example of scientific racism, argues for polygenesis—that is, a theory that the races represent distinct species. This was a claim disputed even by other pro-slavery apologists. Colfax justifies the enslavement of Africans by claiming that the attributes of the African intellect are brutish and, consequently, that blacks are incapable of self-government. The reference near the beginning is to Samuel Thomas von

Sömmerring (1755–1830), who, like many scientists of his day, literally thought that the blood of blacks was darker than the blood of whites. Thus the quote from Thomas Jefferson is not merely moral or metaphysical—the "stain" from intermarriage was physiological, and would introduce into whites the "natural . . . depravity" associated with blacks,[12] a claim that Colfax and many others shared. We've retained the spellings of the original documents.

[T]he chief arguments of the "total abolitionists" are grounded upon the supposition, 1st, That negroes and white men belong to one and the same species, and 2d, that their known want of intellect and mental capacity arises from their deficiency of education and from the peculiar habits that slavery has entailed upon them. The inferences from which are 1st that they should be placed upon a public, as well as private footing of equality with white men; and 2nd, that an exemption from the above deteriorating causes will shew the pristine equality of negro intellect with that of white men.

[W]e feel ourselves competent to overturn the premises of such writers. . . .

This can be done quite effectually . . . by demonstrating to the public, that the physical and mental differences between negroes and white men, are sufficient to warrant us in affirming that they have descended from distinct origins, and that therefore no alteration of the social condition of the negro can be expected to create any change in his *nature*. . . .

[T]he most important conclusions upon this subject, will be drawn from a view of the development of the negro brain, nerves and intellect, as compared with the white man, comprising the

MENTAL DISTINCTIONS

Professor Soemmering long since demonstrated, that the nerves of the negro were much larger than those of white men, and that, in this respect, the negroes make a close approach towards the nature of the inferior classes of animals. For it is an established axiom, that in proportion as the nerves are largely developed, so do the animal attributes exceed the powers of intellect. For that portion of the brain which presides over the organic or animal functions, and from which the nerves have their more immediate origin, will, in the same ratio, exceed in size the superior or thinking portion. . . .

. . . Furthermore, although we are not believers in *physiognomy*, (as a science,) yet we cannot avoid making a remark upon the negro's face, which may not be entirely overlooked. . . .

His lips are thick, his zygomatic muscles, large and full,—his jaws large and projecting,—his chin retreating,—his forehead low, flat, and slanting, and

---

12. See document 10 in Chapter 1.

(as a consequence of this latter character,) his eyeballs are very prominent,—apparently larger than those of white men;—all of these peculiarities at the same time contributing to reduce his *facial angle* almost to a level with that of the brute.—Can any such man become great or elevated?—the history of the Africans will give a decisive answer. . . .

If then it is consistent with science, to believe that the mind will be great in proportion to the size and figure of the brain it is equally reasonable to suppose, that the acknowledged meanness of the negroe's intellect, only coincides with the shape of his head; or in other words, that *his want of capability to receive a complicated education renders it improper and impolitic, that he should be allowed the privileges of citizenship in an enlightened country*! It is in vain for the Amalgamationists to tell us that the negroes have had no opportunity to improve, or have had less opportunities than European nations; the public are well aware that three or four thousand years could not have passed away, without throwing advantages in the way of the Africans; yet in all this time, with every advantage that liberty, and their proximity to refined nations could bestow, they have never even *attempted* to raise themselves above their present equivocal station, in the great zoological chain. . . .

If their physical organization will continually prevent them from attaining a level with the whites, how unreasonable is it in those enemies to our country, called "abolitionists," to unloose within the bosom of this now happy community, a . . . race incapable of receiving education and of comprehending the terrors of religion, much less of perceiving the value of our majestic system of Law. But more than this, when it is objected to this proposal that if it should go into effect we would eternally have our prisons filled and our public charities consumed because of the inability of the negroes to obtain respectable employments, (the result of a well founded prejudice,) it is further proposed that the two races should by intermarriage &c. amalgamate with each other. Would it not be as reasonable to expect the negroes to amalgamate with that equally valuable race of inferiors—the orang-outangs?

The negroes themselves could not feel more righteous indignation at this latter proposal, than we do at the other. "Among the Romans," observes Mr. Jefferson, "emancipation required but *one effort.* The slave, when made free, might mix with, without *staining* the blood of his master. But with us a second is necessary, unknown to history, *When freed he is to be removed beyond the reach of mixture.*" But how agreeably and no less ingeniously have the devout members of the Anti-slavery Society removed all difficulties, "Liberate the negroe *first*," they exclaim, "consider upon the ways, means, and expediency afterwards, and lastly make him by marriage, or otherwise, one of your family." Truly, by complying with this advice, we should after the lapse of a few generations, could we live as long, behold a promising race, having about as much affinity to the present Americans, as the offspring of an African and an orang outang would to a negro. . . .

Perhaps our reasons for showing how many physical and moral arguments there are against the supposition, that the negro race ever will improve, are now more obvious; it may be thought that we wish to keep alive old prejudices, which is partly true; for, although we do not wish to create any rancorous hatred against the negroes, yet it is but proper that they should be viewed according to the intention of nature. . . . —Who does not compassionate [*sic*] the mixture of natural and acquired depravity, which renders the negro when free, far worse than when in chains, an enemy to himself, and a curse to others? . . .

. . . Now if it can be proved that by giving the negroe his liberty we actually do him an injury, it is obvious to us that it is more an act of piety to keep him in slavery—in which situation no one can deny that there is less inducement to crime, for by being well employed he is kept beyond the reach of temptation. . . .

5. Elijah Lovejoy, "To My Fellow Citizens," St. Louis *Observer* (November 5, 1835)

Following warnings from his fellow residents of St. Louis, Missouri, directing him to suppress his criticism of slavery, to which he responds below, abolitionist Elijah Lovejoy (1802–1837) was murdered while defending his print shop against a pro-slavery mob.

. . . [H]ad I desired to send a copy of the *Emancipator* or of any other newspaper to Jefferson City, I should not have taken the pains to box it up. I am not aware that any law of my country forbids my sending what document I please to a friend or citizen. I know, indeed, that mob law has decided otherwise, and that it has become fashionable in certain parts of this country, to break open the Post Office, and take from it such documents as the mob should decide, ought not to pass unburned. But I had never imagined there was a sufficiency of respectability attached to the good citizens of my own state. And grievously and sadly shall I be disappointed to find it otherwise.

In fine, I wish it to be distinctly understood that I have never, knowingly, to the best of my recollections, sent a single copy of the *Emancipator* or any other Abolition publication to a single individual in Missouri, or elsewhere; while yet I claim the right to send ten thousand of them if I choose, to as many of my fellow-citizens. Whether I will exercise that right or not is for me, and not for the mob, to decide. The right to send publications of any sort to slaves, or in any way to communicate with them, without the express permission of their masters, I freely acknowledge that I have not. It is with the master alone, that I would have to do, as one freeman with another; and who shall say me nay? . . .

I come now to the proceedings had at the late meetings of our citizens. . . .

The sixteenth section, article thirteenth, of the Constitution of Missouri, reads as follows:

"That the free communication of thoughts and opinions is one of the invaluable rights of man, and that every person may freely speak, write, and print on any subject, being responsible for the abuse of that liberty."

Here, then, I find my warrant for using, as Paul did, all freedom of speech. If I abuse that right I freely acknowledge myself amenable to the laws.

But it is said that the right to hold slaves is a constitutional one, and therefore not to be called in question. I admit the premise, but deny the conclusion. To put a strong case by way of illustration. The Constitution declares that this shall be a perpetual republic, but has not any citizen the right to discuss, under that Constitution, the comparative merits of despotism and liberty? And if he has eloquence and force of argument sufficient, may he not persuade us all to crown him our king? Robert Dale Owen came to this city, and Fanny Wright, followed him, openly proclaiming the doctrine that the institution of marriage was a curse to any community, and ought to be abolished. It was, undoubtedly, an abominable doctrine, . . . yet who thought of denying Mr. Owen and his disciple, the perfect right of avowing such doctrines, or who thought of mobbing them for the exercise of this right? And yet, most surely, the institution of Slavery [is] not more interwoven with the structure of our society, than those of marriage.

See the danger, and the natural and inevitable result to which the first step here will lead. To-day a public meeting declares that you shall not discuss the subject of Slavery, in any of its bearings, civil or religious. Right or wrong, the press must be silent. To-morrow, another meeting decides that it is against the peace of society, that the principles of Popery shall be discussed, and the edict goes forth to muzzle the press. The next day, it is in a similar manner, declared that not a word must be said against distilleries, dram shops, or drunkenness. And so on to the end of the chapter. The truth is, my fellow-citizens, if you give ground a single inch, there is no stopping place. I deem it, therefore, my duty to take my stand upon the Constitution. Here is firm ground—I feel it to be such. And I do most respectfully, yet decidedly, declare to you my fixed determination to maintain this ground. We have slaves, it is true, but I am not one. I am a citizen of these United States, a citizen of Missouri, free-born; and having never forfeited the inestimable privileges attached to such condition, I cannot consent to surrender them. But while I maintain them, I hope to do it with all that meekness and humility that become a Christian, and especially a Christian minister. I am ready, not to fight, but to suffer, and if need be, to die for them. Kindred blood to that which flows in my veins, flowed freely to water the tree of Christian liberty, planted by the Puritans on the rugged soil of New England. It flowed as freely on the plains of Lexington, the heights of Bunker Hill, and fields of Saratoga. And freely, too, shall mine flow, yea, as freely as if it were so much water, ere I surrender my right to plead the cause of truth and righteousness, before my fellow-citizens, and in the face of all their opposers. . . .

6. Gerrit Smith, Address to the New York Anti-Slavery Society, Peterboro (October 22, 1835; reprinted in *The Liberator*, November 14, 1835)

When members of a New York abolitionist movement seeking statewide support convened a meeting in Utica, they were attacked by a mob. Resuming the next day in Peterboro, New York, Gerrit Smith (1797–1874) submitted a resolution decrying slavery as antithetical to the Constitution. Here he laments that a war over slavery has already erupted.

Mr. President—Allow me to commence a few remarks by stating the history of this resolution. On returning home from Utica last night, my mind was so much excited with the horrid scenes of the day, and the frightful encroachments made on the right of free discussion, that I could not sleep, and at 3 o'clock I left my bed and drafted the resolution. . . .

. . . Let me read the resolution:

Resolved, That the right of free discussion, given to us by our God, and asserted and guarded by the laws of our country, is a right so vital to man's freedom, and dignity, and usefulness, that we can never be guilty of its surrender, without consenting to exchange that freedom for slavery, and that dignity and usefulness for debasement and worthlessness. . . .

I love our free and happy government. But not because it *confers* any new rights upon us. Our rights spring from a nobler source than human constitutions and governments—from the favor of Almighty God. Constitutions and laws are modes of human device for asserting and defining and carrying out the great natural and inherent rights of man, which belong to him as a rational creature of God. We do not learn our rights in the Book of Constitutions. We learn them from the Book of Books, which is the great Charter of man's rights. . . .

This right, so sacred and so essential, is now sought to be trammeled, and is in fact virtually denied. . . . It is generally defended as something which our free government has given us, as what was earned by the toil and purchased by the blood of our fathers. Sir, this is an error. And men in denying this right, are not only guilty of violating the constitution, and destroying the blessings brought by the blood and toil of our fathers, but guilty of making open war with God himself. I want to see this right placed on this true, this infinitely high ground, as a DIVINE right. . . .

We are even now threatened with legislative restrictions on this right. Let us tell our legislators, in advance, that we cannot bear it. . . . Laws to gag men's mouths, to seal up their lips, to freeze up the warm gushings of the heart, are laws which the free spirit cannot brook; they are laws contrary alike to the nature of man and the commands of God; laws destructive of human happiness and the divine constitution, and before God and man they are NULL AND VOID. . . .

And for what purpose are we called to throw down our pens and seal up our lips, and sacrifice our influence over our fellow men . . . ? . . . That the oppressed may lie more passive at the feet of the oppressor; that one sixth of our American people may never know their rights; that two and a half millions of our own countrymen, crushed in the cruel folds of slavery, may remain in all their misery and despair, without pity and without hope. . . .

I knew before that slavery would not survive free discussion. But the demands recently put forth by the south, for our surrender of the *right* of discussion, and the avowed reasons of that demand, involve a full concession of this fact, that free discussion is incompatible with slavery. The South, by her own showing, admits that slavery cannot live, unless the north is tongue-tied. Now you and I, and all these abolitionists have two objections to this: One is, we desire and purpose to employ all our influence lawfully, and kindly, and temperately, to deliver our southern brethren from bondage, and never to give rest to our lips or our pens till it is accomplished. The other objection is, that we are not willing to be slaves ourselves. The enormous and insolent demands put forth by the south, show us that the question is now, not only whether the blacks shall continue to be slaves, but whether our necks shall come under the yoke. . . .

It is not to be disguised, sir, that a war has broken out between the south and the north, not easily to be terminated. Political and commercial men, for their own purposes, are industriously striving to restore peace. But the peace which they may accomplish will be superficial and hollow. True and permanent peace can only be restored by removing the cause of the war—that is, slavery. . . . The sword now drawn will not be sheathed, till victory, entire victory, is ours or theirs. Not until that deep and damning stain is washed out from our nation, or the chains of slavery are riveted afresh where they now are, and on our necks also. . . .

7. George McDuffie, *The Natural Slavery of the Negro* (1835)

In this message directed to the South Carolina Legislature, Governor George McDuffie (1790–1851), a leading defender of slavery and the doctrine of nullification, argues that slavery is "the cornerstone of our republican edifice." According to McDuffie, slavery prevents class warfare among whites and protects the right to property, a right insecure in the North. He also claims that slavery is the destiny of blacks, that the South enjoys "the most perfect system of social and political happiness, that has ever existed," and that slaves are to be envied for their easy, carefree lives.

. . . No human institution, in my opinion, is more manifestly consistent with the will of God, than domestic slavery, and no one of his ordinances is written in more legible characters than that which consigns the African race to this condition, as more conducive to their own happiness, than any other of which they are susceptible. Whether we consult the sacred Scriptures, or the lights of nature and reason, we shall find these truths as abundantly apparent. . . .

That the African Negro is destined by providence to occupy this condition of servile dependence, is . . . manifest. It is marked on the face, stamped on the skin, and evinced by the intellectual inferiority and natural improvidence of this race. They have all the qualities that fit them for slaves, and not one of those that would fit them to be freemen. They are utterly unqualified not only for rational freedom, but for self-government of any kind. . . . It is utterly astonishing that any enlightened American, after contemplating all the manifold forms in which even the white race of mankind are doomed to slavery and oppression, should suppose it possible to reclaim the African race from their destiny. The capacity to enjoy freedom is an attribute not to be communicated by human power. It is an endowment of God, and one of the rarest which it has pleased his inscrutable wisdom to bestow upon the nations of the earth. It is conferred as the reward of merit, and only upon those who are qualified to enjoy it. Until the "Ethiopian can change his skin," it will be in vain to attempt, by any human power, to make freemen of those whom God has doomed to be slaves by all their attributes.

If the benevolent friends of the black race would compare the condition of that portion of them which we hold in servitude, with that which still remains in Africa, totally unblessed by the lights of civilization of Christianity, and groaning under a savage despotism, as utterly destitute of hope as of happiness, they would be able to form some tolerable estimate, of what our blacks have lost by slavery in America, and what they have gained by freedom in Africa. Greatly as their condition has been improved by their subjection to an enlightened and Christian people—the only mode under heaven by which it could have been accomplished—they are yet wholly unprepared for anything like a rational system of self-government. Emancipation would be a positive curse, depriving them of a guardianship essential to their happiness. . . . If emancipated, where would they live and what would be their condition? The idea of their remaining among us is utterly visionary. Amalgamation is abhorrent to every sentiment of nature; and if they remain as a separate caste, whether endowed with equal privileges or not, they will become our masters or we must resume the mastery over them. . . . The only disposition, therefore, that could be made of our emancipated slaves would be their transportation to Africa, to exterminate the natives or be exterminated by them; contingencies either of which may well serve to illustrate the wisdom, if not the philanthropy, of these superserviceable madmen who in the name of humanity would desolate the fairest region of the earth and destroy the most perfect system of social and political happiness, that ever has existed.

. . . The advantage of domestic slavery over the most favorable condition of political slavery, does not admit of a question. It is the obvious interest of the master, not less than his duty, to provide comfortable food and clothing for his slaves; and whatever false and exaggerated stories may be propagated by mercenary travellers, . . . the peasantry and operatives of no country in the world are better provided for, in these respects, than the slaves of our country. In the single empire of Great Britain, the most free and enlightened nation in Europe, there are more wretched paupers and half starving operatives, than there are Negro slaves in the United States. In all respects, the comforts of our slaves are greatly superior to those of the English operatives, or the Irish and continental peasantry, to say nothing of the millions of paupers crowded together in those loathsome receptacles of starving humanity, the public poor-houses. Besides the hardships of incessant toil . . . and the sufferings of actual want . . . , these miserable creatures are perpetually annoyed by the most distressing cares for the future condition of themselves and their children.

From this excess of labor, this actual want, and these distressing cares, our slaves are entirely exempted. They habitually labor from two to four hours a day less than the operatives in other countries, and it has been truly remarked . . . that a Negro cannot be made to injure himself by excessive labor. It may be safely affirmed that they usually eat as much wholesome and substantial food in one day, as English operatives or Irish peasants eat in two. And as it regards concern for the future, their condition may well be envied even by their masters. There is not upon the face of the earth, any class of people, high or low, so perfectly free from care and anxiety. They know that their masters will provide for them under all circumstances, and that in the extremity of old age, instead of being driven to beggary or to seek public charity in a poor-house, they will be comfortably accommodated and kindly treated among their relatives and associates. . . . The government of our slaves is strictly patriarchal, and produces those mutual feelings of kindness which result from a constant interchange of good offices, and which can only exist in a system of domestic or patriarchal slavery. They are entirely unknown either in a state of political slavery, or in that form of domestic servitude which exists in all other communities.

In a word, our slaves are cheerful, contented, and happy, much beyond the general condition of the human race except where those foreign intruders and fatal ministers of mischief, the emancipationists, have tempted them to aspire above the condition to which they have been assigned in the order of providence. . . .

Reason and philosophy can easily explain what experience so clearly testifies. If we look into the elements of which all political communities are composed, it will be found that servitude, in some form, is one of the essential constituents. No community ever has existed without it, and we may confidently assert, none ever will. In the very nature of things there must be classes of persons to discharge all the different offices of society, from the highest to the lowest. Some of those offices are regarded as degrading, though they must and will be performed. Hence those manifold forms of dependent servitude which produces a sense of superiority in the masters or employers, and of inferiority on the part of the servants. Where these offices are performed by members of the political community, a dangerous element is introduced into the body politic. Hence the alarming tendency to violate the rights of property by agrarian legislation, which is beginning to be manifest in the older states, where universal suffrage prevails without domestic slavery, a tendency that will increase in the progress of society with the increasing inequality of wealth. No government is worthy of the name that does not protect the rights of property, and no enlightened people will long submit to such a mockery. Hence it is that in older countries, different political orders are established to effect this indispensable object, and it will be fortunate for the non-slaveholding states, if they are not, in less than a quarter of a century, driven to the adoption of a similar institution, or to take refuge from robbery and anarchy under a military despotism.

But where the menial offices and dependent employments of society are performed by domestic slaves, a class well defined by their color and entirely separated from the political body, the rights of property are perfectly secure, without the establishment of artificial barriers. In a word, the institution of domestic slavery supersedes the necessity of an order of nobility, and all the other appendages of a hereditary system of government. If our slaves were emancipated, and admitted, bleached or unbleached, to an equal participation in our political privileges, what a commentary should we furnish upon the doctrines of the emancipationists, and what a revolting spectacle of republican equality should we exhibit to the mockery of the world! . . .

Domestic slavery, therefore, instead of being a political evil, is the cornerstone of our republican edifice. No patriot who justly estimates our privileges will tolerate the idea of emancipation, at any period, however remote, or on any conditions of pecuniary advantage, however favorable. I would as soon think of opening a negotiation for selling the liberty of the state at once, as for making any stipulations for the ultimate emancipation of our slaves. . . .

8. Angelina E. Grimké, *Appeal to the Christian Women of the South* (1836)

Born and raised in a South Carolina slaveholding family, Angelina Grimké (1805–1879), and her sister, Sarah, eventually moved to Pennsylvania. By the mid-1830s they joined other Garrisonians in demanding racial equality while also advocating women's rights. Testifying against the inhumanity of slavery and chastising Northern complicity, Angelina Grimké here rejects claims grounding slavery in Scripture and challenges descriptions of slavery as the cornerstone of republican government.

[T]he Bible is my ultimate appeal in all matters of faith and practice, and it is to this test I am anxious to bring the subject [of slavery] at issue between us. Let us then begin with Adam and examine the charter of privileges which was given to him. "Have dominion over the fish of the sea, and over the fowl of the air, and over every living thing that moveth upon the earth." . . . In this charter, although the different kinds of irrational beings are so particularly enumerated, and supreme dominion over all of them is granted, yet man is never vested with this dominion over his fellow man; he was never told that any of the human species were put under his feet; it was only all things, and man, who was created in the image of his Maker, never can properly be termed a thing, though the laws of Slave States do call him "a chattel personal;" Man then, I assert never was put under the feet of man, by that first charter of human rights which was given by God. . . .

But it has been urged that the patriarchs held slaves, and therefore, slavery is right. Do you really believe that patriarchal servitude was like American slavery? . . .

I admit that a species of servitude was permitted to the Jews, but in studying the subject I have been struck with wonder and admiration at perceiving how carefully the servant was guarded from violence, injustice and wrong. . . .

. . . To protect servants from violence, it was ordained that if a master struck out the tooth or destroyed the eye of a servant, that servant immediately became free, for such an act of violence evidently showed he was unfit to possess the power of a master. . . . All servants enjoyed the rest of the Sabbath and partook of the privileges and festivities of the three great Jewish Feasts; and if a servant died under the infliction of chastisement, his master was surely to be punished. As a tooth for a tooth and life for life was the Jewish law, of course he was punished with death. . . .

. . . You may observe that I have carefully avoided using the term slavery when speaking of Jewish servitude; and simply for this reason, that no such thing existed among that people. . . .

Shall I ask you now my friends, to draw the parallel between Jewish servitude and American slavery? No! For there is no likeness in the two systems; I ask you rather to mark the contrast. The laws of Moses protected servants in their rights as men and women, guarded them from oppression and defended them from wrong. The Code Noir of the South robs the slave of all his rights as a man, reduces him to a chattel personal, and defends the master in the exercise of the most unnatural and unwarrantable power over his slave. They each bear the impress of the hand which formed them. The attributes of justice and mercy are shadowed out in the Hebrew code; those of injustice and cruelty, in the Code Noir of America. Truly it was wise in the slaveholders of the South to declare their slaves to be "chattels personal;" for before they could be robbed of wages, wives, children, and friends, it was absolutely necessary to deny they were human beings. . . .

But some have even said that Jesus Christ did not condemn slavery. To this I reply that our Holy Redeemer lived and preached among the Jews only. . . . If . . . He did not condemn Jewish servitude this does not prove that he would not have condemned such a monstrous system as that of American slavery, if that had existed among them. But did not Jesus condemn slavery? Let us examine some of his precepts. "Whatsoever ye would that men should do to you, do ye even so to them." Let every slaveholder apply these queries to his own heart; Am I willing to be a slave—Am I willing to see my wife the slave of another—Am I willing to see my mother a slave, or my father, my sister or my brother? If not, then in holding others as slaves, I am doing what I would not wish to be done to me or any relative I have; and thus have I broken this golden rule which was given me to walk by.

But some slaveholders have said, "we were never in bondage to any man," and therefore the yoke of bondage would be insufferable to us, but slaves are accustomed to it, their backs are fitted to the burden. Well, I am willing to admit that you who have lived in freedom would find slavery even more oppressive than the poor slave does, but then you may try this question in another form—Am I willing to reduce my little child to slavery? . . . You start back with horror and indignation at such a question. But why, if slavery is no wrong to those upon whom it is imposed? Why, if as has often been said, slaves are happier than their masters, free from the cares and perplexities of providing for themselves and their families? Why not place your children in the way of being supported without your having the trouble to provide for them, or they for themselves? Do you not perceive that as soon as this golden rule of action is applied to yourselves that you involuntarily shrink from the test. . . ?

But perhaps you will be ready to query, why appeal to women on this subject? We do not make the laws which perpetuate slavery. No legislative power is vested in us; we can do nothing to overthrow the system, even if we wished to do so. To this I reply, I know you do not make the laws, but I also know that you are the wives and mothers, the sisters and daughters of those who do; and if you really suppose you can do nothing to overthrow slavery, you are greatly mistaken. You can do much in every way: four things I will name. 1st. You can read on this subject. 2d. You can pray over this subject. 3d. You can speak on this subject. 4th. You can act on this subject. . . .

The women of the South can overthrow this horrible system of oppression and cruelty, licentiousness and wrong. Such appeals to your legislatures would be irresistible, for there is something in the heart of man which will bend under moral suasion. There is a swift witness for truth in his bosom, which will respond to truth when it is uttered with calmness and dignity. If you could obtain but six signatures to such a petition in only one state, I would say, send up that petition, and be not in the least discouraged by the scoffs and jeers of the heartless, or the resolution of the house to lay it on the table. It will be a great thing if the subject can be introduced into your legislatures in any way, even by women, and they will be the most likely to introduce it there in the best possible manner, as a matter of morals and religion, not of expediency or politics. You may petition, too, the different ecclesiastical bodies of the slave states. Slavery must be attacked with the whole power of truth and the sword of the spirit. You must take it up on Christian ground, and fight against it with Christian weapons, whilst your feet are shod with the preparation of the gospel of peace. . . .

. . . Doubtless you have all heard Anti-Slavery Societies denounced as insurrectionary and mischievous, fanatical and dangerous. It has been said they publish the most abominable untruths, and that they are endeavoring to excite rebellions at the South. . . . You know that I am a Southerner; you know that my dearest relatives are now in a slave State. Can you for a moment believe I would prove so recreant to the feelings of a daughter and a sister, as to join a society which was seeking to overthrow slavery by falsehood, bloodshed, and murder? . . . As a Carolinian, I was peculiarly jealous of any movements on this subject; and before I would join an Anti-Slavery Society, I took the precaution of becoming acquainted with some of the leading Abolitionists, of reading their publications and attending their meetings . . . and it was not until I was fully convinced that their principles were entirely pacific, and their efforts only moral, that I gave my name as a member to the Female Anti-Slavery Society of Philadelphia. Since that time, I have regularly taken the *Liberator*, and read many Anti-Slavery pamphlets and papers and books, and can never read any account of cruelty which I could not believe. Southerners may deny the truth of these accounts, but . . . I lived too long in the midst of slavery, not to know what slavery is. When I speak of this system, "I speak that I do know," and I am not at all afraid to assert, that Anti-Slavery publications have not over-drawn the monstrous features of slavery at all. . . .

But you will probably ask, if Anti-Slavery societies are not insurrectionary, why do Northerners tell us they are? Why, I would ask you in return, did Northern senators and Northern representatives give their votes, at the last sitting of congress, to the admission of Arkansas Territory as a state? Take those men, one by one, and ask them in their parlours, do you approve of slavery? Ask them on Northern ground, where they will speak the truth, and I doubt not, every man of them will tell you, no! . . . Why then, I would ask, do they lend you their help? I will tell you, "they love the praise of men more than the praise of God." The Abolition cause has not yet become so popular as to induce them to believe, that by advocating it in congress they shall sit still more securely in their seats there, and like the chief rulers in the days of our Saviour, though many believed on him, yet they did not confess him, lest they should be put out of the synagogue; John xii, 42, 43. Or perhaps like Pilate, thinking they could prevail nothing, and fearing a tumult, they determined to release Barabbas and surrender the just man, the poor innocent slave to be stripped of his rights and scourged. In vain will such men try to wash their hands, and say, with the Roman governor, "I am innocent of the blood of this just person." Northern American statesmen are no more innocent of the crime of slavery, than Pilate was of the murder of Jesus, or Saul of that of Stephen. . . . Slavery then is a national sin.

But you will say, a great many other Northerners tell us so, who can have no political motives. . . . The Northern merchants and manufacturers are making their fortunes out of the produce of slave labor; the grocer is selling your rice and sugar; how then can these men bear a testimony against slavery without con-demning themselves? But there is another reason, the North is most dreadfully afraid of Amalgamation. She is alarmed at the very idea of a thing so monstrous, as she thinks. And lest this consequence might flow from emancipation, she is determined to resist all efforts at emancipation without expatriation. It is not because she approves of slavery, or believes it to be "the cornerstone of our republic," for she is as much anti-slavery as we are; but amalgamation is too horrible to think of. Now I would ask you, is it right, is it generous, to refuse the colored people in this country the advantages of education and the privilege, or rather the right, to follow honest trades and callings merely because they are colored? . . . Great numbers cannot bear the idea of equality, and fearing lest, if they had the same advantages we enjoy, they would become as intelligent, as moral, as religious, and as respectable and wealthy, they are determined to keep them as low as they possibly can. Is this doing as they would be done by? Is this loving their neighbor as themselves? . . .

9. Theodore S. Wright, Speech of October 20, 1836, to the Meeting of the NY State Anti-Slavery Society Convention (printed in *Friend of Man*, October 27, 1836)

In this speech African American Presbyterian minister Theodore S. Wright (1797–1847) discusses the relationship between racism and slavery. In a similar speech he gave to this organization the following year, Wright observed that "the giant sin of prejudice" was both "the parent and offspring of slavery," and he implored abolition societies to "annihilate in their own bosoms the cord of caste." By the late 1830s, Wright joined more militant voices encouraging slave resistance.

Mr. President . . .

This is a serious business, sir. The prejudice which exists against the colored man, the free man, is like the atmosphere, everywhere felt by him. It is true that in these United States, and in this State, there are men, like myself, colored with the skin like my own, who are not subjected to the lash, who are not liable to have their wives and their infants torn from them; from whose hand the Bible is not taken. It is true that we may walk abroad; we may enjoy our domestic comforts, our families; retire to the closet; visit the sanctuary, and may be permitted to urge on our children and our neighbors in well doing. But sir, still we are slaves—everywhere we feel the chain galling us. It is by that prejudice which the resolution condemns. . . . This spirit is withering all our hopes, and oft times causes the colored parent as he looks upon his child, to wish he had never been born. Often is the heart of the colored mother, as she presses her child to her bosom, filled with sorrow to think that, by reason of this prejudice, it is cut off from all hopes of usefulness in this land. Sir, this prejudice is wicked.

If the nation and church understood this matter, I would not say a word on this question; I would not speak a word about that killing influence that destroys the colored man's reputation. This influence cuts us off from everything; it follows us up from childhood to manhood; it excludes us from all stations of profit, usefulness and honor; takes away from us all motive for pressing forward in enterprises, useful and important to the world and to ourselves.

. . . A colored man can hardly learn a trade, and if he does it is difficult for him to find any one who will employ him to work at that trade, in any part of the State. In most of our large cities there are associations of mechanics who legislate out of their society colored men. And in many cases, where our young men have learned trades, they have had to come to low employments, for want of encouragement in those trades.

It must be a matter of rejoicing to know that in this place, many colored fathers and mothers have the privileges of education. It must be a matter of rejoicing that in this vicinity colored parents can have their children trained up in schools. At present, we find the colleges barred against us.

. . . I will say nothing about the inconvenience of traveling; how we are frowned upon and despised. No matter how we may demean ourselves, we find embarrassments everywhere. . . .

And sir, the manner in which our churches are regulated destroys souls. Whilst the church is thrown open to everybody, and one says come, come in and share the blessings of the sanctuary, this is the gate of heaven—he says to the colored man, *be careful where you take your stand.* I know an efficient church in this State, where a respectable colored man went to the house of God, and was going to take a seat in the gallery, and one of the officers contended with him, and said, "you cannot go there, sir." . . .

Thanks be to God, there is a buoyant principle which elevates the poor down-trodden colored man above all this: It is . . . the fact, that when he looks up to Heaven, he knows that God . . . treats him as a moral agent, irrespective of caste or the circumstances in which he may be placed. Amid the embarrassments which he has to meet, and the scorn and contempt that is heaped upon him, he is cheered by the hope that he will be disenthralled, and soon, like a bird let forth from its cage, wing his flight to Jesus, where he can be happy, and look down with pity upon the man who despises the poor slave for being what God made him, and the man who despises him, because he is identified with the poor slave. Blessed be God for the principles of the Gospel. Were it not for these, and for the fact that a better day is dawning, I would not wish to live. Blessed be God for the antislavery movement. Blessed be God there is a war waging with slavery, that the granite rock is about to be rolled from its base. But as long as the colored man is to be looked upon as an inferior caste, so long will they disregard his cries, his groans, his shrieks. . . .

Let me, through you, sir, request this delegation to take hold of this subject. This will silence the slave holder, when he says where is your love for the slave? Where is your love for the colored man who is crushed at your feet? Talking to us about emancipating our slaves when you are enslaving them by your feelings, and doing more violence to them by your prejudice, than we are to our slaves by our treatment! They call on us to evince our love for the slave, by treating man as man, the colored man as a man, according to his worth.

10. James Henry Hammond, Address before the U.S. House of Representatives (February 1, 1837)

This speech, delivered by committed South Carolina slaveholder James Henry Hammond (1807–1864), was part of a sustained effort to ban any discussion of slavery petitions from the House of Representatives (the infamous "gag rule"). His appeals to Scripture (the story of Ham), and to the welfare and happiness of the slaves, are typical, but he introduces a new angle when he deems slavery to be "the greatest of all the great blessings" which God has bestowed on the South. His reference to a "distinguished Virginian" is to John Randolph; the reference to "Thompson" is to George Thompson, a leading British abolitionist who was forced to cut short his lecture tour of America under threats to his life from slavery advocates, a threat that Hammond embraces.

Mr. Speaker, I object to the reception of these [abolitionist] petitions. . . . [T]hey are sent here by persons who are pursuing a systematic plan of operations intended to subvert the institutions of the South, and which, if carried into effect, must desolate the fairest portion of America, and dissolve in blood the bonds of this confederacy. . . .

[At this point Representative Hammond reads into the record extensive and numerous examples of abolitionist literature that he finds particularly incendiary, and proceeds to further build his case against the reception of abolitionist petitions before the House.—eds.]

. . . I think I may say that any appeal to slaveholders will be in vain. In the whole history of emancipation, in Europe or America, I do not remember a dozen instances of masters freeing their slaves, at least during their own lifetime, from any qualms of conscience. . . .

The abolitionists can appeal only to the hopes or fears or interest of the slaveholder, to induce him to emancipate his slaves. So far as our hopes are concerned, I believe I can say we are perfectly satisfied. We have been born and bred in a slave country. Our habits are accommodated to them, and so far as we have been able to observe other states of society abroad, we see nothing to invite us to exchange our own, but, on the contrary, everything to induce us to prefer it above all others.

As to our fears, I know it has been said by a distinguished Virginian, and quoted on this floor, "that the fire bell in Richmond never rings at night, but the mother presses her infant more closely to her breast, in dread of servile insurrection." Sir, it is all a flourish. There may be nervous men and timid women, whose imaginations are haunted with unwonted fears, among us, as there are in all communities on earth; but in no part of the world have men of ordinary firmness less fear of danger from their operatives than we have. The fires which in a few years have desolated Normandy and Anjou, the great machine burning the heart of England, the bloody and eternal struggles of the Irish Catholics, and the mobs which for some years past have figured in the northern States, burning convents, tearing down houses, spreading dismay and ruin through their cities, and even taking life, are appropriate illustrations of the peace and security of a community whose laborers are all free. On the other hand, during the two hundred years that slavery has existed in this country, there has, I believe, been but one serious insurrection, and that one very limited in its extent.

The appeal, however, to our interest, is that which might appear to promise much success. . . . If you will look over the world, you will find that in all those countries where slavery has been found unprofitable, it has been abolished. In northern latitudes, where no great agricultural staple is produced, and where care, skill, and a close economy, enter largely into the elements of production, free labor has been found more valuable than that of slaves. . . .

. . . But in southern latitudes, where great agricultural staples are produced, . . . domestic slavery is indispensable. To such a country, it is as natural as the clime itself—as the birds and beasts to which that climate is congenial. . . . The system of "strikes," so universally practiced in all other kinds of labor, would desolate a planting country in five years. . . . Sir, it is not in the interest of the planters of the South to emancipate their slaves, and it never can be shown to be so.

Slavery is said to be an evil; that it impoverishes the people, and destroys their morals. If it be an evil, it is one to us alone, and we are contented with it—why should others interfere? But it is no evil. On the contrary, I believe it to be the greatest of all the great blessings which a kind Providence has bestowed upon our glorious region. For without it, our fertile soil and our fructifying climate would have been given to us in vain. And as to its impoverishing and demoralizing influence, the simple and irresistible answer to that is, that the history of the short period during which we have enjoyed it has rendered our southern country proverbial for its wealth, its genius, its manners. . . .

But it is impossible for another reason: the moment this House undertakes to legislate upon this subject, it dissolves the Union. Should it be my fortune to have a seat upon this floor, I will abandon it the instant the first decisive step is taken, looking towards legislation on this subject. I will go home to preach, and if I can, to practice, disunion, and civil war, if needs be. A revolution must ensue, and this republic must sink in blood.

The only remaining chance for the abolitionists to succeed in their nefarious schemes will be by appealing to the slaves themselves . . . in the language of the miscreant Thompson, to "teach the slave to cut his masters throat." . . . This will be no easy task. . . . As a class, . . . there is not a happier, more contended race upon the face of the earth. I have been born and brought in the midst of them, and, so far as my knowledge and experience extend, I should say they have every reason to be happy. Lightly tasked, well clothed, well fed—far better than the free laborers of any country in the world, our own and those perhaps of the other States of this confederacy alone excepted—their lives and persons protected by the law, all their sufferings alleviated by the kindest and most interested care, and their domestic affections cherished and maintained, at least as far as I have known, with conscientious delicacy.

A gentleman from Massachusetts [Mr. John Quincy Adams] has introduced upon this floor the abolition cant of wives and husbands, parents and children, torn from each other's arms, and separated forever. Such scenes but rarely, very rarely, happen. I do not believe such separations are near so common among slaves, as divorces are among white persons, where they can be with much facility obtained. . . . Sir, our slaves are a peaceful, kind-hearted, and affectionate race; satisfied with their lot, happy in their comforts, and devoted to their masters. It will be no easy thing to seduce them from their fidelity. . . .

Sir, I believe that every appeal to the slave to assist, through the horrid process of burning and assassination, in his own emancipation . . . will be without success. I feel firmly convinced that, under any circumstances, emancipation, gradual or immediate, is impossible. [S]lavery can never be abolished. The doom of Ham has been branded on the form and features of his African descendants. The hand of fate has united his color and his destiny. Man cannot separate what God has joined. . . .

What, sir, does the South ask next? She asks—and this at least she has a right to demand—that these petitions be not received here and recorded in your journals. This House at least ought to be a sanctuary, into which no such topic should be allowed to enter. Representatives from every section of the republic ought to be permitted to come here faithfully to perform their duties to their constituents and their country, without being subjected to these incendiary attacks—their feelings insulted, their rights assaulted, and the falsest calumnies of themselves and those they represent thrown on them daily, and perpetuated to their posterity. . . . If these things are to be permitted here, you drive us from your councils. Let the consequences rest on you. . . .

. . . I warn the abolitionists, ignorant, infatuated, barbarians as they are, that if chance shall throw any of them into our hands he may expect a felon's death. No human law, no human influence, can arrest his fate. The superhuman instinct of self-preservation, the indignant feelings of an outraged people, to whose hearth-stones he is seeking to carry death and desolation, pronounce his doom; and if we failed to accord it to him we should be unworthy of the forms we wear, unworthy of the beings whom it is our duty to protect, and we should merit and expect the indignation of offended Heaven.

11. Debates in the U.S. Congress: Senate (February 6, 1837)

These debates in the U.S. Senate are notable for highlighting disparate interpretations of Congress' authority over the interstate slave trade and for inquiring into the extent of congressional authority over slavery in the District of Columbia. This debate includes a remarkable exchange between William Rives (1793–1868) of Virginia, who hewed to an older belief that slavery was a moral evil while construing its basis in the Constitution and recommending its gradual, peaceful abolition, and John C. Calhoun (1782–1850) of South Carolina who held a more novel position that slavery is a "positive good."

Mr. [John] Tipton [of Indiana] said that he was requested to present to the Senate two memorials . . . to abolish slavery in the District of Columbia. . . . I acknowledge (said Mr. T.) the right of the people to petition Congress for a redress of their grievances, and I feel it to be my duty . . . to present their petitions. [B]ut . . . my reflections on this subject have brought me to a conclusion very different from that which they seem to have arrived at. . . .

It is contended that Congress has exclusive legislation over the District of Columbia. If that be granted, it is but a delegated and limited power, not original, derivative. Slavery existed in Virginia, Maryland, and other States, before the federal constitution was adopted. . . . The States of Virginia and Maryland ceded to the Federal Government this ten miles square . . . for a seat of Government, and granted to Congress exclusive legislative powers over it for that purpose. This power was given to Congress by the States for special purposes, and is limited, from the very nature of the grant. Congress cannot abolish the right of trial by jury, abridge the liberty of the press, nor establish a national church, in this District, any more than in any of the States; nor do I believe that Congress has a right to interfere with slavery in the District, while Virginia and Maryland continued to be slave States.

Were it possible that the petitioners could . . . abolish slavery in the District of Columbia, they would erect a receptacle in the midst of two slave-holding States for fanatics, abolitionists, and runaway slaves, who would, from their stronghold here, spread dissatisfaction, death and destruction, through the surrounding country. . . .

Mr. [Thomas] Ewing, of Ohio said . . . I am a citizen of a State in which slavery is not admitted, and all my habits and feelings, and opinions, are averse to it, both in principle and practice; but I do not . . . think, that our National Legislature ought to interfere with the subject. They ought not to interfere with it, for it would exacerbate sectional feelings, which ought to be assuaged rather than excited; and, in justice to the people of the District itself, it ought not, for they are in the midst of a slaveholding population, surrounded with it on all sides. They themselves have been bred up in the same habits. . . .

Mr. [William] Preston [of South Carolina] . . . objected to all interference with the subject in any shape. . . . The South was sore on the subject. The attacks made upon them were violent and incessant. Their nerves were irritated. Propositions to meddle with the slave trade in the District were but an entering wedge. If Congress once tampered with the rights of slaveholders at all; if the subject got the least foothold in the Senate, he would not give a rush for the rights of the South. He complained of the imputations cast by implication, in these petitions, on the people of the South, as violators of the laws of God, and living in open vice and wickedness, practicing a standing sin, corrupting their own morals and those of their children. . . . The charge was individually insulting and was utterly false and calumnious. . . . He denied that the language of the petitions was respectful and decorous; it cast foul and false aspersions on him and his constituents, and ought not to be admitted into the Senate. . . .

Mr. [Alfred] Cuthbert [of Georgia] . . . proceeded to refer to certain resolutions which had been adopted in Boston, in 1819, . . . one of which declared that Congress had authority to act on the subject of slavery in the District of Columbia, and the other that Congress had power to regulate the transfer of slaves from one State to another. He adduced this to show but as fast as one was yielded another was pressed on. . . .

Mr. [Daniel] Webster [of Massachusetts] . . . [T]here was not in his mind a particle of doubt that Congress had an unquestionable right to regulate the subject of slavery in the District of Columbia, simply because they constituted the exclusive Legislature of the District. It appeared to him little short of an absurdity to think that there were certain subjects which must be tied up from all legislation. And as to the other point, the right of regulating the transfer of slaves from one State to another, he did not know that he entertained any doubt, because the constitution gave Congress the right to regulate trade and commerce between the States. Trade in what? In whatever was the subject of commerce and ownership. If slaves were the subjects of ownership, then trade in them between the States was subject to the regulation of Congress. But while he held this opinion, he had expressed none on the one side or the other as to the matter of expediency. . . .

Mr. [William C.] Rives [of Virginia] said he had witnessed the whole course of this discussion with great pain and mortification. . . . [W]ould gentlemen have so little regard to the peace of the whole community as not to abstain from agitating a subject of this kind? The gentleman from Massachusetts had taken occasion not only to read sentiments, from the memorials, which were obnoxious to the South, but had volunteered the expression of his own opinion as to the constitutional power of Congress over the subject of slavery in the District of Columbia. Wherefore introduce that subject again? Why put forward the expression of an opinion in regard to the regulation of trade in slaves between the States, to warrant which the Senator could find nothing in the statute book? He had told the Senate that laws had been passed on that subject, and with the sanction of the South. Mr. R. joined issue with the Senator, and called on him to point to the law. He was very confident there was none. As to the laws to which he presumed the reference had been made, they did not touch the matter. Laws to prevent the escape of slaves, or to secure their restoration, were only in fulfillment of the constitution, which expressly provided for the delivering up of runaways; and so far from being an unfavorable interference with the tenure of slave property, it was, on the contrary, a recognition of the right in slaves, and a guarantee of that right. Mr. R. had no objection that Senators should present their petitions, but he protested against the gratuitous exhibition of these horrid pictures of misery which had no existence. He was not in favor of slavery in the abstract. On that point he differed with the gentlemen from South Carolina [Mr. John C. Calhoun]. But it was an existing institution; it was recognized and protected by the Constitution. . . .

Mr. Calhoun . . . denied having expressed any opinion in regard to slavery in the abstract. He had merely stated . . . that it was an inevitable law of society that one portion of the community depended on the labor of another portion, over which it must unavoidably exercise control. He had not spoken of slavery in the abstract, but of slavery as existing where two races of men, of different color, and striking dissimilarity in conformation, habits, and a thousand other particulars, were placed in immediate juxtaposition. Here the existence of slavery was good to both. Did not the Senator from Virginia [Sen. Rives] consider it as a good?

Mr. Rives said, no. He viewed it as a misfortune and an evil in all circumstances, though, in some, it might be the lesser evil.

Mr. Calhoun insisted on the opposite opinion, and declared it as his conviction that, in point of fact, the Central African race . . . had never existed in so comfortable, so respectable, or so civilized a condition, as that which it now enjoyed in the Southern States. The population doubled in the same ratio with that of the whites—a proof of ease and plenty; while, with respect to civilization, it nearly kept pace with that of the owners; and as to the effect upon the whites, would it be affirmed that they were inferior to others, that they were less patriotic, less intelligent, less humane, less brave, than where slavery did not exist? . . . Both races, therefore, appeared to thrive under the practical operation of this institution. The experiment was in progress, but had not been completed. . . . The social experiment was going on both at the North and at the South—in the one with almost a pure and unlimited democracy, and in the other with a mixed race. Thus far, the results of the experiment had been in favor of the South. Southern society had been far less agitated, and he would venture to predict that its condition would prove by far the most secure, and by far the most favorable to the preservation of liberty. In fact, the defense of human liberty against the aggressions of despotic power had been always the most efficient in States where domestic slavery was found to prevail. He did not admit it to be an evil. Not at all. It was a good—a great good. . . .

Mr. Rives said [that] though he came from a slaveholding State, he did not believe slavery to be a good, either moral, political, or economical; and if it depended on him, and there were any means of effecting it, he would not hesitate to terminate that coexistence of the two races to which the Senator from South Carolina alluded. . . . Yet none had therefore reason to doubt that he should defend the rights growing out of the relations of slavery to the uttermost. No interference with that relation could be attempted without great and abiding mischief. . . . Great as might be the evil, no remedy for it has been found; and if any were to be devised, it must proceed from those only who suffer the evil; nor would the Constitution tolerate the remotest interference by others. When such interference should be forcibly attempted, Mr. R. was prepared to throw himself into the breach, and to perish in the last ditch in defense of the constitutional rights of the South. But he was not on this account going back to the exploded dogmas of Sir Robert Filmer, in order to vindicate the institution of slavery in the abstract.

Mr. Calhoun . . . denied having pronounced slavery in the abstract a good. All he had said of it referred to existing circumstances; to slavery as a practical, not as an abstract thing. It was a good where a civilized race and a race of a different description were brought together. . . . He utterly denied that his doctrine had anything to do with the tenets of Sir Robert Filmer, which he abhorred. So far from holding the dogmas of that writer, he had been the known and open advocate of freedom from the beginning. Nor was there anything in the doctrines he held in the slightest degree inconsistent with the highest and purest principles of freedom. . . .

Mr. Rives . . . [S]ir, while I have been thus prepared and determined to defend the constitutional rights and vital interests of the South at every hazard, I have not felt myself bound to conform my understanding and conscience to the standard of faith that has recently been set up by some gentlemen in regard to the general question of slavery. I have not considered it a part of my duty, as a representative from the South, to deny, as has been done by this new school, the natural freedom and equality of man; to contend that slavery is a positive good; that it is inseparable from the condition of man; that it must exist, in some form or other, in every political community; and that it is even an essential ingredient in republican government. . . .

This is a philosophy to which I have not yet become a convert. It is sufficient for me to know that domestic slavery . . . was an institution existing at the time of the adoption of the constitution; that it is recognized and sanctified by that solemn instrument . . . ; that . . . it was entailed upon them by a foreign and unnatural jurisdiction, in opposition to their own wishes and remonstrances; that there is now no remedy for it, within the reach of any human agency, and, if there were, it must be originated and applied by those only who feel the evil; and that any interference with it by this Government, or the other States, would, in violating the most sacred guarantees of the constitution, rend the Union itself asunder. In pursuing this course, I have the satisfaction of reflecting that I follow the example of the greatest men and the purest patriots who have illustrated the annals of our country—of the fathers of the republic itself. . . .

In following such lights as these, I feel that I sin against no principle of republicanism, against no safeguard of Southern rights and Southern policy, when I frankly say . . . that I do regard slavery as an evil. . . . But, evil as it may be, it is now indissolubly interwoven with the whole frame of our society. . . . [I]t is inviolably protected by the sanctuary of the constitution itself. . . . [B]y putting the defense of Southern rights on the abstract merits of slavery, as a positive good, as a natural and inevitable law of society, you shock the generous sentiments of human nature, you go counter to the common sense of mankind, you outrage the spirit of the age, and alarm the minds of even of the most liberal and patriotic among our fellow citizens of the other States, for those great fundamental truths on which our common political institutions repose. Unfavorable revulsions only, in the public sentiment, can be expected from bold abstractions of this kind; and nothing, I verily believe, has given so strong an impulse to the cause of the abolitionists as the obsolete and revolting theory of human rights and human society, but which, of late, the institution of domestic slavery has been sustained and justified by some of its advocates in a portion of the South. . . .

12. Catharine E. Beecher, *An Essay on Slavery and Abolitionism, Addressed to Miss A. D. Grimké* (1837)

Catharine E. Beecher (1800–1878) acknowledged the evil of slavery from a more conservative perspective with regard to the role of women in public life. This essay, prompted by controversies stirred by Angelina Grimké's recent public appearances before anti-slavery societies, presumes that the subordination of women is a divine mandate. Her invocation of "chivalry" and "romantic gallantry" anticipate sentiments later expressed by defenders of the Lost Cause.

MY DEAR FRIEND,

. . . The object I have in view, is to present some reasons why it seems unwise and inexpedient for ladies of the non-slave-holding States to unite themselves in Abolition Societies; and thus, at the same time, to exhibit the inexpediency of the course you propose to adopt. . . .

I believe, that as a body, Abolitionists are men of pure morals, of great honesty of purpose, of real benevolence and piety, and of great activity in efforts to promote what they consider the best interests of their fellow men. I believe, that, in making efforts to abolish slavery, they have taken measures, which they supposed were best calculated to bring this evil to an end, with the greatest speed, and with the least danger and suffering to the South. I do not believe they ever designed to promote disunion, or insurrection, or to stir up strife. . . . I believe they have been urged forward by a strong feeling of patriotism, as well as of religious duty. [A]ll this can be allowed, and yet the objection I am to urge against joining their ranks may stand in its full force. . . .

The position then I would aim to establish is, that the method taken by the Abolitionists is the one that, according to the laws of mind and past experience, is least likely to bring about the results they aim to accomplish. . . .

It is the maxim . . . of experience, that when men are to be turned from evils, and brought to repent and reform, those only should interfere who are most loved and respected, and who have the best right to approach the offender. While on the other hand, rebuke from those who are deemed obtrusive and inimical, or even indifferent, will do more harm than good.

It is another maxim of experience, that such dealings with the erring should be in private, not in public. The moment a man is publicly rebuked, shame, anger, and pride of opinion, all combine to make him defend his practice, and refuse either to own himself wrong, or to cease from his evil ways.

The Abolitionists have violated all these laws of mind and of experience, in dealing with their southern brethren. . . .

Their course has been most calculated to awaken anger, fear, pride, hatred, and all the passions most likely to blind the mind to truth, and make it averse to duty.

They have not approached them with the spirit of love, courtesy, and forbearance. . . .

While Abolition Societies did not exist, men could talk and write, at the South, against the evils of slavery, and northern men had free access and liberty of speech, both at the South and at the North. But now all is changed. Every avenue of approach to the South is shut. No paper, pamphlet, or preacher, that touches on that topic, is admitted in their bounds. Their own citizens, that once labored and remonstrated, are silenced; their own clergy, under the influence of the exasperated feelings of their people, and their own sympathy and sense of wrong, either entirely hold their peace, or become the defenders of a system they once lamented, and attempted to bring to an end. This is the record of experience as to the tendencies of Abolitionism, as thus far developed. The South are now in just that state of high exasperation, at the sense of wanton injury and impertinent interference, which makes the influence of truth and reason most useless and powerless. . . .

The preceding are some of the reasons which, on the general view, I would present as opposed to the proposal of forming Abolition Societies; and they apply equally to either sex. . . .

To appreciate more fully these objections, it will be necessary to recur to some general views in relation to the place woman is appointed to fill by the dispensations of heaven. . . .

It is the grand feature of the Divine economy, that there should be different stations of superiority and subordination, and it is impossible to annihilate this beneficent and immutable law. On its first entrance into life, the child is a dependent on parental love, and of necessity takes a place of subordination and obedience. As he advances in life these new relations of superiority and subordination multiply. The teacher must be the superior in station, the pupil a subordinate. The master of a family the superior, the domestic a subordinate—the ruler a superior, the subject a subordinate. Nor do these relations at all depend upon superiority either in intellectual or moral worth. However weak the parents, or intelligent the child, there is no reference to this, in the immutable law. However incompetent the teacher, or superior the pupil, no alteration of station can be allowed. However unworthy the master or worthy the servant, while their mutual relations continue, no change in station as to subordination can be allowed. In fulfilling the duties of these relations, true dignity consists in conforming to all those relations that demand subordination, with propriety and cheerfulness. When does a man, however high his character or station, appear more interesting or dignified than when yielding reverence and deferential attentions to an aged parent, however weak and infirm? And the pupil, the servant, or the subject, all equally sustain their own claims to self-respect, and to the esteem of others, by equally sustaining the appropriate relations and duties of subordination. In this arrangement of the duties of life, Heaven has appointed to one sex the superior, and to the other the subordinate station, and this without any reference to the character or conduct of either. It is therefore as much for the dignity as it is for the interest of females, in all respects to conform to the duties of this relation. And it is as much a duty as it is for the child to fulfil similar relations to parents, or subjects to rulers. But while woman holds a subordinate relation in society to the other sex, it is not because it was designed that her duties or her influence should be any the less important, or all-pervading. But it was designed that the mode of gaining influence and of exercising power should be altogether different and peculiar.

It is Christianity that has given to woman her true place in society. And it is the peculiar trait of Christianity alone that can sustain her therein. "Peace on earth and good will to men" is the character of all the rights and privileges, the influence, and the power of woman. A man may act on society by the collision of intellect, in public debate; he may urge his measures by a sense of shame, by fear and by personal interest; he may coerce by the combination of public sentiment; he may drive by physical force, and he does not outstep the boundaries of his sphere. But all the power, and all the conquests that are lawful to woman, are those only which appeal to the kindly, generous, peaceful and benevolent principles.

Woman is to win every thing by peace and love; by making herself so much respected, esteemed and loved, that to yield to her opinions and to gratify her wishes, will be the free-will offering of the heart. But this is to be all accomplished in the domestic and social circle. There let every woman become so cultivated and refined in intellect, that her taste and judgment will be respected; so benevolent in feeling and action; that her motives will be reverenced;—so unassuming and unambitious, that collision and competition will be banished;—so "gentle and easy to be entreated," as that every heart will repose in her presence; then, the fathers, the husbands, and the sons, will find an influence thrown around them, to which they will yield not only willingly but proudly. A man is never ashamed to own such influences, but feels dignified and ennobled in acknowledging them. But the moment woman begins to feel the promptings of ambition, or the thirst for power, her aegis of defence is gone. All the sacred protection of religion, all the generous promptings of chivalry, all the poetry of romantic gallantry, depend upon woman's retaining her place as dependent and defenceless, and making no claims, and maintaining no right but what are the gifts of honour, rectitude and love.

A woman may seek the aid of co-operation and combination among her own sex, to assist her in her appropriate offices of piety, charity, maternal and domestic duty; but whatever, in any measure, throws a woman into the attitude of a combatant, either for herself or others—whatever binds her in a party conflict—whatever obliges her in any way to exert coercive influences, throws her out of her appropriate sphere. If these general principles are correct, they are entirely opposed to the plan of arraying females in any Abolition movement. . . .

13. Alvan Stewart, *A Constitutional Argument, on the Subject of Slavery* (published in *Friend of Man*, October 18, 1837)

Here abolitionist Alvan Stewart (1790–1849) argues that slavery could be abolished by congressional authority. Stewart conceded that a compromise over slavery was struck in 1787, and that the federal government guaranteed to the slaveholding states assistance in the recovery of fugitive slaves and the suppression of slave rebellions. In turn, the North won the concession that men could be enslaved only in accordance with the Constitution's Fifth Amendment. Stewart's argument represents a growing belief that emancipation could be achieved only through direct political and legal action.

Congress, by the power conferred on it by the Constitution, possesses the entire and absolute right to abolish slavery in every state and territory in the Union. This could be effected by the enactment of a . . . law, in pursuance of, and in conformity to the 5th Article of the amendments to the Constitution of the United States. . . .

The latter part of the 5th article . . . says, Nor shall any person "be deprived of life, liberty, or property, without due process of law." . . .

The first inquiry we shall institute, is to know what is meant by the words, "without due process of law." For it is important to know what that "due process of law" can be, which has power to deprive a man of his life, liberty, or property. And on this subject, it is believed no lawyer . . . will deny that the true and only meaning of the phrase, "due process of law," is an indictment or presentment by a grand jury, of not less than twelve, nor more than twenty-three men; a trial by a petit jury of twelve men, and a judgment pronounced on the finding of the jury, by a court. . . .

It must not be forgotten, that before the Revolution which separated us from the British empire, no provision was made, as between the Colonies of this country, for the surrender of fugitive slaves. Neither was there any thing said on the subject of slaves, in the articles of confederation, which lasted twelve years. . . . Therefore, so far as the northern states were concerned, in the adoption of the Constitution, they assumed a new and peculiar position in relation to slavery. . . . The North having agreed to share equal legislative power with the South, in relation to the District of Columbia, and the territories where slaves might be; and having obligated themselves, though free states, to surrender fugitive slaves . . . and . . . to pour [their] blood out in suppression of . . . insurrection: all of these engagements on the part of the man of the North, gave him full power to insist on what forms should be gone through with, to constitute and make the man a slave. . . . The men of the free states being made partakers in the crime of slavery, out of courtesy, might firmly, as they truly did, insist that the Constitution should contain the only mould in which slaves should be run, and if they were not made in that mould, with all its forms, they could not exist.

That constitutional mould was in these words: "Nor shall any person be deprived of his life, liberty, or property, without due process of law." . . .

Thus the great and difficult question was arranged, in the formation of the Constitution. Let it not be said that the master had, antecedent to the Constitution, *vested rights* of property in the slave; for, granting that proposition, still the master, for the *greater* security from his slaves' insurrections and flights, agreed upon a new *criterion*, upon a new definition of slavery, and upon a *slavery* which was first proven by the course of a legal trial. . . .

When the man of South Carolina, pursuing his fugitive slave to New Hampshire, comes and demands his slave to be delivered up; what will the magistrate of the granite state say to the slaveholder of the Palmetto? I acknowledge I am bound to make out an order and deliver up this fugitive to you, as a part of the grand compact of the Constitution, provided the fugitive has been deprived of his "liberty by due process of law." For that is the grand principle on which the men of the free states consented that slavery might exist. . . . Now, says the magistrate, I know slavery, in no form or shape under the Constitution, except where the slave has lost his liberty, by due process of law. . . . [I]f you can produce me a record . . . showing to me, that a court of competent jurisdiction . . . by the indictment or presentment of a grand jury . . . who have found that indictment, and that 12 men on their oath as a jury have said on the trial of the fugitive, that he was a slave, and a court has pronounced judgment thereupon, then I will make an order for you to take the person as your fugitive slave, otherwise not. No matter what evidence you produce to show that you own the slave, if your title be unbroken through five generations of men, and if you have the bill of sale from him who claimed the fugitive's mother and grandmother, that will not answer. The word "person" is used for the fugitive slave, in the 3d clause of the 2d section of the 4th article—"No person held to service" &c. The word "person" here means a slave. . . . The slave is [also] designated under the appellation of "*persons*" in fixing the basis of representation . . . and [thus] the words in the 5th article of amendments of the Constitution, "nor shall any person be deprived of life, liberty or property, without due process of law," must necessarily include slaves. For if it did not, after having previously twice used the word "person" where it meant slaves, if it did not intend to embrace the slave, there would have been an exception in relation to the slave. The words of the Constitution have no exception like the following, "nor shall any person (except slaves) be deprived of their life, liberty and property without due process of law." "Any person," is equivalent to every body. . . .

[W]e may be permitted to assume, at this stage of our reasoning, that there is not a slave at this moment, in the United States upon the terms mutually agreed upon, but the people of this country, at the formation of the Constitution. If this be true, any judge in the United States, who is clothed with sufficient authority to grant a writ of *Habeas Corpus*, and decide upon a return made to such a writ; on the master and slave being brought before said judge, to inquire by what authority, he the master held the slave; if the master could not produce a record of conviction, by which the particular slave had been deprived of his liberty, by indictment, trial, and judgment at a court, the judge would be obliged under the oath which he must have taken, to obey the Constitution of his country, to discharge the slave and give him his full liberty. . . .

14. Theodore Dwight Weld, *The Power of Congress over Slavery in the District of Columbia* (1838)

Theodore Weld (1803–1895) argued that Congress could abolish slavery in the District of Columbia under legislative authority granted by Article I of the Constitution. Weld also argued that slavery, a creature of local law, is antithetical to the Constitution and common law; and he drew on considerable evidence to show that state legislatures—and by analogy, Congress—could regulate and even abolish slavery within their respective jurisdictions.

In the Constitution of the United States, whatever else may be obscure, the clause granting power to Congress over the Federal District may well defy misconstruction. Art. 1, Sec. 8, Clause 18: "The Congress shall have power to exercise exclusive legislation, in all cases whatsoever, over such District." . . .

In common with the legislatures of the States, Congress cannot constitutionally pass ex post facto laws in criminal cases, nor suspend the writ of habeas corpus, nor pass a bill of attainder, nor abridge the freedom of speech and of the press. . . . These are general limitations. Congress cannot do these things anywhere. The exact import, therefore, of the clause "in all cases whatsoever," is, on all subjects within the appropriate sphere of legislation. . . .

. . . Since, then, Congress is the sole legislature within the District, and since its power is limited only by the checks common to all legislatures, it follows that what the law-making power is intrinsically competent to do anywhere, Congress is competent to do in the District of Columbia. . . .

. . . That the abolition of slavery is within the sphere of legislation, I argue . . .

5. *The competency of the law-making power to abolish slavery, HAS BEEN REC-OGNIZED BY ALL THE SLAVEHOLDING STATES, EITHER DIRECTLY OR BY IMPLICATION.* Some States recognize it in their *Constitutions*, by giving the legislature power to emancipate such slaves as may "have rendered the state some distinguished service," and others by express prohibitory restrictions. The Constitution of Mississippi, Arkansas, and other States, restrict the power of the legislature in this respect. Why this express prohibition, if the law-making power cannot abolish slavery? . . . The people of Arkansas, Mississippi, &c. well knew the competency of the law-making power to abolish slavery, and hence their zeal to restrict it. . . .

6. *Eminent statesmen, themselves slaveholders, have conceded THIS POWER.*—
Washington, in a letter to Robert Morris, April 12, 1786, says: "There is not a

man living, who wishes more sincerely than I do, to see a plan adopted for the abolition of slavery; but there is only one proper and effectual mode by which it can be accomplished, and that is by *legislative* authority."[13] In a letter to Lafayette, May 10, 1786, he says: "It (the abolition of slavery) certainly might, and assuredly ought to be effected, and that too by *legislative* authority." . . .

Every slaveholding member of Congress from the States of Maryland, Virginia, North and South Carolina, and Georgia, voted for the celebrated ordinance of 1787, which *abolished* the slavery then existing in the Northwest Territory. Patrick Henry, in his well known letter to Robert Pleasants, of Virginia, January 18, 1773, says: "I believe a time will come when an opportunity will be offered to *abolish* this lamentable evil."[14] . . .

The Virginia Legislature asserted this power in 1832. At the close of a month's debate, the following proceedings were had. I extract from an editorial article in the *Richmond Whig*, Jan. 26, 1832.

"The report of the Select Committee, adverse to legislation on the subject of Abolition, was in these words: *Resolved*, as the opinion of this Committee, that it is INEXPEDIENT FOR THE PRESENT, to make any *legislative enactments for the abolition of slavery.*" . . .

9. *Congress has unquestionable power to adopt the Common Law, as the legal system, within its exclusive jurisdiction.*—This has been done, with certain restrictions, in most of the States, either by legislative acts or by constitutional implication. THE COMMON LAW KNOWS NO SLAVES. Its principles annihilate slavery wherever they touch it. It is a universal, unconditional, abolition act. Wherever slavery is a legal system, it is so only by statute law, and in violation of the common law. . . . Let Congress adopt the common law in the District of Columbia, and slavery there is abolished. Congress may well be at home in common law legislation, for the common law is the grand element of the United States' Constitution. . . . The preamble of the Constitution plants the standard of the Common Law immovably in its foreground. "We, the people of the United States, in order to ESTABLISH JUSTICE, &c., do ordain and establish this Constitution;" thus proclaiming *devotion* to JUSTICE, as the controlling motive in the organization of the Government, and its secure establishment the chief object of its aims. . . .

By adopting the common law within its exclusive jurisdiction Congress would carry out the principles of our glorious Declaration, and follow the highest

---

13. See document 11 in Chapter 1.
14. See document 2 in Chapter 1.

precedents in our national history and jurisprudence. It is a political maxim as old as civil legislation, that laws should be strictly homogeneous with the principles of the government whose will they express, embodying and carrying them out. . . . Who needs be told that slavery makes war upon the principles of the Declaration, and the spirit of the Constitution, and that these and the principles of the common law gravitate towards each other with irrepressible affinities, and mingle into one? . . .

15. Henry Clay, Address before the Senate on Petitions for the Abolition of Slavery (February 7, 1839)

Portending strained political relations between slaveholding and free states, Henry Clay (1777–1852) voiced concern over the growing influence of the Liberty Party and its commitment to abolition through political means. Such efforts, Clay suggested, were ominous, for they could only lead to violence. For Clay, states retained sovereign power to protect slavery, free states having no more authority to interfere with this power than they "would have to interfere with institutions existing in any foreign country." Rejecting the possibility that whites and blacks might coexist as equals, he anticipated a race war as the inevitable result of emancipation.

. . . There are three classes of persons opposed, or apparently opposed, to the continued existence of slavery in the United States. The first are those, who, from sentiments of philanthropy and humanity, are conscientiously opposed to the existence of slavery, but who are no less opposed, at the same time, to any disturbance of the peace and tranquility of the union, or the infringement of the powers of the states composing the confederacy. . . . The next class consists of apparent abolitionists; that is, those who, having been persuaded that the right of petition has been violated by Congress, cooperate with the abolitionists for the sole purpose of asserting and vindicating that right. And the third class are the real ultra-abolitionists, who are resolved to persevere in the pursuit of their object at all hazards, and without regard to any consequences, however calamitous they may be. With them the rights of property are nothing; the deficiency of the powers of the general government is nothing; civil war, a dissolution of the union, and the overthrow of a government in which are concentrated the fondest hopes of the civilized world, are nothing. . . . With this class, the immediate abolition of slavery in the District of Columbia, and in the territory of Florida, the prohibition of the removal of slaves from state to state, and the refusal to admit any new state, comprising within its limits the institution of domestic slavery, are but so many means conducing to the accomplishment of the ultimate but perilous end at which they avowedly and boldly aim. . . . Their purpose is abolition, universal abolition; peaceably if it can, forcibly if it must be. . . . [T]hey . . . promulgate to the world their purpose to be, to manumit forthwith, and without compensation, and without moral preparation, three millions of negro slaves. . . .

. . . They began their operations by professing to employ only persuasive means in appealing to the humanity, and enlightening the understandings, of the slave-holding portion of the union. . . . For some time they continued to make these appeals to our duty and our interest; but impatient with the slow influence of their logic upon our stupid minds, they recently resolved to change their system of action. To the agency of their powers of persuasion, they now propose to substitute the powers of the ballot-box; and he must be blind to what is passing before us, who does not perceive that the inevitable tendency of their proceedings is, if these should be found insufficient, to invoke, finally, the more potent powers of the bayonet.

. . . The Constitution of the United States never could have been formed upon the principle of investing the general government with authority to abolish the institution at its pleasure. It never can be continued for a single day, if the exercise of such a power be assumed or usurped. But it may be contended by these ultra-abolitionists, that their object is, not to stimulate the action of the general government, but to operate upon the states themselves, in which the institution of domestic slavery exists. If that be their object, why are these abolition societies and movements all confined to the free states? Why are the slave states wantonly and cruelly assailed? Why do the abolition presses teem with publications tending to excite hatred and animosity, on the part of the inhabitants of the free states, against those of the slave states? Why is congress petitioned? The free states have no more power or right to interfere with institutions in the slave states, confided to the exclusive jurisdiction of those states, than they would have to interfere with institutions existing in any foreign country. . . .

The next obstacle in the way of abolition, arises out of the fact of the presence in the slave states of three millions of slaves. . . . The slaves are here, and here must remain, in some condition; and, I repeat, how are they to be best governed? What is best to be done for their happiness and our own? In the slave states the alternative is, that the white man must govern the black, or the black govern the white. In several of those states, the number of the slaves is greater than that of the white population. An immediate abolition of slavery in them . . . would be followed by a desperate struggle for immediate ascendency of the black race over the white race, or rather it would be followed by instantaneous collisions between the two races, which would break out into a civil war, that would end in the extermination or subjugation of the one race or the other. . . . Is it not better for both parties that the existing state of things should be preserved, instead of exposing them to the horrible strifes and contests which would inevitably attend an immediate abolition? This is our true ground of defense, for the continued existence of slavery in our country. It is that which our revolutionary ancestors assumed. It is that which, in my opinion, forms our justification in the eyes of all Christendom.

A third impediment to immediate abolition is to be found in the immense amount of capital which is invested in slave property. . . . The total value . . . of the slave property in the United States, is twelve hundred millions of dollars. This property is diffused throughout all classes and conditions of society. It is owned by widows and orphans, by the aged and infirm, as well as the sound and vigorous. It is the subject of mortgages, deeds of trust, and family settlements. It has been made the basis of numerous debts contracted upon its faith, and is the sole reliance, in many instances, of creditors, within and without the slave states for the payment of the debts due to them. And now it is rashly proposed, by a single fiat of legislation, to annihilate this immense amount of property! To annihilate it without indemnity and without compensation to its owners! Does any considerate man believe it to be possible to effect such an object, without convulsion, revolution, and bloodshed? I know that there is a visionary dogma, which holds that negro slaves cannot be the subject of property. I shall not dwell long on this speculative abstraction. That is property which the law declares to be property. . . .

This is not all. The abolitionists strenuously oppose all separation of the two races. . . .

They proclaim . . . that color is nothing; that the organic and characteristic differences between the two races ought to be entirely overlooked and disregarded. And, elevating themselves to a sublime but impracticable philosophy, they would teach us to eradicate all the repugnances of our nature, and to take to our bosoms and our boards, the black man as we do the white, on the same footing of equal social condition. Do they not perceive that in thus confounding all the distinctions which God himself has made, they arraign the wisdom and goodness of Providence itself? It has been his divine pleasure to make the black man black, and the white man white, and to distinguish them by other repulsive constitutional differences. . . .

Abolition should no longer be regarded as an imaginary danger. The abolitionists, let me suppose, succeed in their present aim of uniting the inhabitants of the free states, as one man, against the inhabitants of the slave states. Union on the one side will beget union on the other. And this process of reciprocal consolidation will be attended with all the violent prejudices, embittered passions, and implacable animosities, which ever degraded or deformed human nature. . . . The most valuable element of union, mutual kindness, the feelings of sympathy, the fraternal bonds, which now happily unite us, will have been extinguished forever. . . . The collision of opinion will be quickly followed by the clash of arms. . . .

I am, Mr. President, no friend of slavery. The searcher of all hearts knows that every pulsation of mine beats high and strong in the cause of civil liberty. Wherever it is safe and practicable, I desire to see every portion of the human family in the enjoyment of it. But I prefer the liberty of my own country to that of any other people; and the liberty of my own race to that of any other race. The liberty of the descendants of Africa in the United States is incompatible with the safety and liberty of the European descendants. . . .

16. Theodore Dwight Weld, *Slavery as It Is: The Testimony of a Thousand Witnesses* (1839)

Theodore Weld set out to disprove the conventional view that slave owners treated their slaves like family. Weld (with the help of his wife, Angelina Grimké Weld, and her sister, Sarah Grimké) researched thousands of Southern newspapers and gathered incriminating accounts from the slave owners themselves that reveal in detail the torture and brutalization of their slaves. Distributed by the American Anti-Slavery Society, the book was widely influential. Most notably, Harriet Beecher Stowe drew upon these accounts in writing Uncle Tom's Cabin.

Introduction

READER, you are empanelled as a juror to try a plain case and bring in an honest verdict. The question at issue is not one of law, but of fact—"What is the actual condition of the slaves in the United States?" A plainer case never went to a jury. Look at it. TWENTY-SEVEN HUNDRED THOUSAND PERSONS in this country, men, women and children, are in SLAVERY. Is slavery, as a condition for human beings, good, bad or indifferent? We submit the question without argument. . . . You have a wife, or a husband, a child, a father, a mother, a brother, a sister—make the case your own, make it theirs, and bring in your verdict. . . .

[S]laveholders and their apologists are volunteer witnesses in their own cause, and are flooding the world with testimony that their slaves are kindly treated; that they are well fed, well clothed, well housed, well lodged, moderately worked, and bountifully provided with all things needful for their comfort. . . . We will prove that the slaves in the United States are treated with barbarous inhumanity; that they are overworked, underfed, wretchedly clad and lodged, and have insufficient sleep; that they are often made to wear round their necks iron collars armed with prongs, to drag heavy chains and weights at their feet while working in the field, and to wear yokes, and bells, and iron horns; that they are often kept confined in the stocks day and night for weeks together, made to wear gags in their mouths for hours or days, have some of their front teeth torn out or broken off, that they may be easily detected when they run away; that they are frequently flogged with terrible severity, have red pepper rubbed in their lacerated flesh, and hot brine, spirits of turpentine, &c., poured over the gashes to increase the torture; that they are often stripped naked, their backs and limbs cut with knives, bruised and mangled by scores and hundreds of blows with the paddle, and terribly torn by the claws of cats, drawn over them by their tormentors; that they are often hunted with blood hounds and shot down like beasts, or torn in pieces by dogs; that they are often suspended by the arms and whipped and beaten till they faint, and when revived by restoratives, beaten again till they faint, and sometimes till they die; that their ears are often cut off, their eyes knocked out, their bones broken, their flesh branded with red hot irons, that they are maimed, mutilated and burned to death over slow fires. All these things, and more, and worse, we shall *prove*. [W]e will establish all these facts by the testimony of *slaveholders* in all parts of the slave states. . . . We shall show, not merely that such deeds are committed, but that they are frequent; not done in corners, but before the sun; not in one of the slave states, but in all of them; not perpetrated by brutal overseers and drivers merely, but by magistrates, by legislators, by professors of religion, by preachers of the Gospel, by governors of states, by "gentlemen of property and standing," and by the delicate females moving in the "highest circle of society." . . .

Punishments

I. Floggings.

  . . . We will in the first place, prove by a cloud of witnesses, that the slaves are whipped with such inhuman severity, as to lacerate and mangle their flesh in the most shocking manner, leaving permanent scars and ridges; after establishing this, we will present a mass of testimony, concerning a great variety of other tortures. The testimony, for the most part, will be that of the slaveholders themselves, and in their own chosen words. A large portion of it will be taken from the advertisements, which they have published in their own newspapers, describing by the scars on their bodies made by the whip, their own runaway slaves. . . .

Witness	Testimony
Mr. D, Judd, Jailor, Davidson Co., Tennessee, in the "Nashville Banner," Dec, 10th, 1838.	"Committed to jail as a runaway, a negro woman named Martha, 17 or 18 years of age, *has numerous scars of the whip on her back.*"
Mr. Robert Nicoll, Dauphin st. . . . Mobile, Alabama, in the "Mobile Commercial Advertiser." . . .	"Ten dollars reward for my woman Siby, *very much scarred about the neck and ears by whipping.*" . . .
Maurice Y. Garcia, Sheriff of the County of Jefferson, La., in the "New Orleans Bee," August 14, 1838.	"Lodged in jail, a mulatto boy, *having large marks of the whip,* on his shoulders and other parts of his body." . . .
John A. Rowland, Jailor, Lumberton, North Carolina, in the "Fayetteville (N.C). Observer," June 20, 1838. . . .	"Committed, a mulatto fellow—his back shows *lasting impressions of the whip,* and leaves no doubt of his being A SLAVE."

. . .

III.   Brandings, Maimings, Gun-Shot Wounds, &c.

   The slaves are often branded with hot irons, pursued with fire arms and *shot,* hunted with dogs, and torn by them, shockingly maimed with knives, dirks, &c.; have their ears cut off, their eyes knocked out, their bones dislocated and broken with bludgeons, their fingers and toes cut off, their faces and other parts of their persons disfigured with scars and gashes, *besides* those made with the lash. . . .

Witness	Testimony
Mr. Micajah Ricks, Nash County, North Carolina, in the Raleigh "Standard," July 18, 1838	"Ranaway, a negro woman and two children; a few days before she went off, *I burnt her with a hot iron*, on the left side of her face, *I tried to make the letter M*."
Mr. Asa B. Metcalf, . . . in the "Natchez Courier," June 15, 1832	"Ranaway Mary, a black woman, has a *scar* on her back and right arm near the shoulder, *caused by a rifle ball*."
Madame Burvant . . . New Orleans, the "Bee," Dec. 21, 1838	"Ranaway a negro woman named Rachel, has *lost all her toes* except the large one."
Mr. R. W. Sizer, in the "Grand Gulf" Advertiser," July 8, 1837	"Ranaway my negro man Dennis, . . . has been *shot* in the left arm between the shoulders and elbow, which has paralyzed his left hand."

. . . The preceding are extracts from advertisements published in southern papers, mostly in the year 1838. They are the mere *samples* of hundreds of similar ones published during the same period, with which, as the preceding are quite sufficient to show the *commonness* of inhuman floggings in the slave states, we need not burden the reader. . . .

We will now present the testimony of a large number of individuals, with their names and residences,—persons who witnessed the inflictions to which they testify. Many of them have been slaveholders, and *all* residents for longer or shorter periods in slave states.

Rev. JOHN H. CURTISS, a native of Deep Creek, Norfolk county, Virginia, now a local preacher of the Methodist Episcopal Church in Portage co., Ohio, testifies as follows:—

"In 1829 or 30, one of my father's slaves was accused of taking the key to the office and stealing four or five dollars: he denied it. A constable by the name of Hull was called; he took the negro, very deliberately tied his hands, and whipped him till the blood ran freely down his legs. By this time Hull appeared tired, and stopped; he then took a rope, put a slip noose around his neck, and told the negro he was going to *kill* him, at the same time drew the rope and began whipping: the negro fell; his cheeks looked as though they would burst with strangulation. Hull whipped and kicked him, till I really thought he was going to kill him; when he ceased, the negro was in a complete gore of blood from head to foot." . . .

SAMUEL ELLISON, a member of the Society of Friends, formerly of Southampton county, Virginia, now of Marlborough, Stark county, Ohio, gives the following testimony:—

"While a resident of Southampton county, Virginia, I knew two men, after having been severely treated, endeavor to make their escape. In this they failed—were taken, tied to trees, and whipped to *death* by their overseer. I lived a mile from the negro quarters, and, at that distance, could frequently hear the screams of the poor creatures when beaten, and could also hear the blows given by the overseer with some heavy instrument." . . .

Mr. SAMUEL HALL, a teacher in Marietta College, Ohio, and formerly secretary of the Colonization society in that village, has recently communicated the facts which follow. We quote from his letter. . . .

"The following statement is made by a young man from Western Virginia. He is a member of the Presbyterian Church, and a student in Marietta College. All that prevents the introduction of his *name*, is the peril to his life, which would probably be the consequence, on his return to Virginia. His character for integrity and veracity is above suspicion.

'On the night of the great meteoric shower, in Nov. 1833. I was at Remley's tavern, 12 miles west of Lewisburg, Greenbrier Co., Virginia. A drove of 50 or 60 negroes stopped at the same place that night. They usually 'camp out,' but as it was excessively muddy, they were permitted to come into the house. So far as my knowledge extends, 'droves,' on their way to the south, eat but twice a day, early in the morning and at night. Their supper was a compound of 'potatoes and meal,' and was, without exception, *the dirtiest, blackest looking mess I ever saw.* . . . Such as it was, however, a black woman brought it on her head, in a tray or trough two and a half feet long, where the men and women were promiscuously herded. The slaves rushed up and seized it from the trough in handfulls, before the woman could take it off her head. They jumped at it as if half-famished. . . .

'There were three drivers, one of whom staid in the room to watch the drove, and the other two slept in an adjoining room. Each of the latter took a female from the drove to lodge with him, as is the common practice of the drivers generally. There is no doubt about this particular instance, *for they were seen together.* The mud was so thick on the floor where this *drove* slept, that it was necessary to take a shovel, the next morning, and clear it out. Six or eight in this drove were chained; all were for the south. . . .'"

17. John Quincy Adams, Address at Weymouth (1842)

When John Quincy Adams (1767–1848) delivered this address, he had already served as president and secretary of state, and the previous year he had argued before the U.S. Supreme Court in the famous Amistad case. A committed foe of slavery and the "Slave Power" in Congress, Adams fiercely opposed the annexation of Texas on the grounds that it would fortify slavery in the United States. Here he dismissed the doctrine of nullification as undemocratic and un-Christian. The reference to the "Atherton gag" is to the gag rule written by Congressman Charles G. Atherton (New Hampshire), which imposed a ban on anti-slavery petitions in the House, against which Adams tenaciously and successfully fought.

. . . The severance of Texas from Mexico, and its annexation to the United States, was undoubtedly an object to the colonists who went from the United States to settle there, of earnest desire. . . . In 1834, the revolt of Texas from Mexico was declared; precipitated if not chiefly caused by the abolition of Slavery by the Mexican Government. On the 2d of March, 1836, the Texan Declaration of Independence was issued, and on the 17th of the same month a Constitution of the Republic was proclaimed—framed on the model of those of our Southern States. It re-instituted the law of slavery, which Mexico had abolished—denied to the Legislature the power of emancipating slaves, and to the owners of slaves the power of emancipating them without the consent of the Legislature; it excluded all Africans, and descendants of Africans and Indians, from the name, rights and privileges of citizens, forever. . . . There is a Declaration of Rights annexed to this Constitution, and declared to be a part of it. This declaration embodies all the usual guards for the protection of liberty, but it avoids the base hypocrisy of declaring the equality of rights of all men, which pollutes some of our slavery-sullied Constitutions. The Constitution of the Republic of Texas, more warily worded, virtually repudiates the sublime doctrine of the natural rights of man, by merely saying, "All men, *when they form a social compact*, have equal rights"—and you all see how wide a margin this leaves for slavery and the slave trade, in their most hideous and disgusting forms. . . .

. . . The controlling object of this whole system of policy was, and yet is, to obtain a nursery of slave holding States, to break down forever the ascendant power of the free States, and to fortify, beyond all possibility of reversal, the institution of slavery. . . .

. . . Nullification was generated in the hot-bed of slavery. It drew its first breath in the land, where the meaning of the word democracy is that a majority of the people are the goods and chattels of the minority. That more than one half of the people are not men, women and children, but things to be treated by their owners, not exactly like dogs and horses, but like tables, chairs and joint-stools. That they are not even fixtures to the soil, as in countries where servitude is divested of its most hideous features; not even beings in the mitigated degradation from humanity of beasts, or birds, or creeping things; but destitute not only of the sensibilities of our own race of men, but of the sensations of all animated nature. That is the native land of nullification, and it is a theory of Constitutional law, worthy of its origin. *Democracy*, pure democracy, has at least its foundation in a generous theory of human rights. It is founded on the natural equality of mankind. It is the corner stone of the Christian religion. It is the first *element* of *all* lawful government upon earth. . . .

. . . The Southern or Slave party, outnumbered by the free, are cemented together by a common, intense interest of property to the amount of $1,200,000,000 in human beings, the very existence of which is neither allowed nor tolerated in the North. It is the opinion of many theoretical reasoners on the subject of Government, that whatever may be its form, the ruling power of every nation is its property. . . .

The utter and unqualified inconsistency of slavery . . . with the principles of . . . the Declaration of our Independence, had so forcibly struck the Southern champions of our rights, that the abolition of slavery and the emancipation of slaves was a darling project of Thomas Jefferson. . . . But the associated wealth of the slaveholders outweighed the principles of the Revolution, and by the Constitution of the U. States a compromise was established between slavery and freedom. The extent of the sacrifice of principle made by the North in this compromise, can be estimated only by its practical effects. . . . For practical results, look to the present composition of your Government. . . . The President of the United States—the President of the Senate—the Speaker of the House, all are slaveholders. The Chief Justice, and four other out of the nine Judges of the Supreme Court of the United States, are slaveholders. . . .

. . . By the dismemberment of Mexico, Texas and a territory of five hundred thousand square miles, might be annexed to the Union. Mexico had abolished slavery, but Texas had restored it and made it irrevocable. Ten States, with each a population exceeding that of Virginia, might be carved out of this territory, and place on immoveable foundations the supremacy and perpetuity of the slaveholding power.

[T]he same spell which has been of potency sufficient to fasten the Atherton gag upon the sacred right of petition, will find her equally ready to sacrifice all the inalienable rights of man to the Moloch of slavery, and to fasten, from the plunder of Mexico, ten slave-spotted States upon the Union, to settle for all time, and beyond the possibility of redemption, the preponderancy of Southern slavery over the democracy and the freedom of the North. . . .

18. James Freeman Clarke, Thanksgiving Day Sermon (November 24, 1842)

In this sermon, James Freeman Clarke (1810–1888) argued that slavery is a "soul-destroying system" that degrades the capacity of blacks to live as moral adults, a consequence even worse than the physical abuses they suffer. His sermon exposes the violence permeating slave culture, which, because of general complacency, has diffused into society as a whole.

I. Let us look . . . in the first place, at *the evils* in the system of slavery. . . .

1. First, the evils to the slave are very great. He is not always treated badly, but he is always *liable* to be so treated. He is entirely at the mercy of his master. If his master is passionate, arbitrary, despotical, avaricious, he is liable to be beaten, starved, over-worked, and separated from his family; and whoever knows human nature, knows that such cases will not be rare. . . .

A worse evil to the slave than the cruelties he sometimes endures, is the moral degradation which results from his conditions. Falsehood, theft, licentiousness, are the natural consequences of his situation. He steals,—why should he not?— . . . He lies,—it is the natural weapon of weakness against tyrant strength. He goes to excess in eating and drinking and animal pleasures,—for he has no access to any higher pleasures. And a man cannot be an animal without sinking below an animal,—a brutal man is worse than a brute. An animal cannot be more savage or more greedy than the law of his nature allows. But there seems to be no limit to the degradation of a man. Slavery is the parent of vice; it always has been, and always will be. Cowardice and cruelty, cunning and stupidity, abject submission and deadly vindictiveness are now as they always have been the fruits of slavery. . . .

Masters often can and do preserve their slaves from great immorality by careful superintendence,—but there is one evil so inherent in the system, that no care can obviate it. The slaves' nature never *grows*. The slave is always a child. God has made Progress and Freedom inseparable. You are astonished, when you first go to the South, to hear a grey-headed black man called *boy*, but there is a propriety, though unintended, in the term; they *are* boys always. What is it which turns the white child into a man, but the necessity of looking forward, of preparing *now* for the future? But the slave has no motive to look forward. He has nothing to hope, nothing to fear beyond the present day. If he should ever be so industrious, diligent, skillful and faithful, he would gain nothing by it,—he would only be worth so much more to his master. If he should ever be lazy, stupid, or unfaithful, he loses nothing by it. He must still be fed and clothed. His only ambition, then, is to do as little work as possible today, and to get as much rest, food and sleep as he can. . . .

The system of slavery, then, is a soul-destroying system. . . .

2. . . . The evils to the master are, perhaps, nearly as great. This is admitted by intelligent slaveholders. It was admitted by Mr. Clay, when he said . . . "that he considered the system as a curse to the master as well as a bitter wrong to the slave, and to be justified only by an urgent political necessity." It is an evil to the slaveholder in every way. It impoverishes him. Slave cultivation destroys the value of the soil,—manufactures cannot thrive where slavery exists. . . . It depopulates a country. Kentucky has greater advantages than Ohio . . . and yet the population of Ohio was about double that of Kentucky in 1840. Slavery is a domestic evil. There is no comfort, no cleanliness, no improvement with slaves in your family. It is a perpetual annoyance and vexation. Society is poisoned in its roots by this system. The spirit, tone, and aim of society is incurably bad, wherever slavery is. . . . Public education is out of the question in slave States,—common schools cannot exist except in cities. . . .

With the bloody affrays that are constantly occurring in the Slave states, we are all familiar. There no white man is ever punished for shooting or stabbing his enemy in the street. According to Southern law, to go up to a man in the highway, abuse him till he is provoked to make some violent reply, and then to draw a knife and cut him down, is self-defense. In the city where I lived, three Mississippi gentlemen, one a judge, attacked three unarmed mechanics, who had offended them, in a public bar-room, with dirks and bowie knives. Two of the mechanics were killed, one by the judge. . . . The judge was tried . . . and acquitted.

From the speech of the prosecuting officer . . . I quote the following testimony to the different habits of the South and North.

"If you can go into the Northern States, it is a rare thing if you can find a man in ten thousand with concealed weapons on his person. Go South . . . and though you would be a peaceable man at the North, in these states you may arm yourself to the teeth, and track your steps in blood with impunity." . . .

The cause of this is obvious,—habits of dictation and violence, formed among slaves, cause these affrays among masters. . . .

II. Let us now examine the question of the *sinfulness* of slavery.

There are two theories on this subject which I think extreme,—one, of the Abolitionists who demand immediate emancipation,—the other, of the South Carolina party of slaveholders.

The first theory declares that to hold slaves, or to have anything to do with holding slaves, is always sinful, and to be repented of immediately,—that no slaveholder should be permitted to commune in our churches, and that we should come out and be separate from this unclean thing as far as possible. . . .

The other party . . . declare slavery to be a system which is sanctioned by the Bible, has existed in all times, and is necessary to the progress of the world in freedom and happiness. . . .

Now the true doctrine, I think, is, that slavery as a system is thoroughly sinful and bad,—but it does not follow that every slaveholder commits sin in holding slaves. That the whole spirit of the gospel is opposed to slavery, and that the tendency of Christianity is to break every yoke, is perfectly plain. But the fact . . . that Jesus and his Apostles did not attempt violently to overthrow and uproot this institution, did not denounce all slaveholders, and that while we have catalogues of sins which are to be repented and forsaken, slaveholding is not among them, shows that, under all circumstances, it is not sinful. This is also evident from fact. Here is a young man who inherits a hundred slaves from his father; some are good, some bad; some are industrious, some idle; some young, some old,—shall he tell them they are free, and let them go? Some could do well, but others not,—they are too old, or too idle, or too vicious,— they have been made so by slavery, and it is the duty of the slaveholder to keep them and take care of them, till they can be prepared for freedom. . . .

What is needed more than anything else now . . . is a class of *independent* men—who will not go at all lengths with any party—who will govern themselves by conscience—who will not join the abolitionists in their denunciations and their violence, nor join the South in their defense of slavery—who can be temperate without being indifferent—who can be moderate and zealous also—who can make *themselves felt* as third power, holding the balance between violent parties, and compelling both to greater moderation and justice. . . . We can avoid the fanaticism of the North and the South. We can oppose to the violence and passion of Southern blood, the sterner and more awful face of conscience. . . .

19. Henry Highland Garnet, Address to the Slaves of the United States of America, Speech Delivered to the National Convention of Colored Citizens (August 16, 1843; published in 1848)

Henry Highland Garnet (1815–1882) argued that slaves have a moral obligation to resist their oppressors, shifting the onus for emancipation from whites to blacks themselves. He pointed to a number of resisters, including Nat Turner and Denmark Vesey, as heroic examples of dying for freedom rather than living as slaves.

. . . Two hundred and twenty seven years ago, the first of our injured race were brought to the shores of America. They came not with glad spirits to select their homes in the New World. They came not with their own consent, to find an unmolested enjoyment of the blessings of this fruitful soil. The first dealings they had with men calling themselves Christians, exhibited to them the worst features of corrupt and sordid hearts; and convinced them that no cruelty is too great, no villainy and no robbery too abhorrent for even enlightened men to perform, when influenced by avarice and lust. Neither did they come flying upon the wings of Liberty, to a land of freedom. But they came with broken hearts, from their beloved native land, and were doomed to unrequited toil and deep degradation. Nor did the evil of their bondage end at their emancipation by death. Succeeding generations inherited their chains. . . .

The propagators of the system, or their immediate ancestors, very soon discovered its growing evil, and its tremendous wickedness, and secret promises were made to destroy it. The gross inconsistency of a people holding slaves, who had themselves "ferried o'er the wave" for freedom's sake, was too apparent to be entirely overlooked. The voice of Freedom cried, "Emancipate your slaves." . . . But all was in vain. Slavery had stretched its dark wings of death over the land, the Church stood silently by, the priests prophesied falsely, and the people loved to have it so. Its throne is established, and now it reigns triumphantly. . . .

The colonists threw the blame upon England. They said that the mother country entailed the evil upon them, and that they would rid themselves of it if they could. The world thought they were sincere, and the philanthropic pitied them. But time soon tested their sincerity. In a few years the colonists grew strong, and severed themselves from the British Government. Their independence was declared, and they took their station among the sovereign powers of the earth. The declaration was a glorious document. Sages admired it, and the patriotic of every nation reverenced the God-like sentiments which it contained. When the power of Government returned to their hands, did they emancipate the slaves? No; they rather added new links to our chains. Were they ignorant of the principles of Liberty? Certainly they were not. The sentiments of their revolutionary orators fell in burning eloquence upon their hearts, and with one voice they cried, *Liberty or Death*. Oh what a sentence was that! It ran from soul to soul like electric fire, and nerved the arm of thousands to fight in the holy cause of Freedom. . . .

Slavery! How much misery is comprehended in that single word. What mind is there that does not shrink from its direful effects? Unless the image of God be obliterated from the soul, all men cherish the love of Liberty. . . . In every man's mind the good seeds of liberty are planted, and he who brings his fellow down so low, as to make him contented with a condition of slavery, commits the highest crime against God and man. Brethren, your oppressors aim to do this. They endeavor to make you as much like brutes as possible. . . .

To such Degradation it is sinful in the Extreme for you to make voluntary Submission. The divine commandments you are in duty bound to reverence and obey. If you do not obey them, you will surely meet with the displeasure of the Almighty. He requires you to love him supremely, and your neighbor as yourself—to keep the Sabbath day holy—to search the Scriptures—and bring up your children with respect for his laws, and to worship no other God but him. But slavery sets all these at naught, and hurls defiance in the face of Jehovah. The forlorn condition in which you are placed does not destroy your moral obligation to God. You are not certain of Heaven, because you suffer yourselves to remain in a state of slavery, where you cannot obey the commandments of the Sovereign of the universe. If the ignorance of slavery is a passport to heaven, then it is a blessing, and no curse, and you should rather desire its perpetuity than its abolition. God will not receive slavery, nor ignorance, nor any other state of mind, for love and obedience to him. Your condition does not absolve you from your moral obligation. The diabolical injustice by which your Liberties are cloven down, *neither God; nor angels, or just men, command you to suffer for a single moment. Therefore it is your solemn and imperative duty to use every means, both moral; intellectual and physical that promises success.* . . .

Brethren, the time has come when you must act for yourselves. It is an old and true saying that, "if hereditary bondmen would be free, they must themselves strike the blow." You can plead your own cause, and do the work of emancipation better than any others. . . . Look around you, and behold the bosoms of your loving wives heaving with untold agonies! Hear the cries of your poor children! Remember the stripes your fathers bore. Think of the torture and disgrace of your noble mothers. Think of your wretched sisters, loving virtue and purity, as they are driven into concubinage and are exposed to the unbridled lusts of incarnate devils. Think of the undying glory that hangs around the ancient name of Africa—and forget not that you are native born American citizens, and as such, you are justly entitled to all the rights that are granted to the freest. Think how many tears you have poured out upon the soil which you have cultivated with unrequited toil and enriched with your blood; and then go to your lordly enslavers and tell them plainly, that you *are determined to be free*. Appeal to their sense of justice, and tell them that they have no more right to oppress you, than you have to enslave them. Entreat them to remove the grievous burdens which they have imposed upon you, and to remunerate you for your labor. Promise them renewed diligence in the cultivation of the soil, if they will render to you an equivalent for your services. Point them to the increase of happiness and prosperity in the British West Indies since the Act of Emancipation. Tell them in language which they cannot misunderstand, of the exceeding sinfulness of slavery, and of a future judgment, and of the righteous retributions of an indignant God. Inform them that all you desire is *freedom*, and that nothing else will suffice. Do this, and for ever after cease to toil for the heartless tyrants, who give you no other reward but stripes and abuse. If they then commence the work of death, they, and not you, will be responsible for the consequences. You had far better all *die immediately*, than live slaves and entail your wretchedness upon your posterity. If you would be free in this generation, here is your only hope. However much you and all of us may desire it, there is not much hope of redemption without the shedding of blood. If you must bleed, let it all come at once—rather *die freemen, than live to be slaves.* . . .

Fellow men! patient sufferers! behold your dearest rights crushed to the earth! See your sons murdered, and your wives, mothers and sisters doomed to prostitution! In the name of the merciful God, and by all that life is worth, let it no longer be a debatable question whether it is better to choose *Liberty or death*!

In 1822, Denmark Veazie [Vesey], of South Carolina, formed a plan for the liberation of his fellow men. In the whole history of human efforts to overthrow slavery, a more complicated and tremendous plan was never formed. He was betrayed by the treachery of his own people, and died a martyr to freedom. Many a brave hero fell, but history, faithful to her high trust, will transcribe his name on the same monument with Moses, Hampden, Tell, Bruce and Wallace, Toussaint L'Ouverture, Lafayette and Washington. That tremendous movement shook the whole empire of slavery. The guilty soul thieves were overwhelmed with fear. It is a matter of fact, that at that time, and in consequence of the threatened revolution, the slave States talked strongly of emancipation. But they blew but one blast of the trumpet of freedom and then laid it aside. As these men became quiet, the slaveholders ceased to talk about emancipation; and now behold your condition today! . . .

The patriotic Nathaniel Turner followed Denmark Veazie [Vesey]. He was goaded to desperation by wrong and injustice. By despotism, his name has been recorded on the list of infamy, and future generations will remember him among the noble and brave.

Next arose the immortal Joseph Cinqué, the hero of the *Amistad.* He was a native African, and by the help of God he emancipated a whole ship-load of his fellow men on the high seas. And he now sings of liberty on the sunny hills of Africa and beneath his native palm trees, where he hears the lion roar and feels himself as free as that king of the forest.

Next arose Madison Washington, that bright star of freedom, and took his station in the constellation of true heroism. He was a slave on board the brig *Creole,* of Richmond, bound to New Orleans, that great slave mart, with a hundred and four others. Nineteen struck for liberty or death. But one life was taken, and the whole were emancipated, and the vessel was carried into Nassau, New Providence.

Noble men! Those who have fallen in freedom's conflict, their memories will be cherished by the true hearted and the God-fearing in all future generations; those who are living, their names are surrounded by a halo of glory.

Brethren, arise, arise! Strike for your lives and liberties. Now is the day and the hour. Let every slave throughout the land do this, and the days of slavery are numbered. You cannot be more oppressed than you have been—you cannot suffer greater cruelties than you have already. *Rather die freemen than live to be slaves.* Remember that you are *three millions*!

It is in your power so to torment the God-cursed slaveholders that they will be glad to let you go free. If the scale was turned, and black men were the masters and white men the slaves, every destructive agent and element would be employed to lay the oppressor low. Danger and death would hang over their heads day and night. Yes, the tyrants would meet with plagues more terrible than those of Pharaoh. But you are a patient people. You act as though you were made for the special use of these devils. You act as though your daughters were born to pamper the lusts of your masters and overseers. And worse than all, you tamely submit while your lords tear your wives from your embraces and defile them before your eyes. In the name of God, we ask, are you men? Where is the blood of your fathers? Has it all run out of your veins? Awake, awake; millions of voices are calling you! Your dead fathers speak to you from their graves. Heaven, as with a voice of thunder, calls on you to arise from the dust. . . .

Let your motto be resistance! *Resistance! Resistance!* No oppressed people have ever secured their liberty without resistance. . . .

20. Charles Hodge, "The Integrity of Our National Union vs. Abolitionism," *The Biblical Repertory and Princeton Review* (1844)

In this review of George Junkin's 1843 publication, "The Integrity of Our National Union," Charles Hodge (1797–1878), a leading Presbyterian theologian, took issue with advocates of immediate abolitionism as well as with slavery's most ardent apologists. At the core of his essay is an emphasis on the rights and corresponding duties of Christian slaveholders. Cassius M. Clay, mentioned at the start of the essay, was an abolitionist newspaper editor.

. . . If, in our day, and in this country, you ask a man whether he is an abolitionist, he will promptly answer no, though, he may believe with Jefferson that slavery is the greatest curse that can be inflicted on a nation; or with Cassius M. Clay, that it is destructive of industry, the mother of ignorance, opposed to literature, antagonist to the fine arts; that it corrupts the people, retards population and wealth, impoverishes the soil, destroys national wealth, and is incompatible with constitutional liberty. A man may believe and say all this, as many of the best and wisest men of the South believe and openly avow, and yet be no abolitionist. . . . What then is an abolitionist? He is a man who holds that slaveholding is a great sin; and consequently that slaveholders should not be admitted to the communion of the church, and that slavery should be immediately, under all circumstances, and regardless of all consequences, be abolished. "Slaveholding," says the second article of the American Anti-slavery Society, "is a heinous crime in the sight of God," and "ought therefore to be immediately abolished." . . .

. . . "A slave," says the Reviewer of Dr. Junkin's pamphlet, "is a human being who is made an article of property." And this is the definition usually given by abolitionists. The gravamen of the charge against slavery is, that it makes a man a thing in distinction from a person. This charge is an absurdity in the very terms of it; and yet we doubt not that it is some obscure feeling of outrage to human nature involved in making "a man a thing," that is the source of much of the horror commonly expressed on this subject; and the reason of the ready credence often given to the doctrine that "slaveholding is a heinous crime." It would indeed be a grave crime, and moreover a great miracle, if it involved making things of human beings. The abolitionists impose upon themselves and others by not defining what they mean by property, and by not determining the sense in which one man can be said to be the property of another man. Property is simply the right of possession and use; the right of having and using. From the necessity of the case, as well as from the laws of God, this right must vary according to the nature of its object. If a man has property in land, he must use it as land, and he cannot use it as anything else. If he has property in an animal he can only use it as an animal; and if he has property in a man, he can only use him as a man. And as the use he may make of an animal is regulated by its nature and by the laws of God; so his property in a man gives him no right to treat him contrary to his nature, or to act towards him with injustice. If one man has property in another he must still treat him as a human being. . . . What men have the power to do, in virtue of the relation in which they stand to others, and what they have a right to do in virtue of that relation, are two very different things, which abolitionists constantly confound. . . .

. . . [A]s all slaves in this country were born such, the only practically important question is, whether a constitution of society in which one man is by birth placed in such a relation to another man to be bound to labour for him, upon condition of having all his wants as a human being adequately supplied, is necessarily sinful? That question cannot be answered in the affirmative, without asserting that it is sinful to have the relative position of men in society determined by the accident of birth. And this latter position cannot be maintained, without contradicting the Bible and the common judgment of mankind. . . . Such an arrangement cannot in itself be sinful, because God ordained it; nor does the light of nature contradict this decision of the word of God. . . . Men are left at liberty to determine the mode in which society shall be constituted, guided by the peculiar circumstances of the community, and the immutable obligation to adopt that method which is for the general good. Moreover, neither the church nor world has ever maintained that hereditary monarchy and hereditary nobility, were in their own nature sinful. . . . [E]ven if the monarch were possessed of irresponsible power over the property and lives of his subjects, undesirable and impossible as such a form of government would be, in an advanced state of society, it would not in its nature be sinful. . . . But if the word of God does not condemn as sinful either the possession of unlimited power, or the designation by the accident of birth, of the person who is to hold it; then it is admitted that it is not necessarily sinful that one man should by birth be assigned to the rank of king, noble, or master, and another to that of subject, commoner, or slave. As this diversity of condition among men has always existed, as there has always been masters and servants, if there is nothing sinful in the nature of the relation, neither is there in its being determined by birth.

Does then, the word of God sanction this relation? Did it permit the Israelites to own men, to buy and sell them? If so, then no man who can bow his heart and conscience to the authority of God, can pronounce slaveholding to be a heinous crime. It is conceded that the heathen by whom these patriarchs and their descendants were surrounded, were slaveholders in the strictest sense. . . . Abraham is spoken of as having men servants and maid servants, they are enumerated as a part of his possessions. . . . So in later times we hear of the Hebrews having, buying, and selling slaves. . . . In Numbers xxxi. 26 . . . we have an account of the distribution of the spoil taken from the Midianites, among whom women and children are enumerated, and which were given in certain proportions to the conquerors. . . . As we have in this case one of the ways in which the Hebrews were allowed by God to acquire slaves, so we hear of their possessing them, and buying and selling them. In Lev. xxii. 10, 11, it is said, "A sojourner of a priest, or an hired servant, shall not eat of the holy thing. But if the priest buy any soul with his money he shall eat of it, and he that is born in his house, they shall eat of it. . . ."

We have thought it the less necessary to go into detail on the argument from the Old Testament, because we consider abolitionists as abandoning the whole ground, and conceding the whole question, when they come to the New Testament. . . . The admitted facts of the case are these, 1. That at the time of the introduction of Christianity slavery in its worst form prevailed extensively over the world. . . . 2. That, neither Christ nor his apostles ever denounced slaveholding as a crime. 3. That, they never urged emancipation as an immediate duty. These are the facts, the inference is irresistible, slaveholding cannot be a crime. . . . [T]he apostles, though living under the reign of Nero, while they denounce all injustice and cruelty, whether in despot, master, or parent, never say a word about the sin of despotism. On the contrary, they enjoined the duty of submission to the exercise of that authority; teaching that human government, however constituted, was an ordinance of God. . . .

. . . What the abolitionists, for the most part, really condemn, the true objects of their moral disapprobation, is not slaveholding, but the slave laws; and what the other party vindicate as not necessarily inconsistent with the will of God, is slaveholding, and not the slave laws of this or any other country. It is the want of discrimination between these entirely distinct things, SLAVEHOLDING AND THE SLAVE LAWS, we firmly believe is the cause of a great part of the difference of sentiment which exists on this subject. . . . The abolitionists constantly assume that the incidents of the right of property are the same whatever may be the nature of its object. Hence they infer that if one man may justly hold another man as property, he may justly treat him as he may treat any other article of property; if the validity of the title be acknowledged, it follows that the owner may disregard the nature of his slave; treat him as if he were not a husband, or not a parent; as though he had no social affections; or was not a rational being, and had no soul to be saved or lost. This is what they mean to condemn, and if this was a correct view of what is meant by the right of property in man, there could be no diversity of opinion as to whether slaveholding were a heinous crime. . . .

. . . When they speak of slaveholding as a sin, they mean that it is a sin to do what the slave laws of the south permit to be done; to separate parents and children, or husbands and wives; to treat slaves with injustice and cruelty; to prevent their learning to read the word of God, or attending the preaching of the gospel. And when any man asserts that slaveholding is not a crime, they consider him as saying that it is not a sin thus to trample on the dearest rights of our fellow men. . . . This distinction which is so plain as to be glaring, it is of great importance should be bourne in mind both in the North and South. In the North, to prevent the sin and folly of condemning all slaveholders as criminals, when the slave laws are the real objects meant to be condemned; and in the South, to prevent those who maintain that slaveholding is no sin, from thinking it necessary to defend, and from expecting others to defend the existing laws in relation to that subject. . . .

By slaveholding we understand one man's having the right of property in another man; and by the right of property we understand the right of having and using a thing according to its nature; and consequently the right of property in a man can be nothing more than the right to use him as a man. . . . [A]s the possession of rights implies corresponding duties, the possession of property in a man, imposes the responsibility of providing for his wants as a man. So far, therefore, from maintaining that a master has a right in virtue of his ownership, to prevent his slaves marrying, or to separate them when married, or to keep them in ignorance, or to debar them from the means of grace, we say that it of necessity flows from his right of property in them, that he has no right to do any of these things, but is bound to the direct reverse. . . .

It follows necessarily, from what has been said, that all those laws which are designed to restrict the master in the discharge of the duties, which flow from his relation to his slaves; which forbid his teaching them to read, or which prohibit marriages among them, or which allow of the separation of those who are married . . . or are otherwise in conflict with the word of God, are wicked laws; laws which do not find their justification in the admission of the right of ownership in the master, but are in direct contravention of the obligations which necessarily flow from that right. . . .

The principles above stated we believe to be scriptural and in accordance with the enlightened moral sense of men. . . . The principles and conduct, on the other hand, of our abolitionists, we believe to be unchristian and in the highest degree injurious. If their distinctive doctrine is erroneous, then denouncing slaveholders as such, excluding them from the church, insisting on immediate emancipation as in all cases a duty, are all seen and felt to be unreasonable; and the spirit with which this course is pursued, to be unchristian. The consequence is that opposition and alienation are produced between those who ought to be united; slaveholders who do not belong to the church are exasperated, and become more severe in the treatment of their slaves. . . .

As the cause of temperance was disparaged, weakened, and in some places ruined, by making all use of intoxicating drinks sinful; so the cause of the slave has been injured beyond estimate, by the doctrine that slaveholding is itself a crime, and by the spirit and measures to which that doctrine has given rise.

Any candid man can see . . . that the scriptural doctrine is adapted to promote the best interests of the slave. . . . If a man owns another he is for that very reason bound to feed and clothe him, to provide for him in sickness and old age, to educate him and let the light of truth and saving knowledge in upon his mind, to watch over his rights, to exercise all the power which his ownership gives him in accordance with those rules of mercy and righteousness, which are laid down in the word of God. It is also evident that acting in accordance with these principles would soon so improve the condition of the slaves, would make them intelligent, moral and religious, and thus work out to the benefit of all concerned, and the removal of the institution. For slavery like despotism supposes the actual inferiority, and consequent dependence of those held in subjection. Neither can be permanent. Both may be prolonged by keeping the subject class degraded, that is by committing sin on a large scale, which is only to treasure up wrath for the day of wrath. It is only the antagonistic fanaticism of a fragment of the south, which maintains the doctrine that slavery is in itself a good thing, and ought to be perpetuated. It cannot by possibility be perpetuated. The only question is, how is it to end? All that we are concerned with, is present duty; and that duty, inferred from the nature of the relation, and declared in the word of god, is to instruct, to civilize, to evangelize the slaves, to make them as far as we can, intelligent, moral and religious; good husbands, good fathers, as well as good servants. The consequence of such conduct must be peace, a good conscience, and the blessing of God. . . .

21. Wendell Phillips, *The Constitution, a Pro-Slavery Compact* (1845)

Like other Garrisonians, Wendell Phillips (1811–1884) condemned the Constitution for protecting slavery, rejecting arguments to the contrary. According to Phillips, the Constitution's wording, the way it had been interpreted, even the notes from the Constitutional Convention, are proof enough of its unworthy "compromise between slavery and freedom." Consequently, it was a "covenant with death" that no abolitionist could rightfully support.

. . . The first of these clauses, relating to representation, confers on a slave-holding community additional political power for every slave held among them, and thus tempts them to continue to uphold the system: the second and the last, relating to insurrection and domestic violence, perfectly innocent in themselves—yet being made with the fact directly in view that slavery exists among us, do deliberately pledge the whole national force against the unhappy slave if he imitate our fathers and resist oppression—thus making us partners in the guilt of sustaining slavery: the third, relating to the slave-trade, disgraces the nation by a pledge not to abolish that traffic till after twenty years, *without obliging Congress to do so even then*, and thus the slave-trade may be legalized tomorrow if Congress choose: the fourth is a promise on the part of the whole Nation to return fugitive slaves to their masters, a deed which God's law expressly condemns and which every noble feeling of our nature repudiates with loathing and contempt. . . .

. . . A few persons, to be sure, of late years, to serve the purposes of a party, have tried to prove that the Constitution makes no compromise with slavery. Notwithstanding the clear light of history; the unanimous decision of all the courts in the land, both State and Federal; the action of Congress and the State Legislature; the constant practice of the Executive in all its branches; and the deliberate acquiescence of the whole people for half a century, still they contend that the Nation does not know its own meaning, and that the Constitution does not tolerate slavery!

Every candid mind, however, must acknowledge that the language of the Constitution is clear and explicit. . . .

But granting that the terms of the Constitution are ambiguous—that they are susceptible of two meanings, if the unanimous, concurrent, unbroken practice of every department of the Government, judicial, legislation, and executive, and the acquiescence of the whole people for fifty years do not prove which is the true construction, then how and where can such a question ever be settled? If the people and the Courts of the land do not know what they themselves mean, who has authority to settle their meaning for them?

If then the people and the Courts of a country are to be allowed to determine what their own laws mean, it follows that at this time and for the last half century, the Constitution of the United States has been, and still is, a pro-slavery instrument, and that anyone who swears to support it, swears to do pro-slavery acts, and violates his duty both as a man and as an abolitionist. What the Constitution may become a century hence, we know not; we speak of it *as* it is, and repudiate it *as* it *is*.

. . . Some men, finding the nation unanimously deciding that the Constitution tolerates slavery, have tried to prove that this false construction, as they think *it*, has been hoisted into the instrument by the corrupting influence of slavery itself, tainting all it touches. They assert that the known antislavery spirit of revolutionary times never *could* have consented to so infamous a bargain as the Constitution is represented to be, and has in its present hands become. Now these pages prove the melancholy fact, that willingly, with deliberate purpose, our fathers bartered honesty for gain, and became partners with tyrants, that they might share in the profits of their tyranny. . . .

Besides, the advocates of this new theory of the Anti-slavery character of the Constitution quote some portions of the Madison Papers in support of their views; and this makes it proper that the community should hear *all* that these Debates have to say on the subject. The further we explore them, the clearer becomes the fact, that the Constitution was meant to be, what it has always been esteemed, a compromise between slavery and freedom.

If then the Constitution be, what these Debates show that our fathers intended to make it, and that, too, their descendants, this nation, say they did make it and agreed to uphold, then we affirm that it is a "covenant with death and an agreement with hell," and ought to be immediately annulled. [N]o abolitionist can consistently take office under it, or swear to support it.

But if, on the contrary, our fathers failed in their purpose, and the Constitution is all pure and untouched by slavery, then, the Union itself is impossible, without guilt. . . . To continue this disastrous alliance longer is madness. The trial of fifty years with the best of men and the best of Constitutions, on this supposition, only proves that it is impossible for free and slave States to unite on any terms, without all becoming partners in guilt and responsibility for the sin of slavery. We dare not prolong the experiment, and with double earnestness we repeat our demand upon every honest man to join in the outcry of the American Anti-Slavery Society,—

NO UNION WITH SLAVEHOLDERS!

Chapter Five: 1847–1853

Introduction

Events in the mid-1840s once again thrust the issue of slavery into national politics. Issues related to slavery figured prominently in the presidential contests of 1844 and 1848, shaping the national political conversation. Annexation of the Republic of Texas, which had declared and won independence from Mexico in 1836, was the central issue of the 1844 presidential election. When James K. Polk defeated Henry Clay, the United States Congress passed a joint resolution that brought Texas into the Union directly as a state (bypassing the territorial stage). The full extent of Texas' dominion, however, remained unsettled. Texas claimed southern and western borders that included lands all the way to the Rio Grande—a much larger territory than the former Mexican state of Texas. In acquiring Texas, the United States was thus drawn into a bitter border dispute. In 1845 President Polk sent diplomats to Mexico City with an offer to purchase the disputed territory, along with New Mexico and California. Meanwhile, he deployed United States soldiers into the contested area. Mexico responded by breaking off diplomatic ties, and war rapidly followed. Few doubted that the United States intended to take by force not only the disputed Texas borderlands but also the entire Mexican northwest extending to California.

Many in the North believed that the war with Mexico was part of a Southern conspiracy to seize additional land into which slavery could expand. Abolitionist poet James Russell Lowell captured Northern sentiments well, writing in 1846:

> Them thet rule us, them slave-traders,
> Hain't they cut a thunderin' swarth
> (Helped by Yankee renegaders)
> Thru the vartu o' the North!
> . . . .
> They jest want this Californy
> So 's to lug new slave States in,
> To abuse ye, an' to scorn ye,
> An' to plunder ye like sin.[1]

---

1. "The Biglow Papers," in *The Early Poems of James Russell Lowell, Including The Biglow Papers, with Biographical Sketch by Henry Ketcham* (A. L. Burt, 1900), 39 and 41.

Consequently, Northern politicians endorsed the 1846 proposal by Pennsylvania congressman David Wilmot to ban slavery from territories seized through the war. The Wilmot Proviso failed, but it was supported by state legislatures in every Northern state and by nearly every Northern member of the House of Representatives. In a speech on the proviso, Joshua Giddings from Ohio declared the war with Mexico to be an "aggressive war," aimed at "expending the blood and treasure of the nation for the extension of an institution odious to man and forbidden by the laws of God."[2] Outside the halls of Congress, citizens voiced their objections as well. Influential transcendentalist Henry David Thoreau refused to pay a local poll tax in an act of civil disobedience against the injustice of slavery and institutions that supported it. "When a sixth of the population of a nation which has undertaken to be the refuge of liberty are slaves, and a whole country is unjustly overrun and conquered by a foreign army, and subjected to military law, I think that it is not too soon for honest men to rebel and revolutionize," he later explained. "What makes this duty the more urgent is that fact that the country so overrun is not our own, but ours is the invading army."[3]

For the United States, the outcome of the war against Mexico added vast territories in the west extending to the Pacific Ocean. This raised the issue of the status of slavery in those new territories acquired by conquest. The great national debate of 1819–1820 had previously settled the question, but only for the lands encompassed within the Louisiana Purchase. The conquest of new territories reopened the question, this time in a Union even more fractured by debate over the morality and legality of slavery.

Unlike the Louisiana Territory, where both the French and Spanish empires had enacted positive law that secured property in slaves, Mexico had abolished slavery. Southern proposals to extend slavery into lands conquered from Mexico thus amounted to the reintroduction of slavery into areas where the hard work of abolition was already accomplished. No one could argue that, in the Mexican cessions, slavery was an institution unfortunately inherited from misguided ancestors. Americans now held unqualified responsibility with regard to any designs involving the expansion of slavery.

In the ensuing political debates, four distinct positions emerged. James Buchanan, President Polk's secretary of state and a contender for the Democratic nomination in 1848, suggested that the federal government simply extend the Missouri Compromise line westward to the coast. This would have permitted

---

2. Joshua Giddings, speech to the House of Representatives, *Congressional Globe Appendix*, 29th Cong., 2d Sess., 404 (1847).

3. Henry David Thoreau, "Civil Disobedience," in *The Writings of Henry David Thoreau*, vol. 4, *Cape Cod and Miscellanies*, ed. B. Torrey and F. B. Sanborn (Boston: Houghton Mifflin, 1906), 361.

slavery in present-day Arizona, New Mexico, and southern California. This suggestion was quickly eclipsed by a second proposal, advanced by Michigan senator Lewis Cass. Cass, who eventually secured nomination in 1848 as the Democratic candidate for president, argued that "the theory of our Government presupposes that its various members have reserved to themselves the regulation of all subjects relating to what may be termed their internal police. . . . Local institutions," he explained, "whether they have reference to slavery, or to any other relations, domestic or public, are left to local authority."[4] Accordingly, it was settlers, not Congress, who should determine whether slavery would be permitted in a particular territory. This idea, which in time came to be known as "popular sovereignty," defined the Democratic effort to resolve the question for the next decade.

Southern Democrats articulated a much more aggressive and uncompromising third position. John C. Calhoun argued that slavery was not something on which the federal government was qualified to legislate. Slavery was a matter for the state governments to determine. "As the federal representative of each and all the States," Calhoun argued, the federal government "is bound to deal out, within the sphere of its powers, equal and exact justice and favor to all." Thus, any effort by the federal government to prevent the expansion of slavery into the federal territories would be both unfair and unconstitutional. "What then we do insist on," Calhoun declaimed, "is, not to extend slavery, but that we shall not be prohibited from immigrating with our property, into the Territories of the United States, because we are slaveholders."[5] Unlike Cass' position, which presumably permitted territorial governments to ban slavery, Calhoun insisted that it was simply a matter of fairness for Southern planters to be able to move to the federal territories, and to bring their slaves with them.

Fourth, a newly emergent political party, the Free Soil Party, offered a different kind of uncompromising position. This party coalesced around the earlier Liberty Party, joined by abolitionist "Conscience" Whigs and by anti-slavery Democrats. "Let the soil of our extensive domains be kept free for the hardy pioneers of our own land, and the oppressed and banished of other lands, seeking homes of comfort and fields of enterprise in the new world," Free Soilers proclaimed in their 1848 party platform. "We accept the issue which the Slave power has forced upon us; and to their demand for more slave States, and more slave Territory, our calm but final answer is, no more slave States and no more slave Territory."[6] Under the slogan "Free Soil, Free Speech, Free Labor, and Free Men," the party endorsed the Wilmot Proviso and advocated for a federal homestead law to promote the movement of impoverished Northern families

---

4. See document 1 in this chapter.
5. See document 4 in this chapter.
6. "Free Soil Platform of 1848," *The Platform Text Book* (Vincent Publishing, 1900), 46–48. The quoted passage comes from the eighth resolution.

to newly opened western farmlands. While the party won no Electoral College votes in 1848, 10 percent of the electorate voted for the Free Soil candidate, former Democratic president Martin Van Buren.

The appeal of the Free Soil platform was considerably broader than that of the more committed abolitionists. The Wilmot Proviso attracted a wide range of supporters, including those who were influenced by racial prejudice. Supporters of the Free Soil party did not have to take a stand on the morality of slavery, or express sympathy with slaves or tolerate racial differences. Many who supported the Free Soil platform did so because they wanted to preserve western lands exclusively for white farmers.

In his final months in office President Polk appealed for national harmony. In his fourth annual address, Polk noted that during the war men from the North and South "were all companions in arms and fellow-citizens of the same country, engaged in the same common cause." Now that the war had ended, he continued, "surely a spirit of harmony and concession and of equal regard for the rights of all and of all sections of the Union ought to prevail in providing governments for the acquired territories—the fruits of their common service." Developing this line of argument, Polk's Southern sympathies nonetheless emerged. He advanced claims that verged close to those of Calhoun and other strident Southerners. "The whole people of the United States, and of every State, contributed to defray the expenses of that war," he said, "and it would not be just for any one section to exclude another from all participation in the acquired territory."[7] Northern Democrats opposed such claims and reiterated instead the policy of the Wilmot Proviso to ban slavery in territory obtained in the war. Thus, the conflict over slavery in the territories threatened to split the party.

Polk also noted the discovery of gold in northern California and the urgent necessity of establishing a territorial government there. His successor, Zachary Taylor, a wealthy slave owner, encouraged California (and New Mexico) to hold conventions, and Congress to accept their statehood on the terms agreed upon in those conventions. Thus, for the purposes of California statehood, he endorsed the doctrine of popular sovereignty. In his only annual message to Congress, President Taylor explained that by allowing California and New Mexico to decide the slavery question for themselves, "the introduction of those exciting topics of a sectional character which have hitherto produced painful apprehensions in the public mind" would be avoided, thereby "maintaining the harmony and tranquillity so dear to all."[8]

---

7. James K. Polk, "Fourth Annual Message," December 5, 1848. Online by Gerhard Peters and John T. Woolley, *The American Presidency Project*, http://www.presidency.ucsb.edu/ws/?pid=29489.

8. Zachary Taylor, "Annual Message," December 4, 1849. Online by Gerhard Peters and John T. Woolley, *The American Presidency Project*, http://www.presidency.ucsb.edu/ws/?pid=29490.

As it became increasingly evident that California would request to join the Union as a free state, debate over slavery became heated. Southerners objected that admission of California (and likely New Mexico) would give the free states an advantage in the Senate. Southern congressional Democrats called for and convened a convention in Nashville, in June 1850, to consider how to respond in the event that slavery was banned in the newly acquired territories. The convention resolved that slavery was "recognized by the Constitution" and consequently that "Congress has no power to exclude from the territory of the United States any property lawfully held in the states of the Union." While it warned that "the slaveholding states cannot and will not submit to the enactment by Congress of any law imposing onerous conditions or restraints upon the rights of masters to remove with their property into the territories of the United States," it was, for the sake of the Union, "ready to acquiesce in the adoption of the line of 36 deg. 30 min. north latitude, extending to the Pacific Ocean, as an extreme concession, upon consideration of what is due to the stability of our institution."[9]

California's application for statehood thus provoked a sectional crisis. In Congress, Henry Clay, Daniel Webster, and others searched for a resolution. The result was the Compromise of 1850, which admitted California as a free state. It also allowed for the formal organization of Utah and New Mexico as territories. No restrictions were placed on slavery in those territories, and the acts establishing them explicitly stated that they would be admitted into the Union with or without slavery, as their constitutions "may prescribe at the time of their admission." Texas would give up its extravagant western claims, in exchange for the federal government assuming Texas' remaining debt. Slavery would remain legal in the national capital, but the slave trade across its borders would be abolished. The compromise also contained a new, especially vigorous fugitive slave law.[10]

In the short term, the compromise worked—Congress enacted it, and the immediate crisis was averted. But Americans across the nation were alarmed. In the North, people were now faced with the choice of helping to apprehend runaway slaves or defy federal law. The Wisconsin Supreme Court declared the Fugitive Slave Act of 1850 unconstitutional. Meanwhile, John Calhoun and other slavery advocates rejected the compromise. In a speech on March 4, 1850, Calhoun warned of the "wide-spread discontent which now pervades" the South, and of impending disunion. According to Calhoun, the "southern States . . . cannot remain, as things now are, consistently with honor and safety, in the Union." The admission of California, along with the future addition of

---

9. "Resolves of the Southern Convention at Nashville," June 10–11, 1850, rept. in *State Documents on Federal Relations: The States and the United States*, no. VI, *Slavery and the Union, 1845–1861*, ed. Herman V. Ames (Philadelphia, 1911), 23–24, 26.

10. The various provisions of the compromise, which consisted of five statutes, were passed from September 9 to September 18, 1850. The statutes can be found in *United States Statutes at Large*, 31st Cong., 1st Sess., 446–458, 462–465. The quote is found on page 447.

other states, including Oregon and Minnesota, would "irretrievably destroy the equilibrium . . . between the two sections in the Government, as it stood when the constitution was ratified." Moreover, abolitionist agitation, especially after 1835, was directly threatening slavery. "What is to stop this agitation," Calhoun asked, "before the great and final object at which it aims—the abolition of slavery in the States—is consummated?" If "something decisive is not now done to arrest it," he added, "the South will be forced to choose between abolition and secession." Calhoun left no doubt that if forced to choose between no slavery and no Union, the South would choose no Union. Invoking the memory of George Washington, he made it clear which path the South would follow. "[W]e find much in [Washington's] example to encourage us," he declared, "should we be forced to the extremity of deciding between submission and disunion."[11]

Incensed by passage of the compromise in September, Southern delegates held a second Nashville Convention in November 1850. There they resolved that "the object of those who are urging on the federal government in its aggressive policy upon our domestic institutions is, beyond all doubt, finally to overthrow them, and abolish the existing relation between the master and slave." If "the non-slaveholding states, who are parties to [the Constitution], disregard its provisions and endanger . . . [the] great and vital interest [of slavery], we have a right, as states, there being no common arbiter, to secede."[12] In the immediate aftermath of California's admittance to the Union, Southern representatives talked openly and publicly about secession a full decade before the outbreak of the Civil War.

DOCUMENTS

1. Frederick Douglass, "To Henry Clay" (*The North Star*, December 3, 1847)

In this open letter, Frederick Douglass (c. 1818–1895) charged Henry Clay with hypocrisy, directly confronting a number of claims commonly made by slavery's apologists. To Douglass, slavery was existentially hostile to republican government, and claims favoring state sovereignty are supportive of arbitrary, absolute government. He also rejected the claims that emancipation was

---

11. John C. Calhoun, Address to the U.S. Senate, *Congressional Globe*, 31st Cong., 1st Sess. 451–455 (1850). The quotes are located on pages 451, 453, and 454.
12. See document 10 in this chapter.

*the cause of the violence in Haiti, and that slaves have benefited from their
condition.*

Sir:

I have just received and read your Speech, delivered at the Mass Meeting in
Lexington, Kentucky, 13th November 1847, and, after a careful and candid
perusal of it, I am impressed with the desire to say a few words to you on one
or two subjects which form a considerable part of that speech. . . .

You confess that "Slavery is a great evil, and a wrong to its victims, and
you would rejoice if not a single slave breathed the air within the limits of our
country."

These are noble sentiments, and would seem to flow from a heart overborne
with a sense of the flagrant injustice and enormous cruelty of slavery, and of
one earnestly and anxiously longing for a remedy. Standing alone, it would
seem that the author had long been in search of some means to redress the
wrongs of the "unfortunate victims" of whom he speaks;—that his righteous
soul was, every hour, deeply grieved on account of the foul blot inflicted by this
curse on his country's character.

But what are the facts? You are yourself, at this moment, a slaveholder, and
your words on this point had scarcely reached the outer circle of the vast multitude by which you were surrounded, before you poured forth one of the most
helpless, illogically, and cowardly apologies for this same wrong, and "great
evil," which I remember to have ever read. . . .

In speaking of "the unfortunate victims" of this "great evil," and "wrong,"
you hold this most singular and cowardly excuse for perpetuating the wrongs
of my "unfortunate" race.

"But here they are, to be dealt with as well as we can, with a due consideration of all circumstances affecting the security and happiness of both races."

What do you mean by "the security, safety and happiness of both races?" Do
you mean that the happiness of the slave is augmented by his being a slave? and
if so, why call him an "unfortunate victim." Can it be that this is mere cant by
which to seduce the North into your support, on the ground of your sympathy
for the slave? I cannot believe you capable of such infatuation. I do not wish
to believe that you are capable of either the low cunning or the vanity which
your language on this subject would seem to imply, but will set it down to an
uncontrollable conviction of the innate wickedness of slavery, which forces
itself out and defies even your vast powers of concealment.

But further, you assert that "Every State has the supreme, uncontrolled
and exclusive power to decide for itself whether slavery shall cease or continue
within its limits, without any exterior intervention from any quarter."

Here I understand you to assert the most profligate and infernal doctrine,
that any State in this Union has a right to plunder, scourge and enslave any

part of the human family within its borders, just so long as it deems it for its interest so to do, and that no person or body of persons beyond the limits of said state has a right to interfere by word or deed against it. Is it possible that you hold this monstrous and blood-chilling doctrine? If so, what confidence can any enlightened lover of liberty place in your pretended opposition to Slavery? . . . You go on to say:

"In States where the SLAVES OUTNUMBER THE WHITES, as is the case in several (which I believe are only two out of fifteen) the blacks could not be emancipated without BECOMING THE GOVERNING POWER IN THESE STATES."

. . . You pretend that you are a Republican. You loudly boast of your democratic principles: why, then, do you object to the application of your principles in this case? Is the democratic principle good in one case and bad in another? Would it be worse for a black majority to govern a white minority than it now is for the latter to govern the former? But you conjure up an array of frightful objections in answer to this.

"COLLISIONS AND CONFLICTS BETWEEN THE TWO RACES WOULD BE INEVITABLE," and after shocking scenes of "RAPINE AND CARNAGE, THE EXTINCTION OR EXPULSION OF THE BLACKS WOULD CERTAINLY TAKE PLACE."

How do you know that any such results would be inevitable? Where, on the page of history, do you find anything to warrant even such a conjecture? You will probably point me to the revolution in Santo Domingo, that old and thread-bare falsehood under which democratic tyrants have, for the last forty years, sought a refuge. The facts in that direction are, however, all against you. It has been clearly proven that that revolution was not the result of emancipation, but of a cruel attempt to re-enslave an already emancipated people. I am not aware that you have a single fact to support your truly terrible assertion, while, on the other hand, I have many, all going to show what is equally taught by the voice of reason and of God, "THAT IT IS ALWAYS SAFE TO DO RIGHT." . . .

I now give your argument in support of the morality of your position.

"It may be argued that, in admitting the injustice of slavery, I grant the necessity of an instantaneous separation of that injustice. Unfortunately, however, it is not always safe, practicable or possible, in the great movements of States or public affairs of nations, to remedy or repair the infliction of previous injustice. In the inception of it we may oppose and denounce it by our most strenuous exertions, but, after its consummation, there is often no other alternative left us but to deplore its perpetration, and to acquiesce, as the only alternative, in its existence, as a less evil than the frightful consequences which might ensue from the vain endeavor to repair it. Slavery is one of these unfortunate instances."

The cases which you put in support of the foregoing propositions, are only wanting in one thing, and that is, analogy. The plundering of the Indians of their territory, is a crime to which no honest man can look with any degree of satisfaction. It was a wrong to the Indians then living, and how muchsoever we might seek to repair that wrong, the victims are far beyond the reach of any reparation; but in regard to the slave, the circumstances are different. The wrong to be repaired is a present one; the slave-holder is the every day robber of the slave and of his birthright to liberty, property, and the pursuit of happiness. But his right to be free is unquestionable; the wrong of enslaving him is self evident; the duty of emancipating him is imperative. Are you aware to what your argument on this point leads? Do you not plainly see that the greatest crimes that ever cursed our common earth, may take shelter under your reasoning, and may claim perpetuity on the ground of their antiquity? . . .

"It is a philanthropic and consoling reflection that the moral and physical condition of the African in the United States in a state of slavery is far better than it would have been had their ancestors not been brought from their native land."

I can scarce repress the flame of rising indignation as I read this cold-blooded and cruel sentence; there is so much of Satan dressed in the livery of Heaven, as well as taking consolation from crime, that I scarcely know how to reply to it. Let me ask you what has been the cause of the present unsettled condition of Africa? . . . For three hundred years Christian nations, among whom we are foremost, have looked to Africa only as a place for the gratification of their lust and love of power, and every means have been adopted to stay the onward march of civilization in that unhappy land.

Your declaration on this point places your consolation with that of the wolf in devouring the lamb. You next perpetrate what I conceive to be the most revolting blasphemy. You say:

"And if it should be the decree of the great Ruler of the Universe, that their descendants shall be made instruments in his hands in the establishment of civilization and the Christian religion throughout Africa—our regrets on account of the original wrong will be greatly mitigated."

Here, Sir, you would charge home upon God the responsibility of your own crimes, and would seek a solace from the pangs of a guilty conscience by sacrilegiously assuming that in robbing Africa of her children, you acted in obedience to the great purposes and were but fulfilling the decrees of the Most High God; but as if fearing that this refuge of lies might fail, you try to shuffle off the responsibility of this "great evil" on Great Britain. May I ask if it's honest, if you were fulfilling the great purposes of God in the share you took in this traffic, and can draw consolation from that alleged fact, to make England a sinner above yourselves, and deny her all the mitigating circumstances which you apply to yourselves? . . .

Now, Sir, I have done with your Speech, though much more might be said upon it. I have a few words to say to you personally.

I wish to remind you that you are not only in the "autumn," but in the very WINTER of life. Seventy-one years have passed over your stately brow. You must soon leave this world and appear before God, to render up an account of your stewardship. For fifty years of your life you have been a slave-holder. You have robbed the laborer who has reaped down your fields, of his rightful reward. You are at this moment the robber of nearly fifty human beings, compelling them to live without liberty and in ignorance. Let me ask if you think that God will hold you guiltless in the great day of account, if you die with the blood of these fifty slaves clinging to your garments? I know that you have made a profession of religion and have been baptized, and am aware that you are in good and regular standing in the church, but I have the authority of God for saying that you will stand rejected at his bar, unless you "put away the evil of your doings from before his eyes, cease to do evil, and learn to do well, seek judgment, relieve the oppressed and plead for the widow." You must "break every yoke and let the oppressed go free," or take your place in the ranks of "EVIL DOERS" and expect to "reap the reward of corruption." . . .

Emancipate your own slaves. Leave them not to be held or sold by others. Leave them free, as the Father of his country left his, and let your name go down to posterity, as his has come down to us, a slave-holder to be sure, but a repentant one. Make the noble resolve, that so far as you are personally concerned, "AMERICA SHALL BE FREE." . . .

2. Lewis Cass, Letter to A. P. O. Nicholson (December 24, 1847)

By the time Lewis Cass (1782–1866) captured the Democratic nomination for president in 1848, he had become an important proponent of the doctrine of "popular sovereignty." His argument draws from a construction of the territories clause, combined with his vision of the Union as a confederacy of sovereign states. His position divided his party, spurring anti-slavery Democrats to bolt to the Free Soil Party.

. . . .The Wilmot proviso has been before the country some time. It has been repeatedly discussed in Congress, and by the public press. I am strongly impressed with the opinion, that a great change has been going on in the public mind upon this subject—in my own as well as others; and that doubts are resolving themselves into convictions, that the principle it involves should be kept out of the National Legislature, and left to the people of the confederacy in their respective local governments.

We may well regret the existence of slavery in the southern States, and wish they had been saved from its introduction. But there it is, and not by the act of the present generation; and we must deal with it as a great practical question, involving the most momentous consequences. We have neither the right nor the power to touch it where it exists; and if we had both, their exercise, by any means heretofore suggested, might lead to results which no wise man would willingly encounter, and which no good man could contemplate without anxiety.

The theory of our Government presupposes that its various members have reserved to themselves the regulation of all subjects relating to what may be termed their internal police. They are sovereign within their boundaries, except in those cases where they have surrendered to the General Government a portion of their rights, in order to give effect to the objects of the Union, whether these concern foreign nations or the several States themselves. Local institutions, if I may so speak, whether they have reference to slavery, or to any other relations, domestic or public, are left to local authority. . . .

In various respects the Territories differ from the States. Some of their rights are inchoate, and they do not possess the peculiar attributes of sovereignty. Their relation to the General Government is very imperfectly defined by the Constitution; and it will be found, upon examination, that in that instrument the only grant of power concerning them is conveyed in the phrase, "Congress shall have the power to dispose of and make all needful rules and regulations respecting the territory and other property belonging to the United States." Certainly this phraseology is very loose, if it were designed to include in the grant the whole power of legislation over persons, as well as things. The expression, the "territory and other property," fairly construed, relates to the public lands, as such, to arsenals, dock-yards, forts, ships, and all the various kinds of property, which the United States may and must possess.

But surely the simple authority to dispose of and regulate these, does not extend to the unlimited power of legislation. [T]he object was evidently to enable the General Government, as a property-holder—which, from necessity, it must be—to manage, preserve, and "dispose of" such property as it might possess, and which authority is essential almost to its being. But the lives and persons of our citizens, with the vast variety of objects connected with them, cannot be controlled by an authority which is merely called into existence for the purpose of making rules and regulations for the disposition and management of property.

Such, it appears to me, would be the construction put upon this provision of the Constitution, were this question now first presented for consideration, and not controlled by imperious circumstances. . . . [T]he principle of interference should not be carried beyond the necessary implication which produces it. It should be limited to the creation of proper governments for new countries, acquired or settled, and to the necessary provision for their eventual admission into the Union; leaving, in the meantime, to the people inhabiting them, to regulate their internal concerns in their own way. They are just as capable of doing so as the people of the States; and they can do so, at any rate, as soon as their political independence is recognized by admission into the Union. During this temporary condition, it is hardly expedient to call into exercise a doubtful and invidious authority, which questions the intelligence of a respectable portion of our citizens, and whose limitation, whatever it may be, will be rapidly approaching its termination—an authority which would give to Congress despotic power, uncontrolled by the Constitution, over most important sections of our common country. For, if the relation of master and servant may be regulated or annihilated by its legislation, so may the relation of husband and wife, of parent and child, and of any other condition which our institutions and the habits of our society recognize. What would be thought if Congress should undertake to prescribe the terms of marriage in New York, or to regulate the authority of parents over their children in Pennsylvania? . . .

3. John C. Calhoun, Address before the U.S. Senate on the Oregon Bill (June 27, 1848)

In this 1848 speech, John C. Calhoun (1782–1850) rejected the principle that "all men are created equal." For Calhoun, slavery was consistent with and beneficial to republican government. He charged the North with agitating discord between the two sections, and accused abolitionists of fomenting sectional hatred toward the South. Reiterating his claim that the Union is a compact of sovereign states, he warned that efforts to ban slavery in the nation's capital set a precedent for emancipation, and universal political and social equality, throughout the Union.

. . . [L]et me say to Senators from the North, you make a great mistake in supposing that the portion [of the territories] which might fall to the South, of whatever line might be drawn, if left to soil, and climate, and circumstances to determine, would be closed to the white labor of the North, because it could not mingle with slave labor without degradation. The fact is not so. There is no part of the world where agricultural, mechanical, and other descriptions of labor are more respected than in the South, with the exception of two descriptions of employment—that of menial and body servants. No Southern man—not the poorest or the lowest—will, under any circumstance, submit to perform either of them. He has too much pride for that, and I rejoice that he has. They are unsuited to the spirit of a freeman. But the man who would spurn them feels not the least degradation to work in the same field with his slave, or to be employed to work with them in the same field or in any mechanical operation; and, when so employed, they claim the right, and are admitted, in the country portion of the South, of sitting at the table of their employers. Can as much, on the score of equality, be said of the North? With us, the two great divisions of society are not the rich and poor, but white and black; and all the former, the poor as well as the rich, belong to the upper class, and are respected and treated as equals, if honest and industrious, and hence have a position and pride of character of which neither poverty nor misfortune can deprive them. . . .

Now, let me say, Senators, if our Union and system of government are doomed to perish, and we to share the fate of so many great people who have gone before us, the historian, who, in some future day, may record the events ending in so calamitous a result, will devote his first chapter to the ordinance of 1787, as lauded as it and its authors have been, as the first in that series which led to it. His next chapter will be devoted to the Missouri compromise, and the next to the present agitation. Whether there will be another beyond, I know not. It will depend on what we may do.

If he should possess a philosophical turn of mind, and be disposed to look to more remote and recondite causes, he will trace it to a proposition which originated in a hypothetical truism, but which, as now expressed and now understood, is the most false and dangerous of all political errors. The proposition to which I allude has become an axiom in the minds of a vast many on both sides of the Atlantic, and is repeated daily from tongue to tongue, as an established and incontrovertible truth; it is, that "all men are born free and equal." . . .

Taking the proposition literally (it is in that sense it is understood), there is not a word of truth in it. It begins with "all men are born," which is utterly untrue. Men are not born. Infants are born. They grow to be men. And concludes with asserting that they are born "free and equal," which is not less false. They are not born free. While infants they are incapable of freedom, being destitute alike of the capacity of thinking and acting, without which there can be no freedom. Besides, they are necessarily born subject to their parents, and remain so among all people, savage and civilized, until the development of their intellect and physical capacity enables them to take care of themselves. They grow to all the freedom of which the condition in which they were born permits, by growing to be men. Nor is it less false that they are born "equal." They are not so in any sense in which it can be regarded; and thus, as I have asserted, there is not a word of truth in the whole proposition, as expressed and generally understood.

If we trace it back, we shall find the proposition differently expressed in the Declaration of Independence. That asserts that "all men are created equal." The form of expression, though less dangerous, is not less erroneous. All men are not created. According to the Bible, only two, a man and a woman, ever were, and of these one was pronounced subordinate to the other. All others have come into the world by being born, and in no sense, as I have shown, either free or equal. But this form of expression being less striking and popular, has given way to the present, and under the authority of a document put forth on so great an occasion, and leading to such important consequences, has spread far and wide, and fixed itself deeply in the public mind. It was inserted in our Declaration of Independence without any necessity. It made no necessary part of our justification in separating from the parent country, and declaring ourselves independent. Breach of our chartered privileges, and lawless encroachment on our acknowledged and well-established rights by the parent country, were the real causes, and of themselves sufficient, without resorting to any other, to justify the step. . . .

If the proposition be traced still further back, it will be found to have been adopted from certain writers on government who had attained much celebrity in the early settlement of these States, and with whose writings all the prominent actors in our Revolution were familiar. Among these, Locke and Sidney were prominent. But they expressed it very differently. According to their expression, "all men in the state of nature were free and equal." From this the others were derived; and it was this to which I referred when I called it a hypothetical truism. To understand why, will require some explanation.

Man, for the purpose of reasoning, may be regarded in three different states: in a state of individuality; that is, living by himself apart from the rest of his species. In the social; that is, living in society, associated with others of his species. And in the political; that is, living under government. We may reason as to what would be his rights and duties in either, without taking into consideration whether he could exist in it or not. It is certain, that in the first, the very supposition that he lived apart and separated from all others, would make him free and equal. No one in such a state could have the right to command or control another. Every man would be his own master, and might do just as he pleased. But it is equally clear, that man cannot exist in such a state; that he is by nature social, and that society is necessary, not only to the proper development of all his faculties, moral and intellectual, but to the very existence of his race. Such being the case, the state is a purely hypothetical one; and when we say all men are free and equal in it, we announce a mere hypothetical truism; that is, a truism resting on a mere supposed state that cannot exist, and of course one of little or no practical value.

But to call it a state of nature was a great misnomer, and has led to dangerous errors; for that cannot justly be called a state of nature which is so opposed to the constitution of man as to be inconsistent with the existence of his race and the development of the high faculties, mental and moral, with which he is endowed by his Creator.

Nor is the social state of itself his natural state; for society can no more exist without government, in one form or another, than man without society. It is the political, then, which includes the social, that is his natural state. It is the one for which his Creator formed him, into which he is impelled irresistibly, and in which only his race can exist and all its faculties be fully developed.

Such being the case, it follows that any, the worst form of government, is better than anarchy; and that individual liberty, or freedom, must be subordinate to whatever power may be necessary to protect society against anarchy within or destruction from without; for the safety and well-being of society is as paramount to individual liberty as the safety and well-being of the race is to that of individuals; and in the same proportion, the power necessary for the safety of society is paramount to individual liberty. On the contrary, government has no right to control individual liberty beyond what is necessary to the safety and well-being of society. Such is the boundary which separates the power of government and the liberty of the citizen or subject in the political state, which, as I have shown, is the natural state of man—the only one in which his race can exist, and the one in which he is born, lives, and dies.

It follows from all this, that the quantum of power on the part of the government, and of liberty on that of individuals, instead of being equal in all cases, must necessarily be very unequal among different people, according to their different conditions. For just in proportion as a people are ignorant, stupid, debased, corrupt, exposed to violence within and danger from without, the power necessary for government to possess in order to preserve society against anarchy and destruction, becomes greater and greater, and individual liberty less and less, until the lowest condition is reached, when absolute and despotic power becomes necessary on the part of the government, and individual liberty extinct. So, on the contrary, just as a people rise in the scale of intelligence, virtue, and patriotism, and the more perfectly they become acquainted with the nature of government, the ends for which it was ordered, and how it ought to be administered, and the less the tendency to violence and disorder within, and danger from abroad, the power necessary for government becomes less and less, and individual liberty greater and greater. Instead, then, of all men having the same right to liberty and equality, as is claimed by those who hold that they are all born free and equal, liberty is the noble and highest reward bestowed on mental and moral development, combined with favorable circumstances. Instead, then, of liberty and equality being born with man; instead of all men and all classes and descriptions being equally entitled to them, they are high prizes to be won, and are in their most perfect state, not only the highest reward that can be bestowed on our race, but the most difficult to be won, and when won, the most difficult to be preserved.

They have been made vastly more so, by the dangerous error I have attempted to expose, that all men are born free and equal, as if those high qualities belonged to man without effort to acquire them, and to all equally alike, regardless of their intellectual and moral condition. . . . We now begin to experience the danger of admitting so great an error to have a place in the Declaration of our Independence. For a long time it lay dormant; but in the process of time it began to germinate, and produce its poisonous fruits. It had strong hold on the mind of Mr. Jefferson, the author of that document, which caused him to take an utterly false view of the subordinate relation of the black to the white race in the South, and to hold, in consequence, that the [former], though utterly unqualified to possess liberty, were as fully entitled to both liberty and equality as the [latter], and that to deprive them of it was unjust and immoral. To this error his proposition to exclude slavery from the territory northwest of the Ohio may be traced, and to that the ordinance of 1787, and through it the deep and dangerous agitation which now threatens to ingulf, and will certainly ingulf, if not speedily settled, our political institutions, and involve the country in countless woes.

4. John C. Calhoun, The Address of Southern Delegates in Congress, to Their Constituents (January 22, 1849)

Calhoun delivered this address as a rallying cry to Southerners and a warning to the North. Charging that the North was agitating discord between the two sections and that abolitionists in particular sought to foment Northern hatred of the South, Calhoun restated his claim that the Union is a compact of sovereign states, and he warned that efforts to ban slavery in the nation's capital were a penultimate step to emancipation throughout the Union and the raising of blacks to a condition of political and social equality. This address provided a key theoretical base for the Nashville Convention and the secession movement in 1850.

We, whose names are hereunto annexed, address you in discharge of what we believe to be a solemn duty, on the most important subject ever presented for your consideration. We allude to the conflict between the two great sections of the Union, growing out of a difference of feeling and opinion in reference to the relation existing between the two races, the European and the African, which inhabit the southern section, and the acts of aggression and encroachment to which it has led. . . .

With few exceptions of no great importance, the South had no cause to complain prior to the year 1819—a year, it is to be feared, destined to mark a train of events, bringing with them many, and great, and fatal disasters, on the country and its institutions. With it commenced the agitating debate on the question of the admission of Missouri into the Union. We shall pass by for the present this question . . . and shall proceed to consider the effects of that spirit of discord, which it roused up between the two sections. It first disclosed itself in the North, by hostility to that portion of the Constitution which provides for the delivering up of fugitive slaves. In its progress it led to the adoption of hostile acts, intended to render it of non-effect, and with so much success that it may be regarded now as practically expunged from the Constitution. . . .

We do not deem it necessary to undertake to refute the sophistry and sub-terfuges by which so plain a provision of the Constitution has been evaded, and, in effect, annulled. It constitutes an essential part of the constitutional compact, and of course the supreme law of the land. As such it is binding on all. . . . What that meaning and intent are, there was no diversity of opinion in the better days of the Republic, prior to 1819. . . . During that period none interposed impediments in the way of the owner seeking to recover his fugitive slave; nor did any deny his right to have every proper facility to enforce his claim to have him delivered up. . . .

. . . The citizens of the South, in their attempt to recover their slaves, now meet, instead of aid and co-operation, resistance in every form; resistance from hostile acts of legislation, intended to baffle and defeat their claims by all sorts of devices, and by interposing every description of impediment—resistance from judges and magistrates—and finally, when all these fail, from mobs, com-posed of whites and blacks, which, by threats or force, rescue the fugitive slave from the possession of his rightful owner. The attempt to recover a slave, in most of the Northern States, cannot now be made without the hazard of insult, heavy pecuniary loss, imprisonment, and even of life itself. Already has a wor-thy citizen of Maryland lost his life in making an attempt to enforce his claim to a fugitive slave under this provision. . . .

There remains to be noticed another class of aggressive acts of a kindred character, but which instead of striking at an express and specific provision of the Constitution, aims directly at destroying the relation between the two races at the South. . . . We refer to the systematic agitation of the question by the Abolitionists, which, commencing about 1835, is still continued in all possible forms. Their avowed intention is to bring about a state of things that will force emancipation on the South. To unite the North in fixed hostility to slavery in the South, and to excite discontent among the slaves with their condition, are among the means employed to effect it. With a view to bring about the for-mer, every means are resorted to in order to render the South, and the relation between the two races there, odious and hateful to the North. For this purpose societies and newspapers are everywhere established, debating clubs opened, lecturers employed, pamphlets and other publications, pictures and petitions to Congress, resorted to, and directed to that single point, regardless of truth or decency; while the circulation of incendiary publications in the South, the agitation of the subject of abolition in Congress, and the employment of emissaries are relied on to excite discontent among the slaves. . . . We regard both object and means to be aggressive and dangerous to the rights of the South, and subversive . . . of one of the ends for which the Constitution was established. Slavery is a domestic institution. It belongs to the States, each for itself to decide, whether it shall be established or not; and if it be established, whether it should be abolished or not. Such being the clear and unquestionable right of the States, it follows necessarily that it would be a flagrant act of aggression on a State, destructive of its rights, and subversive of its independence, for the Federal Government, or one or more States, or their people, to undertake to force on it the emancipation of its slaves. . . .

We now return to the question of the admission of Missouri to the Union . . . and the consequences to which it has directly led. . . .

. . . In this agitating debate, the two sections stood arrayed against each other. . . . Fortunately, a . . . Compromise (as it was called) was offered, based on the terms, that the North should cease to oppose the admission of Missouri on the grounds for which the South contended, and that the provisions of the Ordinance of 1787, for the government of the Northwestern Territory, should be applied to all the territory acquired by the United States from France under the treaty of Louisiana lying North of 36°30' except the portion lying in the State of Missouri. The Northern members embraced it; and although not originating with them, adopted it as their own. It was forced through Congress by the almost united votes of the North, against a minority consisting almost entirely of members from the Southern States.

Such was the termination of this, the first conflict, under the Constitution, between the two sections, in reference to slavery in connection with the territories. Many hailed it as a permanent and final adjustment that would prevent the recurrence of similar conflicts; but others, less sanguine, took the opposite and more gloomy view, regarding it as the precursor as a train of events which might rend the Union asunder, and prostrate our political system. One of these was the experienced and sagacious Jefferson. . . .

For many years the subject of slavery in reference to the territories ceased to agitate the country. Indications, however, connected with question of annexing Texas, showed clearly that it was ready to break out again, with redoubled violence, on some future occasion. . . .

The war with Mexico soon followed, and that terminated in the acquisition of New Mexico and Upper California. . . . The near prospect of so great an addition rekindled the excitement between the North and South in reference to slavery in its connection with the territories. . . .

The effects have been to widen the difference between the two sections, and give a more determined and hostile character to their conflict. The North no longer respects the Missouri compromise line, although adopted by their almost unanimous vote. Instead of compromise, they avow that their determination is to exclude slavery from all the territories of the United States, acquired, or to be acquired; and, of course, to prevent the citizens of the Southern States from emigrating with their property in slaves into any of them. Their object, they allege, is to prevent the extension of slavery, and ours to extend it, thus making the issue between them and us to be the naked question, shall slavery be extended or not? . . .

So far from maintaining the doctrine, which the issue implies, we hold that the Federal Government has no right to extend or restrict slavery, no more than to establish or abolish it; nor has it any right whatever to distinguish between the domestic institutions of one State, or section, and another, in order to favor one and discourage the other. As the federal representative of each and all the States, it is bound to deal out, within the sphere of its powers, equal and exact justice and favor to all. . . . Entertaining these opinions, we ask not, as the North alleges we do, for the extension of slavery. That would make a discrimination in our favor, as unjust and unconstitutional as the discrimination they ask against us in their favor. It is not for them, nor for the Federal Government to determine, whether our domestic institution is good or bad; or whether it should be repressed or preserved. It belongs to us, and us only, to decide such questions. What then we do insist on, is, not to extend slavery, but that we shall not be prohibited from immigrating with our property, into the Territories of the United States, because we are slaveholders; or, in other words, that we shall not on that account be disfranchised of a privilege possessed by all others, citizens and foreigners, without discrimination as to character, profession, or color. . . .

We rest our claim, not only on the high grounds above stated, but also on the solid foundation of right, justice, and equality. The territories immediately in controversy—New Mexico and California—were acquired by the common sacrifice and efforts of all the States, towards which the South contributed far more than her full share of men . . . to say nothing of money, and is, of course, on every principle of right, justice, fairness and equality, entitled to participate fully in the benefits to be derived from their acquisition. But as impregnable as is this ground, there is another not less so. Ours is a Federal Government—a Government in which not individuals, but States as distinct sovereign communities, are the constituents. To them, as members of the Federal Union, the territories belong. . . . The States . . . are the joint owners. Now it is conceded by all writers on the subject, that in all such Governments their members are all equal—equal in rights and equal in dignity. . . . To deprive, then, the Southern States and their citizens of their full share in territories declared to belong to them, in common with the other States, would be in derogation of the equality belonging to them as members of a Federal Union, and sink them, from being equals, into a subordinate and dependent condition. . . .

Although Congress has been in session but little more than one month, a greater number of measures of an aggressive character have been introduced. . . .

The first of this series of aggressions is a resolution introduced by a member from Massachusetts, the object of which is to repeal all acts which recognize the existence of slavery, or authorize the selling or disposing of slaves in this District. . . . That was followed by a bill introduced by [a] member from Ohio, to take the votes of the inhabitants of this District, on the question whether slavery within its limits should be abolished.

. . . He was followed by a member from Illinois, who offered a resolution for abolishing slavery in the Territories, and all places where Congress has exclusive powers of legislation, that is, in all forts, magazines, arsenals, dockyards, and other needful buildings, purchased by Congress with the consent of the Legislature of the State. . . .

Little, in truth, would be left to be done after we have been excluded from all the territories, including those to be hereafter acquired; after slavery is abolished in this District and in the numerous places dispersed all over the South, where Congress has the exclusive right of legislation, and after the other measures proposed are consummated. . . . This District, and all places over which Congress has exclusive power of legislation, would be asylums for fugitive slaves, where, as soon as they placed their feet, they would become, according to the doctrines of our Northern assailants, free. . . .

Under such a state of things the probability is, that emancipation would soon follow, without any final act to abolish slavery. The depressing effects of such measures on the white race at the South, and the hope they would create in the black of a speedy emancipation, would produce a state of feeling inconsistent with the much longer continuance of the existing relations between the two. But be that as it may, it is certain, if emancipation did not follow, as a matter of course, the final act in the States would not be long delayed. The want of constitutional power would oppose a feeble resistance. [I]t would indicate a very superficial knowledge of human nature, to think that, after aiming at abolition, systematically, for so many years, and pursuing it with such unscrupulous disregard of law and Constitution, that the fanatics who have led the way and forced the great body of the North to follow them, would, when the finishing stroke only remained to be given, voluntarily suspend it, or permit any constitutional scruples or considerations of justice to arrest it. . . .

But, even if these conclusions should prove erroneous . . . there would still be left one certain way to accomplish their object. . . . [I]f the determination avowed by the North to monopolize all the territories . . . should be carried into effect . . . [t]hat of itself would, at no distant day, add to the North a sufficient number of States to give her three fourths of the whole; when, under the color of an amendment to the Constitution, she would emancipate our slaves. . . .

[E]mancipation . . . can . . . only be effected [here] by the prostration of the white race; and that would necessarily engender the bitterest feelings of hostility between them and the North. But the reverse would be the case between the blacks of the South and the people of the North. Owing their emancipation to them, they would regard them as friends, guardians, and patrons, and centre, accordingly, all their sympathy in them. The people of the North would not fail to reciprocate and to favor them, instead of the whites. Under the influence of such feelings, and impelled by fanaticism and love of power, they would not stop at emancipation. Another step would be taken—to raise them to a political and social equality with their former owners, by giving them the right of voting and holding public offices under the Federal Government. . . . But when once raised to an equality, they would become the fast political associates of the North, acting and voting with them on all questions, and by this political union between them, holding the white race at the South in complete subjection. The blacks, and the profligate whites that might unite with them, would become the principal recipients of federal offices and patronage, and would, in consequence, be raised above the whites of the South in the political and social scale. We would, in a word, change conditions with them—a degradation greater than has ever yet fallen to the lot of a free and enlightened people, and one from which we could not escape, should emancipation take place, (which it certainly will if not prevented), but by fleeing the homes of ourselves and ancestors, and by abandoning our country to our former slaves, to become the permanent abode of disorder, anarchy, poverty, misery, and wretchedness. . . .

5. Frederick Douglass, "Comments on Gerrit Smith's Address" (*The North Star*, March 30, 1849)

In this editorial, Douglass argued that any fair interpretation of the Constitution would prove its complicity with slavery and thus expose it as a "covenant with death." By 1851, Douglass would change his mind and adopt the contrary view.

. . . What a government ought to do, is one thing; but not the thing germane to the question at issue between Mr. Smith and ourselves. That government ought to be just, merciful, holy, is granted. The question is not, however, what a government ought to be, or to do, but what the government of the United States is *authorized to be, and to do, by the Constitution of the United States.* The two questions should be kept separate, that the simplest may understand, as blending them only leads to confusion.

It is because we hold civil government to be solemnly bound to protect the weak against the strong, the oppressed against the oppressor, the few against the many, and to secure the humblest subject in the full possession of his rights of person and of property, that we utterly abhor and repudiate this government and the Constitution as a dark and damning conspiracy against all the purposes of government. Both its framers and administrators were, and have been until now little better than a band of pirates.—We would make clean work of both the government and the Constitution, and not amend or force a new construction upon either, contradicted by the whole history of the nation; but would abolish both, and reconstruct a Constitution and a government which shall better answer the ends of justice. To think of good government in a Union with slaveholders, and under a Constitution framed by slaveholders, the practical operation of which for sixty years has been to strengthen, sustain and spread slavery, does seem to us delusive. We are not for mending old clothes with new cloth, or putting new wine into old bottles, but for starting afresh under a new and higher light than our piratical fathers saw, and form a Constitution and government which shall be so clear and explicit that no doubt can be entertained as to its minutest purposes.

That this cannot be truthfully affirmed of our present Constitution, we need not insist upon at this time. Even our friend Smith virtually admits that it would be dangerous to leave the question of the slave's redemption to be decided in the light of the Constitution. The "old tattered parchment" receives no great deference from him after all. Disdaining it altogether, he says, "*What-ever may be said of the lawfulness of slavery, government must abolish it. If it have a Constitution under which it cannot abolish slavery, then it must override the Constitution, and abolish slavery. But whether under or over the Constitution, it must abolish slavery.*" We like this for its whole-souled devotion to a glorious object. It is revolutionary, and looks as much like the fanaticism of Wendell Phillips and William Lloyd Garrison, as if it had been cast in their mould. In plain terms, Mr. Smith is for the abolition of slavery, whether in accordance with, or in violation of, the Constitution; and while the declaration is worthy of his noble heart, we cannot think such of his head. The doctrine laid down in this declaration, runs through the whole address, and gives it a vigor and warmth from beginning to end. We shall therefore express a few thoughts upon it.

It will be seen that the doctrine in question makes the government superior to, and independent of, the Constitution, which is the very charter of the government, and without which the government is nothing better than a lawless mob, acting without any other or higher authority than its own convictions or impulses as to what is right or wrong. If this doctrine be sound, it is a mere farce to have a written Constitution at all; for if the government can override and violate its Constitution in one point, it may do so in all. . . . All the safe-guards of that instrument, providing for its own interpretation and its own amendment, are worthless and needless, if this doctrine be true, and government will merely be the voice of an ever-shifting majority, be that good or evil. . . .

We hold this doctrine to be radically unsound, (and although brought forward to promote a noble object,) its tendency immoral. We say to our friend Smith, and to all others who sympathize with his views on this subject, If you profess to hold to the Constitution, maintain its provisions. If you cannot, in accordance with your conscience, perform its requirements, or submit to its limitations, then we say, it is your plain duty to come out from it, forsake it, repudiate it, abandon it, do anything rather than seem to be in harmony with an instrument which you would set aside and destroy. Do not, for the sake of honesty and truth, solemnly swear to protect and defend an instrument which it is your firm and settled purpose to disregard and violate in any one particular. Such a course would unsettle all confidence, invert all the principles of trust and reliance which bind society together, and leave mankind to all the horrors of anarchy, and all the confusion of Babel. . . .

It can scarcely be necessary, after what we have already said, to spend much time upon the following extraordinary declaration of Mr. Smith, respecting the Constitution, in which he declares that it "is drawn up with the intelligent and steadfast purpose of having it serve and be forever fully and gloriously identified with the cause of liberty, republicanism and equal rights, must of necessity be shut against the claims and pretensions of slavery." That it was drawn up with the purpose of serving the cause of the white man's liberty, is true; but that it was meant to serve the cause of the black man's liberty, is false. That a Constitution so drawn, must necessarily be shut against the claims of slavery, is an error. We are not deeply skilled in the science of human language, and use language in the sense in which it is generally used, rather than scientifically, and we do know that "Liberty, Republicanism, and Equal Rights," words constantly on the lips of this nation, are deemed to be no more hostile to Negro slavery, than the same words, when used by the Greeks, were supposed to be against the enslavement of the Helots. Ours is not the business of a lexicographer, but to receive the idea meant to be conveyed by the language of those who use it, and condemn or approve accordingly.

In the letter of Mr. Smith which we published last week, he assumes that the material thing for us to prove, in order to establish the wrongfulness of voting and acting under the United States Constitution, is, that the Federal Government has no right to abolish slavery under that instrument. With all deference, we must say, we see no such necessity laid upon us. We might, for argument's sake, grant all that Mr. Smith claims as to the power of the Federal Government to abolish slavery under the Constitution, and yet hold, as we certainly do hold, that it is wrong to vote and take office under the Constitution. It is not enough that a man can demonstrate that his plan will abolish slavery, to satisfy us that his plan is the right and best one to be adopted. Slavery might be abolished by the aid of a foreign arm; but shall we therefore invoke that aid? We might, to feed the hungry and clothe the naked, break into the house of Mr. Smith and steal the wherewithal to do these things, but the question of the rightfulness of such conduct would be still open. If there is one Christian principle more firmly fixed in our heart than another, it is this, that it is wrong to do evil that good may come; and if there is one heresy more to be guarded against than another, it is the doctrine that the end justifies the means. We say, therefore, that it is not incumbent upon us to show that, by a forced and latitudinarian construction of the Constitution, Congress may not abolish slavery in all the slaveholding States, in order to establish the doctrine which we lay down and justify the course which we feel bound to pursue in regard to voting under the Constitution of the United States. It is enough for us to know that the Constitution requires of those who are parties to it to return the fugitive slave to the house of bondage, and to shoot down the slave if he rises to gain his freedom, to justify us in repudiating and forever casting from us, as a covenant with death, the American Constitution. . . .

6. George Fitzhugh, "Slavery Justified" (1849; reprinted as an appendix in his *Sociology for the South, or the Failure of Free Society*, 1854)

Here social theorist George Fitzhugh (1806–1881) argued that any society based on the idea of "universal liberty and equality" is doomed. For Fitzhugh, the liberty trumpeted in the North fostered unbridled competition, with disastrous results. The poor and vulnerable are oppressed, and the boundless pursuit of wealth destroys virtue. By contrast, the master-slave relationship is peaceful and happy. The slaveholder, he claimed, is more virtuous than his Northern counterpart precisely because of his duty to tend to the welfare of his slaves.

Liberty and equality are new things under the sun. The free states of antiquity abounded with slaves. The feudal system that supplanted Roman institutionally changed the form of slavery, but brought with it neither liberty nor equality.

France and the Northern States of our Union have alone fully and fairly tried the experiment of a social organization founded upon universal liberty and equality of rights. . . .

In France and in our Northern States the experiment has already failed. . . .

So much for experiment. We will now endeavor to treat the subject theoretically, and to show that the system is on its face self-destructive and impracticable. When we look to the vegetable, animal and human kingdoms, we discover in them all a constant conflict, war, or race of competition, the result of which is, that the weaker or less healthy genera, species and individuals are continually displaced and exterminated by the stronger and more hardy. . . . So strong is this propensity, and so destructive to human existence, that man has never yet been found so savage as to be without government. Forgetful of this important fact, which is the origin of all governments, the political economists and the advocates of liberty and equality propose to enhance the well being of man by trammeling his conduct as little as possible, and encouraging what they call FREE COMPETITION. Now, free competition is but another name for liberty and equality, and we must acquire precise and accurate notions about it in order to ascertain how free institutions will work. . . . Men are told it is their duty to compete, to endeavor to get ahead of and supplant their fellow men, by the exercise of all the intellectual and moral strength with which nature and education have endowed them. "Might makes right," is the order of creation, and this law of nature, so far as mental might is concerned, is restored by liberty to man. The struggle to better one's condition, to pull others down or supplant them, is the great organic law of free society. All men being equal, all aspire to the highest honors and the largest possessions. Good men and bad men teach their children one and the same lesson— "Go ahead, push your way in the world." In such society, virtue, if virtue there be, loses all her loveliness because of her selfish aims. None but the selfish virtues are encouraged, because none other aid a man in the race of free competition. . . .

The statistics of France, England and America show that pauperism and crime advance *pari passu* with liberty and equality. How can it be otherwise, when all society is combined to oppress the poor and weak minded? The rich man . . . employs the laborer who will work for the least wages. . . . The poor war with one another in the race of competition, in order to get employment, by underbidding; for laborers are more abundant than employers. Population increases faster than capital. Look to the situation of woman when she is thrown into this war of competition, and has to support herself by her daily wages. For the same or equally valuable services she gets not half the pay that man does, simply because the modesty of her sex prevents her from resorting to all the arts and means of competition which men employ. He who would emancipate woman, unless he could make her as coarse and strong in mind and body as man, would be her worst enemy; her subservience to and dependence on man, is necessary to her very existence. . . .

. . . Liberty and equality throw the whole weight of society on its weakest members; they combine all men in oppressing precisely that part of mankind who most need sympathy, aid and protection. . . . The very simple and improvident man is the prey of every body. The simple man represents a class, the common day laborers. The employer cheapens their wages, and the retail dealer takes advantage of their ignorance, their inability to visit other markets, and their want of credit, to charge them enormous profits. They bear the whole weight of society on their shoulders; they are the producers and artificers of all the necessaries, the comforts, the luxuries, the pomp and splendor of the world; they create it all, and enjoy none of it; they are the muzzled ox that treadeth out the straw; they are at constant war with those above them, asking higher wages but getting lower; for they are also at war with each other, underbidding to get employment. This process of underbidding never ceases so long as employers want profits or laborers want employment. It ends when wages are reduced too low to afford subsistence, in filling poor-houses, and jails, and graves. It has reached that point already in France, England and Ireland. A half million died of hunger in one year in Ireland—they died because in the eye of the law they were the equals, and liberty had made them the enemies, of their landlords and employers. Had they been vassals or serfs, they would have been beloved, cherished and taken care of by those same landlords and employers. Slaves never die of hunger, scarcely ever feel want. . . .

The moral effect of free society is to banish Christian virtue, that virtue which bids us love our neighbor as ourself, and to substitute the very equivocal virtues proceeding from mere selfishness. The intense struggle to better each one's pecuniary condition, the rivalries, the jealousies, the hostilities which it begets, leave neither time nor inclination to cultivate the heart or the head. Every finer feeling of our nature is chilled and benumbed by its selfish atmosphere; affection is under the ban, because affection makes us less regardful of mere self; hospitality is considered criminal waste, chivalry a stumbling-block, and the code of honor foolishness; taste, sentiment, imagination, are forbidden ground because no money is to be made by them. . . . What makes money, and what costs money, are alone desired. Temperance, frugality, thrift, attention to business, industry, and skill in making bargains, are virtues in high repute, because they enable us to supplant others and increase our own wealth. . . .

. . . There is but one remedy for this evil, so inherent in free society, and that is, to identify the interests of the weak and the strong, the poor and the rich. Domestic Slavery does this far better than any other institution. . . . To it (slavery) Greece and Rome, Egypt and Judea, and all the other distinguished States of antiquity, were indebted for their great prosperity and high civilization. . . .

But this high civilization and domestic slavery did not merely co-exist, they were cause and effect. Every scholar whose mind is at all imbued with ancient history and literature, sees that Greece and Rome were indebted to this institution alone for the taste, the leisure and the means to cultivate their heads and their hearts; had they been tied down to Yankee notions of thrift, they might have produced a Franklin, with his "penny saved is a penny gained;" they might have had utilitarian philosophers and invented the spinning jenny, but they never would have produced a poet, an orator, a sculptor or an architect; they would never have uttered a lofty sentiment, achieved a glorious feat in war, or created a single work of art. . . .

Domestic slavery in the Southern States has produced the same results in elevating the character of the master that it did in Greece and Rome. He is lofty and independent in his sentiments, generous, affectionate, brave and eloquent; he is superior to the Northerner in every thing but the arts of thrift. History proves this. . . . Scipio and Aristides, Calhoun and Washington, are the noble results of domestic slavery. . . . Adams and Van Buren, cunning, complex and tortuous, are fit exponents of the selfish system of universal liberty. . . .

But the chief and far most important enquiry is, how does slavery affect the condition of the slave? One of the wildest sects of Communists in France proposes not only to hold all property in common, but to divide the profits, not according to each man's in-put and labor, but according to each man's wants. Now this is precisely the system of domestic slavery with us. We provide for each slave, in old age and in infancy, in sickness and in health, not according to his labor, but according to his wants. The master's wants are more costly and refined, and he therefore gets a larger share of the profits. A Southern farm is the beau ideal of Communism; it is a joint concern, in which the slave consumes more than the master, of the coarse products, and is far happier, because although the concern may fail, he is always sure of a support; he is only transferred to another master to participate in the profits of another concern; he marries when he pleases, because he knows he will have to work no more with a family than without one, and whether he live or die, that family will be taken care of; he exhibits all the pride of ownership, despises a partner in a smaller concern, "a poor man's negro," boasts of "our crops, horses, fields and cattle;" and is as happy as a human being can be. . . .

There is no rivalry, no competition to get employment among slaves, as among free laborers. Nor is there a war between master and slave. The master's interest prevents his reducing the slave's allowance or wages in infancy or sickness, for he might lose the slave by so doing. His feeling for his slave never permits him to stint him in old age. The slaves are all well fed, well clad, have plenty of fuel, and are happy. They have no dread of the future—no fear of want. A state of dependence is the only condition in which reciprocal affection can exist among human beings—the only situation in which the war of competition ceases, and peace, amity and good will arise. A state of independence always begets more or less of jealous rivalry and hostility. A man loves his children because they are weak, helpless and dependent; he loves his wife for similar reasons. When his children grow up and assert their independence, he is apt to transfer his affection to his grand-children. He ceases to love his wife when she becomes masculine or rebellious; but slaves are always dependent, never the rivals of their master. Hence, though men are often found at variance with wife or children, we never saw one who did not like his slaves, and rarely a slave who was not devoted to his master. . . . The slave-holder is like other men; he will not tread on the worm nor break the bruised reed. The ready submission of the slave, nine times out of ten, disarms his wrath even when the slave has offended. The habit of command may make him imperious and fit him for rule; but he is only imperious when thwarted or ordered by his equals; he would scorn to put on airs of command among blacks, whether slaves or free; he always speaks to them in a kind and subdued tone. We go farther, and say the slave-holder is better than others—because he has greater occasion for the exercise of the affection. His whole life is spent in providing for the minutest wants of others, in taking care of them in sickness and in health. Hence he is the least selfish of men. . . .

Every social structure must have its substratum. In free society this substratum, the weak, poor and ignorant, is borne down upon and oppressed with continually increasing weight by all above. We have solved the problem of relieving this substratum from the pressure from above. The slaves are the substratum, and the master's feelings and interests alike prevent him from bearing down upon and oppressing them. With us the pressure on society is like that of air or water, so equally diffused as not any where to be felt. With them it is the pressure of the enormous screw, never yielding, continually increasing. Free laborers are little better than trespassers on this earth given by God to all mankind. . . .

More than half of the white citizens of the North are common laborers, either in the field, or as body or house servants. They perform the same services that our slaves do. They serve their employers for hire; they have quite as little option whether they shall so serve, or not, as our slaves, for they cannot live without their wages. Their hire or wages, except with the healthy and able-bodied, are not half what we allow our slaves, for it is wholly insufficent for their comfortable maintenance, whilst we always keep our slaves in comfort, in return for their past, present, or expected labor. The socialists say wages is slavery. It is a gross libel on slavery. Wages are given in time of vigorous health and strength, and denied when most needed, when sickness or old age has overtaken us. The slave is never without a master to maintain him. The free laborer, though willing to work, cannot always find an employer. He is then without a home and without wages! In a densely peopled country, where the supply of laborers exceeds the demand, wages is worse than slavery. Oh! Liberty and Equality, to what a sad pass do you bring your votaries! This is the exact condition to which the mass of society is reduced in France and England, and to which it is rapidly approximating in our Northern States. . . .

> Oh carry, carry me back to old Virginia shore,
> For I am old and feeble grown,
> And cannot work any more. . . .

At the slaveholding South all is peace, quiet, plenty and contentment. We have no mobs, no trades unions, no strikes for higher wages, no armed resistance to the law, but little jealousy of the rich by the poor. We have but few in our jails, and fewer in our poor houses. We produce enough of the comforts and necessaries of life for a population three or four times as numerous as ours. We are wholly exempt from the torrent of pauperism, crime, agrarianism, and infidelity which Europe is pouring from her jails and alms houses on the already crowded North. Population increases slowly, wealth rapidly. . . . Wealth is more equally distributed than at the North, where a few millionaires own most of the property of the country. . . .

In conclusion, we will repeat the propositions, in somewhat different phraseology, with which we set out. First—That Liberty and Equality, with their concomitant Free Competition, beget a war in society that is as destructive to its weaker members as the custom of exposing the deformed and crippled children. Secondly—That slavery protects the weaker members of society just as do the relations of parent, guardian and husband, and is as necessary, as natural, and almost as universal as those relations. . . .

7. Horace Mann, Address before the U.S. House of Representatives (February 15, 1850)

In this speech, delivered as the Crisis of 1850 peaked, Horace Mann (1796–1859) rejected demands by Calhoun and others that slaveholders be allowed to freely transfer their slaves to the West. Alarmed by threats of violence and secession gathering in the South, Mann predicted the consequences that await slaveholders should secession occur. Finally, Mann sarcastically suggested what a Southern confederacy's hypothetical declaration of independence and constitutional preamble might contain.

. . . We of the North, you say, are Abolitionists; but abolitionists of what? Are we abolitionists of the inalienable, indefeasible, indestructible rights of man? Are we abolitionists of knowledge, abolitionists of virtue, of education, and of human culture? Do we seek to abolish the glorious moral and intellectual attributes which God has given to his children, and thus, as far as it lies in our power, make the facts of slavery conform to the law of slavery, by obliterating the distinction between a man and a beast? . . .

But if the word "abolitionist" is to be used in a reproachful and contumelious sense, does it not more properly belong to those who would extend a system which, in its very nature, abolishes freedom, justice, equity, and a sense of human brotherhood? Does it not belong to those who would abolish, not only all social and political, but all natural rights; who would abolish "liberty and the pursuit of happiness;" who would close up all the avenues to knowledge; who would render freedom of thought and liberty of conscience, impossible, by crushing out the faculties by which, alone, we can think and decide; who would rob a fellow-man of his parental rights, and innocent children of the tenderness and joys of a filial love; who would introduce a foul concubinage in place of the institution of marriage; and who would remorselessly trample upon all the tenderest and holiest affections which the human soul is capable of feeling? . . .

If we are abolitionists, then, we are abolitionists of human bondage; while those who oppose us are abolitionists of human liberty. . . . In using this word, therefore, to calumniate us, they put darkness for light, and lightness for dark; good for evil, and evil for good. . . .

. . . The new residents of California have framed a constitution, have applied for admission to this Union, and their application is now pending before us. Of their own accord, they have excluded slavery from their borders by their fundamental law. Until the discovery of gold in that country . . . it was confidently anticipated at the South, and intensely feared at the North, that the whole region would be overrun with slaveholders and slaves. As far back as 1842, Mr. Wise, of Virginia, the administration leader in the House of Representatives, boldly declared that "*slavery should pour itself abroad without restraint, and find no limit but the Southern Ocean.*" The war with Mexico was waged for the twofold purpose of robbing that Republic of its territory, and then of robbing that territory of its freedom. Congressional orators and the Southern press avowed that the object of acquiring territory was to extend the "divine institution." I could quote pages in proof of this assertion. The North had no hope, the South had no fear, if the territories were left without control, that they would first be filled with slaveholders, and would then incorporate slavery into their organic law. While these hopes and apprehensions existed, the South insisted that the territories should be left untrammelled. Distinguished men in this House, Mr. Calhoun and other Senators . . . all proclaimed that the Territories should be left free to institute such government as they might choose. But since California has formed a free constitution, what a sudden change has taken place in the convictions of men! Within the present week we have had three most elaborate speeches in this House, in which the admission of California, with her free constitution, is vehemently opposed on constitutional grounds. . . . While California promised to be a slave State, all interference was unconstitutional. Now, as she desires to be a free State, it has become constitutional to interfere and repel her. Not only so, but, according to the gentleman from Alabama [Mr. Samuel Inge], in swearing to support the Constitution, we have sworn to perpetuate, and not only to perpetuate, but to *extend* slavery. "To those," he says, "who are disposed to resist my views, I commend a more attentive reading of that instrument. They will find that it not only guarantees slavery, but provides for its extension;" or, as he says in another place, it makes provision "to extend the institution indefinitely. . . ."

But I now come to a more substantial part of this great question: The South rests its claims to the new territory upon the great doctrine of equality. There are fifteen slave States; there are only fifteen free States. The South contributed men and money for the conquest, not less than the North. Hence, equal ownership and equal rights of enjoyment. This is the argument. . . .

Now, I admit this principle in its fullest extent, and without hesitation. That country is equally free to all the people of the United States. . . .

And now, practically, what right has the North, or what right is claimed by the North, which the South has not to an equal extent? . . . But, it is said, we can carry our *property* there, and you cannot carry your *property* there. I think those who use this argument, like the old Roman augurs, must smile at each other askance, for the credulity or simplicity of those they beguile by it. Will not every man, even of the feeblest discernment, see the fallacy which is here covered up under the word "*property?*" What is meant by this deceptive term "*property?*" If you mean silver, or gold, or grass, or grain, or sheep, or horses, cannot you carry these there as freely as we can? But you have special laws; local and peculiar laws,—laws contrary to the great principles of the common law, by which you call *men and women* property. And then, forsooth, because we can carry *property* there, when *property* mean grain and cattle, you can carry property there when it means human beings,—perhaps your own brothers, or sisters, or children. Because we can carry property there, when property means inanimate substances, you have only to call a human being *property*, you have only to call a creature, formed in the image of God, *property*,—and then he can be smuggled in under the new name. Why, sir, there is not a respectable village in the country, where, if a juggler or mountebank were to attempt to palm off upon his audience so flimsy a trick as this, he would not be hissed off the stage. . . .

[T]he law of slavery is a *local* law. Like lotteries, or polygamy . . . it can legally exist in no land where the principles of the common law prevail, until it is legalized and sanctioned by a special law. It is then permitted on the simple ground, that so much of the common law as secures liberty and property, the right of habeas corpus, and freedom of speech to each individual, has been cut out and cast away. The Constitution proceeds upon this doctrine when it provides for the recapture of fugitive slaves. Why did it not provide for the recapture of a fugitive horse, or ox? Why did it not provide that, if a horse or an ox should escape from a slave State into a free State, it should be delivered up, or be recoverable by legal process? Because horses and oxen are *property* by the common consent of mankind. It needed no law to make them property. . . . An escaped slave could not be recovered before the adoption of the Constitution. The power to seize upon escaping slaves was one of the motives for adopting it. These considerations demonstrate that slaves are not *property*, within the meaning of this word, when it is affirmed, that if the North can carry its property into the Territories, so can the South. As the Constitution, in terms, adopts the common law, it leaves slavery nothing to stand upon but the local laws of the States where it is established. Freedom is the rule, slavery is the exception. . . .

But gentlemen of the South . . . go farther, and they tell us what they will proceed to do if we do not yield to their demands. A large majority of the southern Legislatures have solemnly "resolved" that if Congress prohibits slavery in the new Territories, they will resist the law "at any and at every hazard." And yet they say they do not mean to threaten us. They desire to abstain from all language of menace, for threats and menaces are beneath the character of gentlemen. Sir, what is the meaning of the terms "threats" and "menaces?" Mr. Troup, formerly Governor of Georgia, speaking of us upon this floor, and of others who resist the extension of slavery, calls each of us a "fanatic." He says it is only the dread of death, that will stay our hands or stop our machinations; and then adds, "THAT DREAD YOU MUST PRESENT TO HIM IN A VISIBLE, PALPABLE FORM." "If," he says, in another place, "the abolitionists resolve to force emancipation, or *to force dishonor upon the southern States, by any act of Congress*, then it is my decided opinion that, with the military preparation here indicated, conjoined to a good volunteer instead of a militia system, THE STATE SHOULD MARCH UPON WASHINGTON AND DISSOLVE THE GOVERNMENT." . . . I could occupy my hour in citing passages of a similar character, from the southern press, and from southern men. . . .

Now, sir, as this event of a dissolution of the Union is so frequently forced upon our contemplation, I propose to occupy the residue of my hour in considering some of its more obvious consequences. Southern papers and southern resolution-writers have a favorite phrase, that if Congress shall pass any laws against the extension of slavery they will resist it "at any and every hazard." Let us inquire, soberly, what a few of those hazards are.

First, as to the recovery, or non-recovery, of fugitive slaves, which is one of the alleged provocatives of dissolution. . . . Remember, [should the southern states dissolve the Union], there is no Constitution of the United States now. That you have broken. The free States are therefore absolved from all obligation to surrender fugitives. . . . The distinguished Senator from Kentucky said, in his late speech, that no instance had ever come to his knowledge, where an action for harboring runaways had not been maintained in the courts of the free States, and damages recovered. But this remedy you will have annulled. The Constitution of the United States and the law of 1793 being at an end, the law of nature revives. By this law, every case of an escaping slave is but *the self-recovery of stolen goods.* When they cross the line into a free State, they are free,—as free as you or I. The States being separated, I would as soon return my own brother or sister into bondage, as I would return a fugitive slave. Before God, and Christ, and all Christian men, they are my brothers and sisters. As our laws make it piracy to kidnap slaves in Africa, or to ship them thence, so it shall be a felony, punishable with death, for any southern master to kidnap a colored man, in a free State, or transport him from it, on the ground of alleged ownership. You are fond of quoting Scripture to us, in justification of slavery. We will retort the Scripture, that "he that stealeth a man, and selleth him, or *if he be found in his hand,* he shall surely be put to death." . . .

In regard to instigating slaves to escape, I acknowledge there have been some instances of it; but they have been few. . . . But I have never known a single case,—and I believe there is no well-authenticated case on record,—where a northern man has instigated the slaves to rise in rebellion, and to retaliate upon their masters, for the wrongs which they and their race have suffered. As I dread indiscriminate massacre and conflagration, I should abhor the perpetrator of such a crime. But will separation bring relief or security? No, sir. It will enhance the danger a myriad fold. Thousands will start up, who will think it as much a duty and an honor to assist the slaves in any contest with their masters, as to assist Greeks, or Poles, or Hungarians, in resisting their tyrants. Two things exist at the North, which the South does not duly appreciate,—the depth and intensity of our abhorrence of slavery, and that reverence for the law which keeps it in check. The latter counterpoises the former. We are a law-abiding people. But release us from our obligations, tear off from the bond with your own hands the signatures which bind our consciences, and repress our feelings, destroy those compensations which the world and which posterity would derive from this Union, and well may you tremble for the result. . . . If agitation and instigation are evils now, woe to those who would seek to mitigate or to repress them by the remedies of disunion and civil war. Let men who live in a powder-mill beware how they madden pyrotechnists.

But it is said, that if dissolution occurs, the "United States South" can form an alliance with Great Britain. And are there no instigators and abolitionists in

England? Yes, sir,—ten in England where there is one at the North. Frederick Douglass has just returned from England, where he has enjoyed the honors of an ovation. William Wells Brown, another fugitive slave, is now traveling in England. His journeys from place to place are like the "Progresses" of one of the magnates of that land,—passing wherever he will, with free tickets, and enjoying the hospitalities of the most refined and educated men. . . . Sir, every man who has travelled in England knows that there are large, wealthy, and refined circles there, no member of whom would allow a slaveholder to sit at his table, or enter his doors. . . . If the South expects to rid itself of agitation and abolitionism, by rupturing its bonds with the North, and substituting an alliance with Great Britain for our present Constitution, they may envy the wisdom of the geese who invited the fox to stand sentinel over them while they slept. Northern interference will increase a hundred fold; and the whole power and wealth of British abolitionism, not only founded on moral principle, but nursed by national pride, will be brought to bear directly upon them. . . .

It surely is not beneath the dignity of the place or the occasion to look at another of those "hazards" which the South are invoking. They are proud of their past history, and I doubt not their reflecting and patriotic men are at least reasonably solicitous of their future fame. When they meet in august council to inaugurate the great event of establishing an Independent Confederacy of slave States, and of dissolving the political bands which now connect them with us, "a decent respect to the opinions of mankind" will "require them to declare the causes which had impelled them to the separation." And will they find a model for their manifesto in that glorious Declaration of American Independence, which their own immortal Jefferson prepared, and to which many of the greatest of all their historic names are subscribed? Alas, they will have to read that Declaration, as the devil reads Scripture,—backwards! I know not what may be the rhetorical terms and phrases of the new Declaration; but I do know that its *historic* form and substance cannot be widely different from this:

"We hold these truths to be self-evident, that men are not created equal; that they are not endowed by their Creator with inalienable rights; that white men, of the Anglo-Saxon race, were born to rob, and tyrannize, and enjoy; and black men, of the African race, to labor, and suffer, and obey; that a man with a drop of African blood in his veins, has no political rights, and therefore shall never vote; that he has no pecuniary rights, and, therefore, whatever he shall earn or receive, belongs to his master; that he has no judicial rights, and, therefore, he shall never be heard, as a witness, to redress wrong, or violence, or robbery, committed by white men upon him; that he has no parental rights, and, therefore, his children may be torn from his bosom, at the pleasure, or caprice, of his owner; that he has no marital rights, and, therefore, his wife may be lawfully sold away into distant bondage, or violated before his eyes; that he has no rights of mind, or of conscience, and, therefore, he shall never be allowed to read, or to think, and all his aspirations for improvement shall be extinguished; that he has no religious rights, and, therefore, he shall never read the Bible; that he has no heaven-descended, God-given rights of freedom, and, therefore, he, and his posterity, shall be slaves forever; we hold that governments were instituted among men, to secure and fortify this ascendancy of one race over another; that this ascendancy has its foundation in force, ratified by law, and, in ignorance and debasement, inflicted by intelligence and superiority; and when any people, with whom we have been politically associated, would debar us from propagating our doctrines, or extending our domination into new realms, and over free territories, it becomes our duty to separate from them, and to hold them, as we hold the rest of mankind, friends when they make slaves, enemies when they make freemen."

I say, sir, of whatever words and phrases the southern "Magna Charta" may consist, this, or something like this, must be its substance and reality.

So the preamble to their constitution must run in this wise: "We, the people of the 'United States South,' in order to form a more perfect conspiracy against the rights of the African race, establish injustice, insure domestic slavery, provide for holding three millions of our fellow-beings, with all the countless millions of their posterity, in bondage, and to secure to ourselves and our posterity the enjoyment of power, and luxury, and sloth, do ordain and establish this constitution for the 'United States South.'" . . .

8. William H. Seward, Address before the U.S. Senate (March 11, 1850)

Objecting to the 1850 compromise, William Seward (1801–1872) of New York argued that slavery violates both natural law and the Constitution. Rejecting Calhoun's compact theory of Union, he identified the people as sovereign and insisted that there is "a higher law than the Constitution" by which all laws must be judged. This latter claim would elicit much response from slavery's advocates, like Alexander Stephens (1812–1883) of Georgia.

Four years ago, California, a Mexican province, scarcely inhabited, and quite unexplored, was unknown even to our usually immoderate desires. . . .

Today, California is . . . more populous than the least, and richer than several of the greatest of our thirty states. This same California, thus rich and populous, is here asking admission into the Union, and finds us debating the dissolution of the Union itself. . . .

. . . Now it seems to me that the perpetual unity of our empire hangs on the decision of this day and of this hour. . . .

[I]t is insisted that the admission of California shall be attended by a COM-PROMISE of questions which have arisen out of SLAVERY.

I AM OPPOSED TO ANY SUCH COMPROMISE, IN ANY AND ALL THE FORMS IN WHICH IT HAS BEEN PROPOSED. . . .

What am I to receive in this compromise? Freedom in California. It is well; it is a noble acquisition; it is worth a sacrifice. But what am I to give as an equivalent? A recognition of the claim to perpetuate slavery in the District of Columbia; forbearance towards more stringent laws concerning the arrest of persons suspected of being slaves found in the free states; forbearance from the *proviso* of freedom in the charters of new territories. None of the plans of com-promise offered demand less than two, and most of them insist on all of these conditions. The equivalent, then, is some portion of liberty—some portion of human rights in one region, for liberty in another region. . . .

Nor would success attend any of the details of the compromise. And, first, I advert to the proposed alteration of the law concerning fugitives from service or labor. . . . It is a law that deprives the alleged refugee . . . of the writ of *habeas corpus*, and of any certain judicial process of examination of the claim set up by his pursuer, and finally degrades him into a chattel which may be seized and carried away peaceably wherever found, even although exercising the rights and responsibilities of a free citizen of the commonwealth in which he resides, and of the United States—a law which denies to the citizen all the safeguards of personal liberty, to render less frequent the escape of the bondman. . . .

We deem the principle of the law for the recapture of fugitives . . . unjust, unconstitutional, and immoral. . . .

Your Constitution and laws convert hospitality to the refugee, from the most degrading oppression on earth, into a crime, but all mankind except you esteem that hospitality a virtue. The right of extradition of a fugitive from jus-tice, is not admitted by the law of nature and of nations, but rests in voluntary compacts. . . .

. . . The law of nations disavows such compacts; the law of nature, writ-ten on the hearts and consciences of freemen, repudiates them. Armed power could not enforce them, because there is no public conscience to sustain them. I know that there are laws of various sorts which regulate the conduct of men. There are constitutions and statutes, codes mercantile and codes civil; but when we are legislating for States, especially when we are founding States, all these laws must be brought to the standard of the laws of God, and must be tried by that standard, and must stand or fall by it. . . .

Another objection arises out of the principle on which the demand for compro-mise rests. . . . The argument is that the States are severally equal, and that these two classes [slave and free states] were equal at the first, and that the Constitution was founded on that equilibrium—that the states being equal . . . , they are to be regarded as constituting an association, in which each State, and each of these classes of States, respectively, contribute in due proportions—that the new territories are a common acquisition, and the people of these several States and classes of States, have an equal right to participate in them respectively—that the right of the people of the slave States to emigrate to the territories with their slaves, as property, is necessary to afford such a participation on their part, inasmuch as the people of the free States emigrate into the same territories with their property. . . .

How is the original equality of the States proved? It rests on a syllogism of Vattel, as follows: All men are equal by the law of nature and of nations. But States are only lawful aggregations of individual men, who severally are equal; therefore States are equal in natural rights. All this is just and sound; but assuming the same premises, to wit: that all men are equal by the law of nature and of nations, the right of property in slaves falls to the ground; for one who is equal to another cannot be the owner or property of that other. But you answer that the Constitution recognizes property in slaves. It would be sufficient, then, to reply, that this constitutional recognition must be void, because it is repugnant to the law of nature and of nations. But I deny that the Constitution recognizes property in man. I submit, on the other hand, most respectfully, that the Constitution not merely does not affirm that principle, but, on the contrary, altogether excludes it.

The Constitution does not *expressly* affirm anything on the subject; all that it contains is two incidental allusions to slaves. These are—first, in the provision establishing a ratio of representation and taxation; and, secondly, in the provision relating to fugitives from labor. In both cases the Constitution designedly mentions slaves, not as slaves, much less as chattels, but as *persons*. . . .

I deem it established, then, that the Constitution does not recognize property in man, but leaves that question . . . to the law of nature and of nations. . . . When God had created the earth, with its wonderful adaptations, He gave dominion over it to Man—absolute human dominion. The title of that dominion, thus bestowed, would have been incomplete, if the Lord of all terrestrial things could himself have been the property of his fellow-man.

The right to *have* a slave implies the right in some one to *make* the slave; that right must be equal and mutual, and this would resolve society into a state of perpetual war. But if we grant the original equality of the States, and grant also the constitutional recognition of slaves as property, still the argument we are considering fails; because the States are not parties to the Constitution as States; it is the Constitution of the People of the United States. . . .

It needs little argument to show that the idea of a joint stock association, or a copartnership, as applicable even by its analogies to the United States, is erroneous, with all the consequences fancifully deduced from it. The United States are a political state, or organized society, whose end is government, for the security, welfare, and happiness of all who live under its protection. The theory I am combating reduces the objects of government to the mere spoils of conquest. Contrary to a theory so debasing, the preamble of the Constitution not only asserts the sovereignty to be, not in the States, but in the people, but also promulgates the objects of the Constitution:

"We, the people of the United States, in order to form a *more perfect union*, establish *justice*, insure *domestic tranquility*, provide for the *common defence*, promote the GENERAL WELFARE, and secure the *blessings of liberty*, do ordain and establish this Constitution."

Objects sublime and benevolent! They exclude the very idea of conquests, to be either divided among States or even enjoyed by them, for the purpose of securing, not the blessings of liberty, but the evils of slavery. . . .

There is another aspect of the principle of compromise, which deserves consideration. It assumes that slavery, if not the only institution in a slave State, is at least a ruling institution, and that this characteristic is recognized by the Constitution. But *slavery* is only *one* of many institutions there—freedom is equally an institution there. Slavery is only a temporary, accidental, partial and incongruous one; freedom, on the contrary, is a perpetual, organic, universal one, in harmony with the Constitution of the United States. . . . You may separate slavery from South Carolina, and the State will still remain; but if you subvert freedom there, the State will cease to exist. But the principle of this compromise gives complete ascendency in the slave State, and in the Constitution of the United States, to the subordinate, accidental, and incongruous institution over its paramount antagonist. To reduce this claim for slavery to an absurdity, it is only necessary to add that there are only two States in which slaves are a majority, and not one in which the slave holders are not a very disproportionate minority.

But there is yet another aspect in which this principle must be examined. It regards the domain only as a possession, to be enjoyed either in common or by partition by the citizens of the old States. It is true, indeed, that the national domain is ours; it is true, it was acquired by the valor and with the wealth of the whole nation; but we hold, nevertheless, no arbitrary power over it. We hold no arbitrary authority over anything, whether acquired lawfully or seized by usurpation. The Constitution regulates our stewardship; the Constitution devotes the domain to union, to justice, to defence, to welfare, and to liberty.

But there is a higher law than the Constitution, which regulates our authority over the domain, and devotes it to the same noble purposes. The territory is a part—no inconsiderable part—of the common heritage of mankind, bestowed upon them by the Creator of the universe. We are his stewards, and must so discharge our trust as to secure, in the highest attainable degree, their happiness. . . .

And now the simple, bold, and even awful question which presents itself to us is this: Shall we, who are founding institutions, social and political, for countless millions—shall we, who know by experience the wise and the just, and are free to choose them, and to reject the erroneous and unjust—shall we establish human bondage, or permit it, by our sufferance, to be established? Sir, our forefathers would not have hesitated an hour. They found slavery existing here, and they left it only because they could not remove it. There is not only no free State which would now establish it, but there is no slave State, which, if it had had the free alternative as we now have, would have founded slavery. Indeed, our revolutionary predecessors had precisely the same question before them in establishing an organic law under which the States of Ohio, Michigan, Illinois, and Wisconsin and Iowa, have since come into the Union, and they solemnly repudiated and excluded slavery from those States forever. I confess that the most alarming evidence of our degeneracy, which has yet been given, is found in the fact that we even debate such a question.

Sir, there is no Christian nation, thus free to choose as we are, which would establish slavery. I speak on due consideration, because Britain, France, and Mexico, have abolished slavery, and all other European States are preparing to abolish it as speedily as they can. We cannot establish slavery, because there are certain elements of the security, welfare, and greatness of nations, which we all . . . recognize as essential; and these are the security of natural rights, the diffusion of knowledge, and the freedom of industry. Slavery is incompatible with all of these, and just in proportion to the extent that it prevails and controls in any republican State, just to that extent it subverts the principle of democracy, and converts the State into an aristocracy or a despotism. . . .

It remains only to remark that our own experience has proved the dangerous influence and tendency of slavery. All our apprehensions of dangers, present and future, begin and end with slavery. If slavery, limited as it yet is, now threatens to subvert the Constitution, how can we, as wise and prudent statesmen, enlarge its boundaries and increase its influence, and thus increase already impending dangers? Whether, then, I regard merely the welfare of the future inhabitants of the new territories, or the security and welfare of the whole people of the United States, or the welfare of the whole family of mankind, I cannot consent to introduce slavery into any part of this continent which is now exempt from what seems to me so great an evil. These are my reasons for declining to compromise the question relating to slavery as a condition of the admission of California. . . .

9. Rev. J. H. Thornwell, *The Rights and the Duties of Masters: A Sermon Preached at the Dedication of a Church, Erected in Charleston, S.C., for the Benefit and Instruction of the Coloured Population* (May 26, 1850)

Presbyterian preacher and writer James Henley Thornwell (1812–1862) argued that rather than dehumanizing slaves, slavery assumes their moral agency. Slaves and masters have responsibilities to each other, and the fulfillment of those responsibilities is how they pay homage to God and achieve that "liberty wherewith Christ has made us free." Slaves must obey their masters; masters should teach slaves the Gospel, which, he assured his readers, will make slaves more content with their condition.

It is common to describe slavery as the property of man in man—as the destruction of all human and personal rights, the absorption of the humanity of one individual into the will and power of another. "The very idea of a slave," says Dr. [William Ellery] Channing, "is that he belongs to another, that he is bound to live and labour for another, to be another's instrument, and to make another's will his habitual law, however adverse to his own." . . . In other words, in every system of slavery, from the operation of its inherent and essential principles, the slave ceases to be a person—a man—and becomes a mere instrument or thing. Dr. Channing does not charge this result upon the relation as it obtains under particular codes, or at particular times, or in particular places. He says, distinctly and emphatically, that it violates all human rights, *not incidentally*, but *necessarily, systematically* from *its very nature*. It belongs to the very essence of slavery to divest its victims of humanity. . . .

If this be a just description of slavery, the wonder is, not that the civilized world is now indignant at its outrages and wrongs, but that it has been so slow in detecting its enormities, that mankind, for so many centuries, acquiesced in a system which contradicted every impulse of nature, every whisper of conscience, every dictate of religion. . . . I have, however, no hesitation in saying, that whatever may be the technical language of the law, in relation to certain aspects in which slavery is contemplated, the ideas of personal rights and personal responsibility pervade the whole system. It is a relation of man to man—a form of civil society, of which persons are the only elements, and not a relation of man to things. . . . Paul treats the services of slaves as *duties*—not like the toil of the ox or the ass—a labor extracted by the stringency of discipline—but a moral debt, in the payment of which they were rendering a homage to God. "Servants," says he, "be obedient to them that

are your masters, according to the flesh, with fear and trembling, in singleness of your heart, as unto Christ; not with eye-service, as men-pleasers, but
as the servants of Christ, doing the will of God from the heart; with good
will doing service, as to the Lord, and not to men; knowing that whatever
good thing any man doeth, the same shall he receive of the Lord, whether he
be bond or free" [Ephes. iv.5–9]. I need not say to those who are acquainted
with the very elements of moral philosophy, that obedience, except as a figured term, can never be applied to any but rational, intelligent, responsible
agents. . . .

The apostle not merely recognizes the moral agency of slaves . . . but treats
them as possessed of conscience, reason and will. . . . He says to them in effect
that their services to their masters are duties which they owe to God—that
a moral character attaches to their works, and that they are the subjects of
praise or blame according to the principles upon which their obedience is rendered. . . . He considered slavery as a social and political economy, in which
relations subsisted betwixt moral, intelligent, responsible beings, involving
reciprocal rights and reciprocal obligations. There was a right to command
on the one hand—an obligation to obey on the other. Both parties might be
guilty of injustice and of wrong—the master might prostitute his power by
tyranny, cruelty, and iniquitous exactions—the servant might evade his duty
from indolence, treachery, or obstinate self-will. . . .

If, then, slavery is not inconsistent with the existence of personal rights
and of moral obligation, it may be asked in what does its peculiarity consist?
What is it that makes a man a slave? We answer, the obligation to labour for
another, determined by the Providence of God, independently of the provisions of a contract. The right which the master has is a right, not to the *man*,
but to his *labour*; the duty which the slave owes is the service which, in conformity with this right, the master exacts. The essential difference betwixt free
and slave-labour is, that one is rendered in consequence of a contract; the
other is rendered in consequence of a command. The labourers in each case are
equally moral, equally responsible, equally men. But they work upon different
principles. . . .

Whatever control the master has over the person of the slave, is subsidiary
to this right to his labour; what he sells is not the man, but the property in his
services. . . . [T]rue he chastises the man, but the punishments inflicted for
disobedience are no more inconsistent with personal responsibilities than the
punishments inflicted by the law for breaches of contract. On the contrary,
punishment in contradistinction from suffering, always implies responsibility. . . . The chastisements of slaves are accordingly no more entitled to awaken
the indignation of loyal and faithful citizens—however pretended philanthropists may describe the horrors of the scourge and the lash—than the penalties
of disgrace, imprisonment, or death, which all nations have inflicted upon

crimes against the State. All that is necessary in any case, is that the punishment should *be just.* . . .

. . . There is a freedom which is the end and glory of man. . . . It is *the* freedom which God approves; which Jesus bought by his blood . . . ; the liberty wherewith Christ has made us free. It consists essentially in the dominion of rectitude, in the emancipation of the will from the power of sin. . . . This freedom makes man truly a man; and it is precisely the assertion of this freedom—this dominion of rectitude—this supremacy of right, which the Apostle enjoins upon slaves—when he exhorts them to obey their masters in singleness of heart as unto Christ—to despise eye-service, but to do their work as in the eye of God. To obey under the influence of these motives, is to be slaves no longer. . . .

Now, unless slavery is incompatible with the habitudes of holiness—unless it is inconsistent with the spirit of philanthropy or the spirit of piety—unless it furnishes no opportunities for obedience to the law, it is not inconsistent with the pursuit or attainment of the highest excellence. It is no abridgement of moral freedom; the slave may come from the probation of *his* circumstances as fully stamped with the image of God, as those who have enjoyed an easier lot. . . .

Hence those moralists are grievously in error, who have represented slavery as inconsistent with the full complement of human duty and as a consequent limitation upon the spiritual freedom of man, because there are duties which God has not connected with this condition of society. To maintain that the same things are universally obligatory, without regard to circumstances or relations, that what is exacted of one must necessarily be exacted from another, however different or even incongruous their outward states, is to confound the obligations of rulers and subjects, of parents and children, of guardians and wards, and to plunge the community into irretrievable confusion. All that can be affirmed is, that the same temper of universal rectitude is equally incumbent upon all, while it must be admitted that the outward forms of its manifestations and expression must be determined by the relations which Providence has actually assigned to our state. The slave is to show his reverence for God—the freedom of his inward man—by a cheerful obedience to the lawful commands of his master;—the master, his regard for one who is his master in heaven, by rendering to the slave that which is just and equal. The character of both is determined, in the sight of God, by the spirit which pervades their single acts, however the acts may differ in themselves. . . .

[W]e hesitate not to affirm that one of the highest and most solemn obligations which rests upon the masters of the South, is to give to their servants, to the utmost extent of their ability, free access to the instructions and institution of the Gospel. The injustice of denying to them food and raiment, and shelter, against which the law effectually guards, is nothing to the injustice of defrauding them of that bread which cometh down from Heaven. [E]very motive of humanity and religion exacts from us, that we should remunerate their services by putting within their reach, the means of securing a blessed immortality. The meanest slave has, in him, a soul of priceless value. . . . That soul has sinned—it is under the curse of the Almighty, and nothing can save it from an intolerable hell but the redemption that is in Christ Jesus. They must hear this joyful sound or perish. For how shall they believe in Him of whom they have not heard, and how shall they hear without a preacher, and how shall they preach except they be sent? Our design in giving them the Gospel, is not to civilize them—not to change their social condition—not to exalt them into citizens or freemen— it is to save them. . . . We have begun a good work, and God grant that it may never cease until every slave in the land is brought under the tuition of Jesus of Nazareth. None need be afraid of His lessons. It was said of Him on earth, that He should not cry, nor lift up, nor cause His voice to be heard in the streets. He was no stirrer up of strife, nor mover of sedition. . . . Insurrection, anarchy and bloodshed—revolt against masters, or treason against States, were never learned in the school of Him, whose Apostles enjoined subjection to the magistrate, and obedience to all lawful authority, as characteristic duties of the faithful. . . . Christian knowledge inculcates contentment with our lot; and in bringing before us the tremendous realities of eternity, renders us comparatively indifferent to the inconveniences and hardships of time. It subdues those passions and prejudices, from which all real danger to the social economy springs. . . .

Our highest security in these States, lies in the confidence and affection of our servants, and nothing will more effectually propitiate their regards than consistent efforts, upon our part, to promote their everlasting good. They will feel that those are not tyrants who are striving to bring them unto God; and they will be slow to cast off a system which has become associated in their minds with their dearest hopes and most precious consolations. Brutal ignorance is indeed to be dreaded—the only security against it, is physical force—it is the parent of ferocity, of rashness, and of desperate enterprizes. But Christian knowledge softens and subdues. Christ Jesus in binding his subjects to God, binds them more closely to each other in the ties of confidence, fidelity and love. We would say, then, to you and to all our brethren of the South, go on in your present undertaking; and though our common enemies may continue to revile, you will be consolidating the elements of your social fabrick, so firmly and compactly, that it shall defy the storms of fanaticism, while the spectacle you will exhibit of union, sympathy and confidence, among the different orders of the community, will be a standing refutation of all their accusations against us. . . .

10. Preamble and Resolutions of the Second Nashville Convention (November 18, 1850)

Delegates from nine slaveholding states met in Nashville in June 1850 to debate the pending Compromise of 1850. Delegates were split between those willing to accept a compromise (extending the 36°30' line to the Pacific Ocean) and those advocating secession if slavery were not permitted throughout the new territories. After President Millard Fillmore signed the compromise, a second, rump convention convened, again in Nashville, resolving to secede from the Union if their "rights" were not restored.

. . . We, the delegates assembled from a portion of the states of this confederacy, make this exposition of the causes which have brought us together, and of the rights which the states we represent are entitled to under the compact of Union.

We have amongst us two races, marked by such distinctions of color and physical and moral qualities as for ever forbid their living together on terms of social and political equality.

The black race have been slaves from the earliest settlement of our country, and our relations of master and slave have grown up from that time. A change in those relations must end in convulsion, and the entire ruin of one or of both races.

When the Constitution was adopted this relation of master and slave, as it exists, was expressly recognised and guarded in that instrument. It was a great and vital interest, involving our very existence as a separate people then as well as now.

The states of this confederacy acceded to that compact, each one for itself, and ratified it as states.

If the non-slaveholding states, who are parties to that compact, disregard its provisions and endanger our peace and existence by united and deliberate action, we have a right, as states, there being no common arbiter, to secede.

The object of those who are urging on the federal government in its aggressive policy upon our domestic institutions is, beyond all doubt, finally to overthrow them, and abolish the existing relation between the master and slave. We feel authorized to assert this from their own declarations, and from the history of events in this country for the last few years. . . .

We make no aggressive move. We stand upon the defensive. We invoke the spirit of the Constitution, and claim its guarantees. Our rights—our independence—the peace and existence of our families, depend upon the issue.

The federal government has within a few years acquired, by treaty and by triumphant war, vast territories. This has been done by the counsels and the arms of all, and the benefits and rights belong alike and equally to all the states.

The federal government is but the common agent of the states united, and represents their conjoined sovereignty over subject-matter granted and defined in the compact.

The authority it exercises over all acquired territory must in good faith be exercised for the equal benefit of all the parties. To prohibit our citizens from settling there with the most valuable part of our property is not only degrading to us as equals, but violates our highest constitutional rights.

Restrictions and prohibitions against the slaveholding states, it would appear, are to be the fixed and settled policy of the government; and those states that are hereafter to be admitted into the Federal Union from their extensive territories will but confirm and increase the power of the majority; and he knows little of history who cannot read our destiny in the future if we fail to do our duty now as free people.

We have been harassed and insulted by those who ought to have been our brethren, in their constant agitation of a subject vital to us and the peace of our families. We have been outraged by their gross misrepresentations of our moral and social habits, and by the manner in which they have denounced us before the world. We have had our property enticed off; and the means of recovery denied us by our co-states in the territories of the Union, which we were entitled to as political equals under the Constitution. Our peace has been endangered by incendiary appeals. The Union, instead of being considered a fraternal bond, has been used as the means of striking at our vital interests.

The admission of California . . . confirms an unauthorized and revolutionary seizure of public domain, and the exclusion of near half the states of the confederacy from equal rights therein destroys the line of thirty-six degrees thirty minutes, which was originally acquiesced in as a matter of compromise and peace, and appropriates to the northern states one hundred and twenty thousand square miles below that line, and is so gross and palpable a violation of the principles of justice and equality as to shake our confidence in any security to be given by that majority who are now clothed with power to govern the future destiny of the confederacy. . . .

We have no powers that are binding upon the states we represent. But, in order to produce system and concerted action, we recommend the following resolutions, viz. . . .

Resolved, That the union of the States is a union of equal and independent sovereignties, and that the powers delegated to the Federal government can be resumed by the several states, whenever it may seem to them proper and necessary.

Resolved, That all the evils anticipated by the South, and which occasioned this Convention to assemble have been realized, by the failure to extend the Missouri line of compromise to the Pacific Ocean; By the admission of California as a state. By the organization of Territorial governments for Utah and New Mexico without giving adequate protection for the property of the

South. By the dismemberment of Texas. By the abolition of the slave trade, and the emancipation of slaves carried into the District of Columbia for sale.

Resolved, That we earnestly recommend to all parties in the slaveholding States, to refuse to go into or countenance any national convention, whose object may be to nominate candidates for the Presidency and Vice-Presidency of the United States, under any party denomination whatever, until our constitutional rights are secured.

Resolved, That in view of these aggressions, and of those threatened and impending, we earnestly recommend to the slaveholding states, to meet in a congress or convention . . . , intrusted with full power and authority to deliberate and act with a view and intention of arresting further aggression, and if possible of restoring the constitutional rights of the South, and if not to provide for their safety and independence. . . .

11. Frederick Douglass, "The U.S. Constitution" (reprinted in *The Liberator*, May 23, 1851)

Douglass met William Lloyd Garrison in 1841 and was influenced initially by the arguments of Garrison, Wendell Phillips, and other abolitionists that the Constitution was a pro-slavery compact. To their minds, the Constitution not only tolerated slavery but supported it, holding that various provisions of the charter legitimized it and ensured for it the full protection of U.S. law. However, by 1851 Douglass embraced the arguments of men like Lysander Spooner and Gerrit Smith who believed otherwise, and he announced his change of mind in the document included here. Slavery, he asserted, is "a system of lawless violence; . . . it never was lawful, and never can be made so."

In the last number of the North Star [May 15, 1851] is a full and comprehensive summary of the proceedings of the annual meeting of the American Anti-Slavery Society, at Syracuse, from the pen of FREDERICK DOUGLASS. Here is an extract:

CHANGE OF OPINION ANNOUNCED

The debate on the resolution relative to anti-slavery newspapers assumed such a character as to make it our duty to define the position of the "North Star" in respect to the Constitution of the United States. The ground having been directly taken, that no paper ought to receive the recommendation of the American Anti-Slavery Society that did not assume the Constitution to be a pro-slavery document, we felt in honor bound to announce at once to our old anti-slavery companions that we no longer possessed the requisite qualification for their official approval and commendation; and to assure them that we had arrived at the firm conviction that the Constitution, construed in the light of well established rules of legal interpretation, might be made consistent in its details with the noble purposes avowed in its preamble; and that hereafter we should insist upon the application of such rules to that instrument, and demand that it be wielded in behalf of emancipation. The change in our opinion on this subject has not been hastily arrived at. A careful study of the writings of Lysander Spooner, of Gerrit Smith, and of William Goodell, has brought us to our present conclusion. We found, in our former position, that, when debating the question, we were compelled to go behind the letter of the Constitution, and to seek its meaning in the history and practice of the nation under it—a process always attended with disadvantages; and certainly we feel little inclination to shoulder disadvantages of any kind, in order to give slavery the slightest protection. In short, we hold it to be a system of lawless violence; that it *never was lawful, and never can be made so*; and that it is the first duty of every American citizen, whose conscience permits so to do, to use his *political* as well as his *moral* power for its overthrow. . . .

12. Samuel A. Cartwright, "Report on the Diseases of and Physical Peculiarities of the Negro Race," *The New-Orleans Medical and Surgical Journal, Devoted to Medicine and the Collateral Sciences*, Volume VII (May 1851; reprinted in *De Bow's Review of the Southern and Western States*, Volume XI [1851])

A renowned physician, Samuel Cartwright (1793–1863) claimed to have proven that the "two races" were fundamentally different and that slavery, while "poisonous" to whites, was "wholesome and beneficial . . . to the negro race." He was known for conjuring the disease "Drapetomania," which he defined as a mental disorder that induced slaves to seek escape.

Drapetomania, or the Disease Causing Slaves to Run Away

Drapetomania . . . is unknown to our medical authorities, although its diagnostic symptom, the absconding from service, is well known to our planters and overseers, as it was the ancient Greeks. . . . I have added to the word meaning runaway slave, another Greek term, to express the disease of the mind causing him to abscond. In noticing a disease not heretofore classed among the long list of maladies that man is subject to, it was necessary to have a new term to express it. The cause, in the most of cases, that induces the negro to run away from service, is as much a disease of the mind as any other species of mental alienation, and much more curable, as a general rule. With the advantages of proper medical advice, strictly followed, this troublesome practice that many negroes have of running away, can be almost entirely prevented, although the slaves be located on the borders of a free state, within a stone's throw of the abolitionists. . . .

To ascertain the true method of governing negroes, so as to cure and prevent the disease under consideration, we must go back to the Pentateuch, and learn the true meaning of the untranslated term that represents the negro race. In the name there given to that race, is locked up the true art of governing negroes in such a manner that they cannot run away. The correct translation of that term declares the Creator's will in regard to the negro; it declares him to be the submissive knee-bender. In the anatomical conformation of his knees, we see "*genu flexit*" written in the physical structure of his knees, being more flexed or bent, than any other kind of man. If the white man attempts to oppose the Deity's will, by trying to make the negro anything else than "*the submissive knee-bender,*" (which the Almighty declared he should be), by trying to raise him to a level with himself, or by putting himself on an equality with the negro; or if he abuses the power which God has given him over his fellow-man, by being cruel to him, or punishing him in anger, or by neglecting to protect him from the wanton abuses of his fellow-servants and all others, or by denying him the usual comforts and necessaries of life, the negro will run away; but if he keeps him in the position that we learn from the Scriptures he was intended to occupy, that is, the position of submission; and if his master or overseer be kind and gracious in his bearing towards him, without condescension, and at the same time ministers to his physical wants, and protects him from abuses, the negro is spell-bound, and cannot run away. "*He shall serve* Japeth; he shall be his servant of servants," on the conditions above mentioned. . . . According to my experience, the "genu flexit"—the awe and reverence, must be exacted from them, or they will despise their masters, become rude and ungovernable, and run away. On Mason and Dixon's line, two classes of persons were apt to lose their negroes; those who made themselves too familiar with them, treating them as equals, and making little or no distinction in regard to color; and, on the other hand, those who treated them cruelly, denied them the common necessaries of life, neglected to protect them against the abuses of others, or frightened them by a blustering manner of approach, when about to punish them for misdemeanors. Before negroes run away, unless they are frightened or panic-struck, they become sulky and dissatisfied. The cause of this sulkiness and dissatisfaction should be inquired into and removed, or they are apt to run away or fall into the negro consumption. When sulky and dissatisfied without cause, the experience of those on the line and elsewhere was decidedly in favor of whipping them out of it, as a preventive measure against absconding or other bad conduct. It was called whipping the devil out of them.

If treated kindly, well fed and clothed, with fuel enough to keep a small fire burning all night—separated into families, each family having its own house—not permitted to run about at night to visit their neighbors, to receive visits or use intoxicating liquors, and not overworked or exposed too much to the weather, they are very easily governed—more so than any other people in the world. When all this is done, if any one or more of them, at any time, are inclined to raise their heads to a level with their master or overseer, humanity and their own good require that they should be punished until they fall into that submissive state which it was intended for them to occupy in all after-time, when their progenitor received the name of Canaan or "submissive knee-bender." They have only to be kept in that state and treated like children, with care, kindness, attention and humanity, to prevent and cure them from running away.

Dysesthesia Æthiopis, or Hebetude of Mind and Obtuse Sensibility of Body. . . .

Dysaesthesia Aethiopica is a disease peculiar to negroes. . . . It is much more prevalent among free negroes living in clusters by themselves, than among slaves on our plantations, and attacks only such slaves as live like free negroes in regard to diet, drinks, exercise, etc. . . . I propose only to describe its symptoms among slaves.

From the careless movements of the individuals affected with the complaint, they are apt to do much mischief, which appears as if intentional, but is mostly owing to the stupidity of mind and insensibility of the nerves induced by the disease. Thus, they break, waste and destroy everything they handle, . . . They wander about at night, and keep in a half-nodding sleep during the day. They slight their work,—cut up corn, cane, cotton or tobacco when hoeing it, as if for pure mischief. They raise disturbances with their overseers and fellow-servants without cause or motive, and seem to be insensible to pain when subjected to punishment. . . . The northern physicians and people have noticed the symptoms, but not the disease from which they spring. They ignorantly attribute the symptoms to the debasing influence of slavery on the mind, without considering that those who have never been in slavery, or their fathers before them, are the most afflicted. . . . The disease is the natural offspring of negro liberty—the liberty to be idle, to wallow in filth, and to indulge in improper food and drinks. . . .

According to unalterable physiological laws, negroes . . . can only have their intellectual faculties awakened in a sufficient degree to receive moral culture, and to profit by religious or other instruction, when under the compulsory authority of the white man; because, as a general rule . . . they will not take sufficient exercise, when removed from the white man's authority, to vitalize and decarbonize their blood by the process of full and free respiration, that active exercise of some kind alone can effect. . . . From their natural indolence, unless under the stimulus of compulsion, they doze away their lives with the capacity of their lungs for atmospheric air only half expanded from the want of exercise to superinduce full and deep respiration. The inevitable effect is, to prevent a sufficient atmospherization or vitalization of the blood, so essential to the expansion and freedom of action of the intellectual faculties. The black blood distributed to the brain chains the mind to ignorance, superstition, and barbarism, and bolts the door against civilization, moral culture and religious truth. The compulsory power of the white man, by making the slothful negro take active exercise, puts into active play the lungs, through whose agency the vitalized blood is sent to the brain, to give liberty to the mind, and open the door to intellectual improvement. The very exercise, so beneficial to the negro, is expended in cultivating . . . cotton, sugar, rice and tobacco, which, but for his labor, would, from the heat of the climate, go uncultivated, and their products lost to the world. Both parties are benefitted—the negro as well as his master. . . . But there is a third party benefitted—the world at large. . . . The laboring classes of all mankind, having less to pay for clothing, have more money to spend in educating their children, and in intellectual, moral and religious progress. . . .

Our Declaration of Independence . . . is often quoted in support of the false dogma that all mankind possess the same mental, physiological and anatomical organization, and that the liberty, free institutions, and whatever else would be a blessing to one portion, would, under the same external circumstances, be to all, without regard to any original or internal differences. . . . The dysaesthesia ethiopis adds another to the many ten thousand evidences of the fallacy of the dogma that abolitionism is built on; for here, in a country where two races of men dwell together . . . liberty, which is elevating the one race of people above all other nations, sinks the other into beastly sloth and torpidity; and the slavery, which the one would prefer death rather than endure, improves the other in body, mind and morals; thus proving the dogma false, and establishing the truth that there is a radical, internal, or physical difference between the two races, so great in kind, as to make what is wholesome and beneficial for the white man, as liberty, republican or free institutions, etc., not only unsuitable to the negro race, but actually poisonous to its happiness.

13. Martin R. Delany, *The Condition, Elevation, Emigration, and Destiny of the Colored People of the United States* (1852)

An early voice for black nationalism, Martin R. Delany (1812–1885) criticized African Americans for their passive acceptance and internalization of black inferiority. The salvation of black Americans, he argued, can only result from "self-effort." Choosing to remain in America means accepting degradation; thus, all blacks should renounce America and emigrate.

IV. OUR ELEVATION IN THE UNITED STATES

. . . That all men and women, should be moral, upright, good and religious— we mean *Christians*—we would not utter a word against, and could only wish that it were so; but, what we here desire to do is to correct the long standing error among a large body of the colored people in this country, that the cause of our oppression and degradation, is the displeasure of God towards us, because of our unfaithfulness to Him. This is not true; because if God is just—and he is—there could be no justice in prospering white men with his fostering care, for more than two thousand years, in all their wickedness, while dealing out to the colored people, the measure of his displeasure, for not half the wickedness as that of the whites. Here then is our mistake, and let it forever henceforth be corrected. We are no longer slaves, believing any interpretation that our oppressors may give the word of God, for the purpose of deluding us to the more easy subjugation; but freemen, comprising some of the first minds of intelligence and rudimental qualifications, in the country. What then is the remedy, for our degradation and oppression? This appears now to be the only remaining question—the means of successful elevation in this our own native land? This depends entirely upon the application of the means of Elevation.

V. MEANS OF ELEVATION

Moral theories have long been resorted to by us, as a means of effecting the redemption of our brethren in bonds, and the elevation of the free colored people in this country. Experience has taught us, that speculations are not enough; that the *practical* application of principles adduced, the thing carried out, is the only true and proper course to pursue. . . .

Cast our eyes about us and reflect for a moment, and what do we behold! every thing that presents to view gives evidence of the skill of the white man. Should we purchase a pound of groceries, a yard of linen, a vessel of crockeryware, a piece of furniture, the very provisions that we eat,—all, all are the products of the white man, purchased by us from the white man, consequently, our earnings and means, are all given to the white man.

. . . Look as you pass along through the cities, at the great and massive buildings . . . , all standing as mighty living monuments, of the industry, enterprise, and intelligence of the white man. . . . How do we compare with them? Our fathers are their coachmen, our brothers their cookmen, and ourselves their waiting men. Our mothers their nurse-women, our sisters their scrub-women, our daughters their maid-women, and our wives their washer-women. . . .

. . . Until we are determined to change the condition of things, and raise ourselves above position in which we are now prostrated, we must hang our heads in sorrow, and hide our faces in shame. It is enough to know that these things are so; the causes we care little about. Those we have been examining, complaining about, and moralizing over, all our life time. This we are weary of. What we desire to learn now is, how to effect a *remedy*; this we endeavored to point out. Our elevation must be the result of *self-efforts*, and work of our *own hands*. . . .

. . . The means are at hand, within our reach. Are we willing to try them? Are we willing to raise ourselves superior to the condition of slaves, or continue the meanest underlings, subject to the beck and call of every creature bearing a pale complexion? If we are, we had as well remained in the South, as to have come to the North in search of more freedom. What was the object of our parents in leaving the South, if it were not for the purpose of attaining equality in common with others of their fellow citizens, by giving their children access to all the advantages enjoyed by others? Surely this was their object. They heard of liberty and equality here, and they hastened on to enjoy it, and no people are more astonished and disappointed than they, who for the first time, [behold] the position we occupy here in the free North. . . . They at once tell us, that they have as much liberty in the South as we have in the North. . . . Indeed, if our superior advantages of the free States do not induce and stimulate us to the higher attainments in life, what in the name of degraded humanity will do it? Nothing, surely nothing. . . . The degradation of the slave parent has been entailed upon the child, induced by the subtle policy of the oppressor, in regular succession handed down from father to son—a system of regular submission and servitude, menialism and dependence, until it has become almost a physiological function of our system, an actual condition of our nature. Let this no longer be so, but let us determine to equal the whites among whom we live, not by declarations and unexpressed self-opinion, for we have always had enough of that, but by actual proof in acting, doing, and carrying out practically, the measures of equality. Here is our nativity, and here have we the natural right to abide and be elevated through the measures of our own efforts. . . .

XVI. NATIONAL DISFRANCHISEMENT OF COLORED PEOPLE

We give below the Act of Congress, known as the "Fugitive Slave Law," for the benefit of the reader, as there are thousands of the American people of all classes, who have never read the provisions of this enactment, and consequently, have no conception of its enormity. . . .

By the provisions of this bill, the colored people of the United States are positively degraded beneath the level of the whites—are made liable at any time, in any place, and under all circumstances, to be arrested—and upon the claim of any white person, without the privilege, even of making a defence, sent into endless bondage. Let no visionary nonsense about *habeas corpus*, or a *fair trial* deceive us; there are no such rights granted in this bill. . . .

We are slaves in the midst of freedom, waiting patiently, and unconcern-edly—indifferently, and stupidly, for masters to come and lay claim to us, trusting to their generosity whether or not they will own us and carry us into endless bondage. . . .

A people capable of originating and sustaining such a law as this, are not the people to whom we are willing to entrust our liberty at discretion.

What can we do?—What shall we do? This is the great and important ques-tion:—Shall we submit to be dragged like brutes before heartless men, and sent into degradation and bondage?—Shall we fly, or shall we resist? . . .

This is the law of the land and must be obeyed; and we candidly advise that it is useless for us to contend against it. To suppose its repeal, is to anticipate an overthrow of the Confederate Union; and we must be allowed an expres-sion of opinion, when we say, that candidly we believe, the existence of the Fugitive Slave Law *necessary* to the continuance of the National Compact. This Law is the foundation of the Compromise—remove it, and the consequences are easily determined. We say necessary to the continuance of the National Compact: certainly we will not be understood as meaning that the enactment of such a Law was *really* necessary, . . . but we speak logically and politically, leaving morality and right out of the question—taking our position on the acknowledged popular basis of American Policy; arguing from premise to con-clusion. We must abandon all vague theory, and look at *facts* as they really are, viewing ourselves in our true political position in the body politic. To imagine ourselves to be included in the body politic . . . is at war with common sense, and contrary to fact. Legislation, the administration of the laws of the country, and the exercise of rights by the people, all prove to the contrary. We are politi-cally, not of them, but aliens to the laws and political privileges of the country. These are truths—fixed facts, that quaint theory and exhausted moralising, are impregnable to, and fall harmlessly before. . . .

What then shall we do?—what is the remedy—is the important question to be answered?

This important inquiry we shall answer, and find a remedy in when treating of the emigration of the colored people. . . .

XXII. THINGS AS THEY ARE

. . .

We have been standing comparatively still for years, following in the footsteps of our friends, believing that what they promise us can be accomplished, just because they say so, although our own knowledge should long since have satisfied us to the contrary. Because even were it possible, with the present hate and jealousy that the whites have towards us in this country, for us to gain equality of rights with them, we never could have an equality of the exercise and enjoyment of those rights—because, the great odds of numbers are against us. . . .

Let our young men and women, prepare themselves for usefulness and business; that the men may enter into merchandise, trading, and other things of importance; the young women may become teachers of various kinds, and otherwise fill places of usefulness. Parents must turn their attention more to the education of their children. We mean, to educate them for useful practical business purposes. Educate them for the Store and the Counting House—to do every-day practical business. Consult the children's propensities, and direct their education according to their inclinations. It may be that there is too great a desire on the part of parents to give their children a professional education, before the body of the people, are ready for it. A people must be a business people, and have more to depend upon than mere help in people's houses and Hotels, before they are either able to support, or capable of properly appreciating the services of professional men among them. This has been one of our great mistakes—we have gone in advance of ourselves. We have commenced at the superstructure of the building, instead of the foundation—at the top instead of the bottom. We should first be mechanics and common tradesmen, and professions as a matter of course would grow out of the wealth made thereby. Young men and women, must now prepare for usefulness—the day of our Elevation is at hand—all the world now gazes at us—and Central and South America, and the West Indies, bid us come and be men and women, protected, secure, beloved and Free. . . .

XXIII. A GLANCE AT OURSELVES—CONCLUSION

. . .

One of our great temporal curses is our consummate poverty. . . . To compete now with the mighty odds of wealth, social and religious preferences, and political influences of this country, at this advanced stage of its national existence, we never may expect. A new country, and new beginning, is the only true, rational, politic remedy for our disadvantageous position. . . .

When such great worth and talents . . . of men like Rev. Jonathan Robinson, Robert Douglass, Frederick A. Hinton, and a hundred others that might be named, were permitted to expire in a barber-shop . . . certainly the necessity of such a course as we have pointed out, must be cordially acknowledged. . . . These minds must become "unfettered," and have "space to rise." This cannot be in their present positions. A continuance in any position, becomes what is termed "Second Nature"; it begets an *adaptation*, and *reconciliation of mind* to such condition. It changes the whole physiological condition of the system, and adapts man and woman to a higher or lower sphere in the pursuits of life. The offsprings of slaves and peasantry, have the general characteristics of their parents; and nothing but a different course of training and education, will change the character.

The slave may become a lover of his master, and learn to forgive him for continual deeds of maltreatment and abuse; just as the Spaniel would couch and fondle at the feet that kick him; because he has been taught to reverence them, and consequently, becomes adapted in body and mind to his condition. . . . It has been so with us in our position among our oppressors; we have been so prone to such positions, that we have learned to love them. When reflecting upon this all important, and to us, all absorbing subject, we feel in the agony and anxiety of the moment, as though we could cry out in the language of a Prophet of old: "Oh that my head were waters, and mine eyes a fountain of tears, that I might weep day and night for the" degradation "of my people! . . ."

A child born under oppression, has all the elements of servility in its constitution; who when born under favorable circumstances, has to the contrary, all the elements of freedom and independence of feeling. Our children then, may not be expected to maintain that position and manly bearing, born under the unfavorable circumstances with which we are surrounded in this country, that we so much desire. To use the language of the talented Mr. Whipper, "they cannot be raised in this country, without being stoop shouldered." Heaven's pathway stands unobstructed, which will lead us into a Paradise of bliss. Let us go on and possess the land, and the God of Israel will be our God. . . .

Chapter Six: 1854–1865

Introduction

According to Carl von Clausewitz, war "always starts from a political condition, and is called forth by a political motive." War itself is never the goal. Rather, it's a means invoked in pursuit of some political end. And thus, as he famously concluded, "War is not merely a political act, but also a real political instrument, a continuation of political commerce, a carrying out of the same by other means."[1] If so, then the American Civil War began at least as early as May 1856, when "border ruffians" from Missouri sacked the town of Lawrence, Kansas. The use of violence was the means. The political objective was admission of Kansas to the Union as a slave state.

The immediate cause of the armed conflict in the Kansas Territory (and for that matter, of the Civil War) was slavery. The proximate cause was passage of the Kansas-Nebraska Act in 1854, which opened up that territory to slavery. The principal author of the 1854 law was Stephen Douglas, leader of the Democratic Party in the U.S. Senate, advocate for the transcontinental railroad, and presidential aspirant. Southern support was necessary to pass any new territorial measure, and southern senators made it clear that they would oppose any legislation that did not guarantee slaveholders equal rights in the Kansas and Nebraska territories. Their concern was that if legislation remained silent on the slavery issue, the provisions of the 1820 Missouri Compromise would operate, banning (as a matter of law) the introduction of slaves into the two territories.

Douglas met Southern demands by writing the principle of popular sovereignty into the bill. This principle declared that local territorial populations should decide for themselves whether a territory would enter the Union as a free or slave state. The doctrine of popular sovereignty appeared to be a way to mend the Democratic Party division over slavery while keeping the issue from reemerging as a divisive congressional issue. It had been central to the Compromise of 1850, and when Douglas began to craft the 1854 legislation, Southerners again demanded slaveholder equality in federal territories—including lands covered by the 1820 law. Douglas willingly obliged, and accordingly the bill declared the anti-slavery provision of the Missouri

---

1. Carl Von Clausewitz, *On War*, vol. 1, trans. J. J. Graham (London: N. Trübner, 1873), 11–12.

Compromise "inoperative and void."[2] Douglas was in fact an ardent supporter of the principle, both as a statement of a core democratic value as well as for its value as a political expedient. As he told an audience in Chicago, "If there is any one principle dearer and more sacred than all others in free governments, it is that which asserts the exclusive right of a free people to form and adopt their own fundamental law, and to manage and regulate their own internal affairs and domestic institutions."[3] Additionally, as his biographer has noted, Douglas was committed to the principle because he "recognized in it a formula that would (he hoped) bridge the differences between the North and South on the slavery question, thus preserving the Union that was so essential to his national faith."[4] The bill passed through the Congress with near unanimous support from Southern Democrats. But Douglas was quickly to realize the cost of soliciting that support. His expectation that the principle would help maintain party unity while easing tensions between the North and South proved misguided.

Just days after the bill's introduction, several members of the Free Soil Party, including Salmon Chase, Gerrit Smith, and Charles Sumner published the "Appeal of the Independent Democrats in Congress, to the People of the United States," in which they warned that the proposed bill posed an "imminent danger [to] the freedom of our institutions [and] the permanency of our Union." They labeled the bill a "gross violation of a sacred pledge" and a "plot to exclude from a vast unoccupied region . . . free laborers from our own States, and convert it into a dreary region of despotism, inhabited by masters and slaves." Reviewing legislation dating back to the Continental Congress, they declared that the "original settled policy of the United States, clearly indicated by the Jefferson proviso of 1784, and by the ordinance of 1787, was non-extension of slavery." That pledge was embraced by the 1820 compromise, which they declared a "solemn compact against the extension of slavery into any part of the territory acquired from France" and which "consecrated beyond question . . . the whole remainder of the territory to freedom and free institutions forever."[5] The 1854 bill thus raised the ire of Free Soilers who saw the western lands as a place where white settlers could go; and of abolitionists, who

---

2. See section 14 of the Act of May 30, 1854, in *United States Statutes at Large*, 33rd Cong., 1st Sess., 59:283.

3. Stephen A. Douglas, speech at Chicago, July 9, 1858, in *Political Debates between Abraham Lincoln and Stephen A. Douglas, in the Celebrated Campaign of 1858 in Illinois* (O. S. Hubbell & Company, 1895), 8.

4. Robert W. Johannsen, *The Frontier, the Union, and Stephen A. Douglas* (Champaign: University of Illinois Press, 1989), 96.

5. "Appeal of the Independent Democrats in Congress, to the People of the United States. Shall Slavery Be Permitted in Nebraska?" January 19, 1854 (Towers' Printers), 1–3.

sought to stop the extension of slavery as a precursor to the eradication of the institution.

The Kansas-Nebraska bill fractured American politics. The Whig Party, which found its Northern members voting against the bill and its Southern members for it, split on the issue. Northern Whigs, along with Free Soilers, would help to establish the Republican Party. Douglas' own party felt the strain as well.

The success of the 1854 bill and of the principle of popular sovereignty more broadly—particularly as applied to slavery in the territories—depended on its ambiguity. The principle didn't specify *when* territorial settlers could decide on the slavery question. Could settlers actively discourage slavery from a territory, thereby deciding the slavery question long before statehood? Or were slave owners free to bring slaves to a territory, with the question being decided only during the process of applying for statehood? Southerners maintained that slavery could not be prohibited from a territory until a state government had been formed. Northerners operated on the assumption that slavery could be effectively barred from a region throughout its territorial period.

This ambiguity quickly inflamed tensions in Kansas. Pro-slavery and anti-slavery settlers poured into the territory, intent on securing a majority of the voting population and thereby determining whether Kansas would enter the Union as a free or a slave state. Tensions escalated into violence, with pro-slavery advocates sacking the town of Lawrence and attacking anti-slavery settlers. More famously, John Brown and anti-slavery settlers massacred five pro-slavery settlers near Pottawatomie Creek. More deaths related to the slavery crisis would occur in Kansas in the months to come.

Those battles were part of ongoing efforts by pro- and anti-slavery settlers to determine the future status of the state. Pro-slavery and anti-slavery advocates formed competing governments (pro-slavery forces in Lecompton, anti-slavery forces in Topeka) and drafted respective constitutions. Despite fraud surrounding the drafting of the Lecompton version, both constitutions were sent to Washington. President James Buchanan, a Democrat, supported the Lecompton constitution, as did the Southern wing of the party. But Senator Douglas opposed it on the grounds that it was not a true expression of the will of the people of Kansas. "Why force this constitution down the throats of the people of Kansas in opposition to their wishes?" he asked. Violating the principle of popular sovereignty, he insisted, would destroy the party and harm the Union. "It is not satisfactory to me to have the President [Buchanan] say in his message that [the Lecompton] constitution is an admirable one. . . . Whether good or bad, whether obnoxious or not, is none of my business and none of yours. . . . You have no more right to force a free-State constitution on Kansas than a slave-State constitution. If Kansas wants a slave-State constitution she has a right to it; if she wants a free-State constitution she has a right to it. It is none of my business which way the slavery clause is decided. I care not whether it is voted down or voted up."[6]

In a debate with Douglas ten months later, Abraham Lincoln declared that this conception of popular sovereignty had "*been nothing but a living, creeping lie from the time of its introduction till to-day.*"[7] "Every thing that emanates from [Douglas] or his coadjutors in their course of policy," he asserted in a speech at Galesburg, "carefully excludes the thought that there is any thing wrong in slavery." He explained,

> If you will take the Judge's speeches, and select the short and pointed
> sentences expressed by him—as his declaration that he "don't care
> whether slavery is voted up or down"—you will see at once that
> this is perfectly logical, if you do not admit that slavery is wrong. If
> you do admit that it is wrong, Judge Douglas cannot logically say
> he don't care whether a wrong is voted up or voted down. Judge
> Douglas declares that if any community wants slavery they have a
> right to have it. He can say that logically, if he says that there is no
> wrong in slavery; but if you admit that there is a wrong in it, he
> cannot logically say that any body has a right to do wrong.[8]

Moreover, Lincoln charged that Douglas was in fact part of a broader effort to nationalize the institution of slavery. According to Lincoln, Negroes were included in the Declaration's reference to "all men." "Mr. Calhoun and all the politicians of his school," however, "denied the truth of the Declaration."[9] By denying Negroes a share, "humble though it may be, in the Declaration," Douglas, too, was helping to nationalize slavery. He was, Lincoln charged, "blowing out the moral lights around us, when he contends that whoever wants slaves has a right to hold them. . . . [H]e is penetrating, so far as lies in his power, the human soul, and eradicating the light of reason and the love of liberty, when he is in every possible way preparing the public mind, by his vast influence, for making the institution of slavery perpetual and national."[10]

Douglas insisted that the principle of popular sovereignty was not pro-slavery, a claim that Southern politicians like Calhoun and Alexander Stephens echoed. The principle was neutral toward the institution and for that reason would

---

6. Stephen A. Douglas, speech to the U.S. Senate, December 9, 1857, *Congressional Globe*, 35th Cong., 1st Sess., 17–18.

7. Lincoln's reply at Alton, October 15, 1858, in *Political Debates between Abraham Lincoln and Stephen A. Douglas*, 228.

8. Lincoln's Reply at Galesburg, Illinois, October 7, 1858. See document 6 in this chapter.

9. Lincoln's reply at Alton, October 15, 1858, in *Political Debates between Abraham Lincoln and Stephen A. Douglas*, 225.

10. Lincoln's Reply at Galesburg, Illinois, October 7, 1858. See document 6 in this chapter.

alleviate agitation over the issue. Stephens and others further argued that Congress lacked the authority to ban slavery in the territories. The constitutional power to govern the territories, Stephens argued, was "but an incident merely to some of the expressly granted powers, and cannot go beyond the *necessities* attending the execution of the express powers. . . . The exclusion or restraining of slavery in the Territories . . . was not amongst any of those objects, and is not a necessary incident in carrying any of them out." Additionally, Stephens argued that territorial governments had no authority to ban slavery. "To protect property is the duty of Government," he stated, "and the power to do this does not include the power or right to destroy it." Thus, in addition to inflaming sectional tensions, efforts like the 1820 Missouri Compromise and the Wilmot Proviso were unconstitutional. With the 1854 law, Stephens proclaimed, sectionalism was "signally rebuked and constitutionalism gloriously triumphant." In short, the principle of popular sovereignty was "essential to the peace of the country and the ultimate security of the rights of the South."[11]

Two months later, in his *Dred Scott* ruling, Chief Justice Roger Taney affirmed these legal claims. According to Taney, Congress lacked the authority to ban slavery in the territories. The right to own slaves, he wrote, was expressly declared in the Constitution. Thus, the 1820 law was unconstitutional and slave owners were constitutionally guaranteed the right to bring slaves into federal territories. Frederick Douglass and others condemned the ruling. "I ask any man to read the Constitution," Douglass declared in a May 1857 speech, "and tell me where, if he can, in what particular that instrument affords the slightest sanction of slavery?" The Constitution did not sanction slavery. On the contrary, it was an anti-slavery document. "Your fathers have said that man's right to liberty is self-evident," Douglass declared. "There is no need of argument to make it clear. . . . Man was born with it. . . . To decide against this right in the person of Dred Scott or the humblest and most whip-scarred bondman in the land, is to decide against God." Nonetheless, Douglass was sanguine about the future. He declared that his "hopes were never brighter than now." The *Dred Scott* ruling had ensured that "the National Conscience will [not] be put to sleep," and he was "morally certain that, sooner or later, by fair means or foul means, in quiet or in tumult, in peace or in blood, in judgment or in mercy, slavery is doomed to cease out of this otherwise goodly land, and liberty is destined to become the settled law of this Republic."[12]

---

11. Alexander Stephens, speech before the U.S. House of Representatives, January 6, 1857, *Congressional Globe Appendix*, 34th Cong., 3rd Sess., 4, 8, 10.

12. Frederick Douglass, "The Dred Scott Decision," speech delivered before the American Anti-Slavery Society, New York, May 14, 1857, in *Frederick Douglass: Selected Speeches and Writings*, ed. Philip S. Foner (Chicago: Lawrence Hill Books, 1999), 347–348, 350, 354.

Lincoln agreed with Douglass' reading of the Constitution. Like Douglass, Lincoln held that "fathers of this government" had intended to put slavery on a course of "ultimate extinction."[13] Like Douglass, Lincoln believed that it was the "moral blindness" of the American people, not the "peculiar character of our Constitution," that preserved the institution of slavery; and like Douglass, Lincoln rejected Garrison's call for disunion.[14] But Lincoln was less willing to embrace violence as a means of abolition, and he expressed grave concerns about the future of slavery in the Union. For Lincoln, it was clear only that the Union would cease to be half slave and half free—not that it would necessarily become all free.

According to Lincoln, the principle of popular sovereignty and the *Dred Scott* ruling diminished the moral argument against slavery. Additionally, he worried that by lifting the ban on slavery in the territories, Douglas and the Supreme Court had in fact promoted the spread of slavery. For if slave owners could not be legally barred from bringing slaves into the territories, what would prevent them from doing so? "It is argued that slavery will not go to Kansas and Nebraska, *in any event*," Lincoln observed in 1854. "This is a *palliation—a lullaby*. I have some hope that it will not; but let us not be too confident." Climate, he insisted, would not keep slavery out of the new territories. Nor would the lack of any pro-slavery laws. "Wherever slavery is," Lincoln argued, "it has been first introduced without law."

> A white man takes his slave to Nebraska now; who will inform the negro that he is free? Who will take him before court to test the question of his freedom? In ignorance of his legal emancipation, he is kept chopping, splitting and plowing. Others are brought, and move on in the same track. At last, if ever the time for voting comes, on the question of slavery, the institution already in fact exists in the country, and cannot well be removed. The facts of its presence, and the difficulty of its removal will carry the vote in its favor. . . . To get slaves into the country simultaneously with the whites, in the incipient stages of settlement, is the precise stake played for, and won in this Nebraska measure.[15]

---

13. Lincoln's reply at Alton, October 15, 1858, in *Political Debates between Abraham Lincoln and Stephen A. Douglas*, 228. Lincoln makes this claim repeatedly during this period. See, for example, his speech at Chicago, Illinois (July 10, 1858), and his speech at Columbus, Ohio (September 16, 1859), in ibid., 18 and 244, respectively.

14. The quotes are from Frederick Douglass, "The Dred Scott Decision," 351. For Lincoln, see for example his Address at Peoria, Illinois, October 16, 1854, document 3 in this chapter.

15. Abraham Lincoln, Address at Peoria, Illinois, October 16, 1854. See document 3 in this chapter.

Lincoln pressed Senator Douglas on this point. If as the Court claimed the Constitution guaranteed the right to own slaves, then did not federal officials have a legal obligation to provide legal protections of this property right? Douglas demurred, insisting that regardless of the Court's ruling, local populations could effectively prevent slavery from entering a territory. "What is the right to carry your property into the Territory worth to either, when unfriendly legislation in the Territory renders it worthless after you get it there," Douglas asked? "The slaveholder when he gets his slaves there finds that there is no local law to protect him in holding them, no slave code, no police regulation maintaining and supporting him in his right, and he discovers at once that the absence of such friendly legislation excludes his property from the Territory, just as irresistibly as if there was a positive Constitutional prohibition excluding it." According to Douglas, if the people in a territory withheld "friendly legislation," slavery could never take root there.[16]

By pressing Douglas on the inherent tension between his principle and the *Dred Scott* ruling, Lincoln succeeded in driving a wedge into the Democratic Party and undermining Douglas' presidential ambitions for 1860. Dividing the Democrats into two sectional parties was instrumental to Lincoln's victory. That victory, along with Republican majorities in both houses of Congress, likely made secession inevitable. For years, slavery advocates from the South had pushed for the institution's expansion. That aim was demonstrated by their insistence on the right to bring slaves into the territories, by their insistence that the United States annex Cuba as a slave state, and by their serious consideration of secession as early as 1850. Lincoln consistently promised not to interfere with slavery where it already existed, a point he reiterated upon taking the oath of office in 1861. "I have no purpose, directly or indirectly, to interfere with the institution of slavery in the States where it exists," he said at the beginning of his First Inaugural Address. "I believe I have no lawful right to do so, and I have no inclination to do so."[17] But given Lincoln's claim that the Constitution did not recognize a right to own slaves, along with his consistent assertions that slavery was a moral and political anathema, that it contradicted the intent of the Framers, and that its spread must be halted, Southerners could understandably worry that a Lincoln presidency would in fact seek to abolish slavery everywhere. Barely two months after he took office, the attack on Fort Sumter would announce the start of the Civil War.

---

16. Stephen A. Douglas, speech at Galesburg, October 7, 1858, in *Political Debates between Abraham Lincoln and Stephen A. Douglas*, 267. Douglas makes this claim repeatedly during this period. See, for example, his speech at Springfield, Illinois (July 17, 1858) and his speech at Freeport, Illinois (August 27, 1858), in ibid., 74 and 144, respectively.

17. Abraham Lincoln, First Inaugural Address, March 4, 1861, in *Lincoln: Selected Speeches and Writings*, ed. Don E. Fehrenbacher (New York: Library of America, 1992), 284.

DOCUMENTS

1. William Lloyd Garrison, Address before the Anti-Slavery Society, New York City (February 14, 1854)

This address captures William Lloyd Garrison's (1805–1879) moral outrage regarding slavery and his insistence that to do what is morally right trumps all claims of political expediency. For Garrison, the North and South were equally culpable for the perpetuation and growth of slavery, as evidenced by their compromise over slavery in the West, and only disunion from slaveholders would free the North from its complicity in the "sin of this nation."

. . . Let me define my positions, and at the same time challenge any one to show wherein they are untenable.

. . . I am a believer in that portion of the Declaration of American Independence in which it is set forth, as among self-evident truths, "that all men are created equal; that they are endowed by their Creator with certain inalienable rights; that among these are life, liberty, and the pursuit of happiness." Hence, I am an Abolitionist. Hence, I cannot but regard oppression in every form—and most of all, that which turns a man into a thing—with indignation and abhorrence. Not to cherish these feelings would be recreancy to principle. They who desire me to be dumb on the subject of Slavery, unless I will open my mouth in its defense, ask me to give the lie to my professions, to degrade my manhood, and to stain my soul. I will not be a liar, a poltroon, or a hypocrite, to accommodate any party, to gratify any sect, to escape any odium or peril, to save any interest, to preserve any institution, or to promote any object. Convince me that one man may rightfully make another man his slave, and I will no longer subscribe to the Declaration of Independence. Convince me that liberty is not the inalienable birthright of every human being, of whatever complexion or clime, and I will give that instrument to the consuming fire. I do not know how to espouse freedom and slavery together. I do not know how to worship God and Mammon at the same time. If other men choose to go upon all-fours, I choose to stand erect, as God designed every man to stand. If, practically falsifying its heaven-attested principles, this nation denounces me for refusing to imitate its example, then, adhering all the more tenaciously to those principles, I will not cease to rebuke it for its guilty inconsistency. . . . My crime is, that I will not go with the multitude to do evil. My singularity is, that when I say that Freedom is of God, and Slavery is of the devil, I mean just what I say. My fanaticism is, that I insist on the American people abolishing Slavery, or ceasing to prate of the rights of man. . . .

Notwithstanding the lessons taught us by Pilgrim Fathers and Revolutionary Sires, at Plymouth Rock, on Bunker Hill, at Lexington, Concord and Yorktown; notwithstanding our Fourth of July celebrations, and ostentatious displays of patriotism; in what European nation is personal liberty held in such contempt as in our own? Where are there such unbelievers in the natural equality and freedom of mankind? Our slaves outnumber the entire population of the country at the time of our revolutionary struggle. In vain do they clank their chains, and fill the air with their shrieks, and make their supplications for mercy. In vain are their sufferings portrayed, their wrongs rehearsed, their rights defended. . . . For one impeachment of the slave system, a thousand defenses are made. For one rebuke of the man-stealer, a thousand denunciations of the Abolitionists are heard. For one press that bears a faithful testimony against Slavery, a score are ready to be prostituted to its service. For one pulpit that is not "recreant to its trust," there are ten that openly defend slaveholding as compatible with Christianity, and scores that are dumb. For one church that excludes the human enslaver from its communion table, multitudes extend to him the right hand of religious fellowship. The wealth, the enterprise, the literature, the politics, the religion of the land, are all combined to give extension and perpetuity to the Slave Power. . . . The two great parties which absorb nearly the whole voting strength of the Republic are pledged to be deaf, dumb and blind to whatever outrages the Slave Power may attempt to perpetrate. . . . The tremendous power of the Government is actively wielded to "crush out" the little Anti-Slavery life that remains in individual hearts, and to open new and boundless domains for the expansion of the Slave system. . . .

The Abolitionism which I advocate is as absolute as the Law of God, and as unyielding as His throne. It admits of no compromise. Every slave is a stolen man; every slaveholder is a man stealer. By no precedent, no example, no law, no compact, no purchase, no bequest, no inheritance, no combination of circumstances, is slaveholding right or justifiable. While a slave remains in his fetters, the land must have no rest. Whatever sanctions his doom must be pronounced accursed. The law that makes him a chattel is to be trampled underfoot; the compact that is formed at his expense, and cemented with his blood, is null and void; the church that consents to his enslavement is horribly atheistical; the religion that receives to its communion the enslaver is the embodiment of all criminality. Such, at least, is the verdict of my own soul, on the supposition that I am to be the slave; that my wife is to be sold from me for the vilest purposes; that my children are to be torn from my arms, and disposed of to the highest bidder, like sheep in the market. And who am I but a man? What right have I to be free, that another man cannot prove himself to possess by nature? . . .

How has the slave system grown to its present enormous dimensions? Through compromise. How is it to be exterminated? Only by an uncompromising spirit. This is to be carried out in all the relations of life—social, political, religious. Put not on the list of your friends, nor allow admission to your domestic circle, the man who on principle defends Slavery, but treat him like a moral leper. . . .

. . . A sordid, trucking, cowardly, compromising spirit, is everywhere seen. No insult or outrage, no deed of impiety or blood, on the part of the South, can startle us into resistance, or inspire us with self-respect. We see our free coloured citizens incarcerated in Southern prisons, or sold on the auction-block, for no other crime than that of being found on Southern soil; and we dare not call for redress. Our commerce with the South is bound with the shackles of the plantation—"Free-Trade and Sailors'-Rights" are every day violated in Southern ports; and we tamely submit to it as the slave does to the lash. Our natural, God-given right of free-speech . . . can be exercised in the slaveholding States only at the peril of our lives. Slavery cannot bear one ray of light, or the slightest criticism. . . . Gov. Lumpkin, of Georgia, says: "The weapons of reason and argument are insufficient to put down discussion; we can therefore hear no argument upon the subject, for our opinions are unalterably fixed." And he adds, that the Slave States "will provide for their own protection, and those who speak against Slavery will do well to keep out of their bounds, or they will punish them." The Charleston *Courier* declares, "The gallows and the stake (*i.e.*, burning alive and hanging) await the Abolitionists who shall dare to appear in person among us." The Columbia *Telescope* says: "Let us declare through the public journals of our country, that the question of Slavery is not and shall not be open to discussion; that the system is too deep-rooted among us, and must remain forever; that the very moment any private individual attempts to lecture us upon its evils and immorality, and the necessity of putting means in operation to secure us from them, in the same moment his tongue shall be cut out and cast upon the dunghill." . . .

Whatever may be the guilt of the South, the North is still more responsible for the existence, growth and extension of Slavery. In her hand has been the destiny of the Republic from the beginning. She could have emancipated every slave, long ere this, had she been upright in heart and free in spirit. She has given respectability, security, and the means of sustenance and attack to her deadliest foe. She has educated the whole country, and particularly the Southern portion of it, secularly, theologically, religiously; and the result is, three millions and a half of slaves, increasing at the appalling rate of one hundred thousand a year, three hundred a day, and one every five minutes—the utter corruption of public sentiment, and general skepticism as to the rights of man—the inauguration of Mammon in the place of the living God—the loss of all self-respect, all manhood, all sense of shame, all regard for justice—the Book styled holy, and claimed to be divinely inspired, everywhere expounded and enforced in extenuation or defense of slaveholding . . . —colour-phobia infecting the life-blood of the people . . . —the pulpits, with rare exceptions, filled with men as careful to consult the popular will as though there were no higher law . . . and now, the repeal of the Missouri Compromise, and the consecration of five hundred thousand square miles of free territory forever to the service of the Slave Power!

And what does all this demonstrate? That the sin of this nation is not geographical—is not specially Southern—but deep-seated and universal. . . . It proves, too, the folly of all plasters and palliatives. Some men are still talking of preventing the spread of the cancer, but leaving it just where it is. They admit that, constitutionally, it has now a right to ravage two-thirds of the body politic—but they protest against its extension. This is moral quackery. Even some, whose zeal in the Anti-Slavery cause is fervent, are so infatuated as to propose no other remedy for Slavery but its non-extension. Give it no more room, they say, and it may be safely left to its fate. Yes, but who shall "bell the cat?" Besides, with fifteen Slave States, and more than three millions of Slaves, how can we make any moral issue with the Slave Power against its further extension? Why should there not be twenty, thirty, fifty Slave States, as well as fifteen? Why should not the star-spangled banner wave over ten, as well as over three millions of Slaves? Why should not Nebraska be cultivated by Slave labour, as well as Florida or Texas? If men, under the American Constitution, may hold slaves at discretion and without dishonor in one-half of the country, why not in the whole of it? . . . I do not understand the moral code of those who, screaming in agony at the thought of Nebraska becoming a Slave Territory, virtually say to the South: "Only desist from your present designs, and we will leave you to flog, and lacerate, and plunder, and destroy the millions of hapless wretches already within your grasp. If you will no longer agitate the subject, we will not." There is no sense, no principle, no force in such an issue. Not a solitary slaveholder will I allow to enjoy repose on any other condition than instantly ceasing to be one. Not a single slave will I leave in his chains, on any conditions, or under any circumstances. I will not try to make as good a bargain for the Lord as the Devil will let me, and plead the necessity of a compromise, and regret that I cannot do any better, and be thankful that I can do so much. The Scriptural injunction is to be obeyed: "Resist the devil, and he will flee from you." My motto is, "No union with slaveholders, religiously or politically." Their motto is "Slavery forever!" . . .

While the present Union exists, I pronounce it hopeless to expect any repose, or that any barrier can be effectually raised against the extension of Slavery. With two thousand million dollars' worth of property in human flesh in its hands, to be watched and wielded as one vast interest for all the South—with forces never divided, and purposes never conflictive—with a spurious, negrohating religion universally diffused, and everywhere ready to shield it from harm—with a selfish, sordid, divided North, long since bereft of its manhood, to cajole, bribe and intimidate—with its foot planted on two-thirds of our vast national domains, and there unquestioned, absolute and bloody in its sway—with the terrible strength and boundless resources of the whole country at its command—it cannot be otherwise than that the Slave Power will consummate its diabolical purposes to the uttermost. . . .

These are solemn times. It is not a struggle for national salvation; for the nation, as such, seems doomed beyond recovery. The reason why the South rules, and North falls prostrate in servile terror, is simply this: With the South, the preservation of Slavery is paramount to all other considerations—above party success, denominational unity, pecuniary interest, legal integrity, and constitutional obligation. With the North, the preservation of the Union is placed above all other things—above honor, justice, freedom, integrity of soul, the Decalogue and the Golden Rule—the Infinite God himself. All these she is ready to discard for the Union. Her devotion to it is the latest and the most terrible form of idolatry. She has given to the Slave Power a *carte blanche*, to be filled as it may dictate—and if, at any time, she grows restive under the yoke, and shrinks back aghast at the new atrocity contemplated, it is only necessary for that Power to crack the whip of Disunion over her head, as it has done again and again, and she will cower and obey like a plantation slave—for has she not sworn that she will sacrifice everything in heaven and on earth, rather than the Union?

What then is to be done? Friends of the slave, the question is not whether by our efforts we can abolish Slavery, speedily or remotely—for duty is ours, the result is with God; but whether we will go with the multitude to do evil, sell our birthright for a mess of pottage, cease to cry aloud and spare not, and remain in Babylon when the command of God is, "Come out of her, my people, that ye be not partakers of her sins, and that ye receive not of her plagues." Let us stand in our lot, "and having done all, to stand." At least, a remnant shall be saved. Living or dying, defeated or victorious, be it ours to exclaim, "No compromise with Slavery! Liberty for each, for all, forever! Man above all institutions! The supremacy of God over the whole earth!"

2. Frederick Douglass, The Claims of the Negro Ethnologically Considered, Western Reserve College (July 12, 1854)

In this commencement address, Douglass attacked decades of "scientific moonshine" that have "read the negro out of the human family." He further argued that blacks, who are men, will and should by right remain inhabitants of their country, the United States.

. . . Man is distinguished from all other animals, by the possession of certain definite faculties and powers, as well as by physical organization and proportions. He is the only two-handed animal on the earth—the only one that laughs, and nearly the only one that weeps. Men instinctively distinguish between men and brutes. Common sense itself is scarcely needed to detect the absence of manhood in a monkey, or to recognize its presence in a negro. His speech, his reason, his power to acquire and to retain knowledge, his heaven-erected face, his habitudes, his hopes, his fears, his aspirations, his prophecies, plant between him and the brute creation, a distinction as eternal as it is palpable. Away, therefore, with all the scientific moonshine that would connect men with monkeys; that would have the world believe that humanity, instead of resting on its own characteristic pedestal—gloriously independent—is a sort of sliding scale, making one extreme brother to the ourang-ou-tang, and the other to angels, and all the rest intermediates! Tried by all the usual, and all the unusual tests, whether mental, moral, physical, or psychological, the negro is a MAN—considering him as possessing knowledge, or needing knowledge, his elevation or his degradation, his virtues, or his vices—whichever road you take, you reach the same conclusion, the negro is a MAN. His good and his bad, his innocence and his guilt, his joys and his sorrows, proclaim his manhood in speech that all mankind practically and readily understand.

The temptation, therefore, to read the negro out of the human family is exceedingly strong, and may account somewhat for the repeated attempts on the part of Southern pretenders to science, to cast a doubt over the Scriptural account of the origin of mankind. If the origin and motives of most works, opposing the doctrine of the unity of the human race, could be ascertained, it may be doubted whether one such work could toast an honest parentage. Pride and selfishness, combined with mental power, never want for a theory to justify them—and when men oppress their fellow-men, the oppressor ever finds, in the character of the oppressed, a full justification for his oppression. Ignorance and depravity, and the inability to rise from degradation to civilization and respectability, are the most usual allegations against the oppressed. The evils most fostered by slavery and oppression, are precisely those which slaveholders and oppressors would transfer from their system to the inherent character of their victims. Thus the very crimes of slavery become slavery's best defense. By making the enslaved a character fit only for slavery, they excuse themselves for refusing to make the slave a freeman. A wholesale method of accomplishing this result, is to overthrow the instinctive consciousness of the common brotherhood of man. For, let it be once granted that the human race are of multitudinous origin, naturally different in their moral, physical, and intellectual capacities, and at once you make plausible a demand for classes, grades and conditions, for different methods of culture, different moral, political, and religious institutions, and a chance is left for slavery, as a necessary institution. . . .

. . . I have said that the negro and white man are likely ever to remain the principal inhabitants of this country. I repeat the statement now, to submit the reasons that support it. The blacks can disappear from the face of the country by three ways. They may be colonized,—they may be exterminated,—or, they may die out. Colonization is out of the question; for I know not what hardships the laws of the land can impose, which can induce the colored citizen to leave his native soil. He was here in its infancy; he is here in its age. Two hundred years have passed over him, his tears and blood have been mixed with the soil, and his attachment to the place of his birth is stronger than iron. It is not probable that he will be exterminated; two considerations must prevent a crime so stupendous as that—the influence of Christianity on the One hand, and the power of self interest on the other; and, in regard to their dying out, the statistics of the country afford no encouragement for such a conjecture. The history of the negro race proves them to be wonderfully adapted to all countries, all climates, and all conditions. Their tenacity of life, their powers of endurance, their maleable toughness, would almost imply especial interposition on their behalf. The ten thousand horrors of slavery, striking hard upon the sensitive soul, have bruised, and battered, and stung, but have not killed. The poor bondman lifts a smiling face above the surface of a sea of agonies, hoping on, hoping ever. . . . All the facts in his history mark out for him a destiny, united to America and Americans. Now, whether this population shall, by FREEDOM, INDUSTRY, VIRTUE and INTELLIGENCE, be made a blessing to the country and the world, or whether their multiplied wrongs shall kindle the vengeance of an offended God, will depend upon the conduct of no class of men so much as upon the Scholars of the country. The future public opinion of the land, whether anti-slavery or pro slavery, whether just or unjust, whether magnanimous or mean, must redound to the honor of the Scholars of the country or cover them with shame. There is but one safe road for nations or for individuals. The fate of a wicked man and of a wicked nation is the same. The flaming sword of offended justice falls as certainly upon the nation as upon the man. God has no children whose rights may be safely trampled upon. The sparrow may not fall to the ground without the notice of his eye, and men are more than sparrows. . . .

3. Abraham Lincoln, Address at Peoria, Illinois (October 16, 1854)

In this major speech, Abraham Lincoln (1809–1865) argued that the Kansas-Nebraska bill represents a categorical change in U.S. policy toward slavery. He explained that the nation's Founders believed slavery to be immoral and endeavored to put slavery on a political and constitutional path toward extinction. Allowing slaves to be brought into the western territories was a means of extending and perpetuating the institution of slavery nationwide, which Lincoln perceived to be the greatest threat to American democracy.

The repeal of the Missouri Compromise, and the propriety of its restoration, constitute the subject of what I am about to say. . . .

Before proceeding, let me say I think I have no prejudice against the Southern people. They are just what we would be in their situation. If slavery did not now exist amongst them, they would not introduce it. If it did now exist amongst us, we should not instantly give it up. This I believe of the masses north and south. . . .

When southern people tell us they are no more responsible for the origin of slavery, than we; I acknowledge the fact. When it is said that the institution exists; and that it is very difficult to get rid of it, in any satisfactory way, I can understand and appreciate the saying. I surely will not blame them for not doing what I should not know how to do myself. If all earthly power were given me, I should not know what to do, as to the existing institution. My first impulse would be to free all the slaves, and send them to Liberia,—to their own native land. But a moment's reflection would convince me, that whatever of high hope, (as I think there is) there may be in this, in the long run, its sudden execution is impossible. . . . What then? Free them all, and keep them among us as underlings? Is it quite certain that this betters their condition? I think I would not hold one in slavery, at any rate; yet the point is not clear enough for me to denounce people upon. What next? Free them, and make them politically and socially, our equals? My own feelings will not admit of this; and if mine would, we well know that those of the great mass of white people will not. Whether this feeling accords with justice and sound judgment, is not the sole question, if indeed, it is any part of it. A universal feeling, whether well or ill-founded, cannot be safely disregarded. We cannot, then, make them equals. It does seem to me that systems of gradual emancipation might be adopted; but for their tardiness in this, I will not undertake to judge our brethren of the south.

When they remind us of their constitutional rights, I acknowledge them, not grudgingly, but fully, and fairly; and I would give them any legislation for the reclaiming of their fugitives, which should not, in its stringency, be more likely to carry a free man into slavery, than our ordinary criminal laws are to hang an innocent one.

But all this; to my judgment, furnishes no more excuse for permitting slavery to go into our own free territory, than it would for reviving the African slave trade by law. . . .

[I]t is said that the compromises of '50 and the ratification of them by both
political parties, in '52, established a *new principle*, which required the repeal
of the Missouri Compromise. . . . I deny it, and demand the proof. I have
already stated fully what the compromises of '50 are. The particular part of
those measures, for which the virtual repeal of the Missouri Compromise is
sought to be inferred . . . is the provision in the Utah and New Mexico laws,
which permits them when they seek admission into the Union as States, to
come in with or without slavery as they shall then see fit. Now I insist this provision was made for Utah and New Mexico, and for no other place whatever.
It had no more direct reference to Nebraska than it had to the territories of
the moon. But, say they, it had reference to Nebraska, *in principle*. Let us see.
The North consented to this provision, not because they considered it right in
itself; but because they were compensated—paid for it. They, at the same time,
got California into the Union as a free State. This was far the best part of all
they had struggled for by the Wilmot Proviso. They also got the area of slavery
somewhat narrowed in the settlement of the boundary of Texas. Also, they got
the slave trade abolished in the District of Columbia. For all these desirable
objects the North could afford to yield something; and they did yield to the
South the Utah and New Mexico provision. . . . Now can it be pretended that
the *principle* of this arrangement requires us to permit the same provision to be
applied to Nebraska, *without any equivalent at all*? Give us another free State;
press the boundary of Texas still further back, give us another step toward the
destruction of slavery in the District, and you present us a similar case. . . .

. . . It is argued that slavery will not go to Kansas and Nebraska, *in any event*.
This is a *palliation*—a *lullaby*. I have some hope that it will not; but let us not
be too confident. As to climate, a glance at the map shows that there are five
slave States—Delaware, Maryland, Virginia, Kentucky, and Missouri—and
also the District of Columbia, all north of the Missouri Compromise line. The
census returns of 1850 show that, within these, there are 867,276 slaves—
being more than one-fourth of all the slaves in the nation.

It is not climate, then, that will keep slavery out of these territories. Is there
any thing in the peculiar nature of the country? . . . No peculiarity of the country will—nothing in *nature* will. Will the disposition of the people prevent it?
Those nearest the scene, are all in favor of the extension. The yankees, who are
opposed to it may be more numerous; but in military phrase, the battle-field is
too far from *their* base of operations.

But it is said, there now is *no* law in Nebraska on the subject of slavery;
and that, in such case, taking a slave there, operates his freedom. That *is* good
book-law; but is not the rule of actual practice. Wherever slavery is, it has been
first introduced without law. The oldest laws we find concerning it, are not
laws introducing it; but *regulating* it, as an already existing thing. A white man
takes his slave to Nebraska now; who will inform the negro that he is free? Who

will take him before court to test the question of his freedom? In ignorance of his legal emancipation, he is kept chopping, splitting and plowing. Others are brought, and move on in the same track. At last, if ever the time for voting comes, on the question of slavery, the institution already in fact exists in the country, and cannot well be removed. The facts of its presence, and the difficulty of its removal will carry the vote in its favor. Keep it out until a vote is taken, and a vote in favor of it, can not be got in any population of forty thousand, on earth, who have been drawn together by the ordinary motives of emigration and settlement. To get slaves into the country simultaneously with the whites, in the incipient stages of settlement, is the precise stake played for, and won in this Nebraska measure. . . .

Equal justice to the south, it is said, requires us to consent to the extending of slavery to new countries. That is to say, inasmuch as you do not object to my taking my hog to Nebraska, therefore I must not object to you taking your slave. Now, I admit this is perfectly logical, if there is no difference between hogs and negroes. But while you thus require me to deny the humanity of the negro, I wish to ask whether you of the south yourselves, have ever been willing to do as much? . . . The great majority, south as well as north, have human sympathies, of which they can no more divest themselves than they can of their sensibility to physical pain. These sympathies in the bosoms of the southern people, manifest in many ways, their sense of the wrong of slavery, and their consciousness that, after all, there is humanity in the negro. If they deny this, let me address them a few plain questions. In 1820 you joined the north, almost unanimously, in declaring the African slave trade piracy, and in annexing to it the punishment of death. Why did you do this? If you did not feel that it was wrong, why did you join in providing that men should be hung for it? The practice was no more than bringing wild negroes from Africa, to sell to such as would buy them. But you never thought of hanging men for catching and selling wild horses, wild buffaloes or wild bears. . . .

And yet again; there are in the United States and territories, including the District of Columbia, 433,643 free blacks. At $500 per head they are worth over two thousand millions of dollars. How comes this vast amount of property to be running about without owners? We do not see free horses or free cattle running at large. How is this? All these free blacks are the descendants of slaves now, but for SOMETHING which has operated on their white owners, inducing them, at vast pecuniary sacrifices, to liberate them. What is that SOMETHING? Is there any mistaking it? In all these cases it is your sense of justice, and human sympathy, continually telling you, that the poor negro has some natural right to himself—that those who deny it, and make mere merchandise of him, deserve kickings, contempt and death. . . .

But one great argument in the support of the repeal of the Missouri Compromise, is still to come. That argument is "the sacred right of self-government." . . .

The doctrine of self-government is right—absolutely and eternally right—but it has no just application, as here attempted. Or perhaps I should rather say that whether it has such just application depends on whether a negro is *not* or *is* a man. If he is *not* a man, why in that case, he who *is* a man may, as a matter of self-government, do just as he pleases with him. But if the negro *is* a man, is it not to that extent, a total destruction of self-government, to say that he too shall not govern *himself?* When the white man governs himself, and also governs *another* man, that is *more* than self-government—that is despotism. If the negro is a *man*, why then my ancient faith teaches me that "all men are created equal;" and that there can be no moral right in the connection with one man's making a slave of another. . . .

Let it not be said I am contending for the establishment of political and social equality between the whites and blacks. I have already said the contrary. I am not now combating the argument of NECESSITY, arising from the fact that the blacks are already amongst us; but I am combating what is set up as MORAL argument for allowing them to be taken where they have never yet been—arguing against the EXTENSION of a bad thing, which where it already exists, we must of necessity, manage as best we can. . . .

But you say this question should be left to the people of Nebraska, because they are more particularly interested. . . .

Whether slavery shall go into Nebraska, or other new territories, is not a matter of exclusive concern to the people who may go there. The whole nation is interested that the best use shall be made of these territories. We want them for the homes of free white people. This they cannot be, to any considerable extent, if slavery shall be planted within them. Slave States are places for poor white people to remove FROM; not to remove TO. New free States are the places for poor people to go to and better their condition. For this use, the nation needs these territories. . . .

. . . I insist that, if there is ANY THING which it is the duty of the WHOLE PEOPLE to never entrust to any hands but their own, that thing is the preservation and perpetuity, of their own liberties, and institutions. And if they shall think, as I do, that the extension of slavery endangers them, more than any, or all other causes, how recreant to themselves, if they submit the question, and with it, the fate of their country, to a mere hand-full of men, bent only on temporary self-interest. . . . But Nebraska is urged as a great Union-saving measure. Well I too, go for saving the Union. Much as I hate slavery, I would consent to the extension of it rather than see the Union dissolved, just as I would consent to any GREAT evil, to avoid a GREATER one. But when I go to Union saving, I must believe, at least, that the means I employ has some adaptation to the end. To my mind, Nebraska has no such adaptation.

"It hath no relish of salvation in it."

It is an aggravation, rather, of the only one thing which ever endangers the Union. When it came upon us, all was peace and quiet. The nation was looking to the forming of new bonds of Union; and a long course of peace and prosperity seemed to lie before us. In the whole range of possibility, there scarcely appears to me to have been anything, out of which the slavery agitation could have been revived, except the very project of repealing the Missouri Compromise. Every inch of territory we owned, already had a definite settlement of the slavery question, and by which, all parties were pledged to abide. . . .

. . . Slavery is founded in the selfishness of man's nature—opposition to it, is his love of justice. These principles are an eternal antagonism; and when brought into collision so fiercely, as slavery extension brings them, shocks, and throes, and convulsions must ceaselessly follow. . . .

The structure, too, of the Nebraska bill is very peculiar. The people are to decide the question of slavery for themselves; but WHEN they are to decide; or HOW they are to decide . . . the law does not say. . . . Is it to be decided by a vote of the people? or a vote of the legislature? or, indeed by a vote of any sort? To these questions, the law gives no answer. . . . This fact is worth remembering. Some Yankees, in the east, are sending emigrants to Nebraska, to exclude slavery from it; and, so far as I can judge, they expect the question to be decided by voting, in some way or other. But the Missourians are awake too. They are within a stone's throw of the contested ground. They hold meetings, and pass resolutions, in which not the slightest allusion to voting is made. They resolve that slavery already exists in the territory; that more shall go there; that they, remaining in Missouri will protect it; and that abolitionists shall be hung, or driven away. Through all this, bowie-knives and six-shooters are seen plainly enough; but never a glimpse of the ballot-box. And, really, what is to be the result of this? Each party WITHIN, having numerous and determined backers WITHOUT, is it not probable that the contest will come to blows, and bloodshed? Could there be a more apt invention to bring about collision and violence, on the slavery question, than this Nebraska project is? I do not charge, or believe, that such was intended by Congress; but if they had literally formed a ring, and placed champions within it to fight out the controversy, the fight could be no more likely to come off, than it is. And if this fight should begin, is it likely to take a very peaceful, Union-saving turn? Will not the first drop of blood so shed, be the real knell of the Union?

The Missouri Compromise ought to be restored. For the sake of the Union, it ought to be restored. . . .

I particularly object to the NEW position which the avowed principle of this Nebraska law gives to slavery in the body politic. I object to it because it assumes that there CAN be MORAL RIGHT in the enslaving of one man by another. . . . I object to it because the fathers of the republic eschewed, and rejected it. The argument of "Necessity" was the only argument they ever admitted in favor of slavery. . . . They found the institution existing among us, which they could not help; and they cast blame upon the British King for having permitted its introduction. BEFORE the constitution, they prohibited its introduction into the north-western Territory—the only country we owned, then free from it. AT the framing and adoption of the Constitution, they forbore to so much as mention the word "slave" or "slavery" in the whole instrument. . . . [T]he thing is hid away, in the constitution, just as an afflicted man hides away a wen or a cancer, which he dares not cut out at once, lest he bleed to death; with the promise, nevertheless, that the cutting may begin at the end of a given time. Less than this our fathers COULD not do; and MORE they WOULD not do. Necessity drove them so far, and farther, they would not go. But this is not all. The earliest Congress, under the constitution, took the same view of slavery. They hedged and hemmed it in to the narrowest limits of necessity. . . .

In 1794, they prohibited an out-going slave-trade—that is, the taking of slaves FROM the United States to sell.

In 1798, they prohibited the bringing of slaves from Africa, INTO the Mississippi Territory—this territory then comprising what are now the States of Mississippi and Alabama. This was TEN YEARS before they had the authority to do the same thing as to the States existing at the adoption of the constitution.

In 1800 they prohibited AMERICAN CITIZENS from trading in slaves between foreign countries—as, for instance, from Africa to Brazil.

In 1803 they passed a law in aid of one or two State laws, in restraint of the internal slave trade.

In 1807, in apparent hot haste, they passed the law, nearly a year in advance to take effect the first day of 1808—the very first day the constitution would permit—prohibiting the African slave trade by heavy pecuniary and corporal penalties.

In 1820, finding these provisions ineffectual, they declared the trade piracy, and annexed to it, the extreme penalty of death. While all this was passing in the general government, five or six of the original slave States had adopted systems of gradual emancipation; and by which the institution was rapidly becoming extinct within these limits.

Thus we see, the plain unmistakable spirit of that age, towards slavery, was hostility to the PRINCIPLE, and toleration, ONLY BY NECESSITY.

But NOW it is to be transformed into a "sacred right." Nebraska brings it forth, places it on the high road to extension and perpetuity; and, with a pat on its back, says to it, "Go, and God speed you." Henceforth it is to be the chief jewel of the nation—the very figure-head of the ship of State. Little by little, but steadily as man's march to the grave, we have been giving up the OLD for the NEW faith. Near eighty years ago we began by declaring that all men are created equal; but now from that beginning we have run down to the other declaration, that for SOME men to enslave OTHERS is a "sacred right of self-government." These principles can not stand together. They are as opposite as God and mammon; and whoever holds to the one, must despise the other. When Pettit, in connection with his support of the Nebraska bill, called the Declaration of Independence "a self-evident lie" he only did what consistency and candor require all other Nebraska men to do. Of the forty odd Nebraska Senators who sat present and heard him, no one rebuked him. Nor am I apprized that any Nebraska newspaper, or any Nebraska orator, in the whole nation, has ever yet rebuked him. . . . If it had been said in old Independence Hall, seventy-eight years ago, the very door-keeper would have throttled the man, and thrust him into the street.

Let no one be deceived. The spirit of seventy-six and the spirit of Nebraska, are utter antagonisms; and the former is being rapidly displaced by the latter.

Fellow countrymen—Americans, south, as well as north, shall we make no effort to arrest this? . . . Is there no danger to liberty itself, in discarding the earliest practice, and first precept of our ancient faith? In our greedy chase to make profit of the Negro, let us beware, lest we "cancel and tear to pieces" even the white man's charter of freedom.

Our republican robe is soiled, and trailed in the dust. Let us repurify it. Let us turn and wash it white, in the spirit, if not the blood, of the Revolution. Let us turn slavery from its claims of "moral right," back upon its existing legal rights, and its arguments of "necessity." Let us return it to the position our fathers gave it; and there let it rest in peace. Let us re-adopt the Declaration of Independence, and with it, the practices, and policy, which harmonize with it. Let north and south—let all Americans—let all lovers of liberty everywhere—join in the great and good work. If we do this, we shall not only have saved the Union; but we shall have so saved it, as to make, and to keep it, forever worthy of the saving. We shall have so saved it, that the succeeding millions of free happy people, the world over, shall rise up, and call us blessed, to the latest generations. . . .

4. **Roger Taney,** *Dred Scott v. Sandford* **(1857)**

Dred Scott sued for his freedom on the grounds that he had been illegally enslaved in Illinois and the Wisconsin Territory. Controversially, the Supreme Court ruled that African Americans were not citizens under the Constitution and thus had no standing to sue in federal courts. The Court further ruled that slavery could not be banned in those territories acquired by the government after the Constitution's ratification in 1788.

Mr. Chief Justice Roger Taney delivered the opinion of the court.

The question is simply this: can a negro whose ancestors were imported into this country and sold as slaves become a member of the political community formed and brought into existence by the Constitution of the United States, and as such become entitled to all the rights, and privileges, and immunities, guarantied by that instrument to the citizen. . . ?

In discussing this question, we must not confound the rights of citizenship which a State may confer within its own limits and the rights of citizenship as a member of the Union. It does not by any means follow, because he has all the rights and privileges of a citizen of a State, that he must be a citizen of the United States. He may have all of the rights and privileges of the citizen of a State and yet not be entitled to the rights and privileges of a citizen in any other State. For, previous to the adoption of the Constitution of the United States, every State had the undoubted right to confer on whomsoever it pleased the character of citizen, and to endow him with all its rights. But this character, of course, was confined to the boundaries of the State, and gave him no rights or privileges in other States beyond those secured to him by the laws of nations and the comity of States. Nor have the several States surrendered the power of conferring these rights and privileges by adopting the Constitution of the United States. Each State may still confer them upon an alien, or anyone it thinks proper, or upon any class or description of persons, yet he would not be a citizen in the sense in which that word is used in the Constitution of the United States, nor entitled to sue as such in one of its courts, nor to the privileges and immunities of a citizen in the other States. The rights which he would acquire would be restricted to the State which gave them. . . .

The question then arises, whether the provisions of the Constitution, in relation to the personal rights and privileges to which the citizen of a State should be entitled, embraced the negro African race, at that time in this country or who might afterwards be imported, who had then or should afterwards be made free in any State, and to put it in the power of a single State to make him a citizen of the United States and endue him with the full rights of citizenship in every other State without their consent? Does the Constitution of the United States act upon him whenever he shall be made free under the laws of a State, and raised there to the rank of a citizen, and immediately clothe him with all the privileges of a citizen in every other State, and in its own courts?

The court think the affirmative of these propositions cannot be maintained. And if it cannot, the plaintiff in error could not be a citizen of the State of Missouri within the meaning of the Constitution of the United States, and, consequently, was not entitled to sue in its courts. . . .

It becomes necessary, therefore, to determine who were citizens of the several States when the Constitution was adopted. . . .

It is difficult at this day to realize the state of public opinion in relation to that unfortunate race which prevailed in the civilized and enlightened portions of the world at the time of the Declaration of Independence and when the Constitution of the United States was framed and adopted. But the public history of every European nation displays it in a manner too plain to be mistaken.

They had for more than a century before been regarded as beings of an inferior order, and altogether unfit to associate with the white race either in social or political relations, and so far inferior that they had no rights which the white man was bound to respect, and that the negro might justly and lawfully be reduced to slavery for his benefit. He was bought and sold, and treated as an ordinary article of merchandise and traffic whenever a profit could be made by it. This opinion was at that time fixed and universal in the civilized portion of the white race. It was regarded as an axiom in morals as well as in politics which no one thought of disputing or supposed to be open to dispute. . . .

The legislation of the different colonies furnishes positive and indisputable proof of this fact. . . .

[T]hese laws . . . show, too plainly to be misunderstood, the degraded condition of this unhappy race. They were still in force when the Revolution began, and are a faithful index to the state of feeling towards the class of persons of whom they speak, and of the position they occupied throughout the thirteen colonies, in the eyes and thoughts of the men who framed the Declaration of Independence and established the State Constitutions and Governments. They show that a perpetual and impassable barrier was intended to be erected between the white race and the one which they had reduced to slavery, and governed as subjects with absolute and despotic power, and which they then looked upon as so far below them in the scale of created beings, that intermarriages between white persons and negroes or mulattoes were regarded as unnatural and immoral, and punished as crimes, not only in the parties, but in the person who joined them in marriage. . . .

The language of the Declaration of Independence is equally conclusive . . . :

> We hold these truths to be self-evident: that all men are created equal; that they are endowed by their Creator with certain unalienable rights; that among them is life, liberty, and the pursuit of happiness; that to secure these rights, Governments are instituted, deriving their just powers from the consent of the governed.

The general words above quoted would seem to embrace the whole human family, and if they were used in a similar instrument at this day would be so understood. But it is too clear for dispute that the enslaved African race were not intended to be included, and formed no part of the people who framed and adopted this declaration, for if the language, as understood in that day, would embrace them, the conduct of the distinguished men who framed the Declaration of Independence would have been utterly and flagrantly inconsistent with the principles they asserted, and instead of the sympathy of mankind to which they so confidently appealed, they would have deserved and received universal rebuke and reprobation.

Yet the men who framed this declaration were great men—high in literary acquirements—high in their sense of honor, and incapable of asserting principles inconsistent with those on which they were acting. They perfectly understood the meaning of the language they used, and how it would be understood by others, and they knew that it would not in any part of the civilized world be supposed to embrace the negro race, which, by common consent, had been excluded from civilized Governments and the family of nations, and doomed to slavery. . . .

This state of public opinion had undergone no change when the Constitution was adopted. . . .

Indeed, when we look to the condition of this race in the several States at the time, it is impossible to believe that these rights and privileges were intended to be extended to them. . . .

The legislation of the States . . . shows in a manner not to be mistaken the inferior and subject condition of that race at the time the Constitution was adopted . . . and it is hardly consistent with the respect due to these States to suppose that they regarded at that time as fellow citizens and members of the sovereignty, a class of beings whom they had thus stigmatized . . . and upon whom they had impressed such deep and enduring marks of inferiority and degradation, or, that, when they met in convention to form the Constitution, they looked upon them as a portion of their constituents or designed to include them in the provisions so carefully inserted for the security and protection of the liberties and rights of their citizens. . . . More especially, it cannot be believed that the large slaveholding States regarded them as included in the word citizens, or would have consented to a Constitution which might compel them to receive them in that character from another State. For if they were so received, and entitled to the privileges and immunities of citizens, it would exempt them from the operation of the special laws and from the police regulations which they considered to be necessary for their own safety. It would give to persons of the negro race, who were recognised as citizens in any one State of the Union, the right to enter every other State whenever they pleased, singly or in companies, without pass or passport, and without obstruction, to sojourn there as long as they pleased, to go where they pleased at every hour of the day or night without molestation . . . ; and it would give them the full liberty of speech in public and in private upon all subjects upon which its own citizens might speak; to hold public meetings upon political affairs, and to keep and carry arms wherever they went. And all of this would be done in the face of the subject race of the same color, both free and slaves, and inevitably producing discontent and insubordination among them, and endangering the peace and safety of the State. . . .

[U]pon a full and careful consideration of the subject, the court is of opinion, that, upon the facts stated in the plea in abatement, Dred Scott was not a citizen of Missouri within the meaning of the Constitution of the United States, and not entitled as such to sue in its courts, and consequently that the Circuit Court had no jurisdiction of the case. . . .

[T]he plaintiff . . . admits that he and his wife were born slaves, but endeavors to make out his title to freedom and citizenship by showing that they were taken by their owner to certain places, hereinafter mentioned, where slavery could not by law exist, and that they thereby became free, and, upon their return to Missouri, became citizens of that State.

We proceed, therefore, to inquire whether the facts relied on by the plaintiff entitled him to his freedom. . . .

The act of Congress upon which the plaintiff relies declares that slavery and involuntary servitude, except as a punishment for crime, shall be forever prohibited in all that part of the territory ceded by France, under the name of Louisiana, which lies north of thirty-six degrees thirty minutes north latitude, and not included within the limits of Missouri. And the difficulty which meets us at the threshold of this part of the inquiry is whether Congress was authorized to pass this law under any of the powers granted to it by the Constitution. . . .

The counsel for the plaintiff has laid much stress upon that article in the Constitution which confers on Congress the power "to dispose of and make all needful rules and regulations respecting the territory or other property belonging to the United States," but, in the judgment of the court, that provision has no bearing on the present controversy, and the power there given, whatever it may be, is confined, and was intended to be confined, to the territory which at that time belonged to, or was claimed by, the United States, and was within their boundaries as settled by the treaty with Great Britain, and can have no influence upon a territory afterwards acquired from a foreign Government. It was a special provision for a known and particular territory, and to meet a present emergency, and nothing more. . . .

[T]he power of Congress over the person or property of a citizen can never be a mere discretionary power under our Constitution and form of Government. . . . It has no power of any kind beyond it, and it cannot, when it enters a Territory of the United States, put off its character and assume discretionary or despotic powers which the Constitution has denied to it. . . . The Territory being a part of the United States, the Government and the citizen both enter it under the authority of the Constitution, with their respective rights defined and marked out, and the Federal Government can exercise no power over his person or property beyond what that instrument confers, nor lawfully deny any right which it has reserved. . . .

For example, no one, we presume, will contend that Congress can make any law in a Territory respecting the establishment of religion, or the free exercise thereof, or abridging the freedom of speech or of the press, or the right of the people of the Territory peaceably to assemble and to petition the Government for the redress of grievances. . . .

These powers, and others in relation to rights of person which it is not necessary here to enumerate, are, in express and positive terms, denied to the General Government, and the rights of private property have been guarded with equal care. Thus, the rights of property are united with the rights of person, and placed on the same ground by the fifth amendment to the Constitution, which provides that no person shall be deprived of life, liberty, and property, without due process of law. And an act of Congress which deprives a citizen of the United States of his liberty or property merely because he came himself or brought his property into a particular Territory of the United States, and who had committed no offence against the laws, could hardly be dignified with the name of due process of law. . . .

Now, as we have already said in an earlier part of this opinion upon a different point, the right of property in a slave is distinctly and expressly affirmed in the Constitution. The right to traffic in it, like an ordinary article of merchandise and property, was guarantied to the citizens of the United States in every State that might desire it for twenty years. And the Government in express terms is pledged to protect it in all future time if the slave escapes from his owner. This is done in plain words—too plain to be misunderstood. And no word can be found in the Constitution which gives Congress a greater power over slave property or which entitles property of that kind to less protection than property of any other description. The only power conferred is the power coupled with the duty of guarding and protecting the owner in his rights.

Upon these considerations, it is the opinion of the court that the act of Congress which prohibited a citizen from holding and owning property of this kind in the territory of the United States north of the line therein mentioned is not warranted by the Constitution, and is therefore void, and that neither Dred Scott himself nor any of his family were made free by being carried into this territory, even if they had been carried there by the owner with the intention of becoming a permanent resident. . . .

5. James Henry Hammond, Address before the U.S. Senate (March 4, 1858)

In his infamous "mud-sill speech," James Henry Hammond argued that slavery's economic clout makes it invincible to any nation—including the Northern states—waging "war" upon it. Echoing earlier arguments, he claimed that every society requires a subordinate class to perform necessary, menial labor. Southern society is superior because it depends on a naturally inferior race well-suited to such work.

[T]he strength of a nation depends in a great measure upon its wealth, and the wealth of a nation, like that of a man, is to be estimated by its surplus production. . . . If a man possess millions of dollars and consumes his income, is he rich? Is he competent to embark in any new enterprises? Can he long build ships or railroads? And could a people in that condition build ships and roads or go to war without a fatal strain on capital? All the enterprises of peace and war depend upon the surplus productions of a people. They may be happy, they may be comfortable, they may enjoy themselves in consuming what they make; but they are not rich, they are not strong. It appears, by going to the reports of the Secretary of the Treasury, which are authentic, that last year the United States exported in round numbers $279,000,000 worth of domestic produce. . . . Of this amount $158,000,000 worth is the clear produce of the South; articles that are not and cannot be made at the North. There are then $80,000,000 worth of exports of products of the forest, provisions and breadstuffs. If we assume that the South made but one third of these, and I think that is a low calculation, our exports were $185,000,000, leaving to the North less than $95,000,000.

In addition to this, we sent to the North $30,000,000 worth of cotton, which is not counted in the exports. We sent to her $7 or $8,000,000 worth of tobacco, which is not counted in the exports. We sent naval stores, lumber, rice, and many other minor articles. There is no doubt that we sent to the North $40,000,000 in addition; but suppose the amount to be $35,000,000, it will give us a surplus production of $220,000,000. . . . If I am right in my calculations as to $220,000,000 of surplus produce, there is not a nation on the face of the earth, with any numerous population, that can compete with us in produce per capita. . . .

With an export of $220,000,000 under the present tariff, the South organized separately would have $40,000,000 of revenue. With one-fourth the present tariff, she would have a revenue . . . adequate to all her wants, for the South would never go to war; she would never need an army or a navy, beyond a few garrisons on the frontiers and a few revenue cutters. It is commerce that breeds war. It is manufactures that require to be hawked about the world, and that give rise to navies and commerce. But we have nothing to do but to take off restrictions on foreign merchandise and open our ports, and the whole world will come to us to trade. They will be too glad to bring and carry us, and we never shall dream of a war. Why the South has never yet had a just cause of war except with the North. Every time she has drawn her sword it has been on the point of honor, and that point of honor has been mainly loyalty to her sister colonies and sister States, who have ever since plundered and calumniated her.

But if there were no other reason why we should never have war, would any sane nation make war on cotton? Without firing a gun, without drawing a sword, should they make war on us we could bring the whole world to our feet. The South is perfectly competent to go on, one, two, or three years without planting a seed of cotton. I believe that if she was to plant but half her cotton, for three years to come, it would be an immense advantage to her. I am not so sure but that after three years' entire abstinence she would come out stronger than ever she was before, and better prepared to enter afresh upon her great career of enterprise. What would happen if no cotton was furnished for three years? I will not stop to depict what every one can imagine, but this is certain: England would topple headlong and carry the whole civilized world with her, save the South. No, you dare not make war on cotton. No power on earth dares to make war upon it. Cotton is king. . . .

But, sir, the greatest strength of the South arises from the harmony of her political and social institutions. This harmony gives her a frame of society, the best in the world, and an extent of political freedom, combined with entire security, such as no other people ever enjoyed upon the face of the earth. . . .

. . . In all social systems there must be a class to do the menial duties, to perform the drudgery of life. That is, a class requiring but a low order of intellect and but little skill. Its requisites are vigor, docility, fidelity. Such a class you must have, or you would not have that other class which leads progress, civilization, and refinement. It constitutes the very mud-sill of society and of political government; and you might as well attempt to build a house in the air, as to build either the one or the other, except on this mud-sill. Fortunately for the South, she found a race adapted to that purpose to her hand. A race inferior to her own, but eminently qualified in temper, in vigor, in docility, in capacity to stand the climate, to answer all her purposes. We use them for our purpose, and call them slaves. We found them slaves by the common "consent of mankind," which, according to Cicero, "lex naturae est." The highest proof of what is Nature's law. We are old-fashioned at the South yet; slave is a word discarded now by "ears polite;" I will not characterize that class at the North by that term; but you have it; it is there; it is everywhere; it is eternal.

The Senator from New York said yesterday that the whole world had abolished slavery. Aye, the name, but not the thing; all the powers of the earth cannot abolish that. God only can do it when he repeals the fiat, "the poor ye always have with you;" for the man who lives by daily labor, and scarcely lives at that, and who has to put out his labor in the market, and take the best he can get for it; in short, your whole hireling class of manual laborers and "operatives," as you call them, are essentially slaves. The difference between us is, that our slaves are hired for life and well compensated; there is no starvation, no begging, no want of employment among our people, and not too much employment either. Yours are hired by the day, not cared for, and scantily compensated, which may be proved in the most painful manner, at any hour in any street in any of your large towns. Why, you meet more beggars in one day, in any single street of the city of New York, than you would meet in a lifetime in the whole South. We do not think that whites should be slaves either by law or necessity. Our slaves are black, of another and inferior race. The status in which we have placed them is an elevation. They are elevated from the condition in which God first created them, by being made our slaves. None of that race on the whole face of the globe can be compared with the slaves of the South. They are happy, content, unaspiring, and utterly incapable, from intellectual weakness, ever to give us any trouble by their aspirations. Yours are white, of your own race; you are brothers of one blood. They are your equals in natural endowment of intellect, and they feel galled by their degradation. Our slaves do not vote. We give them no political power. Yours do vote, and, being the majority, they are the depositories of all your political power. If they knew the tremendous secret, that the ballot-box is stronger than "an army with banners," and could combine, where would you be? Your society would be reconstructed, your government overthrown, your property divided, not as they have mistakenly attempted to initiate such proceedings by meeting in parks, with arms in their hands, but by the quiet process of the ballot-box. You have been making war upon us to our very hearthstones. How would you like for us to send lecturers and agitators North, to teach these people this, to aid in combining, and to lead them?

6. Abraham Lincoln and Stephen Douglas, Debate at Galesburg, Illinois (October 7, 1858)

In this excerpt from the famous Lincoln-Douglas debates, Stephen Douglas (1813–1861)—senator from Illinois—defended the 1854 Kansas-Nebraska Act on the principle of popular sovereignty, and on the grounds that the Constitution was "made by our fathers on the white basis." Denouncing those claims, Abraham Lincoln reasoned that any defense of the 1854 law is logical only if slavery is not wrong. He also denounced the Supreme Court's Dred Scott ruling, perceiving in that ruling, and in Douglas' arguments, a design to force slavery upon the entire nation.

Mr. Douglas' Speech:

Ladies and Gentlemen . . .

The Kansas and Nebraska bill declared, in so many words, that it was the true intent and meaning of the act not to legislate slavery into any State or Territory, nor to exclude it therefrom, but to leave the people thereof perfectly free to form and regulate their domestic institutions in their own way, subject only to the Constitution of the United States. For the last four years I have devoted all my energies . . . to commend that principle to the American people. . . .

During the last year a question arose in the Congress of the United States whether or not that principle would be violated by the admission of Kansas into the Union under the Lecompton Constitution. . . . It is proper that I should remark here, that my opposition to the Lecompton Constitution did not rest upon the peculiar position taken by Kansas on the subject of slavery. I held then, and hold now, that if the people of Kansas want a slave State, it is their right to make one and be received into the Union under it; if, on the contrary, they want a free State, it is their right to have it, and no man should ever oppose their admission because they ask it under the one or the other. I hold to that great principle of self-government which asserts the right of every people to decide for themselves the nature and character of the domestic institutions and fundamental law under which they are to live. . . .

Now, let me ask you whether the country has any interest in sustaining this organization, known as the Republican party. That party is unlike all other political organizations in this country. All other parties have been national in their character—have avowed their principles alike in the slave and free States, in Kentucky as well as Illinois, in Louisiana as well as in Massachusetts. Such was the case with the old Whig party, and such was and is the case with the Democratic party. . . .

But now you have a sectional organization, a party which appeals to the Northern section of the Union against the Southern. . . . The leaders of that party hope that they will be able to unite the Northern States in one great sectional party, and inasmuch as the North is the strongest section, that they will thus be enabled to out vote, conquer, govern, and control the South. Hence you find that they now make speeches advocating principles and measures which cannot be defended in any slaveholding State of this Union. . . . Permit me to say to you in perfect good humor, but in all sincerity, that no political creed is sound which cannot be proclaimed fearlessly in every State of this

Union. . . . Not only is this Republican party unable to proclaim its principles alike in the North and in the South, in the free States and in the slave States, but it cannot even proclaim them in the same forms and give them the same strength and meaning in all parts of the same State. My friend Lincoln finds it extremely difficult to manage a debate in the center part of the State, where there is a mixture of men from the North and the South. In the extreme Northern part of Illinois he can proclaim as bold and radical Abolitionism as ever Giddings, Lovejoy, or Garrison enunciated, but when he gets down a little further South he claims that he is an old line Whig, (great laughter,) a disciple of Henry Clay, (cries of "that's so,") and declares that he still adheres to the old line Whig creed, and has nothing whatever to do with Abolitionism, or negro equality, or negro citizenship. . . .

Fellow-citizens . . . I tell you that this Chicago doctrine of Lincoln's—declaring that the negro and the white man are made equal by the Declaration of Independence and by Divine Providence—is a monstrous heresy. The signers of the Declaration of Independence never dreamed of the negro when they were writing that document. They referred to white men, to men of European birth and European descent, when they declared the equality of all men. I see a gentleman there in the crowd shaking his head. Let me remind him that when Thomas Jefferson wrote that document, he was the owner, and so continued until his death, of a large number of slaves. Did he intend to say in that Declaration, that his negro slaves, which he held and treated as property, were created his equals by Divine law, and that he was violating the law of God every day of his life by holding them as slaves? It must be borne in mind that when that Declaration was put forth, every one of the thirteen Colonies were slaveholding Colonies, and every man who signed that instrument represented a slave-holding constituency. Recollect, also, that no one of them emancipated his slaves, much less put them on an equality with himself, after he signed the Declaration. On the contrary, they all continued to hold their negroes as slaves during the revolutionary war. Now, do you believe—are you willing to have it said—that every man who signed the Declaration of Independence declared the negro his equal, and then was hypocrite enough to continue to hold him as a slave, in violation of what he believed to be the Divine law? And yet when you say that the Declaration of Independence includes the negro, you charge the signers of it with hypocrisy.

[T]his Government was made by our fathers on the white basis. It was made by white men for the benefit of white men and their posterity forever, and was intended to be administered by white men in all time to come. But while I hold that under our Constitution and political system the negro is not a citizen, cannot be a citizen, and ought not to be a citizen, it does not follow by any means that he should be a slave. On the contrary it does follow that the negro, as an inferior race, ought to possess every right, every privilege, every immunity which he can safely exercise consistent with the safety of the society in which he lives. Humanity requires, and Christianity commands, that you shall extend to every inferior being, and every dependent being, all the privileges, immunities and advantages which can be granted to them consistent with the safety of society. If you ask me the nature and extent of these privileges, I answer that that is a question which the people of each State must decide for themselves. . . . The great principle of this Government is, that each State has the right to do as it pleases on all these questions, and no other State, or power on earth has the right to interfere with us, or complain of us merely because our system differs from theirs. . . .

Mr. Lincoln's Reply:

. . . The Judge has alluded to the Declaration of Independence, and insisted that negroes are not included in that Declaration; and that it is a slander upon the framers of that instrument, to suppose that negroes were meant therein; and he asks you: Is it possible to believe that Mr. Jefferson, who penned the immortal paper, could have supposed himself applying the language of that instrument to the negro race, and yet held a portion of that race in slavery? Would he not at once have freed them? I only have to remark upon this part of the Judge's speech . . . , that I believe the entire records of the world, from the date of the Declaration of Independence up to within three years ago, may be searched in vain for one single affirmation, from one single man, that the negro was not included in the Declaration of Independence; I think I may defy Judge Douglas to show that he ever said so, that Washington ever said so, that any President ever said so, that any member of Congress ever said so, or that any living man upon the whole earth ever said so, until the necessities of the present policy of the Democratic party, in regard to slavery, had to invent that affirmation. And I will remind Judge Douglas and this audience, that while Mr. Jefferson was the owner of slaves, as undoubtedly he was, in speaking upon this very subject, he used the strong language that "he trembled for his country when he remembered that God was just;" and I will offer the highest premium in my power to Judge Douglas if he will show that he, in all his life, ever uttered a sentiment at all akin to that of Jefferson. . . .

[T]he Judge will have it that if we do not confess that there is a sort of inequality between the white and black races, which justifies us in making them slaves, we must, then, insist that there is a degree of equality that requires us to make them our wives. . . . I have all the while maintained, that in so far as it should be insisted that there was an equality between the white and black races that should produce a perfect social and political equality, it was an impossibility. This you have seen in my printed speeches, and with it I have said, that in their right to "life, liberty and the pursuit of happiness," as proclaimed in that old Declaration, the inferior races are our equals. And these declarations I have constantly made in reference to the abstract moral question, to contemplate and consider when we are legislating about any new country which is not already cursed with the actual presence of the evil—slavery. I have never manifested any impatience with the necessities that spring from the actual presence of black people amongst us, and the actual existence of slavery amongst us where it does already exist; but I have insisted that, in legislating for new countries, where it does not exist, there is no just rule other than that of moral and abstract right! With reference to those new countries, those maxims as to the right of a people to "life, liberty and the pursuit of happiness," were the just rules to be constantly referred to. There is no misunderstanding this, except by men interested to misunderstand it. . . .

The Judge tells, in proceeding, that he is opposed to making any odious distinctions between free and slave States. I am altogether unaware that the Republicans are in favor of making any odious distinctions between the free and slave States. But there still is a difference, I think, between Judge Douglas and the Republicans in this. I suppose that the real difference between Judge Douglas and his friends, and the Republicans on the contrary, is, that the Judge is not in favor of making any difference between slavery and liberty—that he is in favor of eradicating, of pressing out of view, the questions of preference in this country for free or slave institutions; and consequently every sentiment he utters discards the idea that there is any wrong in slavery. . . . If you will take the Judge's speeches, and select the short and pointed sentences expressed by him—as his declaration that he "don't care whether slavery is voted up or down"—you will see at once that this is perfectly logical, if you do not admit that slavery is wrong. If you do admit that it is wrong, Judge Douglas cannot logically say he don't care whether a wrong is voted up or voted down. Judge Douglas declares that if any community wants slavery they have a right to have it. He can say that logically, if he says that there is no wrong in slavery; but if you admit that there is a wrong in it, he cannot logically say that any body has a right to do wrong. He insists that, upon the score of equality, the owners of slaves and owners of property—of horses and every other sort of property—should be alike and hold them alike in a new Territory. That is perfectly logical, if the two species of property are alike and are equally founded in right. But if you admit that one of them is wrong, you cannot institute any equality between right and wrong. . . . Now, I confess myself as belonging to that class in the country who contemplate slavery as a moral, social and political evil, having due regard for its actual existence amongst us and the difficulties of getting rid of it in any satisfactory way, and to all the Constitutional obligations which have been thrown about it; but, nevertheless, desire a policy that looks to the prevention of it as a wrong, and looks hopefully to the time when as a wrong it may come to an end. . . .

While we were at Freeport, in one of these joint discussions, I answered certain interrogatories which Judge Douglas had propounded to me, and there in turn propounded some to him, which he in a sort of way answered. The third . . . was in these words: "If the Supreme Court of the United States shall decide that the States cannot exclude slavery from their limits, are you in favor of acquiescing in, adhering to and following such decision, as a rule of political action?"

To this interrogatory Judge Douglas made no answer in any just sense of the word. He contented himself with sneering at the thought that it was possible for the Supreme Court ever to make such a decision. . . . I wish now to address to this audience some remarks upon it. . . .

The essence of the Dred Scott case is compressed into the sentence which I will now read: "Now, as we have already said in an earlier part of this opinion, upon a different point, the right of property in a slave is distinctly and expressly affirmed in the Constitution." I repeat it, *"The right of property in a slave is distinctly and expressly affirmed in the Constitution!"* What is it to be *"affirmed"* in the Constitution? Made firm in the Constitution—so made that it cannot be separated from the Constitution without breaking the Constitution—durable as the Constitution, and part of the Constitution. Now, remembering the provision of the Constitution which I have read, affirming that that instrument is the supreme law of the land; that the Judges of every State shall be bound by it, any law or Constitution of any State to the contrary notwithstanding . . . —what follows as a short and even syllogistic argument from it? I think it follows, and I submit to the consideration of men capable of arguing, whether as I state it, in syllogistic form, the argument has any fault in it?

Nothing in the Constitution or laws of any State can destroy a right distinctly and expressly affirmed in the Constitution of the United States.

The right of property in a slave is distinctly and expressly affirmed in the Constitution of the United States.

Therefore, nothing in the Constitution or laws of any State can destroy the right of property in a slave.

I believe that no fault can be pointed out in that argument; assuming the truth of the premises, the conclusion, so far as I have capacity at all to understand it, follows inevitably. There is a fault in it as I think, but the fault is not in the reasoning; but the falsehood in fact is a fault of the premises. I believe that the right of property in a slave *is not* distinctly and expressly affirmed in the Constitution, and Judge Douglas thinks it *is.* I believe that the Supreme Court and the advocates of that decision may search in vain for the place in the Constitution where the right of a slave is distinctly and expressly affirmed. I say, therefore, that I think one of the premises is not true in fact. But it is true with Judge Douglas. It is true with the Supreme Court who pronounced it. They are estopped from denying it, and . . . being affirmed in the decision that the right of property in a slave is distinctly and expressly affirmed in the Constitution, the conclusion inevitably follows that no State law or constitution can destroy that right. I then say to Judge Douglas and to all others, that I think it will take a better answer than a sneer to show that those who have said that the right of property in a slave is distinctly and expressly affirmed in the Constitution, are not prepared to show that no constitution or law can destroy that right. . . . This is but an opinion, and the opinion of one very humble man; but it is my opinion that the Dred Scott decision, as it is, never would have been made in its present form if the party that made it had not been sustained previously by the elections. My own opinion is, that the new Dred Scott decision, deciding against the right of the people of the States to exclude slavery, will never be made, if that party is not sustained by the elections. I believe, further, that it is just as sure to be made as tomorrow is to come, if that party shall be sustained. I have said, upon a former occasion, and I repeat it now, that the course of argument that Judge Douglas makes use of upon this subject (I charge not his motives in this), is preparing the public mind for that new Dred Scott decision. . . .

So far in this controversy I can get no answer at all from Judge Douglas upon these subjects. Not one can I get from him, except that he swells himself up and says, "All of us who stand by the decision of the Supreme Court are the friends of the Constitution; all you fellows that dare question it in any way, are the enemies of the Constitution." Now, in this very devoted adherence to this decision . . . there is something very marked. And the manner in which he adheres to it—not as being right upon the merits . . . but as being absolutely obligatory upon every one simply because of the source from whence it comes—. . . this is another marked feature of his adherence to that decision. It marks it in this respect, that it commits him to the next decision, whenever it comes, as being as obligatory as this one, since he does not investigate it, and won't inquire whether this opinion is right or wrong. So he takes the next one without inquiring whether it is right or wrong. He teaches men this doctrine, and in so doing prepares the public mind to take the next decision when it comes, without any inquiry. In this I think I argue fairly (without questioning motives at all), that Judge Douglas is more ingeniously and powerfully preparing the public mind to take that decision when it comes; and not only so, but he is doing it in various other ways. In these general maxims about liberty—in his assertions that he "don't care whether slavery is voted up or voted down;" that "whoever wants slavery has a right to have it;" that "upon principles of equality it should be allowed to go every where;" that "there is no inconsistency between free and slave institutions." In this he is also preparing (whether purposely or not) the way for making the institution of slavery national! . . .

I have said once before, and I will repeat it now, that Mr. Clay, when he was once answering an objection to the Colonization Society, that it had a tendency to the ultimate emancipation of the slaves, said that "those who would repress all tendencies to liberty and ultimate emancipation must do more than put down the benevolent efforts of the Colonization Society—they must go back to the era of our liberty and independence, and muzzle the cannon that thunders its annual joyous return—they must blot out the moral lights around us—they must penetrate the human soul, and eradicate the light of reason and the love of liberty!" And I do think . . . that Judge Douglas, and whoever like him teaches that the negro has no share, humble though it may be, in the Declaration of Independence, is going back to the era of our liberty and independence, and, so far as in him lies, muzzling the cannon that thunders its annual joyous return; that he is blowing out the moral lights around us, when he contends that whoever wants slaves has a right to hold them; that he is penetrating, so far as lies in his power, the human soul, and eradicating the light of reason and the love of liberty, when he is in every possible way preparing the public mind, by his vast influence, for making the institution of slavery perpetual and national. . . .

7. John A. Bingham, Address before the U.S. House of Representatives (February 11, 1859)

When Oregon applied for statehood, its constitution banned black immigration, denied blacks their property rights, and excluded them from state courts. John A. Bingham (1815–1900), future author of the Fourteenth Amendment, objected on grounds that these exclusions violated the U.S. Constitution's privileges and immunities clause, which applied to all citizens—both black and white.

Mr. Speaker, . . . there is a still more objectionable feature . . . in this Oregon constitution. That is the provision . . . which declares that large numbers of the citizens of the United States shall not, after the admission of the proposed State of Oregon, come or be within said State; that they shall hold no property there; and that the Legislature shall, by statute, make it a penal offense for any person to harbor any of the excluded class of their fellow-citizens who may thereafter come or be within the State. This provision seems to me in its spirit and letter, to be injustice and oppression incarnate. This provision, sir, excludes from the State of Oregon eight hundred thousand of the native-born citizens of the other States, who are, therefore, citizens of the United States. I grant you that a State may restrict the exercise of the elective franchise to certain classes of citizens of the United States, to the exclusion of others; but I deny that any State may exclude a law abiding citizen of the United States from coming within its Territory, or abiding therein or acquiring and enjoying property therein, or from the enjoyment therein of the "privileges and immunities" of a citizen of the United States. What says the Constitution:

> The citizens of each state shall be entitled to all privileges and immunities of citizens in the several States.—Article 4, section 2.

Here is no qualification, as in the clause guarantying suffrage or an elective representation to the people; here is no room for that refined construction, that each State may exclude all or any of the citizens of the United States from its territory. The citizens of each State, all the citizens of each State, being citizens of the United States, shall be entitled to "all privileges and immunities of citizens in the several States." Not to the rights and immunities which result exclusively from State authority or State legislation; but to "all privileges and immunities" of citizens of the United States in the several States. . . .

This guaranty of the Constitution of the United States is senseless and a mockery, if it does not limit State sovereignty and restrain each and every State from closing its territory and its courts of justice against citizens of the United States. Lest it may be said that I have overstated the odious provisions of this Oregon constitution, I read the entire provisions of this section . . . which is expressly declared to be "a part of this constitution."

> Sec. 4. No free negro or mulatto, not residing in this State at the time of the adoption of this constitution, shall ever come, reside or be, within this State, or hold any real estate, or make any contract, or maintain any suit therein; and the Legislative Assembly shall provide by penal laws for the removal by public officers of all such free negroes and mulattoes, and for their effectual exclusion from the State, and for the punishment of persons who shall bring them into the State, or employ or harbor them therein. . . .

Gentlemen say that we violate the ordinance of 1787, which, by the act of 1848, was extended over Oregon, by resisting the admission of Oregon upon this constitution. I very much fear that gentlemen who say this, have never read the ordinance of 1787. I mean no disrespect, sir; but I say the veriest dolt cannot fail to see that this provision of the Oregon constitution is in direct conflict with, and violative of, the second article of that great ordinance. That article declares that the inhabitants of that Territory shall always be entitled to the benefit of the writ of habeas corpus and of trial by jury. The constitution of Oregon denies both these rights to some of the inhabitants. That article declares that no man shall be deprived of his liberty or property but by the judgment of his peers or the law of the land. This sacred provision is also violated by this constitution of Oregon, unless, indeed, gentlemen say a negro or mulatto is no man, but only a brute. . . .

Sir, if the persons thus excluded from the right to maintain any suit in the courts of Oregon were not citizens of the United States; if they were not natives born of free parents within the limits of the Republic, I should oppose this bill; because I say that a State which, in its fundamental law, denies to any person, or to a large class of persons, a hearing in her courts of justice, ought to be treated as an outlaw, unworthy a place in the sisterhood of the Republic. A suit is the legal demand of one's right, and the denial of this right by the judgment of the American Congress is to be sanctioned by law! But sir, I maintain that the persons thus excluded from the State by this section of the Oregon constitution, are citizens by birth of the several States, and therefore are citizens of the United States, and as such are entitled to all the privileges and immunities of citizens of the United States, amongst which are the rights of life and liberty and property, and their due protection in the enjoyment thereof by law; and therefore I hold this section for their exclusion from that State and its courts, to be an infraction of that wise and essential provision of the national Constitution to which I before referred, to wit:

The citizens of each State shall be entitled to all privileges and immunities of citizens IN THE SEVERAL STATES.

Who, sir, are citizens of the United States? First, all free persons born and domiciled within the United States—not all free white persons but all free persons. You will search in vain, in the Constitution of the United States, for that word *white*; it is not there. . . .

At the time of the adoption of the Constitution, only some States, South Carolina, Virginia, and Delaware, made *color* a qualification of basis of suffrage. In five of the others the elective franchise was exercised by free inhabitants, black and white; and therefore, in five of the States, black men cooperated with white men in the elections, and in the formation of the Constitution of the United States. Inasmuch as black men helped to make the Constitution, as well as to achieve the independence of the country by the terrible trial by battle, it is not surprising that the Constitution of the United States does not exclude them from the body politic, and the privileges and immunities of citizens of the United States. That great instrument included in the new body politic, by the name of "the people of the United States," all the then free inhabitants or citizens of the United States, whether white or black, not even excepting, as did the Articles of Confederation, paupers, vagbonds, or fugitives from justice. Thenceforward all these classes, being free inhabitants, irrespective of age, or sex, or complexion, and their descendants, were citizens of the United States. No distinctions were made against the poor and in favor of the rich, or against the freeborn blacks and in favor of the whites. This Government rests upon the absolute equality of natural rights amongst men. . . .

[T]he elective franchise is a political right, which all cannot exercise, and is therefore limited to some citizens to the exclusion of others. An infant in its cradle, the child of a citizen of the United States, is also a citizen of the United States, but has not the capacity to exercise this political right, and is therefore excluded from it. Practically, political rights are exercised only by the majority of the male population, and are subject to just such limitations as the majority see fit to impose. To this I have and can have, no objection. Gentlemen need not trouble themselves, therefore, about the demagogue cry of "the political equality of the negro." Nobody proposes or dreams of political equality any more than of physical or mental equality. It is as impossible for men to establish equality in these respects as it is for "the Ethiopian to change his skin." Who would say that all men are equal in stature, in weight, and in physical strength; or that all are equal in natural mental force, or in intellectual acquirements? Who, on the other hand, will be bold enough to deny that all persons are equally entitled to the enjoyment of the rights of life and liberty and property; and that no one should be deprived of life or liberty, but as punishment for crime; nor of his property, against his consent and without due compensation.

But it is not necessary to take time in demonstrating that all free persons born and domiciled within the United States are citizens of the United States. The fact is notorious that, at the formation of the Constitution, but few of the States made color the basis of suffrage, and all of them, either by the words or the construction of their constitutions, affirmed the fact that all native-born free persons were citizens. . . . New Hampshire, by her constitution of 1792, declared that every male inhabitant of the State, twenty-one years of age and upwards, except paupers and persons excused from paying taxes at their own request, shall have a right to vote at all elections. This was construed to admit all but aliens. . . .

Rhode Island, under the charter of Charles II, allowed negroes to vote, and recognized them as citizens.

Connecticut, under her charter did the same.

New York, by the constitution of 1777, gave suffrage to "every male inhabitant" upon six months' residence, and a property qualification.

All free persons, then, born and domiciled in any State of the Union, are citizens of the United States; and, although not equal in respect of political rights, are equal in respect of natural rights. . . .

While, therefore, I recognize the obligation of the majority to extend political privileges, so far as consistent with the stability of good government, to the large number of citizens, I as fully recognize the fact that all political privileges are, and ought to be, under the absolute control of the majority in a republican government; and their will is, and should be, the law. But, sir, while this is cheerfully conceded, I cannot, and will not, consent that the majority of any republican State may, in any way, rightfully restrict the humblest citizen of the United States in the free exercise of any one of his natural rights; those rights common to all men, and to protect which, not to confer, all good government, are instituted; and the failure to maintain which inviolate furnishes, at all times, a sufficient cause for the abrogation of such government; and, I may add, imposes a necessity for such abrogation, and the reconstruction of the political fabric on a juster basis, and with surer safeguards. . . .

The equality of all to the right to live; to the right to know; to argue and to utter, according to conscience; to work and enjoy the project of their toil, is the rock on which the Constitution rests—its sure foundation and defense. Take this away, and that beautiful and wise and just structure, so full of the goodness and truth of our fathers, falls. The charm of that Constitution lies in the great democratic idea which it embodies, that all men, before the law, are equal in respect of those rights of person which God gives and no man or State may rightfully take away, except as a forfeiture for crime. Before your constitution, sir, as it is, as I trust it ever will be, all men are sacred, whether white or black, rich or poor, strong or weak, wise or simple. Before its divine rule of justice and equality of natural rights, Lazarus in his rags is as sacred as the rich man clothed in purple and fine linen; the peasant in his hovel, as sacred as the prince in his palace, or the king on his throne. . . .

This provision, sir, which denies a fair trial in the courts of justice, excludes the same class of our fellow-citizens, native born, forever from the territory of that State. This is not only a violation of . . . the Constitution of the United States . . . but it is, I maintain, a flagrant violation of the law of nature, as recognized by every civilized nation on the globe. It is, sir, the public law of the civilized world, that every free man is entitled to live in the land of his birth. Oregon, by becoming incorporated into the Union, becomes part of the country of every American citizen, and therefore no citizen of the United States can rightfully be excluded from it. If any one State may rightfully do this, every State may; if it be right for one State thus to violate this law of domicile, acknowledged by all the world, it would be right for every State in the Union to exclude every native-born colored man in America. What, in the name of God, would you do with these men, these eight hundred thousand free, native-born men, of our common country! In the name of eternal justice, I deny this pretended State [the] right to exile any of its native-born freemen, or deny them a fair hearing in maintenance of their rights in the courts of justice.

. . . It was not to this end that the fathers of the Republic put forth their great Declaration, and in defense of it walked through the fire and storm and darkness of a seven years' war. It was not to this end that God gave them victory, and set him his bow in the cloud like a brightness out of heaven, giving token that the wild deluge of oppression and blood should not again sweep over their habitations. It was not to this end that, after the victory was thus achieved, those brave old men, with the dust of Yorktown yet fresh upon their brows, and the blood of Yorktown yet fresh upon their garments, proclaimed to the world, and asked it to be held in everlasting remembrance, "that the rights for which America had contended were the rights of human nature."

8. Abraham Lincoln, Address to the Wisconsin State Agricultural Society at Milwaukee (September 30, 1859)

> *In this address Lincoln refuted the "mud-sill theory" put forth by Fitzhugh, Hammond, and others. Echoing the call for "Free Labor, Free Soil," and universal education, this speech might be read alongside his Peoria address, noting his claim there that the territories promise the poor a place to "better their condition."*

. . . The world is agreed that labor is the source from which human wants are mainly supplied. There is no dispute upon this point. From this point, however, men immediately diverge. Much disputation is maintained as to the best way of applying and controlling the labor element. By some it is assumed that labor is available only in connection with capital—that nobody labors, unless somebody else, owning capital, somehow, by the use of that capital, induces him to do it. Having assumed this, they proceed to consider whether it is best that capital shall hire laborers, and thus induce them to work by their own consent; or buy them, and drive them to it without their consent. Having proceeded so far they naturally conclude that all laborers are necessarily either hired laborers, or slaves. They further assume that whoever is once a hired laborer, is fatally fixed in that condition for life; and thence again that his condition is as bad as, or worse than that of a slave. This is the "mud-sill" theory.

But another class of reasoners hold the opinion that there is no such relation between capital and labor, as assumed; and that there is no such thing as a freeman being fatally fixed for life, in the condition of a hired laborer, that both these assumptions are false, and all inferences from them groundless. They hold that labor is prior to, and independent of, capital; that, in fact, capital is the fruit of labor, and could never have existed if labor had not first existed—that labor can exist without capital, but that capital could never have existed without labor. Hence they hold that labor is the superior—greatly the superior—of capital.

They do not deny that there is, and probably always will be, a relation between labor and capital. The error, as they hold, is in assuming that the whole labor of the world exists within that relation. A few men own capital; and that few avoid labor themselves, and with their capital, hire, or buy, another few to labor for them. A large majority belong to neither class—neither work for others, nor have others working for them. Even in all our slave States, except South Carolina, a majority of the whole people of all colors, are neither slaves nor masters. In these Free States, a large majority are neither hirers or hired. Men, with their families—wives, sons and daughters—work for themselves, on their farms, in their houses and in their shops, taking the whole product to themselves, and asking no favors of capital on the one hand, nor of hirelings or slaves on the other. It is not forgotten that a considerable number of persons mingle their own labor with capital; that is, labor with their own hands, and also buy slaves or hire freemen to labor for them; but this is only a mixed, and not a distinct class. No principle stated is disturbed by the existence of this mixed class. Again, as has already been said, the opponents of the "mud-sill" theory insist that there is not, of necessity, any such thing as the free hired laborer being fixed to that condition for life. There is demonstration for saying this. Many independent men, in this assembly, doubtless a few years ago were hired laborers. And their case is almost if not quite the general rule.

The prudent, penniless beginner in the world, labors for wages awhile, saves a surplus with which to buy tools or land, for himself; then labors on his own account another while, and at length hires another new beginner to help him. This, say its advocates, is free labor—the just and generous, and prosperous system, which opens the way for all—gives hope to all, and energy, and progress, and improvement of condition to all. If any continue through life in the condition of the hired laborer, it is not the fault of the system, but because of either a dependent nature which prefers it, or improvidence, folly, or singular misfortune. I have said this much about the elements of labor generally, as introductory to the consideration of a new phase which that element is in process of assuming. The old general rule was that educated people did not perform manual labor. They managed to eat their bread, leaving the toil of producing it to the uneducated. This was not an insupportable evil to the working bees, so long as the class of drones remained very small. But now, especially in these free States, nearly all are educated—quite too nearly all, to leave the labor of the uneducated, in any wise adequate to the support of the whole. It follows from this that henceforth educated people must labor. Otherwise, education itself would become a positive and intolerable evil. No country can sustain, in idleness, more than a small percentage of its numbers. The great majority must labor at something productive. From these premises the problem springs, "How can labor and education be the most satisfactory combined?"

By the "mud-sill" theory it is assumed that labor and education are incompatible; and any practical combination of them impossible. According to that theory, a blind horse upon a tread-mill, is a perfect illustration of what a laborer should be—all the better for being blind, that he could not tread out of place, or kick understandingly. According to that theory, the education of laborers, is not only useless, but pernicious, and dangerous. In fact, it is, in some sort, deemed a misfortune that laborers should have heads at all. Those same heads are regarded as explosive materials, only to be safely kept in damp places, as far as possible from that peculiar sort of fire which ignites them. A Yankee who could invent strong handed man without a head would receive the everlasting gratitude of the "mud-sill" advocates.

But Free Labor says "no!" Free Labor argues that, as the Author of man makes every individual with one head and one pair of hands, it was probably intended that heads and hands should cooperate as friends; and that that particular head, should direct and control that particular pair of hands. As each man has one mouth to be fed, and one pair of hands to furnish food, it was probably intended that that particular pair of hands should feed that particular mouth—that each head is the natural guardian, director, and protector of the hands and mouth inseparably connected with it; and that being so, every head should be cultivated, and improved, by whatever will add to its capacity for performing its charge. In one word Free Labor insists on universal education.

I have so far stated the opposite theories of "Mud-Sill" and "Free Labor" without declaring any preference of my own between them. On an occasion like this I ought not to declare any. I suppose, however, I shall not be mistaken, in assuming as a fact, that the people of Wisconsin prefer free labor, with its natural companion, education. . . .

9. Alexander Stephens, Speech to the Virginia Secession Convention (April 23, 1861)

In this speech, given two months after his "Cornerstone Speech," Alexander Stephens (1812–1883) agreed with William Seward that the Constitution must accord with a higher law; but Stephens argued that "it is the fanatics of the North, who are warring against the decrees of God Almighty" in their efforts to overturn slavery and elevate blacks to a condition of equality.

. . . One good and wise feature in our new or revised Constitution is, that we have put to rest the vexed question of slavery forever, so far as the Confederate legislative halls are concerned. On this subject, from which sprung the immediate cause of our late troubles and threatened dangers, you will indulge me in a few remarks as not irrelevant to the occasion. The condition of the negro race amongst us presents a peculiar phase of republican civilization and constitutional liberty. To some, the problem seems hard to understand. The difficulty is in theory, not in practical demonstration; that works well enough—theories in government, as in all things else, must yield to facts. No truth is clearer than that the best form or system of government for any people or society is that which secures the greatest amount of happiness, not to the greatest number, but to all the constituent elements of that society, community or State. If our system does not accomplish this; if it is not the best for the negro as well as for the white man; for the inferior as well as the superior race, it is wrong in principle. But if it does, or is capable of doing this, then it is right, and can never be successfully assailed by reason or logic. That the negroes with us, under masters who care for, provide for and protect them, are better off, and enjoy more of the blessings of good government than their race does in any other part of the world, statistics abundantly prove. As a race, the African is inferior to the white man. Subordination to the white man is his normal condition. He is not his equal by nature, and cannot be made so by human laws or human institutions. Our system, therefore, so far as regards this inferior race, rests upon this great immutable law of nature. It is founded not upon wrong or injustice, but upon the eternal fitness of things. Hence, its harmonious working for the benefit and advantage of both. Why one race was made inferior to another, is not for us to inquire. The statesman and the Christian, as well as the philosopher, must take things as they find them, and do the best he can with them as he finds them.

The great truth, I repeat, upon which our system rests, is the inferiority of the African. The enemies of our institutions ignore this truth. They set out with the assumption that the races are equal; that the negro is equal to the white man. If their premises were correct, their conclusions would be legitimate. But their premises being false, their conclusions are false also. Most of that fanatical spirit at the North on this subject, which in its zeal without knowledge, would upturn our society and lay waste our fair country, springs from this false reasoning. Hence so much misapplied sympathy for fancied wrongs and sufferings. These wrongs and sufferings exist only in their heated imaginations. There can be no wrong where there is no violation of nature's laws. We have heard much of the higher law. I believe myself in the higher law. We stand upon that higher law. I would defend and support no Constitution that is against the higher law. I mean by that the law of nature and of God. Human Constitutions and human laws that are made against the law of nature or of God, ought to be overturned; and if Seward was right the Constitution which he was sworn to support, and is now requiring others to swear to support, ought to have been overthrown long ago. It ought never to have been made. But in point of fact it is he and his associates in this crusade against us, who are warring against the higher law—we stand upon the laws of the Creator, upon the highest of all laws. It is the fanatics of the North, who are warring against the decrees of God Almighty, in their attempts to make things equal which he made unequal. My assurance of ultimate success in this controversy is strong from the conviction, that we stand upon the right. . . . The controlling laws of nature regulate the difference between them as absolutely as the laws of gravitation control whatever comes within their action—and until he could change the laws of gravitation, or any other law of nature, he could never make the negro a white man or his equal. No human efforts or human laws can change the leopard's spots or the Ethiopian's skin. These are the works of Providence—in whose hands are the fortunes of men as well as the destiny of nations and the distinctions of races. . . .

10. Abraham Lincoln, Address Delivered at the Dedication of the Cemetery at Gettysburg (November 19, 1863)

With sublime oratory, Lincoln renewed the principal themes that persistently guided his thoughts and actions: that the United States is predicated on the truth that all men are created equal, and on the fact that slavery alone had the strength to destroy the great experiment in democracy that the nation promised.

Four score and seven years ago our fathers brought forth on this continent, a new nation, conceived in Liberty, and dedicated to the proposition that all men are created equal.

Now we are engaged in a great civil war, testing whether that nation, or any nation so conceived and so dedicated, can long endure. We are met on a great battle-field of that war. We have come to dedicate a portion of that field, as a final resting place for those who here gave their lives that that nation might live. It is altogether fitting and proper that we should do this.

But, in a larger sense, we can not dedicate—we can not consecrate—we can not hallow—this ground. The brave men, living and dead, who struggled here, have consecrated it, far above our poor power to add or detract. The world will little note, nor long remember what we say here, but it can never forget what they did here. It is for us the living, rather, to be dedicated here to the unfinished work which they who fought here have thus far so nobly advanced.

It is rather for us to be here dedicated to the great task remaining before us—that from these honored dead we take increased devotion to that cause for which they gave the last full measure of devotion—that we here highly resolve that these dead shall not have died in vain—that this nation, under God, shall have a new birth of freedom—and that government of the people, by the people, for the people, shall not perish from the earth.

11. Abraham Lincoln, Second Inaugural Address (March 4, 1865)

In his Second Inaugural, Lincoln plainly said what everyone always knew to be true—that the "peculiar interest" of slavery "was somehow the cause of the war." Lincoln echoed warnings sounded by generations before him, that slavery was a national sin, and he saw in the Civil War the chastisement of the Almighty. In the end, Lincoln enjoined both sides to abandon malice, embrace charity, and restore friendship among all Americans in "binding up the nation's wounds."

Fellow-Countrymen:

At this second appearing to take the oath of the Presidential office there is less occasion for an extended address than there was at the first. Then a statement somewhat in detail of a course to be pursued seemed fitting and proper. Now, at the expiration of four years, during which public declarations have been constantly called forth on every point and phase of the great contest which still absorbs the attention and engrosses the energies of the nation, little that is new could be presented. The progress of our arms, upon which all else chiefly depends, is as well known to the public as to myself, and it is, I trust, reasonably satisfactory and encouraging to all. With high hope for the future, no prediction in regard to it is ventured.

On the occasion corresponding to this four years ago all thoughts were anxiously directed to an impending civil war. All dreaded it, all sought to avert it. While the inaugural address was being delivered from this place, devoted altogether to saving the Union without war, insurgent agents were in the city seeking to destroy it without war—seeking to dissolve the Union and divide effects by negotiation. Both parties deprecated war, but one of them would make war rather than let the nation survive, and the other would accept war rather than let it perish, and the war came.

One-eighth of the whole population were colored slaves, not distributed generally over the Union, but localized in the southern part of it. These slaves constituted a peculiar and powerful interest. All knew that this interest was somehow the cause of the war. To strengthen, perpetuate, and extend this interest was the object for which the insurgents would rend the Union even by war, while the Government claimed no right to do more than to restrict the territorial enlargement of it. Neither party expected for the war the magnitude or the duration which it has already attained. Neither anticipated that the cause of the conflict might cease with or even before the conflict itself should cease. Each looked for an easier triumph, and a result less fundamental and astounding. Both read the same Bible and pray to the same God, and each invokes His aid against the other. It may seem strange that any men should dare to ask a just God's assistance in wringing their bread from the sweat of other men's faces, but let us judge not, that we be not judged. The prayers of both could not be answered. That of neither has been answered fully. The Almighty has His own purposes. "Woe unto the world because of offenses; for it must needs be that offenses come, but woe to that man by whom the offense cometh." If we shall suppose that American slavery is one of those offenses which, in the providence of God, must needs come, but which, having continued through His appointed time, He now wills to remove, and that He gives to both North and South this terrible war as the woe due to those by whom the offense came, shall we discern therein any departure from those divine attributes which the believers in a living God always ascribe to Him? Fondly do we hope, fervently do we pray, that this mighty scourge of war may speedily pass away. Yet, if God wills that it continue until all the wealth piled by the bondsman's two hundred and fifty years of unrequited toil shall be sunk, and until every drop of blood drawn with the lash shall be paid by another drawn with the sword, as was said three thousand years ago, so still it must be said "the judgments of the Lord are true and righteous altogether."

With malice toward none, with charity for all, with firmness in the right as God gives us to see the right, let us strive on to finish the work we are in, to bind up the nation's wounds, to care for him who shall have borne the battle and for his widow and his orphan, to do all which may achieve and cherish a just and lasting peace among ourselves and with all nations.

Bibliography

Baker, H. Robert. *Prigg v. Pennsylvania: Slavery, the Supreme Court, and the Ambivalent Constitution.* Lawrence: University Press of Kansas, 2012.

Baptist, Edward E. *The Half Has Never Been Told: Slavery and the Making of American Capitalism.* New York: Basic Books, 2014.

Berlin, Ira. *Many Thousands Gone: The First Two Centuries of Slavery in North America.* Cambridge, MA: Belknap Press, 2000.

———. *Slaves without Masters: The Free Negro in the Antebellum South.* New York: Random House, 1974.

Blackburn, Robin. *The American Crucible: Slavery, Emancipation, and Human Rights.* London: Verso, 2013.

Boles, John. *Black Southerners, 1619–1869.* Lexington: University Press of Kentucky, 1984.

———. *Masters & Slaves in the House of the Lord: Race and Religion in the American South, 1740–1870.* Lexington: University Press of Kentucky, 1990.

Briggs, John Channing. *Lincoln's Speeches Reconsidered.* Baltimore: Johns Hopkins University Press, 2005.

Brooks, Corey M. *Liberty Power: Antislavery Third Parties and the Transformation of American Politics.* Chicago: University of Chicago Press, 2016.

Burin, Eric. *Slavery and the Peculiar Solution: A History of the American Colonization Society.* Gainesville: University Press of Florida, 2008.

Cox, LaWanda. *Lincoln and Black Freedom: A Study in Presidential Leadership.* Columbia: University of South Carolina Press, 1981.

Dain, Bruce. *A Hideous Monster of the Mind: American Race Theory in the Early Republic.* Cambridge, MA: Harvard University Press, 2002.

Davis, David Brion. *Inhuman Bondage: The Rise and Fall of Slavery in the New World.* New York: Oxford University Press, 2008.

———. *The Problem of Slavery in the Age of Emancipation.* New York: Oxford University Press, 2014.

———. *The Problem of Slavery in the Age of Revolution, 1770–1823.* New York: Oxford University Press, 1999.

Dew, Charles B. *Apostles of Disunion: Southern Secession Commissioners and the Causes of the Civil War.* Charlottesville: University of Virginia Press, 2001.

Drescher, Seymour. *Abolition: A History of Slavery and Antislavery.* New York: Cambridge University Press, 2009.

Ellis, Richard E. *The Union at Risk: Jacksonian Democracy, States' Rights, and the Nullification Crisis.* New York: Oxford University Press, 1987.

Ely, Melvin. *Israel on the Appomattox: A Southern Experiment in Black Freedom from the 1790s to the Civil War.* New York: Vintage Books, 2005.

Etcheson, Nicole. *Bleeding Kansas: Contested Liberty in the Civil War Era.* Lawrence: University of Kansas Press, 2004.

Faust, Drew Gilpen. *A Sacred Circle: The Dilemma of the Intellectual in the Old South, 1840–1860.* Baltimore: Johns Hopkins University Press, 1977; Philadelphia: University of Pennsylvania Press, 1986.

Fehrenbacher, Don E. *The Dred Scott Case: Its Significance in American Law and Politics.* New York: Oxford University Press, 1978.

———. *Prelude to Greatness: Lincoln in the 1850s.* Redwood City, CA: Stanford University Press, 1962.

———. *The Slaveholding Republic: An Account of the United States Government's Relations to Slavery.* Completed and edited by Ward M. McAfee. New York: Oxford University Press, 2002.

Finkelman, Paul. *Slavery and the Founders: Race and Liberty in the Age of Jefferson.* 3rd ed. Armonk, NY: M. E. Sharpe, 2014.

Foner, Eric. *The Fiery Trial: Abraham Lincoln and American Slavery.* New York: Norton, 2010.

———. *Free Soil, Free Labor, Free Men: The Ideology of the Republican Party before the Civil War.* New York: Oxford University Press, 1995.

Forbes, Robert Pierce. *The Missouri Compromise and Its Aftermath: Slavery and the Meaning of America.* Chapel Hill: University of North Carolina Press, 2007.

Franklin, John Hope. *The Militant South: 1800–1861.* Boston: Beacon Press, 1956.

Fredrickson, George. *The Black Image in the White Mind: The Debate on Afro-American Character and Destiny, 1817–1914.* New York: Harper & Row, 1971.

Freehling, William. *Prelude to the Civil War: The Nullification Crisis in South Carolina, 1816–1836.* New York: Harper & Row, 1966.

———. *The Road to Disunion.* Vol. 1, *Secessionists at Bay, 1776–1854.* New York: Oxford University Press, 1991.

Genovese, Eugene D. *Roll, Jordan, Roll: The World the Slaves Made.* New York: Pantheon Books, 1974.

Graber, Mark A. *Dred Scott and the Problem of Constitutional Evil.* New York: Cambridge University Press, 2006.

Higginbotham, A. Leon, Jr. *In the Matter of Color: Race & the American Legal Process: The Colonial Period.* New York: Oxford University Press, 1978.

Holt, Michael F. *The Political Crisis of the 1850s.* New York: Norton, 1983.

Horne, Gerald. *The Counter-Revolution of 1776: Slave Resistance and the Origins of the United States of America.* New York: New York University Press, 2014.

Jaffa, Harry V. *Crisis of the House Divided: An Interpretation of the Lincoln-Douglas Debates.* Chicago: University of Chicago Press, 1959.

Johannsen, Robert W. *The Frontier, the Union, and Stephen A. Douglas.* Champaign: University of Illinois Press, 1989.

Jordan, Winthrop D. *White over Black: American Attitudes toward the Negro, 1550–1812.* Chapel Hill: University of North Carolina Press, 1968.

Kolchin, Peter. *American Slavery, 1619–1877.* Rev. ed. New York: Hill and Wang, 2003.

Lauer, Bruce. *Beyond Garrison: Antislavery and Social Reform.* New York: Cambridge University Press, 2005.

Levine, Bruce. *Half Slave, Half Free: The Roots of the Civil War.* Rev. ed. New York: Hill and Wang, 2005. First published 1992.

Levine, Robert S. *Martin Delany, Frederick Douglass, and the Politics of Representative Identity.* Chapel Hill: University of North Carolina Press, 1997.

Litwack, Leon F. *North of Slavery: The Negro in the Free States, 1790–1860.* Chicago: University of Chicago Press, 1961.

Maltz, Earl M. *Slavery and the Supreme Court, 1825–1861.* Lawrence: University of Kansas Press, 2009.

Mason, Matthew. *Slavery and Politics in the Early Republic.* Chapel Hill: University of North Carolina Press, 2008.

McKivigan, John R., and Mitchell Snay, eds. *Religion and the Antebellum Debate over Slavery.* Athens: University of Georgia Press, 1998.

Melish, Joanne Pope. *Disowning Slavery: Gradual Emancipation and "Race" in New England.* Ithaca, NY: Cornell University Press, 2000.

Newman, Richard S. *The Transformation of American Abolitionism: Fighting Slavery in the New Republic.* Chapel Hill: University of North Carolina Press, 2002.

Noll, Mark A. *America's God: From Jonathan Edwards to Abraham Lincoln.* New York: Oxford University Press, 2005.

Oakes, James. *The Radical and the Republican: Frederick Douglass, Abraham Lincoln, and the Triumph of Antislavery Politics.* New York: Norton, 2007.

———. *Slavery and Freedom: An Interpretation of the Old South.* New York: Knopf, 1990.

Quarles, Benjamin. *Black Abolitionists.* New York: Oxford University Press, 1969.

Rael, Patrick. *Eighty-Eight Years: The Long Death of Slavery in the United States, 1777–1865.* Athens: University of Georgia Press, 2015.

Robinson, Donald L. *Slavery in the Structure of American Politics, 1765–1820.* New York: Harcourt Brace Jovanovich, 1971.

Rothman, Adam. *Slave Country: American Expansion and the Origins of the Deep South.* Cambridge, MA: Harvard University Press, 2005.

Sinha, Manisha. *The Slave's Cause: A History of Abolition.* New Haven, CT: Yale University Press, 2016.

Smith, Mark M. *Debating Slavery: Economy and Slavery in the Antebellum American South.* Cambridge: Cambridge University Press, 1998.

Stampp, Kenneth M. *America in 1857: A Nation on the Brink.* New York: Oxford University Press, 1990.

———. *The Peculiar Institution: Slavery in the Ante-Bellum South.* New York: Vintage Books, 1956.

Stanton, William. *The Leopard's Spots: Scientific Attitudes toward Race in America, 1815–1859.* Chicago: University of Chicago Press, 1960.

Stewart, James Brewer. *Holy Warriors: The Abolitionists and American Slavery.* New York: Hill and Wang, 1976.

Striner, Richard. *Father Abraham: Lincoln's Relentless Struggle to End Slavery.* New York: Oxford University Press, 2006.

Sweet, John Wood. *Bodies Politic: Negotiating Race in the American North, 1730–1830.* Philadelphia: University of Pennsylvania Press, 2006.

TenBroek, Jacobus. *Equal Under Law.* Enlarged ed. New York: Collier Books, 1965.

Tise, Larry. *Proslavery: A History of the Defense of Slavery in America, 1701–1840.* Athens: University of Georgia Press, 2004.

Tushnet, Mark V. *Slave Law in the American South:* State v. Mann *in History and Literature.* Lawrence: University Press of Kansas, 2003.

Van Cleve, George William. *A Slaveholders' Union: Slavery, Politics, and the Constitution in the Early American Republic.* Chicago: University of Chicago Press, 2010.

Walters, Ronald G. *American Reformers: 1815–1860.* Rev. ed. New York: Hill and Wang, 1997.

Wiecek, William M. *The Sources of Antislavery Constitutionalism in America, 1760–1848.* Ithaca, NY: Cornell University Press, 1977.

Yellen, Jean Fagan, and John C. Van Horne, eds. *The Abolitionist Sisterhood: Women's Political Culture in Antebellum America.* Ithaca, NY: Cornell University Press, 1994.

Young, Jeffrey Robert, ed. *Proslavery and Sectional Thought in the Early South, 1740–1829.* Columbia: University of South Carolina Press, 2006.

Zilversmit, Arthur. *The First Emancipation: The Abolition of Slavery in the North.* Chicago: University of Chicago Press, 1967.

Index

abolition, xiv, xx, 118, 120, 189, 250; gradual, 82, 119, 127, 132; immediate, 125–26, 130, 131, 164–66, 181; is progressing, 64, 65; laws of enacted, xv, 2, 26, 69

abolitionist movements, xiv, 137, 145, 148, 204; British Quakers establish, 2; confined to free states, 165; and constitutionality of slavery, xx; emergence of, xiii, 3; in Southern states, 55; women involved in, 159

abolitionist newspapers, 118, 120, 135, 181, 234

abolitionists, xix, 135, 151, 159, 181–83, 189; appeal to slaveholders, 149; appeal to slaves, 150; are denounced, 253; are enemies to the country, 134; are threatened, 254, 263; asked to surrender right of discussion, 138; attacked by mobs, 120, 135, 137; as class of slavery opponents, 164; and the Declaration of Independence, 252; definition of, 218; demand immediate emancipation, 176; duty of, 186; in England, 221–22; evidence against, 132; fear divine national punishments, 8; foment sectional hatred toward the South, 200, 204, 205; and human rights, 156; oppose separation of races, 166; press Congress, 31; principles and conduct of, 184; publications and readings of, 145; recklessly undermine abolition, 128; renounce colonization, 111; resolve to force emancipation, 220; seek to stop extension of slavery, 246–47; threaten slavery, 194; and U.S. constitution, 185–87, 234–35, 255; violate laws of mind and

experience, 157; in Whig Party, 191; wish to operate on states, 165; would spread dissatisfaction, death and destructions, 152

abolitionists, Garrisonian, xvii, xx, 120, 142, 185

Adam, John, 15

Adams, John Quincy, 150, 172, 215

Africa, 5–6, 23, 47, 56, 82, 112, 140; Christianity should be disseminated throughout, 103, 111; colonizing free blacks to, 65–66, 69, 106–7, 113–15; freedom in, 99; glory of, 179; persecuted, 102; slave trade stifles Christianity in, 4

African American women, 16, 22, 117, 242; as slaves, 167, 171, 173, 219, 240

African Americans. *See* blacks

Alabama, 69, 84, 264

Allen, Richard, xvii, 107, 113, 115

American Colonization Society (ACS), 33, 102, 111, 117, 118; embrace colonization of free blacks, xvii, 64, 69

American Revolution. *See* Revolution, American

Amistad, 172, 180

Anglicans, 2

anti-slavery associations, movements, organizations. *See* abolitionist movements

Articles of Confederation, xv, 2, 14, 30, 160, 282

Atherton, Charles G., 172, 174

Bacon, Leonard, 120, 128

Baptists, 105

Barbour, Philip, xix, 76, 78, 93, 95

Beecher, Catharine E., 120, 156